Ants of Britain and Europe

BLOOMSBURY WILDLIFE
Bloomsbury Publishing Plc
50 Bedford Square, London, WC1B 3DP, UK

BLOOMSBURY, BLOOMSBURY WILDLIFE and the Diana logo are trademarks of Bloomsbury Publishing Plc

First published in 2016 in France as *Fourmis d'Europe occidentale* by Delachaux et Niestlé
This edition published in Great Britain, 2019

A catalogue record for this book is available from the British Library

ISBN: PB: 978-1-4729-5408-4; ePub: 978-1-4729-5407-7; ePDF: 978-1-4729-5406-0

2 4 6 8 10 9 7 5 3 1

English language translation by Tony Williams
Design by Rod Teasdale
Printed and bound in France by Imprimerie Pollina

Front cover (main): Naturfoto Honal/Getty
Front cover (bottom, left to right): Scott Tilley/Getty; Viktoria Rodriguez/EyeEm/Getty; Oxford Scientific/Getty.
Back cover (left to right): Shutterstock; Ian_Redding/iStock; Shutterstock.

To find out more about our authors and books visit www.bloomsbury.com and sign up for our newsletters

C. **LEBAS**
C. **GALKOWSKI**
R. **BLATRIX**
P. **WEGNEZ**

Ants of Britain and Europe

PHOTOGRAPHS :
C. **LEBAS**
R. BLATRIX

BLOOMSBURY WILDLIFE
LONDON • OXFORD • NEW YORK • NEW DELHI • SYDNEY

Contents

Opposite: *Formica sanguinea* on umbelliferae.

Introduction

There are many works on the life of ants but relatively few that summarise our present knowledge of the group's systematics. Despite a long myrmecological tradition, this is true for the whole of Europe: there is currently no taxonomical summary for the area and very few countries have recent and complete lists of their species. However, there are exceptions – for example Germany (Seifert, B., 2007, *Die Ameisen Mittelund Nordeurops*, Tauter, Lutra Verlagsund Vertriebsgesellschaft, 368 pp.) and Poland (Czechowski, W., Radchenko, A., Czechowska W., Vepsäläinen, K., 2012, *The Ants of Poland with Reference to the Myrmecofauna of Europe*, Warsaw, Natura optima dux Foundation, Faunia Poloniae, vol. 4, 496 pp.). Even though these books are very helpful, especially for Central Europe, their technical nature and systems of organisation mean that they are not easily used by amateur or field naturalists. The amateur naturalist in the field thus has no tool for identifying ants encountered on a walk, and often has to juggle between works that are generally very technical and different scientific publications in order to identify specimens. The object of this guide is two-fold. Firstly, it aims to satisfy both the curious observer and the knowledgeable naturalist by presenting a systematic account of all the ant species that occur in Europe in a simplified manner. Each section describes a species or group of very similar species, and photographs allow for rapid comparison. Identification keys, based on morphological features with diagnostic illustrations, enable the reliable identification of the majority of European species. The aim is to provide a tool that will allow a broad public to identify ant species. We hope this will serve the increasing numbers of people interested in these fascinating insects. Secondly, the wider diffusion of knowledge and a public better informed on ant diversity is, we hope, a good means of helping in the conservation of ants.

Systematics

There are more than 13,000 species of ants described throughout the world. This number may seem small compared to the millions of insect species presently known, but their combined biomass is far higher than that of the majority of other groups. Ants colonise nearly every type of terrestrial habitat and are present on all continents except Antarctica. They are, however, much more diverse and numerous in the tropics. In certain parts of the Amazon a few hectares of forest can be home to nearly 500 ant species, about as many as in the whole of Europe. In our present understanding, Europe contains some 480 native species.

Globally, there are 16 subfamilies within the *Formicidae* family, eight of which occur in Europe: *Myrmicinae*, *Formicinae*, *Dolichoderinae*, *Ponerinae*, *Leptanillinae*, *Proceratiinae*, *Amblyoponinae* and *Dorylinae*.

Ant classification

Kingdom: Animal

Phylum: Arthropod

Class: Insect (three pairs of articulated legs)

Order: Hymenoptera (two pairs of membrane wings; the smaller hindwings are attached to the forewings by a series of hooks. Ant workers never have wings).

Suborder: Apocrita (narrow separation between the thorax and abdomen)

Infraorder: Aculeata

Family: Formicidae (= ants)

The principal hierarchic levels that follow are: subfamily, genus, subgenus and species. According to recognised zoological nomenclature, a species should be designated by the name of its genus and specific name, followed by the name of the person who first described the species (the authority), followed by the year of its description. Often, however, for simplicity's sake the authority and year of description are omitted. In scientific language the names of genus and species should be written in italics.

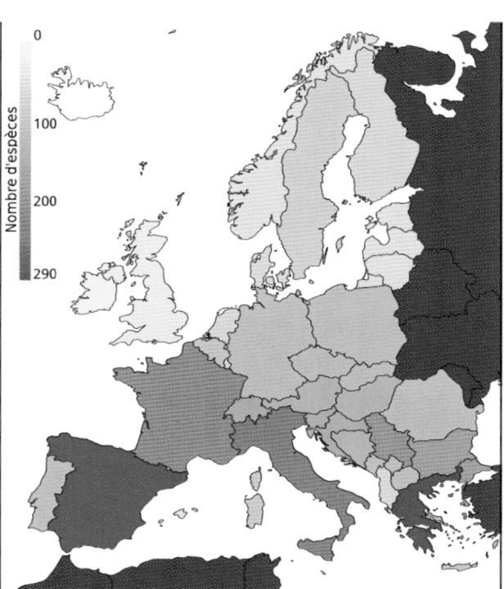

Map of the area covered in this volume, showing the number of ant species for each country. Those countries shown in dark brown are not treated here.

In 2014 Myrmicinae nomenclature underwent modifications due to the emergence of new phytogenetic data. The major changes for the European fauna particularly concerned the *Chalepoxenus* and *Myrmoxenus* genera, which were incorporated into the genus *Temnothorax*, whilst the *Anergates* and *Teleutomyrmex* genera shifted into the genus *Tetramorium*. Thus, all species of *Chalepoxenus* and *Myrmoxenus* should now have the generic name *Temnothorax*, and those of *Anergates* and *Teleutomyrmex* are now *Tetramorium*. This situation has troubled many myrmecologists, as each of these four former genera comprised a homogenous entity: they consist of species that parasitise other *Temnothorax* species (for *Chalepoxenus* and *Myrmoxenus*) and *Tetramorium* species (for *Anergates* and *Teleutomyrmex*), and have morphological particularities that distinguish them from their host genus. Moreover, these changes have caused nomenclature conflicts as the same species name is applied to two different genera that are now synonymous. So, to avoid conflict, the following changes concerning the European fauna have been made: *Myrmoxenus kraussei* (Emery, 1915), becomes *Temnothorax kraussei* (Emery, 1915) and consequently *Temnothorax kraussei* (Emery, 1916) has become *Temnothorax mediterraneus* (Ward, Brady, Fischer & Schultz, 2014); *Teleutomyrmex schneideri* (Kutter, 1950) has become *Tetramorium inquilinum* (Ward, Brady, Fischer & Schultz, 2014). These name changes have been taken into account in the table of genera presented in the introduction. However, due to a major risk of confusion for readers already familiar with the study of ants, we have chosen to conserve

Numbers of genera and species for each subfamily present in Europe
(not including introduced species that are not definitively installed in natural habitats)

Family	Subfamily	Genus (number of species)	
Formicidae (8 subfamilies, 50 genera, 486 species)	Amblyoponinae (1 genus, 4 species)	*Stigmatomma* (4)	
	Dolichoderinae (6 genera, 15 species)	*Bothriomyrmex* (4) *Dolichoderus* (1) *Linepithema* (1)	*Liometopum* (1) *Tapinoma* (7) *Technomyrmex* (1)
	Dorylinae (1 genus, 1 species)	*Aenictus* (1)	
	Formicinae (14 genera, 156 species)	*Acropyga* (1) *Camponotus* (42) *Cataglyphis* (15) *Formica* (33) *Iberoformica* (1) *Lasius* (35) *Lepisiota* (6)	*Nylanderia* (2) *Paratrechina* (1) *Plagiolepis* (9) *Polyergus* (1) *Prenolepis* (1) *Proformica* (8) *Rossomyrmex* (1)
	Leptanillinae (1 genus, 7 species)	*Leptanilla* (7)	
	Myrmicinae (22 genera, 290 species)	*Aphaenogaster* (38) *Cardiocondyla* (7) *Carebara* (1) *Crematogaster* (11) *Formicoxenus* (1) *Goniomma* (7) *Harpagoxenus* (1) *Leptothorax* (6) *Manica* (1) *Messor* (19) *Monomorium* (10)	*Myrmecina* (3) *Myrmica* (34) *Oxyopomyrmex* (5) *Pheidole* (3) *Solenopsis* (9) *Stenamma* (7) *Strongylognathus* (11) *Strumigenys* (5) *Temnothorax* (80) *Tetramorium* (30) *Trichomyrmex* (1)
	Ponerinae (4 genera, 9 species)	*Anochetus* (1) *Cryptopone* (1)	*Hypoponera* (5) *Ponera* (2)
	Proceratiinae (6 genera, 15 species)	*Proceratium* (4)	

throughout the rest of the publication the genera *Chalepoxenus*, *Myrmoxenus*, *Anergates* and *Teleutomyrmex*, whilst at the same time mentioning the name changes as far as possible.

Worker morphology

The body of an insect is composed of several segments grouped into three sections: head, thorax and abdomen. In ants the thorax is fused with the

Principal terms used in the naming of the body parts of a worker

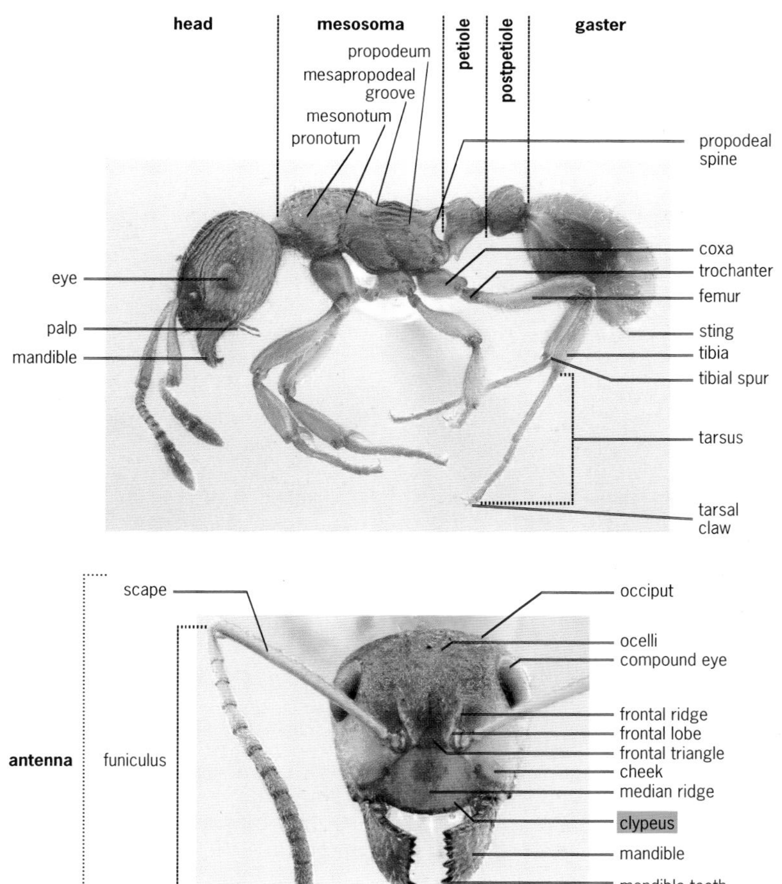

first abdominal segment to form what is termed the mesosoma. For simplicity, the term thorax is sometimes used to describe this assembly in its entirety. The legs are attached to the thorax. The second and sometimes the third abdominal segments are considerably reduced in size; they are termed respectively the petiole and postpetiole. The rest of the abdominal segments together form the gaster. The membranes connecting the different gastral segments to each other – the inter-segmental membranes – are supple and very thin. They allow for great variation in the size of the gaster, which contains the viscera, according to the amount of food ingested. As in all aculeates, the ovipositor of workers is transformed into a sting that is connected to a venom gland. According to the nature and quantity of venom injected, the sting is more or less painful to humans. In Europe-dwelling ant species, stings are present in the following subfamilies: Leptanillinae, Myrmicinae, Ponerinae, Proceratiinae, Amblyoponinae and Dorylinae. They are used in defence or to neutralise prey. In certain Myrmicinae species, the sting is modified and does not sting (in the genus *Crematogaster*, for example). In the Dolichoderinae and Formicinae subfamilies, it is atrophied and the chemical components that serve in neutralising prey or defence are not injected. In the Formicinae these components exit by a circular pore characteristic of the subfamily: the acidopore. The best example of this is the extrusion of formic acid in the genus *Formica*. Certain species can project their venom – composed essentially of formic acid (about 60%) – up to a distance of 20 cm. This acid penetrates the body of captured arthropods by crossing inter-segment membranes and killing them. It also aids in the repulsion of vertebrate predators as it irritates their respiratory passages.

Stages of individual development

There are several developmental stages in ants: egg, larva, pupa and adult. Eggs are small and usually white. A few days after being laid, a tiny larva emerges. It is only during the larval phase that the young ant gains size. This period lasts several weeks, during which there are different larval stages (3–5 depending on species) with a moult between each stage. At the end of its development, in the last larval stage, it transforms into a pupa. In certain species the larva forms a silk cocoon in which it passes the entire pupal stage (this cocoon is often incorrectly called an 'ant egg'). In the Myrmicinae the larvae never make a cocoon, so the pupa is always 'uncovered'. The pupa is immobile and never feeds. It is during this period, which lasts some 15 days, that the larva undergoes important internal and external modifications in order to become an adult. The pupa has the appearance of being curled up on itself. It starts off white and gradually acquires colour. Once its development is finished, the pupa undergoes its final moults (this is

Crematogaster auberti. Some eggs, small and white, can be seen lower right, among a group of larvae.

Lasius emarginatus. Different larval stages. The smallest have just hatched from the egg.

As they change into pupae, the larvae of certain species, such as *Camponotus sylvaticus*, build a silk cocoon. This one has been cut open to show the pupa inside.

As in numerous species of the Formicinae subfamily, *Lasius flavus* pupae are protected in a silk cocoon. The smaller ones will produce workers, the medium ones males and the largest will be future queens.

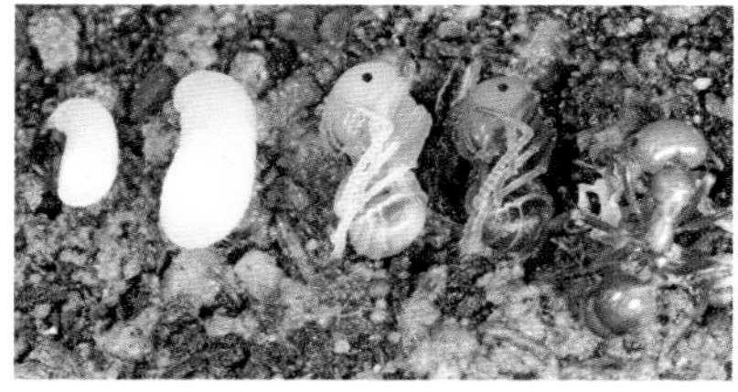

Messor barbarus. The larvae, on the left, are white. Pupae, on the right, become progressively more coloured as they mature.

termed the imago moult) to become an adult ant. From then on it will no longer increase in size. A worker's lifespan varies from a few months to two years, depending on the species. Queens live for much longer, approximately between five and 20 years. Males generally live for just one season at the adult stage – the time needed to reproduce.

Social structure and breeding cycle

Each ant species has three different types of individual: workers, queens and males. As in all Hymenoptera, functional males arise from non-fertilised eggs. On occasion, males can arise from fertilised eggs, but they are not fertile. A fertilised egg normally gives rise to a queen or a worker: the conditions during larval development (essentially the amount of food they receive and the temperature) decide their outcome.

All ant species are eusocial and live in colonies in which there is an unequal share of work between fertile females (queens), males that ensure reproduction and more or less sterile females (workers). A colony is composed of a large number of workers and one or more queens. The queens ensure reproduction by producing workers, future queens and males. Workers, always female, work to rear the brood – that is the eggs, larvae and pupae – to care for and defend the nest, and to find food.

The three castes in *Crematogaster auberti*: worker at the bottom, male on the right and queen top left.

Generally, only queens reproduce, but there are a few species in which workers can also produce other workers or future queens. In Europe this process has only been observed in *Cataglyphis* species. In most species, workers have functional ovaries but cannot be fertilised. They thus have the possibility to produce males from non-fertilised eggs. This process is generally inhibited by the presence of a queen. Consequently, once a queen dies the colony produces males before all the workers themselves die. There are also a few species, such as those of the genus *Pheidole*, in which workers' ovaries are not functional so they cannot even produce males.

In the majority of species there is only one functional queen in a colony. The colony is thus said to be 'monogynous'. After several years of existence, the colony will produce sexual individuals: males and future queens. These are generally winged, whereas workers are never so. The swarming or nuptial flight by the males and future queens is locally synchronised in colonies of the same species. Mating occurs during these nuptial flights, which are the only time that winged ants are seen outside the nest. The synchronised swarming flights ensure cross-fertilisation of males and females from different nests. In most species males and females from the same colony are closely related, and so synchronised swarming avoids inbreeding. The factors that set off swarming are not well known but they often occur before or just after a thunderstorm in hot, muggy weather.

Swarming occurs from spring until autumn. In certain species it can happen over several months but generally it occurs at a precise time of the year, which differs according to species. The winged ants exit from the nest and come together in large numbers around the entrance or on nearby plants, then take flight. According to the species, the queen can mate with one or several males but she will be fertilised by just one during her life, conserving the spermatozoids in her spermathecae. Generally, males die soon after mating. When she has been fertilised, the new queen breaks off her wings at their base and digs in the ground or searches for a crevice where she will form a new colony. Once sheltered, she starts laying. In certain species the queen regularly leaves the site to feed during the growth of the first larvae, but in many other species she does not leave the nest at all. In this last case, metabolic processes dissolve the queen's

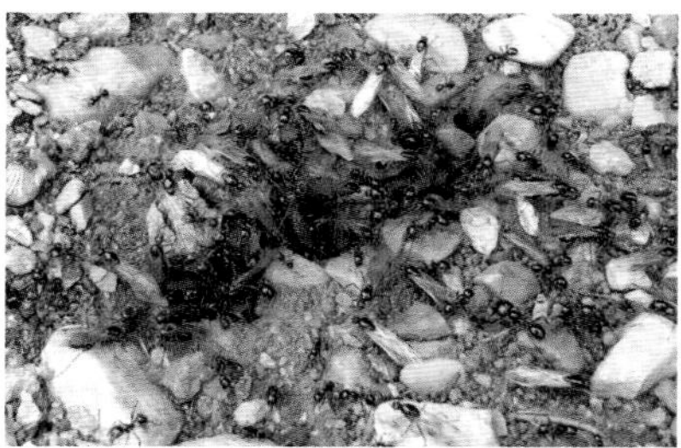

Messor Barbarus nest. During the swarming, large numbers of sexual individuals (future queens and winged males) are escorted by workers as they leave the nest.

Pheidole pallidula mating.

Sexual individuals climb onto surrounding vegetation to leave the nest. Here, three queens (*Lasius paralienus*) make their way to the end of a blade of grass to prepare to depart.

Lasius sp queen. A fertilised queen will establish a new colony by digging a hole in the ground where she can lay and shelter her eggs.

wing muscles, which are no longer of any use. The queen thus has access to an energy supply that allows her to survive and to lay nutritive eggs (without embryos) with which she feeds her larvae until the emergence of the first workers. These workers will then forage for food outside the nest.

Before leaving her natal nest for the nuptial flight, the queen feeds copiously and will be able to use the contents of her gizzard to feed her first larvae. The workers will increase the size of the nest as their numbers increase. After a few years the colony arrives at maturity, meaning that it will now produce sexual individuals. Of the new queens produced by a colony, it is calculated that less than 5% will eventually produce a mature colony. The majority of queens are eaten by predators.

There are many variations on this general theme. Several queens may come together to form a new colony. The first workers to hatch will generally kill all queens except one. This is the case in certain *Lasius* species. In other cases, the newly fertilised queen is accepted into an already formed colony. A colony can therefore become 'polygynous' (with more than one queen) by the adoption of new queens each breeding season. This is the case for various *Formica* and *Myrmica* species. In *Cataglyphis* species and certain *Proformica* species, queens are wingless and are fertilised at the nest entrance by males (which are winged) from nearby nests. In this case, the queen does not found a colony alone but is accompanied by workers from the original colony. Dispersal is thus much reduced, as the group moves by walking on the ground. This is also the case in *Aphaenogaster senilis*, where the queen has reduced wings that do not allow for flight. *Formicoxenus nitidulus*, *Anergates atratulus* and some *Cardiocondyla* and *Hypoponera* males are wingless. These males generally live longer and can mate several times.

Labour division

One of the most surprising characteristics of ant societies is labour division between workers. When observing the activities of a colony at any one moment, it can be seen that each worker is specialised in a certain task. The different behavioural categories are usually: care of the queen, care of the brood, looking after the nest, defence, nest entry surveillance and foraging for food. There is always quite a large proportion of relatively inactive workers that spend most of their time idly in the nest. These workers play an important role, though, as they are crucial in the event of an accidental disappearance of a large proportion of workers of the same behavioural caste (foragers may be destroyed en masse by a predator lying in wait at the nest entrance).

In most species, workers change function according to age. As soon as they hatch they are active in the centre of the colony (caring for the queen and brood and looking after the nest), then after several days they go out of the nest on defensive duties and to forage for food.

Cataglyphis piliscapa worker carrying material whilst caring for the nest.

A *Proformica* worker feeding a larva by regurgitating liquid contained in its gizzard.

To defend their dome, red ant workers eject formic acid at any intruder.

Trophallaxis between two *Camponotus aethiops* workers.

Given that only a small proportion of workers participate in searching for food, these workers have to share and distribute nourishment between all members of the colony. In most species, workers accumulate food in liquid form in a special part of their digestive tract, the gizzard. The nutritive liquid is carried to the nest and regurgitated in the form of droplets to other members of the colony: queens, larvae and workers inside or outside the nest. This process is termed 'trophallaxis'. It implies the presence of a donor, which has a full gizzard, and one or more receivers that need food. The latter use their antennae to tap the mouthparts of the donor with a rapid, rhythmic movement. The donor then opens its mandibles and regurgitates a drop of liquid, which the receiver swallows as quickly as it is provided. Trophallaxis thus provides a quick way of distributing food between members of the colony and in particular between workers charged with providing food and those caring for the brood. In many species, the queen is fed mainly in this manner. However, some species do not practise trophallaxis, as in the case of species in the Ponerinae subfamily and of the

Proformica species 'honeypot' worker, recognised by its extended gaster.

In colonies of species of the *Temnothorax* genus, here *T. tuberum*, all workers are the same size. This species is said to be 'monomorph'.

genus *Aphaenogaster*, for example. Food distribution can also sometimes be done by transporting a droplet in the mandibles.

In other species, workers ingest such large quantities of liquid that their gizzard becomes so dilated as to impede their movement. When food is scarce, these workers, named 'honeypots', regurgitate food that is distributed to other members of the colony. This strategy is most notable in species that occupy very dry, desert areas, such as of the genus *Proformica*.

Polymorphism

Ant species are either monomorph, without any variation in size between workers, or polymorph, with an important variation in size and morphology between workers, which allows for their being divided into subcastes. For example, in *Pheidole pallidula*, workers are differentiated into minor (normal) and major (soldier) forms, the latter with disproportionately large heads. In other forms, variation is continuous, such as in species of the *Cataglyphis*, *Camponotus* and *Messor* genera. Morphological variation is associated with behavioural differences. In *Pheidole pallidula*, soldiers are mainly occupied with nest defence. Laboratory experiments have shown that colonies that are exposed to the presence of other highly competitive species produce more majors. In species of the granivorous genus *Messor*, large workers, specialised in the breaking open of large seeds, have very big heads which contain strong muscles that power their mandibles. In most ants, the factors that determine size variation within a species are not genetic. The worker's caste is not predetermined in the egg, which can produce any of the morphologically different castes; rather, differentiation occurs during the larval stages. The amount of food provided by workers and temperature are the two most important determining factors. Worker size also varies according to the colony's age, which determines the number of

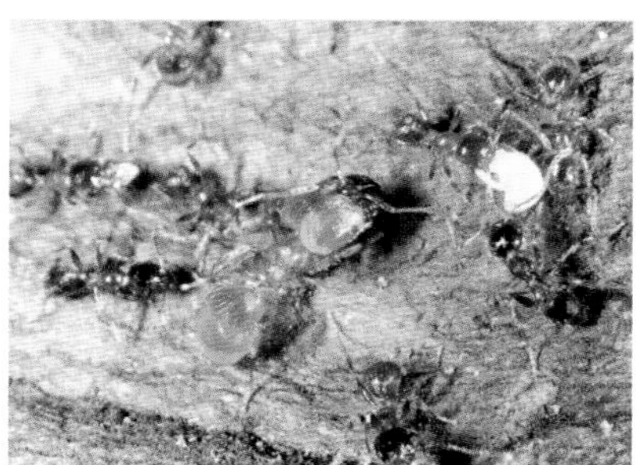

In *Pheidole pallidula* there are two morphologically distinct categories of workers: majors (individual in the centre) with a very big head, and minors (all others).

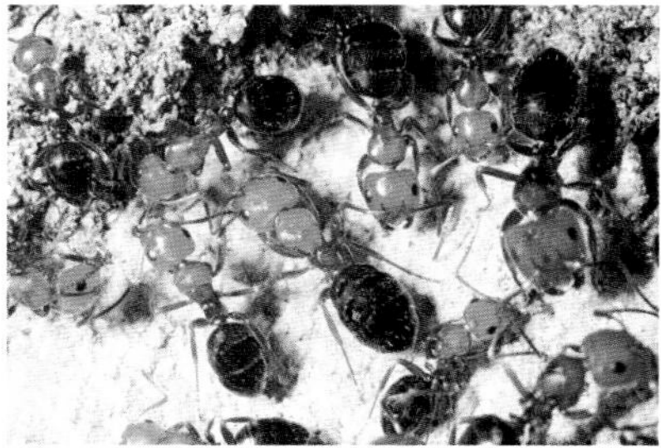

In *Camponotus lateralis* there is significant variation in the size of workers of the same colony. All intermediate sizes exist between the smallest and the largest.

workers bringing back food. Young colonies produce smaller workers than older colonies. This tendency is found as much in monomorph as in polymorph species; young colonies of the latter do not produce large workers.

Colony recognition

In the vast majority of species, colonies are termed 'closed'. This means that workers belonging to the same colony cooperate between themselves but are aggressive towards strangers, even if they are individuals of the same species. This discrimination between members from the same nest and outsiders operates by smell. Each colony possesses its own odour, which is termed the 'colony visa', and is made up of a cocktail of hydrocarbons carried on the cuticle. The colony visa may be composed of several dozen different chemicals. Frequent grooming between different members of the same colony allows for a permanent homogenisation of the colony odour by the transfer of these hydrocarbons from one individual to another. Ants are able to perceive variations in the relative proportions of these compositions, which allows for an infinite number of different combinations and thus avoiding two colonies having the same odour. Ants perceive this odour through sensors on their antennae when in contact with the cuticle of another ant. The reaction of an ant on sensing that another individual has a different colony odour depends on the context, and varies from one species to another. As an example, workers of species in the genus *Temnothorax* that encounter a stranger far from their nest are more likely to do an about-turn, whereas red ant workers (of the subgenus *Formica sensu stricto*) will attack. All species react in the same way when confronted with a stranger trying to penetrate their nest: they attack!

There are a few exceptions to this general rule. The most notable is that

Two *Camponotus cruentatus* workers inspecting each other. The 'colony visa' is detected via the antennae.

of the Argentinian species *Linepithema humile*, considered to be one of the most invasive species of ant globally. Within its natural range, in South America, it is considered to have 'closed' colonies. But in areas where it has been introduced, individuals from different nests are not aggressive towards each other and will even exchange broods or queens. This phenomenon is particularly spectacular along the Mediterranean coast, where it appears that there is a super-colony stretching from Italy to Portugal.

This brings us to the important distinction between 'nest' and 'colony'. A nest is a well-defined space in which individuals of the same colony occur (individuals that are not aggressive towards each other). But a colony may contain several nests. For example, in *Crematogaster scutellaris*, which builds a nest in natural cavities (trees, bark, rocks, stone walls, etc.), the main nest containing the queen can be surrounded by several satellite nests, essentially used for rearing broods. The different nests are linked by chemically marked trails along which workers carry broods. During the winter, the ants in some species come together in the main nest and abandon the satellite nests.

Communication

Communication in ants is principally based on the presence of chemical compounds. Ants have many exocrine glands (which excrete chemicals to the outside of the body). Substances excreted by these glands, pheromones, are the basis of a complex means of communication. The two main types of information transmitted by pheromones pertain to the locality of food sources and the presence of danger.

The glands used in trail pheromone production are at the extreme back of the gaster or on the rear legs of a worker. They produce non-volatile chemical compounds that are placed on the ground and designed to stay for several hours, even days. This method

Three *Messor barbarus* workers bring seeds back to the nest following a chemical trail connecting the nest and a seed-rich area.

of communication allows for those species using it to be quick and efficient in capitalising on important food resources, thus making them more competitive than the species that do not employ it.

Alarm pheromones are produced when workers perceive danger, and are designed to inform other colony members. The workers perceiving the pheromone react either by releasing alarm pheromones in turn and becoming more aggressive, or by fleeing with the brood in order to try to protect it. Alarm pheromones are composed of very volatile chemicals that enable extremely rapid transfer of information. Worker coordination when confronted by a perceived enemy is thus very efficient. These pheromones are released from glands in the gaster or the head. Their effect is particularly obvious in *Crematogaster scutellaris*. When a nest is disturbed, workers lift their gasters in a characteristic manner, and it is possible to see a silvery droplet at the tip of the sting; this is not functional but allows for precise placing of the alarm pheromone. The workers can then be seen hurrying in numbers towards the perceived threat.

In the event of danger, *Crematogaster scutellaris* workers raise the alarm by producing a pheromone droplet from the end of their gaster.

Providing food

A diverse diet

Ancestral ants probably preyed on other arthropods, but their diet has become more diverse over the course of their evolution. The majority of species are omnivorous, as happy with dead animals as sugary liquids. The spectrum of potential prey species is broad (insects, spiders, myriapods, molluscs, etc.). Ants also eat vertebrates and dead invertebrates. In the wild, their main source of sugary liquids is honeydew from sap-sucking Hemiptera. These insects suck the sap from plants, which has a high sugar content but is poor in amino acids. They must therefore absorb a large quantity of sap in order to fulfil their needs, excreting excess sugar and water in the form of honeydew. Many species of ant are highly dependent on honeydew. This is the case with the red ants (*Formica* subgenus in the strict sense), for which honeydew makes up more than half their food intake. Black *Lasius* species (*Lasius* subgenus) are regular aphid visitors too. They protect 'their' aphids from predators (such as ladybirds) and parasites. Root-dwelling aphids are used by several ant genera with underground habits such as *Tetramorium* species, *Crematogaster sordidula* and yellow *Lasius* species (*Cautolasius* and *Chthonolasius* subgenera). Non-floral nectar and, to

Formica lugubris workers visiting an aphid colony to harvest their excretions, commonly named 'honeydew'.

Messor barbarus worker bringing a seed back to the nest. All *Messor* species are granivorous.

Camponotus cruentatus worker drinking nectar from an Apiaceae flower.

a lesser extent, flower nectar may also be sought after by ants. Certain *Camponotus* species, such as *C. aethiops* and *C. piceus*, often inspect the flowerheads of euphorbias or Apiaceae species (umbellifers) in search of nectar.

Other ant species have very specialised diets. The *Messor*, for example, even though they occasionally accept animal prey, are almost exclusively granivorous. On the other hand, the Ponerinae feed mainly on small arthropods living in the soil or ground litter. *Cataglyphis* species that only occupy open areas in the Mediterranean zone feed mainly on insect corpses that they collect during the hottest part of the day, when there is the least competition. The habits of species of the genus *Solenopsis* are still hardly known, but it appears clear that they steal the broods of larger ant species in order to feed on them. The same sorts of raids on neighbouring ant colonies also occur in species of the genus *Formica*.

Methods of harvesting and predation

There are two main ways in which ants collect food: individually or as a group. In the first case, each individual forages, captures and brings food back to the nest independently. Target prey items are relatively small, with choice limited by the workers' capacity. This type of foraging is characteristic of members of the Ponerinae but exists in other genera too, for example species of *Cataglyphis*, *Proformica*, *Camponotus* and *Temnothorax*. In the second case, workers forage individually for prey or sugary substances, but recruit

Temnothorax aveli workers hunt alone. The size of the prey is therefore limited by the size of the worker (about 2.5 mm).

Several *Formica lugubris* workers carrying a large insect.

A *Cataglyphis* worker helping another worker to carry its prey back to the nest.

A group of *Tapinoma nigerrimum* workers cut a large food source into pieces that are easier to transport.

further nest members once a food source has been found. Thus, prey capture and food carrying is the cooperative action of several workers. On the edge of red ant (*Formica* subgenus) nests, it is easy to observe several workers carrying, in a more or less coordinated way, a newly killed large insect. Recruitment to the group may be passive, in which a worker tries to bring the food back to the nest alone but is aided by others encountered along the way, as in *Cataglyphis* and *Formica* species. Alternatively, recruitment may be active, in which the worker returns to the nest without food and incites other workers in the nest to follow it to recover the food, as in *Lasius* and *Myrmica* species.

Cooperative food carrying by a group allows for much larger prey items to be dealt with. This strategy is therefore more effective than individual foraging. In the case of a large, immobile food sources that cannot be transported back to the nest in one piece, such as the body of a vertebrate or large invertebrate or a squashed fruit, labour division may be used. Certain workers will defend the food source whilst others carry the food in pieces back to the nest. In *Pheidole* species, for example, soldiers will defend the resource and cut it into pieces, whereas minor workers carry the pieces off. The same species may harvest food either as individuals or as a group, depending on the type of food source. For instance, species of the *Camponotus*, *Myrmica* and *Temnothorax* genera normally carry food items back to the nest individually, but rely on recruitment when a large sugary resource has been found.

Orientation

Depending on the species, harvesting workers orientate themselves using visual or chemical markers. The presence of chemical trails is an easily observed and spectacular phenomenon. When a worker detects a source of food it returns directly to the nest using visual markers, integrating the trail used when leaving the nest whilst also forming a pheromone trail. Recruited workers then follow this trail themselves, releasing their own trail pheromones along the way. Once the food source is finished, the workers no longer release pheromones, so the trail quickly disappears through evaporation. The most spectacular trails are those of black *Lasius* species, red ants (of the *Formica* subgenus), *Messor* species and *Crematogaster scutellaris*. In these last two examples they can continue for several days and are visible on the ground, as there is less vegetation and a change in the particle size of the surface due to the ants' activities. In

Messor barbatus workers follow a chemical trail to a food source. These trails appear as 'highways' and are perfectly visible on the ground.

the red ants (*Formica* subgenus) the most important trails generally lead to trees in which the ants are using aphids. In the genus *Messor*, large trails become progressively more separated the further they are from the nest, and lead to areas with many seeds. Chemical trails are usually the result of collective effort, although it is thought probable that individual chemical trails exist in certain species, such as *Temnothorax unifasciatus*.

In species that forage individually, orientation is essentially visual. Orientation processes have long been studied in *Cataglyphis* species. These ants generally occur in poor desert-type habitats with few visual markers, in which orientation can be a real challenge. Moreover, the nest entrance is a simple hole in the ground and difficult to see. So, the ants combine several sources of information to find their nest after long excursions. They use celestial clues (the sun's position) in order to judge which direction to take successively, and will remember certain visual markers if they exist. They also estimate the distance they have covered in the number of 'strides'. Thanks to the incorporation of all these sources of information, ants are capable of returning directly, in a straight line, to their nests. It also appears that once an ant approaches the nest entrance, finding it is made easier by the presence of pheromones.

The few studies that have covered the individual development of exploration and harvesting capacities in worker ants indicate that young workers need several days of exploration to be efficient. Their first outings are strictly limited to the immediate area around the nest entrance. Then they go progressively further from the nest on longer explorations. Their first outings allow them to learn the topography of the nearby area. Capturing prey also involves a learning process, young workers being far less adept than older ones.

Social parasitism

The term 'social parasitism' in the context of ants is used when a society of one species lives at the expense of the society of another or the same species. More than 200 species of ants practise social parasitism (about 70 occur in Europe). It is a strategy that appears rare, as there are more than 13,000 species of ants worldwide, but it seems to be commoner in temperate areas. Colonies used as hosts by social parasites can be either of the same species, 'intraspecific parasitism', or of a different species, 'interspecific'. The second type is the most interesting, as it results in colonies containing more than one species (usually two). The term 'parasitism' is used to describe these interactions because it accords with two particular characteristics: the two species live together (it is thus symbiotic), and this interaction is beneficial for one of the set of individuals and harmful for the other. The characteristic of living together distinguishes social parasitism from predation. Indeed, certain species of ant raid other colonies, trying to take their brood which will later be eaten (predation). This occurs in *Solenopsis* species, for example. A different strategy is used by slavemaker species: these capture broods from other species in order to increase the work output of their colony (parasitism). Several types of parasitic strategies exist in ants. For simplicity we have placed these in four broad categories, but in reality the situation is more complex, and intermediate situations exist.

Xenobiosis

Ants that perform xenobiosis live within the colony of another species but in a separate compartment. They raise their own brood independently and do not mix with that of their host, but they depend on the host for a nest and for provision of food. In Europe, there is just one xenobiotic species, *Formicoxenus nitidulus*. These ants construct their nests in the walls of *Formica* (essentially subgenus *Formica* and maybe subgenus *Coptoformica*) species' nest domes. It is not fully known how they acquire food, as this cannot be observed in the field (*Formicoxenus* ants rarely occur outside the dome). It is possible that they steal their host's brood and hunt small arthropods within the dome's decomposing plant material. The energy cost of the presence of a *Formicoxenus* colony for a *Formica* colony is not known but is probably very low due to the great difference between the two genera: *Formicoxenus* ants measure 3 mm, and their colonies include at most a few hundred relatively inactive workers, whereas *Formica* species are two to three times bigger and colonies contain several tens of thousands of very active workers.

Formicoxenus nitidulus (worker indicated by an arrow) is a small ant species that lives exclusively in the domes of ants of the genus *Formica* (the two large workers in the photo).

Temporary parasitism

Temporary parasitism corresponds to the usurpation of a colony by a founding queen. The founding parasite queen enters the host colony, kills the resident queen and takes advantage of those workers present to rear its own brood. It is not able to found its own colony independently. Once all the host workers have died, there are sufficient parasite workers to assure the autonomous functioning of the colony. Temporary parasitic species only need a host species when founding a colony, and it is only at this stage in their development that the two species occur together (parasite and host species). In Europe, all species of the genus *Bothriomyrmex* are temporary parasites that use *Tapinoma* species as hosts. *Lasius fuliginosus* and *Lasius* species of the subgenus *Chthonolasius* parasitise

Ants of the genus *Bothriomyrmex* (the brown workers) are temporary parasites of *Tapinoma* species (black worker). The young colonies contain both species.

In the genus Lasius, certain species such as those of the subgenus *Chthonolasius* (yellow workers) are temporary parasites of other *Lasius* species (black workers) such as *L. psammophilus* shown here.

other *Lasius* species. It is also the case that *Formica* species of the subgenus *Coptoformica* and *Formica* species *sensu stricto* use *Formica* species of the subgenus *Serviformica* as hosts.

Certain species are optional temporary parasites and use a colony of the same species as a host. This is the case in *Temnothorax nylanderi*, of which a certain proportion establish colonies in this way.

Slavemakers

In general, queens of so-called 'slavemaker' species do not found colonies independently but replace the queen of a host colony, as in temporary parasites. During its entire life the colony raids host colonies in order to capture broods. Once the host workers hatch in the parasite colony, they work at the different tasks necessary for colony life as if they were in their own colony. The first naturalists to observe this behaviour were fascinated by its similarity to the slavery practised by humans, and thus used the same term. Despite its human and historical connotations, and the efforts of some of the scientific community to change it, the term still remains in common use. Generally, slavemaker species cannot survive without their hosts, as the parasite workers are usually ineffective in the everyday tasks of the colony, such as caring for the brood and the nest, providing food, nest defence and so on. Some species are completely dependent on trophallaxis for nourishment, food being solicited from host workers.

Different founding methods may result in physiological and behavioural adaptations in queens. These adaptations have particularly been studied in *Polyergus rufescens*, an Amazonian species. When she looks to found a new colony, the young *Polyergus rufescens* queen secretes an incredibly small amount of cuticular hydrocarbons, allowing her to escape the attentions of the workers of the host nest she enters. She can also emit repellent substances. Once inside the nest she kills the host queen and actively licks her in order to acquire her odour, which facilitates the invading queen's acceptance by host workers. Another behavioural adaptation is seen in queens of species of the genus *Myrmoxenus* (all members of this genus are now considered to be in the genus *Temnothorax*): when they feel that they are being investigated by host workers they roll up, taking the form of a pupa, which decreases the aggressiveness of the workers. Certain host workers go as far as grabbing queens adopting this posture and taking them into the nest. Finally, in *Myrmoxenus ravouxi* (now renamed *Temnothorax ravouxi*) the queen engages in a body fight with a host worker, during which she rubs herself on the worker, without doubt allowing her to acquire the colony odour and penetrate the nest more easily. However, the percentage of founding failures in slavemaker species seems to be very high. Once in the nest, the new parasite queen must kill the host queen. In *Myrmoxenus* species the parasite queen grips the host queen by the neck with her mandibles. This strangling, which probably severs the nervous system, may last several days, even several weeks, and results in the host queen's death.

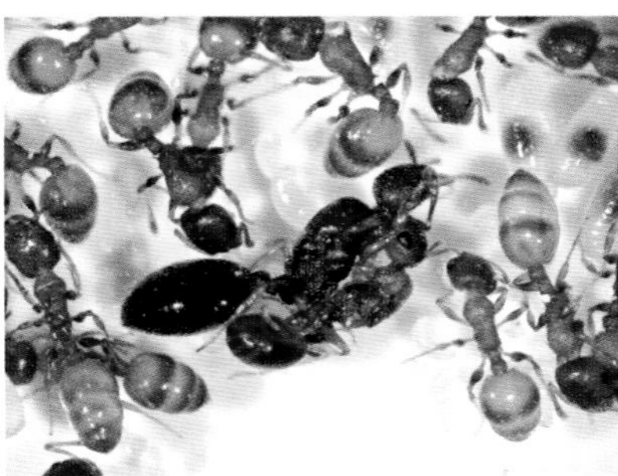

A queen (small queen on the underside) of the slavemaker species *Myrmoxenus ravouxi* takes possession of a *Temnothorax* nest, here *T. aveli*, and replaces the host queen (the large queen on the top) after having strangled her.

In most slavemaker species, workers have morphological and physiological characteristics that equip them for fighting. Of the morphological characters, mandibles are the most spectacular. In *Polyergus rufescens* and species of the genus *Strongylognathus* they are sabre-shaped, which allows them to easily pierce their victim's cuticle. In *Harpagoxenus sublaevis* they have a wide cutting edge, without teeth, which allows for the effective slicing of antennae and legs. Among other adaptations, workers of certain slavemaker species have thick antennae, petioles and postpetioles. These parts of the body are often the target of mandibles during fighting and their thickness probably makes them more resistant. *Harpagoxenus sublaevis* workers produce a substance that, once placed on a host worker, increases aggressiveness in host co-workers. Workers of the host nest then end up attacking each other.

In most species, raids follow the same sequence. First, a few workers leave individually in search of a host nest. Once this is detected, each worker returns to its colony, recruits co-workers, and leads them to the host nest on a raid. Members of the genus *Polyergus* practise mass recruitment and make spectacular raids involving hundreds of workers.

They move rapidly in a straight line towards the targeted nest that may be several dozen metres away.

Once the slavemaker workers have brought a brood back to their nest, it is taken over and looked after by the host workers. In ants, colony recognition partly occurs by learning the colony odour from hatching. Thus, when the host workers hatch in the parasite colony, they are familiar with that colony's odour and consider it as their own. This is probably why they work and behave just as they would in their own colony.

In slavemaker species there are different degrees of specialisation. The least specialised are exemplified by *Formica sanguinea*, a species in which the proportion of slave workers in the nest is very variable. There are even colonies without any slave workers, which are not therefore practising slavery. This species is thus an optional slavemaker (the only such species in Europe). *Formica sanguinea* workers show no morphological slavemaker adaptations. In all other European slavemaker species, colonies cannot survive without the presence of host workers – the parasite workers being specialised in performing raids. This is the case in about 20 European species: *Chalepoxenus kutteri*, *C. muellerianus*, *Harpagoxenus sublaevis*, *Myrmoxenus bernardi*, *M. gordiagini*, *M. kraussei*, *M. ravouxi*, *M. stumperi*, *Polyergus rufescens*, *Rossomyrmex minuchae* and the 11 species of the genus *Strongylognathus*.

In general, the number of slave workers in a nest is far higher than

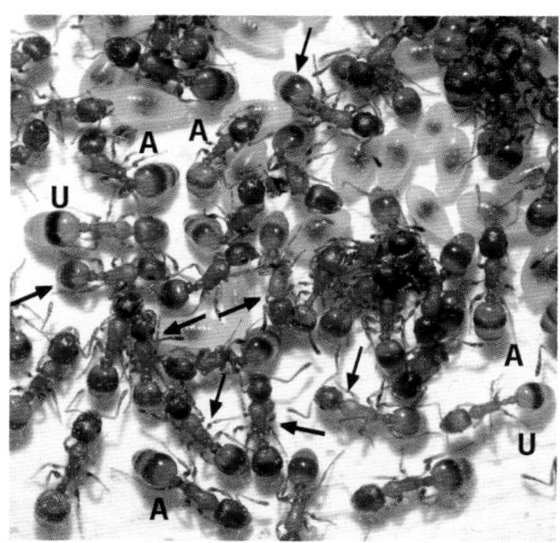

Myrmoxenus ravouxi is a slavemaker species in which the workers (arrowed) very much resemble host workers. Several different host species can be found in the same nest. Here, for example, is a mix of *Temnothorax aveli* (A) and *T. unifasciatus* (U) workers.

that of the slavemaker workers that only leave the nest to perform raids. Coupled with the fact that they are quite rare, this means that they are difficult to detect in the field. In *Myrmoxenus kraussei* (now *Temnothorax kraussei*), the very few parasite workers apparently do not perform raids. However, they are capable of doing so in laboratory conditions, which suggests that slavemaking is an ancestral state of this species but that the species' evolution has tended towards the disappearance of performing raids, giving rise to a different strategy: inquilinism.

Inquilinism

Inquiline species tend to produce only sexual individuals, which are reared by the workers of a host colony. In most species the worker caste does not exist. In Europe this is the case for the following species: *Anergates atratulus* (now *Tetramorium atratulum*), *Teleutomyrmex kutteri* (now *Tetramorium kutteri*), *Teleutomyrmex schneideri* (now *Tetramorium inquilinum*), *Myrmoxenus corsica* (now *Temnothorax corsicus*), *Myrmica lemasnei*, *M. karavajevi*, *Leptothorax pacis*, *L. goesswaldi*, *L. kutteri* and *Plagiolepis xene*. The vast majority of inquiline species do not kill the reigning queen of the host colony, as these species produce no or few workers and need the host queen in order to produce workers that will rear their own brood. There are, however, some well-documented, notable exceptions where the host queen is systematically killed: *Myrmoxenus corsica* and *M. kraussei*. In these two species the host queen is strangled by the parasite queen using her mandibles at the time of founding, as in other species in the genus *Myrmoxenus*. This genus, containing only parasitic species, presents different levels of social parasitism: slavemaking (*M. gordiagini*, *M. ravouxi* and *M. stumperi*), inquilism (*M. corsica*) and what appears to be an intermediate level (*M. kraussei* and *M. bernardi*) in which the queens have a typically inquiline mode of life (producing sexual individuals in their first year, but with no renewing of host workers) but themselves produce a few workers that still have the capacity to make raids. This situation would indicate that, in this group, inquilinism has derived directly from slavemaking during their evolution. However, in most cases inquiline species seem to have evolved from a non-parasitic species. The reproductive strategy of *Myrmica rubra* illustrates what could be the emergence of an inquiline species. This polygynous species has macrogynes (large queens producing many workers) and microgynes (much smaller queens that essentially produce new microgynes and males). The two may coexist in the same nest but are not closely related. The microgyne strategy is similar to inquilism, as queens use those workers produced by macrogynes to rear their sexual offspring. The question as to whether macrogynes and microgynes represent different species is always an object of debate in the scientific community. In this matter, genetic analysis has not provided a clear answer. It is quite possible that at the moment they are a single species and the two reproductive systems are still diverging. The hypothesis that inquilism can evolve from a duo of reproductive strategies in this way requires further discussion.

The different forms of social parasitism described earlier are known in groups of taxonomically very different ants. Temporary parasitism, slavemaking and inquilinism have each evolved independently in at least two subfamilies. The similarities seen in certain behavioural and morphological adaptations, no matter how surprising they seem, are due to convergent evolution. An obvious example is the killing of the host queen by strangulation, common in the temporary parasites of the genus *Bothrio-*

myrmex (Dolichoderinae subfamily) and the slavemakers of the genus *Myrmoxenus* (Myrmicinae). Another example is that of the sabre-shaped mandibles which occur in the slave-maker species of the *Polyergus* (Formicinae) and *Strongylognathus* (Myrmicinae) genera. Despite being fascinating, the biology of many social parasite species remains little known. This is, for instance, the case in parasitic species of the *Myrmica*, *Strongylognathus* and *Plagiolepis* genera. There is a serious lack of field observations for parasitic species; their study should be encouraged.

Interactions between ants and other arthropods

Trophobiosis

Trophobiosis is an association in which ants obtain food from another arthropod without killing it. This concerns two groups of insects: Hemiptera and Lepidoptera. These arthropods produce sugary substances appreciated by ants, which, in exchange, protect them from predators and parasites.

Hemiptera – This insect order contains four suborders, two of which are connected to ants through trophobiosis: the Auchenorrhyncha (spittlebugs, leafhoppers, planthoppers, etc.) and the Sternorrhyncha (aphids, scale insects or mealy bugs, etc.). All Hemiptera that have a trophic relationship with ants are sap-suckers. They have a diet very rich in sugar and water. These two components are found in quantity in their excrement, which forms what is termed 'honeydew'. It is very easy to find ants active in aphid or scale insect colonies, harvesting honeydew. After a few minutes of observation an ant may be seen tapping an aphid's abdomen tip with its antennae. The aphid then excretes a drop of honeydew which is immediately absorbed by the ant. Honeydew of aphids and scale insects is a very important food source for ants. In certain species, such as the red ants (*Formica* genus, *Formica* subgenus), honeydew represents more than half their food intake. Other species, such as those of the *Lasius* and *Tetramorium* genera, manage aphid and scale insect colonies on roots and may carry them from one site to another. The presence of sap-sucking Hemiptera contribute to there being high concentrations of ants. The best way of observing such interactions is to look for aphid colonies on new plant shoots. Certain ant species protect aphid colonies by attacking all intruders trying to get too close (ladybirds, lacewings, Syrphidae fly larvae). The relationship appears to be mutually beneficial: it is termed 'trophic mutualism'. However, when prey is short, ants may prey on aphids. They are thus comparable to cattle used by humans to produce milk and also meat.

Lepidoptera – In Europe, many ants have trophic relationships with butterflies of the Lycaenidae family. Trophobiosis is practised by about three-quarters of Lycaenidae species.

Many ant species, such as *Formica rufibarbis*, visit aphid colonies to collect honeydew (sap-sucking Hemiptera excrement).

This *Lasius* sp. worker has just taken a drop of honeydew excreted by an aphid.

A *Crematogaster scutellaris* worker taking a drop of honeydew excreted by a scale insect.

An ant of the genus *Tetramorium* rearing a root-sucking aphid.

Trophic Hemiptera in a *Formica lemani* nest.

Caterpillars of these Lepidoptera have an exocrine gland at the rear end of their body, which extrudes a sugary substance appreciated by ants. Instead of treating the caterpillar as a prey item, the ants protect it from potential predators in order to ensure access to the liquid. Indeed, caterpillars of certain Lycaenidae species are capable of emitting substances that mimic the alarm pheromones of ants in order to alert them to potential danger.

The majority of interactions between Lycaenidae species and ants are of the mutualism type, but certain Lycaenidae species have evolved towards a parasitic strategy. This is true for the five species of the genus *Phengaris* (previously *Maculinea*) present in Europe, whose caterpillars begin their development by feeding on their host plant. They then emit an odour attractive to species of *Myrmica* ants, which carry them into the ants' nest. The caterpillars finish their development within the ants' nest, either by feeding on the ants' brood or being fed by workers by trophallaxis. Only ants of the genus *Myrmica* are concerned with the development of *Phengaris* species caterpillars. For a long time it was supposed that each *Phengaris* species used just one species of *Myrmica*. In fact, each *Phengaris* species is able to use several species as a host but only parasitises one or two at the same site. Those *Myrmica* species most commonly exploited as hosts are: *M. sabuleti*, *M. scabrinodis*, *M. ruginodis* and *M. schencki*.

Myrmecophily

A species is said to be 'myrmecophile' if it gains advantage from ants' activities. This term incorporates a large range of invertebrates that interact with ants. Due to their social organisation in colonies, ants concentrate certain resources in one site – the nest. The brood, food brought to the nest and waste from the colony may all be exploited by other organisms. It is therefore not surprising that many animals, particularly arthropods, are specialised in using these resources. The different interactions that exist between ants and other arthropods are very varied and thus difficult to categorise. Furthermore, the nature of the interactions between two particular species may vary according to environmental conditions. It is thus not helpful to classify these interactions according to their functional characteristics. We have chosen to divide them into two categories: relationships that occur around the nest, and those that occur in the nest. In the first case, interactions last a short time. In the second, any individual must penetrate the nest and thus be specifically adapted to avoid rejection by the workers.

Arthropods living in the environs of the nest – Numerous species of spiders, bugs and rove beetles are myrmecophile and very much resemble ants. This resemblance allows some of these species to approach ants more easily in order to catch them. Given that ants are efficient predators of other arthropods, it is probable that for most myrmecophile species such a resemblance has evolved because they have gained protection from it. Indeed, it has been shown that certain predatory arthropods more readily attack morphologically distinct species rather than other myrmecophile species.

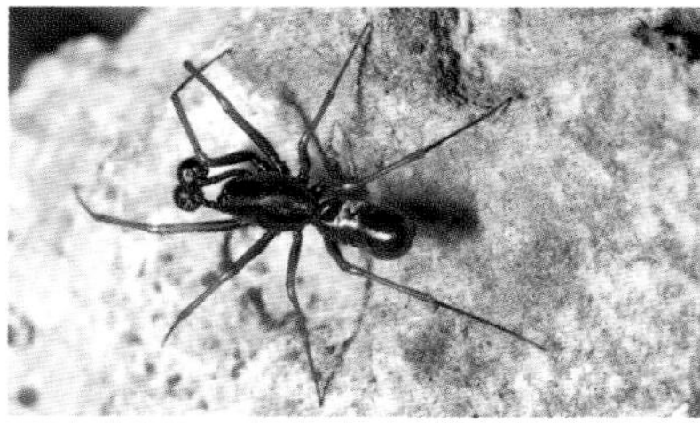

A myrmecophilic spider.

A myrmecophilic bug.

Many beetles follow ant trails to steal and eat prey that the ants have captured.

Arthropods living in the nest – Ant societies are said to be closed, which is to say that workers will kill all individuals not belonging to the colony. However, several arthropod species are capable of entering ants' nests and becoming more or less closely integrated into the colony. As well as gaining food from the ants or their activities, these intruders benefit indirectly from their protection from potential predators, parasites and parasitoids. Integration into the colony occurs either by the production of calming substances, such as by attaining the colony odour from the host workers (chemical camouflage), or by the production of an odour similar to that of the host colony (chemical mimicry).

Woodlice of the genus *Platyarthrus* live in the nests of a variety of ants; here a species of the genus *Tetramorium*.

Several species of silverfish occur only in ants' nests. They frequently appear in the nests of *Messor* species; here *Messor minor*, in Corsica.

Small white woodlice (isopod crustaceans) such as *Platyarthrus hoffmannseggi* or *P. schobli* and pale yellow silverfish (wingless insects) only occur in ants' nests, of various species. Apparently they survive on ants' nest rejections and thus are not at all harmful to the ant colony.

In Orthoptera, the ant-crickets of the genus *Myrmecophilus* are of course myrmecophile. These small crickets, less than 3 mm in length, can only live in association with ants; they complete their whole life cycle within the nest. They are especially found in the nests of *Pheidole pallidula* and species of the *Crematogaster*, *Camponotus* and *Messor* genera. They can solicit workers to feed them by regurgitation. They partly acquire the odour of the colony they inhabit, but the chemical camouflage is not perfect and they are sometimes attacked by workers. They can change host species during the course of their life, in which case their odour also changes. Young may occasionally be seen following *Crematogatser scutellaris* trails.

In certain hoverfly species of the genus *Microdon* (Syrphidae family, Microdontinae subfamily), larval development occurs at a cost to the ants. Their large hemispherical larvae

Small ant-crickets of the genus *Myrmecophilus* live exclusively in ants' nests; here *Messor structor*.

A large *Microdon* (hoverfly) larva attended by workers from the *Myrmica scabrinodis* host colony.

are sometimes integrated into the colony, allowing them to feed on the brood throughout their development. They produce an odour similar to that of the host species and thus are one of the rare examples of chemical mimicry. Adults leave the nest straight after hatching. In the most studied European species, *Microdon mutabilis*, the hoverfly's eggs are laid at the *Formica lemani* nest entrance and the young larvae crawl into the nest. The eggs' odour corresponds to that of the parasitised host ants and if placed into a different ant population, they are detected and destroyed by the workers. Thus, each *Microdon mutabilis* population is adapted to the local population of the *Formica lemani* host.

There exists a large diversity of myrmecophile beetles. The rove beetle *Atemeles pubicollis*, a Staphylinid, develops during the summer in a *Formica polyctena* dome, and during the winter period in a *Myrmica* sp. nest. The adult has three types of gland that permit it to be adopted by the ants: secretions from the appeasement glands calm workers when the beetle approaches the nest; those of the adoption glands incite the ants to carry them into the nest; and secretions of the defensive glands repel any ants that are too aggressive in the nest. Larvae and adults feed on the regurgitations of host workers, which they actively solicit. The larvae also possess glands which produce substances that make them attractive to workers. The Staphylinid beetle *Lomechusa strumosa* also uses the same strategy for integration into the host colony. It only occurs in *Formica sanguinea* nests, in which it completes its whole life cycle.

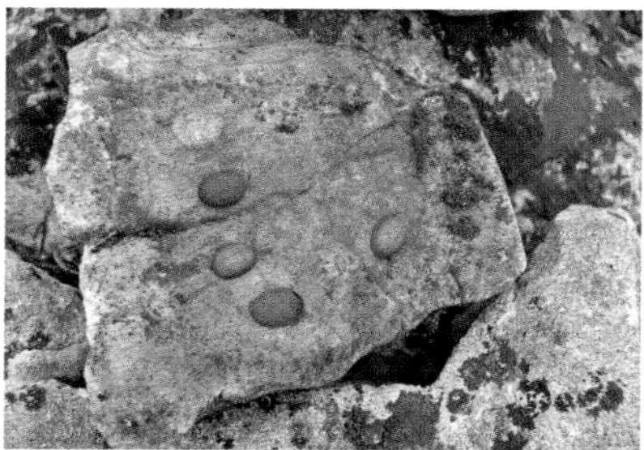

A few *Microdon analis* (hoverfly) larvae under a stone protecting a *Lasius* sp. nest in which they are developing.

A myrmecophile beetle (left) in a *Strongylognathus testaceus* colony.

The myrmecophile Hymenoptera *Solenopsia imitatrix* lives in *Solenopsis* sp. colonies.

The Staphylinid *Lomechusa strumosa* (centre) is dependent on a *Formica sanguinea* colony.

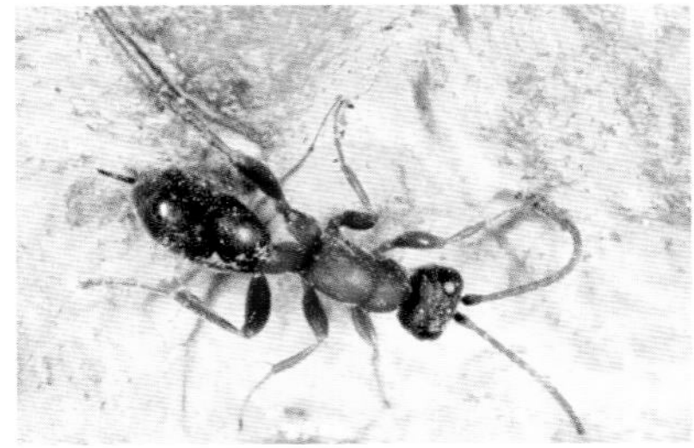

A myrmecophile Ichneumon (Hymenoptera).

A large variety of Hymenoptera species can be found in ants' nests, and their relationships with their hosts have been little studied. A small wasp of the Diapriidae family, *Plagiopria passerai*, completes its whole life cycle in *Plagiolepis pygmaea* colonies. This parasitoid's development takes place on the pupa of a host ant. Two other Diapriidae species, *Solenopsia imitatrix* and *Lepidopria pedestris* nests are found in *Solenopsis* nests. The adults closely resemble their hosts in size and shape but are almost black, whereas *Solenopsis* workers are yellow. Their biology is not well known but it appears that their larvae do not develop within the host colony. The Ichneumonidae family also contains numerous myrmecophile species but their relationships with the species they mimic are largely unknown.

Interactions between plants and ants

Interactions between plants and ants are one of those natural processes that fascinated the first naturalists. The omnipresence and abundance of these two groups in most ecosystems explain the repeated evolution of plant/ant interaction, sometimes very specific and specialised. Despite such interactions being most spectacular in tropical habitats, those of temperate regions are often worthy of interest. The most important are the feeding on and dispersal of seeds by ants, and the protection termed 'mutualism'. This latter interaction implies the protection to plants afforded by ants in exchange for nutritive substances produced by their extrafloral nectaries.

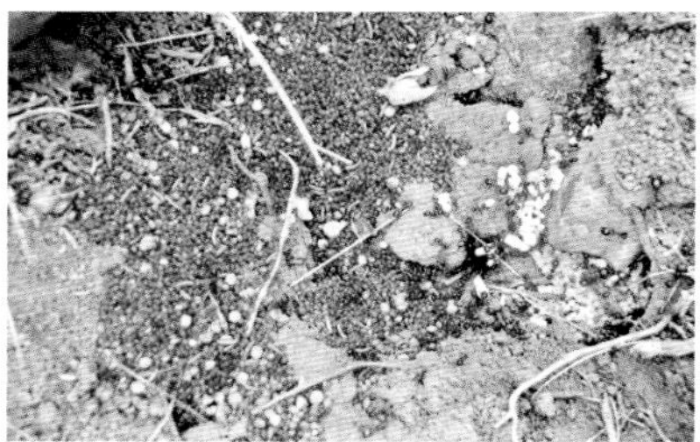

An opened *Messor structor* nest, bringing to light a 'grain store' – a chamber in which the ants store harvested seeds.

Seed eating

Ants do not directly consume either leaves or the wood of trees. Yet certain species are specialised in using seeds as almost their sole food source. In general, seed-eating ants are much more numerous in habitats of short vegetation, rich in herbaceous species, such as meadows, steppe, garrigue, deserts and so on. In Europe the most spectacular and easily observed granivorous ants are those species of the genus *Messor*. These ants of warm, dry habitats are very common in the Mediterranean region. They form populous colonies whose workers show a great variation in size and a morphological adaptation to seed eating. The largest workers have robust mandibles, and an abnormally large head containing the big muscles necessary for breaking seeds. Workers of certain *Messor* species have a series of long, forward-curving 'bristles' under the head (the psammophore) which probably serve in holding and manipulating seeds. *Messor* workers form long harvesting trails when carrying seeds back to the nest. Nests contain several grain stores in which seeds are stored until eaten. Given the large size of colonies and high density of nests in certain habitats, it is not at all surprising that ants can have an important impact on the structure and makeup of the plant community.

Ants of the *Oxyopomyrmex* and *Goniomma* genera are also essentially granivorous. *Pheidole pallidula* and species of the *Tetramorium* genus are occasional seed eaters. When returning to the nest, ants often lose seeds along the harvesting trails, thus contributing to their dispersion. For the plants, it seems highly likely that the disadvantage of consumption by ants far outweighs the advantage they gain from dispersion of their seeds.

Seed dispersion (myrmecochory)

Seeds of certain plants have an elaiosome. These small, fleshy outgrowths, rich in lipids and very attractive to ants, are difficult to dislodge. The diaspore assembly (seed + elaiosome) is carried back to the nest in order to feed the larvae with the elaiosome, a part not at all necessary for germination. This type of interaction differs considerably from the previous one as the ants do not eat the actual seed, only the elaiosome. Being very attractive to ants is an important advantage to the attached seed. In carrying the seed to the nest, the ants help in its dispersion, reducing competition between seeds of the same plant. In addition, once in the nest the seed is no longer visible, protected from fires (especially in dry areas) and a great number of seed-eaters such as birds. Finally, once the elaiosome is eaten, the ants reject the seed into the rest of their waste, which is generally a compost rich in organic matter and particularly suitable for plant development. Myrmecochory is thus an interaction beneficial to both parties, plants and ants. This is non-specific mutualism, that is to say that a large variety of these seeds can attract a wide variety of ant species, and a single species of ant can harvest a large variety of different plant seeds. The presence of one particular species of myrmecochorial plant does not allow for the prediction of the presence of a certain species of ant in that area.

Myrmecochory has evolved independently several times during the course of evolution and occurs in numerous plant families, evidence of the considerable potential benefits. The Western Palearctic region is especially rich in myrmecochorial plants. There are more than 250 species of plant with seeds with an elaiosome in Europe which may be carried by an ant. Observations of ants carrying seeds are relatively rare in non-granivorous species, but it would appear that this does occur more commonly in species of the *Myrmica*, *Tetramorium*, *Lasius* and *Formica* genera. In dry Mediterranean habitats where ants are not that abundant, it is mainly species of the *Tapinoma*, *Aphaenogaster*, *Messor* and *Pheidole* genera that disperse seeds.

Myrmecochory is quite difficult to observe in strictly natural conditions. The most efficient way is to collect

The elaiosome of *Euphorbia helioscopia* (the white part on the left).

A *Messor barbarus* worker attracted by a seed's elaiosome.

seeds of myrmecochoric plants (some species are very common), place them near an ants' nest entrance and wait for the workers to find them. This method requires the observer to intervene and is not truly natural. The greater celandine *Chelidonium majus* (Papaveraceae family) and the annual and dog's Mercuries (*Mercuralis annua* and *perennis*, Euphorbiaceae) are very suitable for this experiment as they are common in gardens and scrub, and their seeds can be collected for a long period of the year. Ants of the *Lasius* and *Myrmica* genera are probably the most suitable as they are also common in gardens. More generally, observations can be carried out on Euphorbiaceae, a family with many myrmecochoric species. There are also many species of violets (*Viola* genus, Violaceae) that are myrmecochoric, their seeds being distributed by species of *Myrmica* and *Tetramorium* in particular.

Myrmecophile plants

Ants may provide plants with efficient protection against the attacks of plant-eating insects. In effect, many species have a varied diet and harvest sugary substances as well as predating other invertebrates. Worker ants are also wingless; they walk along the plant's surface, exploring it more closely than a flying insect would. Furthermore, their ubiquity in most habitats means that the presence of such partners can be relied upon. At various times throughout evolution plants have thus refined different strategies to attract ants. In temperate regions many plants produce non-floral nectar on various structures such as leaves and stipules. This extrafloral nectar, rich in sugars and also sometimes amino acids, serves to attract ants. These plants are considered myrmecophilous.

In searching for extrafloral nectar the ants protect the plant either by capturing plant-eating insects as well as their larvae and eggs, or by changing the behaviour of certain insects when they try to land on the plant. Finally, experiments have shown that flying insects are capable of detecting the presence of ants at a distance and choose plants with the fewest ants. Extrafloral nectar is consumed by other insects such as bees and flies, but they probably do not provide any protection for the plant. As in myrmecochory, this mutualism is not species specific: a species of ant can feed on the extrafloral nectar of several plant species and a single species of plant may be visited by a large variety of ant

A *Lasius* genus worker attracted by the sugary secretions of extrafloral nectar.

species. But, contrary to myrmecochory, the relationship between ants and myrmecophile plants is much more developed in tropical habitats than in temperate regions. Among common myrmecophile species in Europe can be cited all trees in the genus *Prunus* (Rosaceae family). This includes many fruit trees which have two nectar-bearing glands at the base of the leaf stalk, and several species of the genus *Vicia* (Fabaceae family) which include the broad bean *Vicia faba*, common vetch *Vicia sativa* and the tufted vetch *Vicia cracca*, which have nectar-bearing glands near the stipules.

Pollination

Although many ants visit flowers to take nectar, they do not make any significant contribution to pollination. As workers are wingless, they are much less efficient than winged insects in visiting a good number of flowers in a short time and over large distances.

Moreover, ants produce antibiotic substances (specially secreted by the metapleural gland) which could well harm pollen grains. In some cases, ants may even have a negative effect on pollination by chasing away pollinating insects when they are visiting flowers and looking for nectar.

Where to find ants

Ants are found everywhere, except in aquatic environments. They occupy a wide variety of habitats and occur through much of Europe, from sea level to an altitude of 3,000 m. They can also be found in towns: in parks and gardens, on pavements and in buildings. Some are readily observed and easy to record, even though the inventory may not be complete; the finding of more secretive species can be much more difficult. Many ant species stay in their nest or move

Trees of the genus *Prunus* produce nectar at the base of the leaf, on the stalk. This nectar attracts various species of ants; here, a worker of the genus *Lasius*.

A *Crematogaster auberti* worker visiting a flower that finds itself covered in pollen. However, ants participate little in pollination.

about discreetly. Two methods allow them to be investigated: one is passive, by trapping; the other active, by direct observation.

Trapping

Pitfall trap – A receptacle (plastic cup) is sunk into the ground to its rim. It is filled with soapy water (5–10% concentration). Alcohol would scare ants away. Workers walking over the cup drop in and are trapped, and the soapy water prevents them from escaping. In order to avoid deterioration of trapped ants, the cups need to be inspected regularly. This is a non-selective method that may also catch many other arthropods and small invertebrates (frogs, lizards, shrews...). It should therefore not be employed in sites inhabited by rare or protected arthropods (especially beetles). It is, however, very useful for nocturnal species such as certain members of the *Camponotus*, *Formica*, *Lasius* and *Messor* genera.

Baiting – Ants are rapidly attracted to tuna and sardines in oil due to the lipids and proteins they contain. Peanut butter, composed of lipids, carbohydrates and proteins is probably the most effective bait. The inconvenience of this method is the rapidity with which the bait is found (*Lasius* and *Tapinoma* species) and their efficiency in excluding other species. Thus, the ants found at bait are not usually representative of a site's real diversity. Bait, if visited regularly by the observer, may well reveal the presence of species that would not otherwise be found when searching for nests (*Myrmica* species and *Crematogaster sordidula*). Baiting is complementary to other methods in assessing a site's diversity.

Light – Yellow or blue receptacles filled with soapy water are used by entomologists to capture flying insects and especially ants when swarming. Even though they allow for the capture of nocturnal species, they have the inconvenience of being non-selective.

On summer nights, a simple sheet hung behind a strong lamp will attract sexual ants. The vicinity of strong lights from towns or houses can also be inspected. Winged females and males often occur at the base of lights during or just after mating.

Swimming pools may also attract numerous sexual individuals; an ant that falls into water can spend the whole night there without drowning.

By sight – Locating ants by sight is one of the easiest and most efficient ways of finding them. Effectiveness increases with experience. This does not necessarily involve the use of specialised equipment and can be done without any special preparation, when convenient. To find a greater variety of species it is best to cover diverse habitats: sunny sites, rocks, edge habitats, tracks, embankments, set-aside, heath, etc. In urban areas pavements and green areas should be inspected.

Sieving the ground litter – Place the litter and surface soil in a 3–5 mm mesh sieve, then shake it over a light-coloured tray (preferably white, to facilitate finding the dark invertebrates). The smallest animals fall through with the finest particles; ants should then be removed for inspection and the rest released. This is an effective method for finding the smaller species whose nests can be very hard to locate, such as species in the Ponerinae family, the *Myrmecina*, *Stenamma*, *Strumigenys*, *Solenopsis* and certain of the *Lasius* and *Temnothorax* genera. At the foot of rock piles it is often possible to find species in the Ponerinae family, as well as some of those in the *Myrmecina* and *Stenamma* genera.

Beating vegetation – Beating vegetation with a white tray placed underneath can be very useful in finding many ant species, especially those that search for sugary substances and particularly the honeydew of sap-sucking Hemiptera. Beating high branches can lead to the trapping of tree-dwelling species such as *Dolichoderus quadripunctatus*, some *Camponotus* species (*C. fallax* and *C. truncatus*), *Temnothorax* species (*T. affinis*, *T. aveli* and species of the *T. angustulus* group) and *Lasius brunneus*. It is best to concentrate on oaks and fruit trees.

The sweep net – The herbaceous level of meadows and embankments provides food for many ant species. Using a sweep net is a rapid way of prospecting these habitats. It is especially good for finding species of the genus *Temnothorax*.

Food sources – Searching for aphids and scale insects is an excellent way of finding ants. The ants solicit sap-sucking Hemiptera, touching them with their antennae in order to receive drops of honeydew and at the same time protect them from potential predators (ladybirds and various parasitoids, for example). It is useful to search for food sources on umbellifers, grasses, teasels, fruit trees, new shoots of various plants and so forth. Species of the *Tapinoma* and *Lasius* genera form mounds of soil at the base of grasses in which they raise aphids on the plant's roots and stem without their being exposed to predators.

Extrafloral nectaries at the base of fruit tree leaves are especially attractive to species of the *Lasius*, *Crematogaster*, *Formica*, *Tapinoma* and sometimes *Plagiolepis* genera, which visit these trees to take nectar.

Flower nectar is also very attractive to many ants (species of the *Camponotus*, *Temnothorax* genera and others). Fruit trees, rock roses, myrtles, umbellifers, euphorbias, etc. are regularly visited.

Species of the genus *Messor*, termed 'harvester ants', collect a large quantity of seeds and carry them in long processions. They are most common around the Mediterranean, on tracks, in vegetable gardens after sowing, in crops after harvesting, on lanes bordered by plane trees and so on. In autumn they can be observed collecting seeds at the base of common purslane, fennel and various other umbellifers.

It is not uncommon to observe species of the *Formica*, *Lasius* and *Tem-*

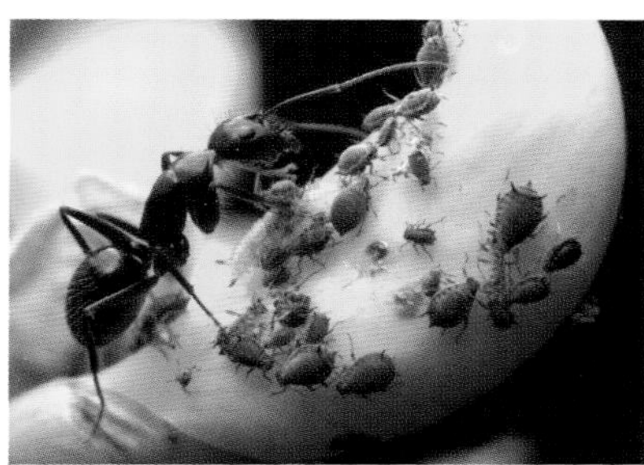

Camponotus aethiops worker visiting an aphid colony on a flower.

Cataglyphis cursor worker on excrement.

Mound of soil built above a nest by a *Tapinoma* species. It probably houses sap-sucking Hemiptera on the grasses.

nothorax genera collecting fragments or liquid from vertebrate excrement. Bird droppings, rich in nitrogen, are particularly attractive.

Searching according to the weather – After rain, ants clean their nests. Soil excavated when making nest galleries is deposited in a mound at the nest entrance, and easily differentiated from earthworm casts. Ants always eject very small particles to the surface, the size of a small grain of sand. Particle size is very much correlated to the size of the ants. It is therefore quite possible to guess the size of an ants' nest's occupants by looking closely at the mound at the entrance. One by one, the workers move to and fro between the bottom of the nest and the ground surface, where they create a typical and easily seen mound. These mounds can be quite remarkable in size and there may be numerous evacuation holes. Such mounds are produced by species that build nests directly in the ground, particularly some of those of the *Pheidole*, *Messor*, *Lasius*, *Cataglyphis*, *Tetramorium*, *Proformica* and *Goniomma* genera.

The *Tapinoma*, with their populous colonies just under the ground surface, spread extracted soil around the nest. They make numerous outings and the workers are very active on the surface.

Small species, such as those of the genus *Temnothorax*, forage on well-exposed rock surfaces. During sunny weather, an observer waiting patiently on flat ground, preferably in a natural habitat, will sooner or later see workers passing, foraging and returning to the nest with small arthropods in their mandibles.

A *Messor barbarus* nest after rain. Workers have extracted soil from the nest galleries and rejected it on the ground surface.

The cleaning of nest galleries by *Pheidole pallidula* workers results in the formation of small piles of soil particles at the surface.

Observing during swarming – Finding swarming ants may be facilitated by the presence of hunting swallows, dragonflies or, in the evening, low-flying bats. It is easier to observe and collect sexual ants on tarmac (road, pavement, terrace, etc.) or on the surface of a swimming pool. As with the sexual individuals, workers of underground species (*Chthonolasius* subgenus, for example) exit the nest and are more easily found at this time. **NB:** swarming of *Solenopsis* species is sometimes confused with gnat clouds.

Galls, beechmast, walnuts, hazelnuts, acorns – All are potential shelters used by colonies of small species of ant (particularly *Temnothorax* species) or by young founding queens that will later move elsewhere (*Crematogaster scutellaris*, *Camponotus truncatus*, *Dolichoderus quadripunctatus*). Searching in such places can considerably disturb colonies or founding queens, which, once disturbed, will have to search for another site.

Snail shells – These can be shelters for *Temnothorax* colonies.

Hollow stems – Dry, hollow stems or those hollowed out by other insects (beetle larvae) are perfect sites for a nest of ant species that are not particular about the site's humidity. They are used mainly by *Temnothorax* species. Species occupying this type of ecological niche are termed 'rubicole' (nesting in stems). They can be found in various types of stems: stubble, brambles, ivy and reeds.

Various waste – All sorts of 'rubbish' from human activity: planks, metal sheets, rubble, cardboard, tyres and the like are used. They all absorb heat and conserve the ground humidity. As such, these sites are favourable for ant brood development. They are especially favourable for ants that form large colonies, such as species of the *Tapinoma*, *Tetramorium*, *Messor*,

Colonies of small ants of the genus *Temnothorax* often nest in hollow stems. This bramble stem has been opened to expose the ant colony. The queen is in the centre.

Temnothorax recedens colony inside a piece of straw.

Aphaenogaster, *Lasius* and *Formica* genera, and *Pheidole pallidula*.

Embankments – Stones on the sides of embankments capture the sun's rays and provide excellent sites for galleries and chambers of the nests of many ant species, including various species of the *Myrmica*, *Lasius*, *Tetramorium* and *Tapinoma* genera, and *Pheidole pallidula*. There may also be small colonies of *Temnothorax* species between stones or in cracks in stones.

Stones – A stone provides a particularly good site for installing a nest. It captures heat, conserves it during the day and releases it at night. Humidity is relatively high under stones throughout the year, which is especially important in summer. A stone can also protect the colony against extreme weather conditions (thunderstorms) and from certain predators. Denser grass growth and the presence of small grains of evacuated soil around a stone are indications of the presence of an ants' nest. Stone size is often proportional to that of the ant. Although small species such as those of the genus *Plagiolepis* need a stone no bigger than a coin, the larger species such as those of the genus *Camponotus* need more space and install their nests under much larger stones; species of an intermediate size such as those of the *Lasius*, *Myrmica*, *Tetramorium* genera and a few *Formica* species (*F. lemani*, *F. sanguinea*, etc.) use medium-sized stones.

Drystone walls can provide sites for species with very populous colonies such as *Camponotus lateralis* and *Crematogaster scutellaris,* and certain *Lasius* and *Temnothorax* species seal the entrance to their nests with

The presence of agglomerations of small soil particles against a stone indicates the presence of an ants' nest.

minute pieces of dry vegetation. Old drystone walls with crumbling stones are especially suitable for all these species.

Ants appreciate vegetation next to stones at the foot of rocky outcrops, often putting their brood there on sunny days. Effectively, the interface between stones and vegetation means that temperature increases quickly, humidity is maintained by the vegetation and thus the site is favourable for brood development. This is particularly true at higher altitudes, where nests are often temporary, for species of the *Myrmica*, *Formica*, *Leptothorax*, *Temnothorax* and *Tetramorium* genera.

Rock crevices – Small colonies of *Temnothorax* species (*T. nigriceps*, *T. recedens* and *T. unifasciatus*) as well as their social parasites, readily install their nests in rock crevices and under flakes on well-exposed rocks. In Southern Europe most sites used by these species have some shade.

A *Temnothorax tuberum* nest exposed by lifting a splinter of rock under which it was located.

Moss – Whether on trees or rocks, mosses often serve as a temporary site for founding queens and their broods. Species such as *Myrmecina graminicola* and of the genus *Ponera* and founding queens of the *Lasius* and *Formica* genera are often found under mosses.

Trees – Trees are a support for many food sources (aphids, caterpillars, etc.) exploited by ants. The ants form long processions between the

The bark of a dead conifer has been lifted to show part of a *Camponotus vagus* nest.

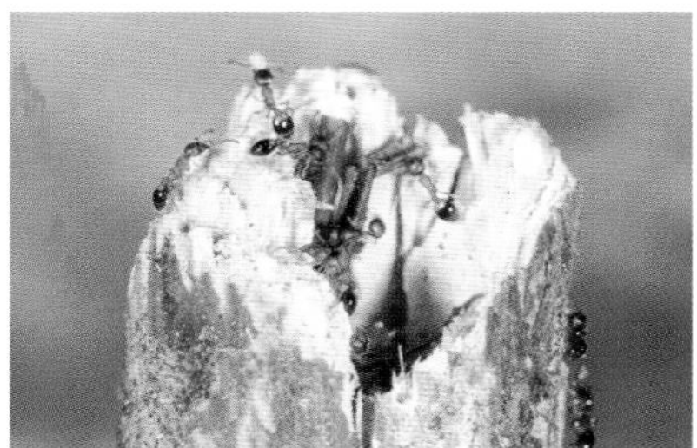

A *Temnothorax nylanderi* colony found in a small dead branch on the ground.

nest and aphid colonies that they visit. This is often seen in *Crematogaster scutellaris* and certain species in the *Lasius* (*L. fuliginosus*, *L. brunneus*) and *Formica* genera (subgenus *Serviformica* and genus *Formica sensu stricto*).

Species such as *Camponotus vagus*, *C. herculeanus*, *C. ligniperda*, *Formica fusca*, various *Lasius* (*L. brunneus*, *L. lasioides*, *L. emarginatus*, *L. platythorax*) and *Crematogaster scutellaris* use dead trunks, either upright or on the ground, in which to build their nests. Depending on their size, dead branches on the ground provide nest sites for species in the *Myrmica*, *Lasius* and *Temnothorax* genera, and for *Formica lemani* and *Aphaenogaster subterranea*. Small dead branches on the ground are the best places to find *Temnothorax* species; they may occupy small pieces of wood at the base of trees or bushes. Dead branches invaded by fungi are not used by ants. Old, cracked stumps are mainly used by *Leptothorax acervorum*.

Dead branches still attached to live trees, and especially those of oaks, walnuts and fruit trees, are occupied by tree-dwelling species such as *Temnothorax affinis*, *T. aveli*, *Temnothorax* species of the *angustulus* group, *Crematogaster scutellaris*, *Camponotus fallax*, *Camponotus lateralis*, *Camponotus truncatus* and *Dolichoderus quadripunctatus*. In certain conifers, the bark is thick and composed of several layers: the space between these layers may be occupied by *Temnothorax* and *Leptothorax* species, at the trunk's base.

Summary of the ants of Britain and Europe (workers)

The reader will find definitions of terms that are useful in describing an ant's morphology in the section 'worker morphology' on pp. 9 and 10, as well as in the glossary, pp. 410 and 411.

Identification may be made either by consulting this chapter (pp. 47–53), or using the subfamily, genus and species identification keys (pp. 54–103).

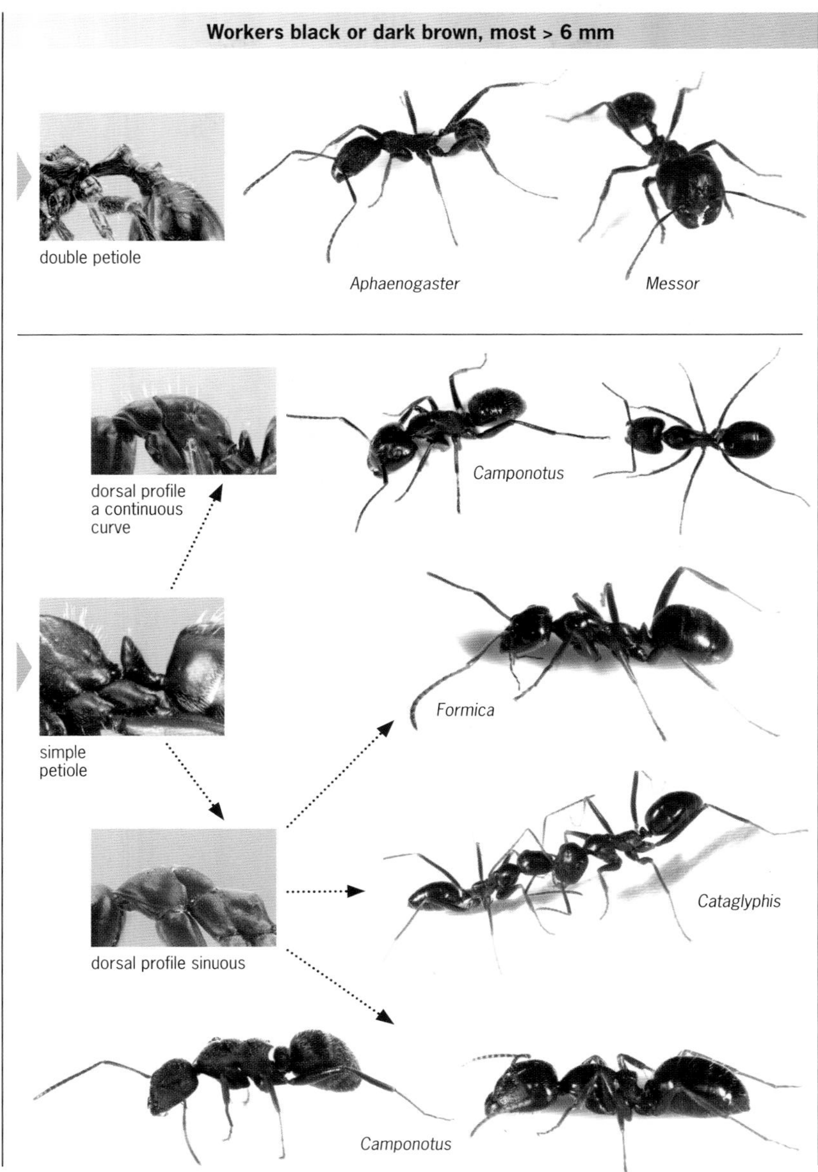
Workers black or dark brown, most > 6 mm
double petiole
Aphaenogaster
Messor
dorsal profile a continuous curve
Camponotus
simple petiole
Formica
dorsal profile sinuous
Cataglyphis
Camponotus

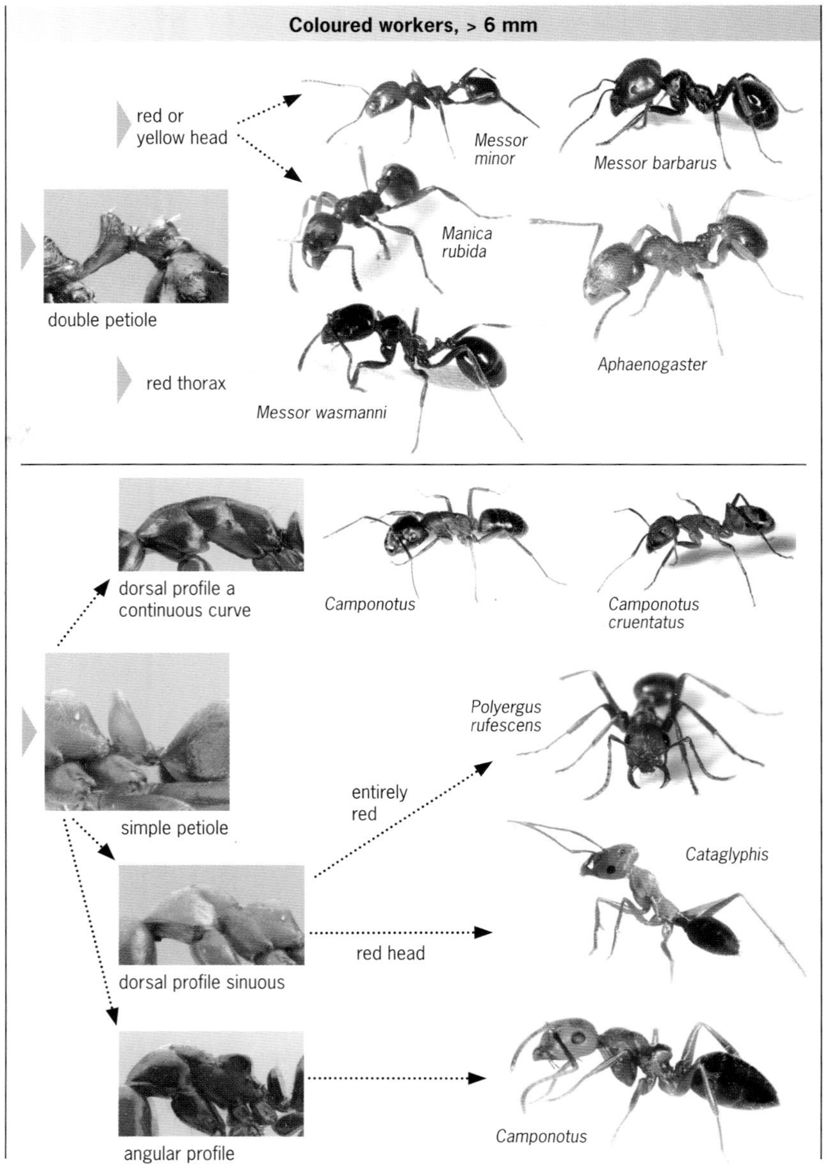
Coloured workers, > 6 mm
red or yellow head
Messor minor
Messor barbarus
Manica rubida
double petiole
Aphaenogaster
red thorax
Messor wasmanni
dorsal profile a continuous curve
Camponotus
Camponotus cruentatus
Polyergus rufescens
simple petiole
entirely red
Cataglyphis
red head
dorsal profile sinuous
angular profile
Camponotus

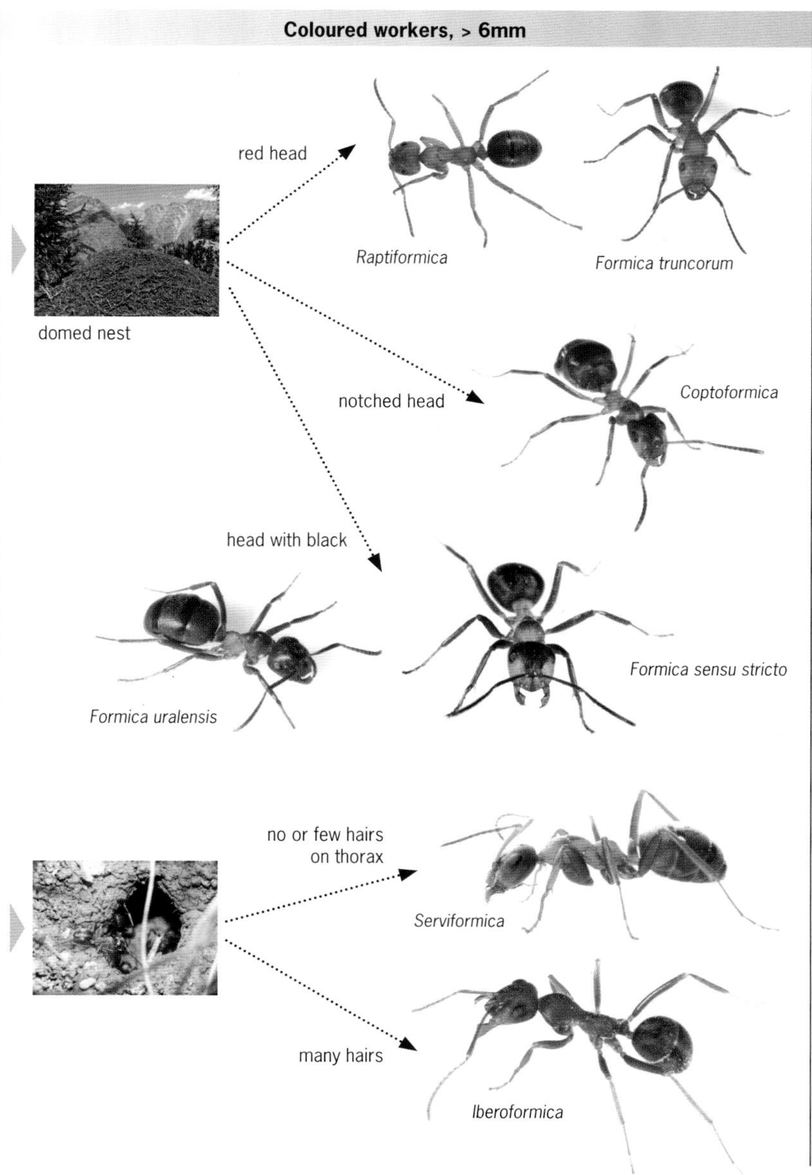
Coloured workers, > 6mm
red head
Raptiformica
Formica truncorum
domed nest
notched head
Coptoformica
head with black
Formica uralensis
Formica sensu stricto
no or few hairs
on thorax
Serviformica
many hairs
Iberoformica

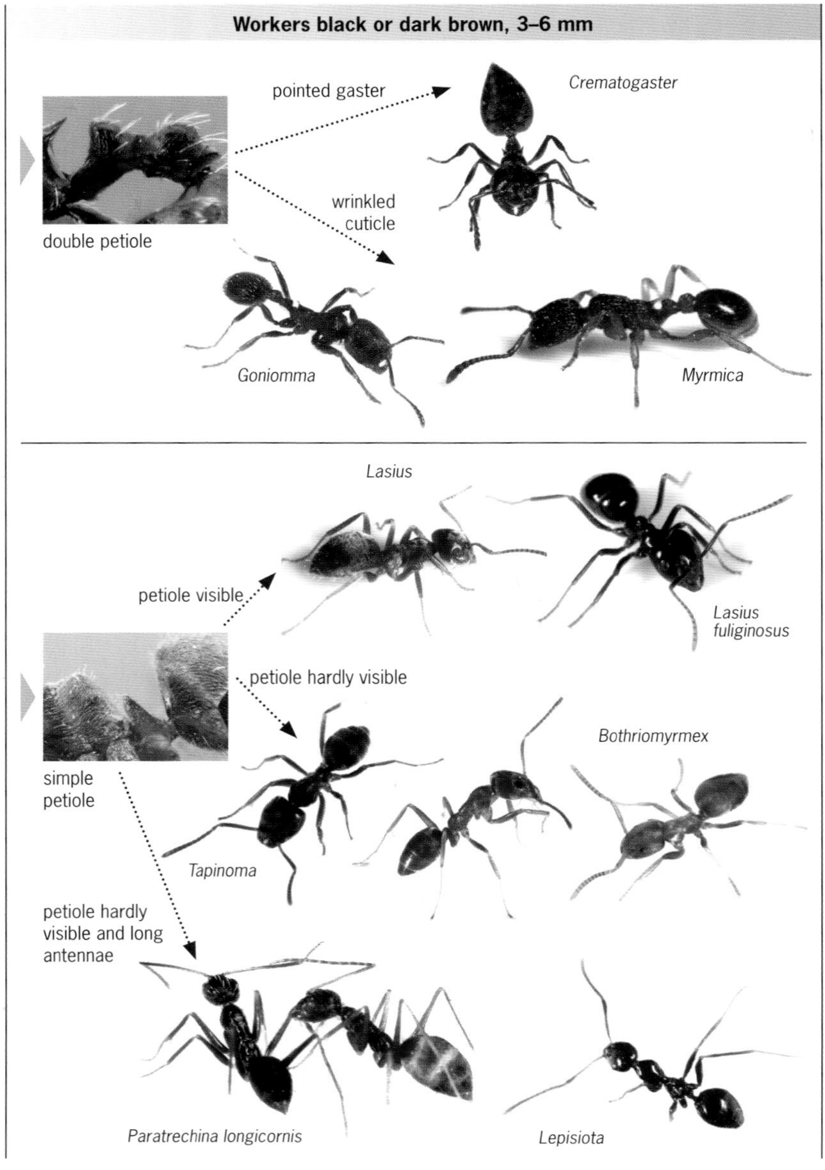
Workers black or dark brown, 3–6 mm
pointed gaster
Crematogaster
wrinkled cuticle
double petiole
Goniomma
Myrmica
Lasius
petiole visible
Lasius fuliginosus
petiole hardly visible
Bothriomyrmex
simple petiole
Tapinoma
petiole hardly visible and long antennae
Paratrechina longicornis
Lepisiota

Coloured workers, 3–6 mm

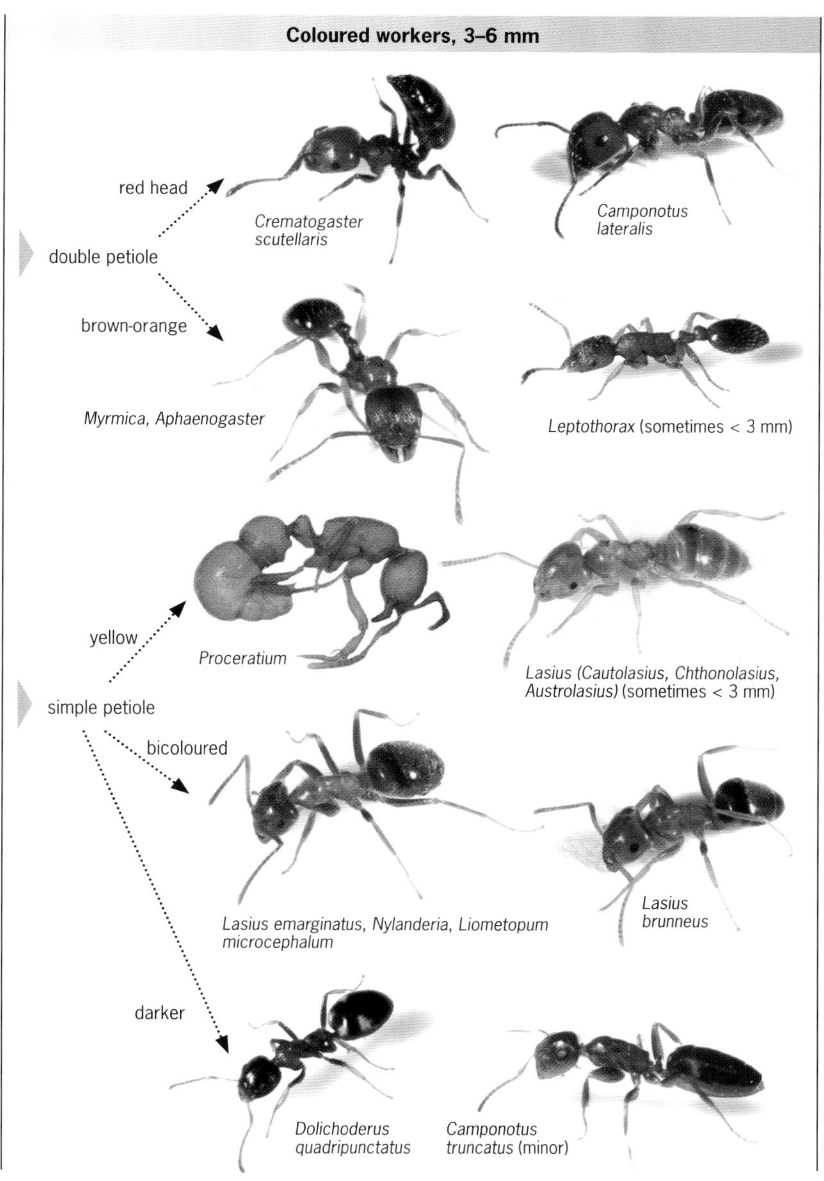

Crematogaster scutellaris

Camponotus lateralis

Myrmica, Aphaenogaster

Leptothorax (sometimes < 3 mm)

Proceratium

Lasius (Cautolasius, Chthonolasius, Austrolasius) (sometimes < 3 mm)

Lasius emarginatus, Nylanderia, Liometopum microcephalum

Lasius brunneus

Dolichoderus quadripunctatus

Camponotus truncatus (minor)

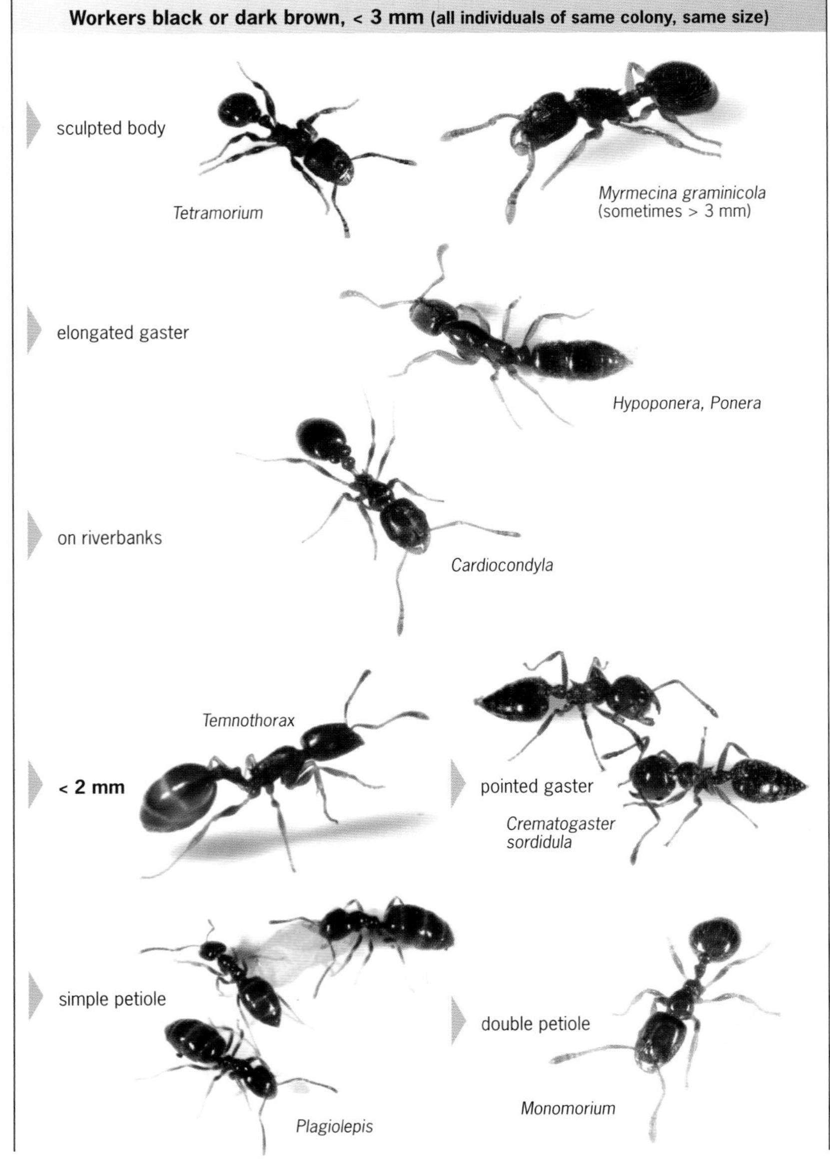
Workers black or dark brown, < 3 mm (all individuals of same colony, same size)
sculpted body
Tetramorium
Myrmecina graminicola (sometimes > 3 mm)
elongated gaster
Hypoponera, Ponera
on riverbanks
Cardiocondyla
Temnothorax
< 2 mm
pointed gaster
Crematogaster sordidula
simple petiole
Plagiolepis
double petiole
Monomorium

Coloured workers, < 3 mm

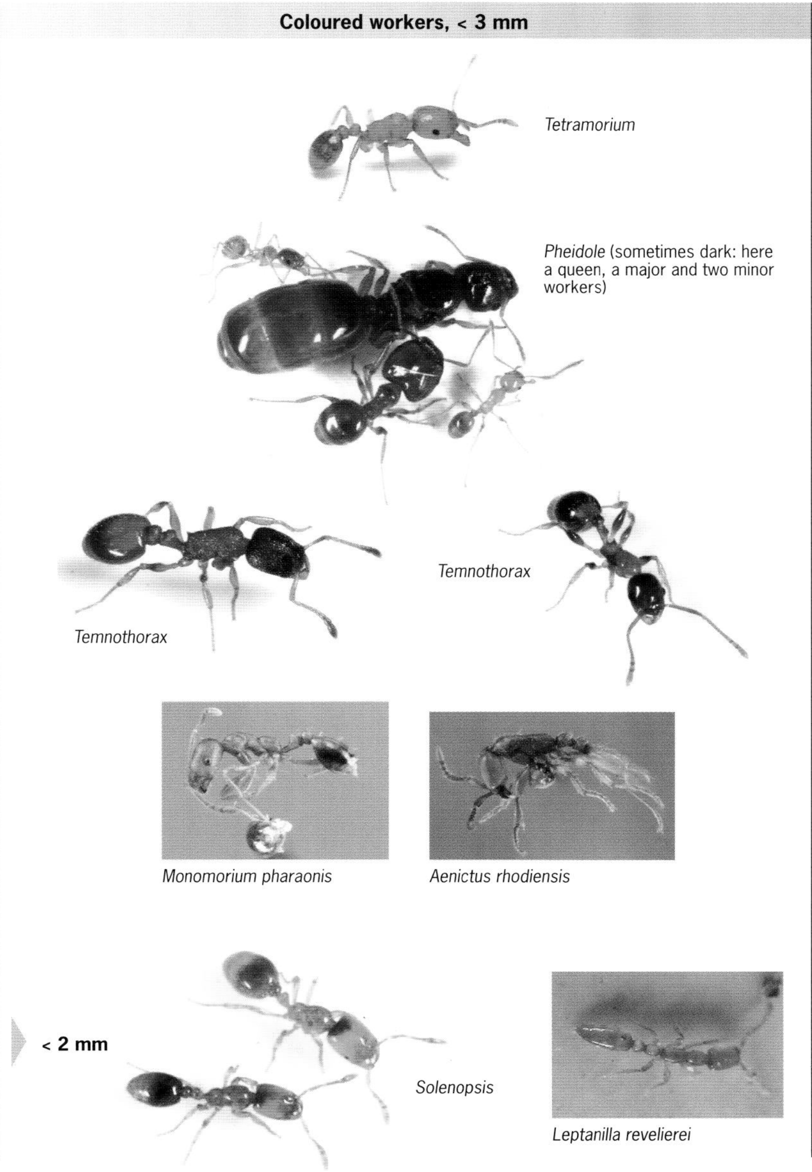

Tetramorium

Pheidole (sometimes dark: here a queen, a major and two minor workers)

Temnothorax

Temnothorax

Monomorium pharaonis

Aenictus rhodiensis

< 2 mm

Solenopsis

Leptanilla revelierei

Key to subfamilies

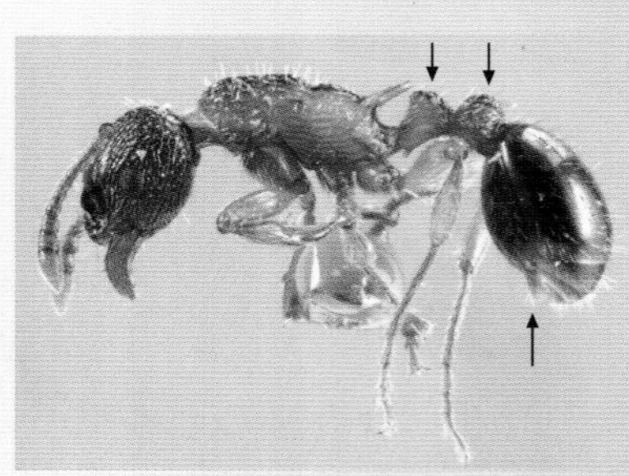

Myrmicinae (see page 80)
- Two segments (petiole and postpetiole) between the mesosoma and the gaster.
- Spine present.
- Compound eyes present.

Amblyoponinae (see page 106)
- A single segment (the petiole) between the mesosoma and the gaster.
- Massive petiole, widely attached to the gaster's first segment.
- 12 segments to the antennae.
- Spine present.

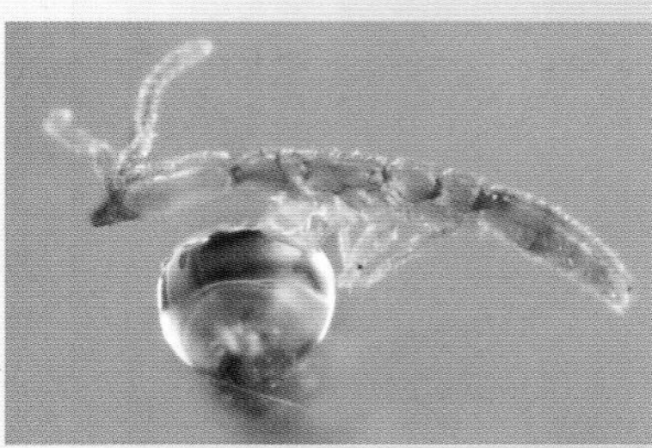

Leptanillinae (see page 244)
- Two segments (petiole and postpetiole) between the mesosoma and the gaster.
- Absence of compound eyes.
- 12 segments to the antennae.
- Very small ants, less than 2 mm.

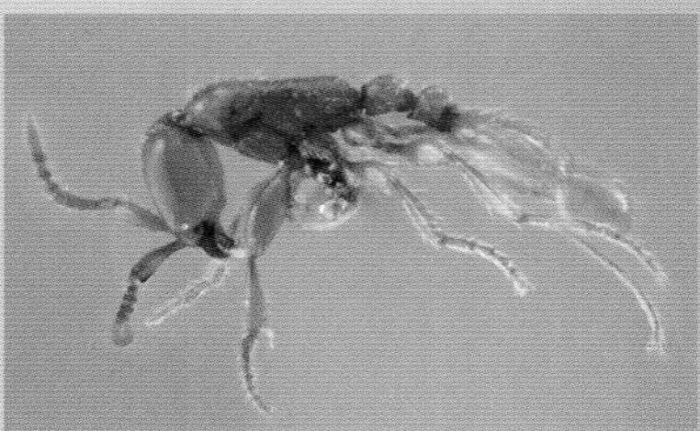

Dorylinae (Aenictus genus) (see page 124)
- Two segments (petiole and postpetiole) between the mesosoma and the gaster.
- Absence of compound eyes.
- Ten segments to the antennae.
- Small ants, 2–3 mm.

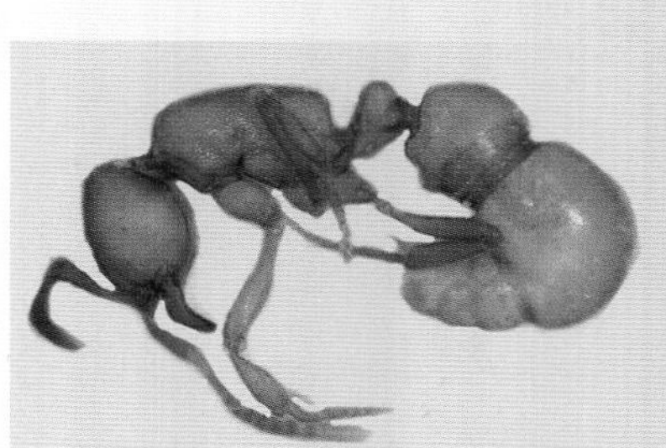

Proceratiinae (see page 408)
– A single segment (petiole) between the mesosoma and the gaster.
– Ten segments to the antennae.
– Bent gaster.
– Spine present.

Formicinae (see page 62)
– A single segment (petiole) between the mesosoma and the gaster, usually quite high.
– The tip of the gaster with circular pore (acidopore) surrounded by hair.
– No spine.

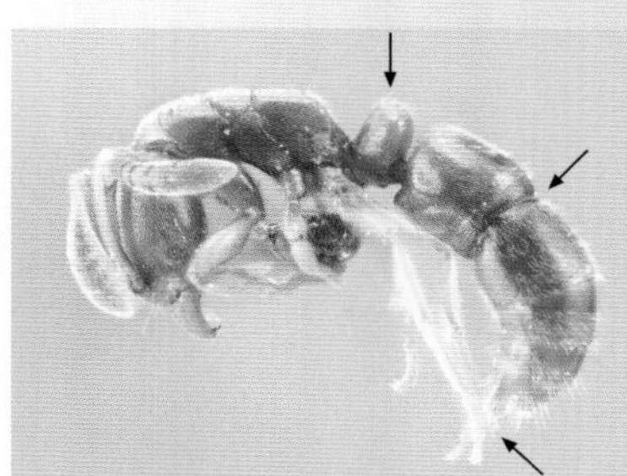

Ponerinae (see page 56)
– A single segment (petiole) between the mesosoma and the gaster, generally high and thick.
– Visible constriction between the first and second gaster segments.
– Spine present.
– 12 segments to the antennae.

Dolichoderinae (see page 58)
– A single segment (petiole) between the mesosoma and the gaster, generally quite low.
– A hardly visible transversal slit at the tip of the gaster.
– No spine.

Key to the identification of British and European ants (workers)

Key to the genera of the subfamily Ponerinae

The Ponerinae form a very large subfamily within the Formiidae, including nearly 50 genera, most occupying the tropics. Certain genera contain very large species. In Europe this subfamily contains just four genera of small underground-dwelling species (forest ground litter, under large stones, etc.).

1 : seen from the front the head is hexagonal, with slender, elongated mandibles that have three teeth at the extremity. Medium-sized ants. Dark in colour. In Europe only occur in the very south, e.g. near Gibraltar (photo 1) .... **Anochetus genus (see page 400)**

1': seen from the front the head is rectangular, the mandibles triangular. The eyes are often reduced to just a few ommatidia, or absent. Ants widely distributed in Southern Europe (photo 2) **2**

2 : mandibles generally with seven distinct teeth all about the same size (photo 3); the base of the mandible, on its lateral side, has a small circular depression on its surface. Eyes absent or reduced to one or two ommatidia in workers. Quite a pale colour, entirely yellowish-red.. **Cryptopone genus (see page 402)**

2': mandibles generally with two or three distinct terminal teeth, preceded by about ten small, more or less blunt teeth (photo 4); the mandible base has no small circular depression. Variable colour, entirely black, brown or reddish................................. **3**

3 : seen in profile the underside and back of the petiole show a small, circular, transparent 'window' and two small backward-pointing spines (photo 5)... **Ponera genus (see page 406)**

3': seen in profile the underside and back of the petiole is entire, without the small, circular 'window' and without small spines (photo 6) .... **Hypoponera genus (see page 404)**

Note: In certain species of the genus *Hypoponera*, such as *H. eduardi*, there exist ergatoid males that can easily be confused with workers. These males differ in being a yellowish colour, by having very short antennae scapes, reduced mandibles and their genital appendages are visible at the gaster tip.

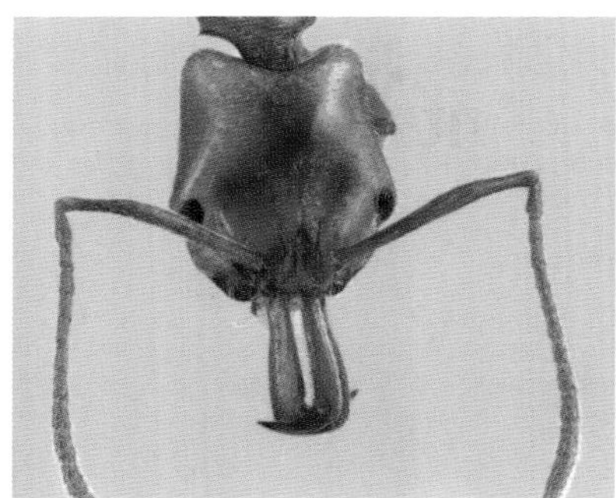
PHOTO 1. *Anochetus ghilianii*

PHOTO 2. *Ponera coarctata*

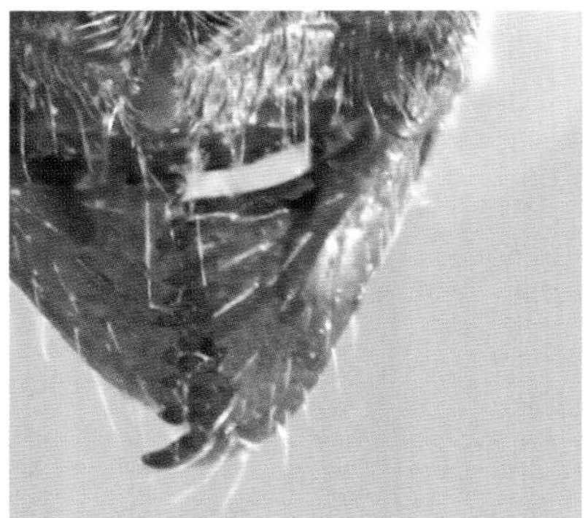
PHOTO 3. The mandibles of *Cryptopone ochracea.*

PHOTO 4. The mandibles of *Hypoponera eduardi.*

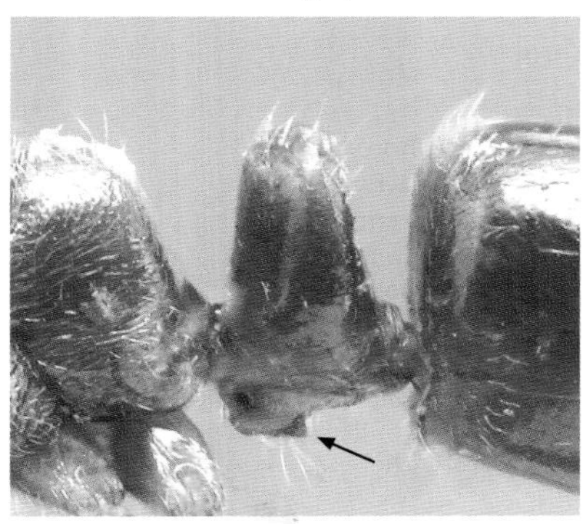
PHOTO 5. Profile of the petiole of a *Ponera* sp.

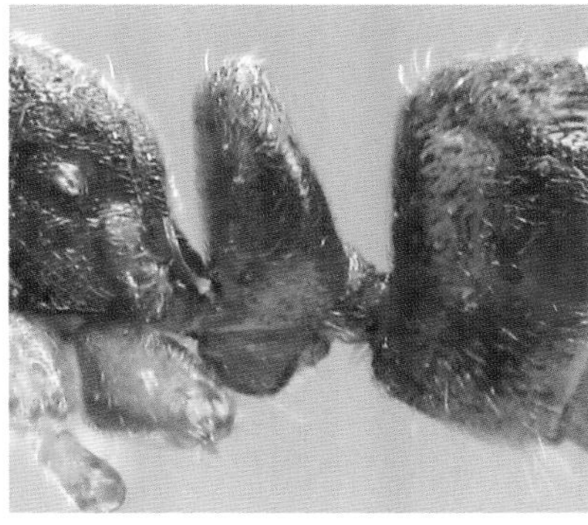
PHOTO 6. Profile of the petiole of a *Hypoponera* worker.

Key to the genera of the subfamily Dolichoderinae

The subfamily Dolichoderinae contains 30 genera and some 1,000 species with a maximum diversity in the Australian and South-east Asian regions. In Europe this subfamily is presented by six genera and 19 species (four restricted to heated buildings). The genus *Tapinoma* is the most important.

1: the tegument surface is very spotted, well-developed mesopropodeal grove and markedly concave propodeum. Gaster has characteristic pale spotting (photo 7)...... .... ***Dolichoderus*** **genus (see page 110)**

1': smooth tegument surface. Rounded propodeum, never concave.............................. **2**

2 : the petiole scale is low and inclined. It is covered by the front of the gaster and is invisible when the worker is seen from above (photo 8); generally black. **3**

2': inclined but distinct petiole scale, not covered by the front of the gaster. There is never an incision in the clypeus. Yellow or pale brown in colour, never entirely black. **4**

3 : no erect hairs on pronotum. Seen from above gaster has four visible segments (photo 8). Most species have an incision in the front of the clypeus..................................... .... ***Tapinoma*** **genus (see key, page 60)**

3': pronotum with a few erect hairs. Seen from above gaster has five visible segments (sometimes the fifth segment is retracted) (photo 9).. .... ***Technomyrmex*** **genus (see page 122)**

4 : in profile the mesosoma forms a continuous curve, without a mesopropodeal grove (photo 10). Pronotum has erect hairs. Polymorph workers. Ocelli visible in larger workers. Only in Eastern Europe. .... ***Liometopum*** **genus (see page 114)**

4': in profile the mesosoma has a more or less well-defined mesopropodeal groove. All workers in the nest the same size. No ocelli. **5**

5 : well-developed eyes, their diameter larger than the width of the scape. Elongated, narrow mesosoma with pronounced mesopropodeal groove (photo 11). .... **Linepithema genus (see page 112)**

5': reduced eyes, their diameter less or equal to the width of the scape. Bigger mesosoma with less pronounced mesopropodeal groove (photo 12)... .... ***Bothriomyrmex*** **genus (see page 108)**

PHOTO 7. *Dolichoderus quadripunctatus*

PHOTO 8. *Tapinoma nigerrimum*

PHOTO 9. *Technomyrmex difficilis*

PHOTO 10. *Liometopum microcephalum*

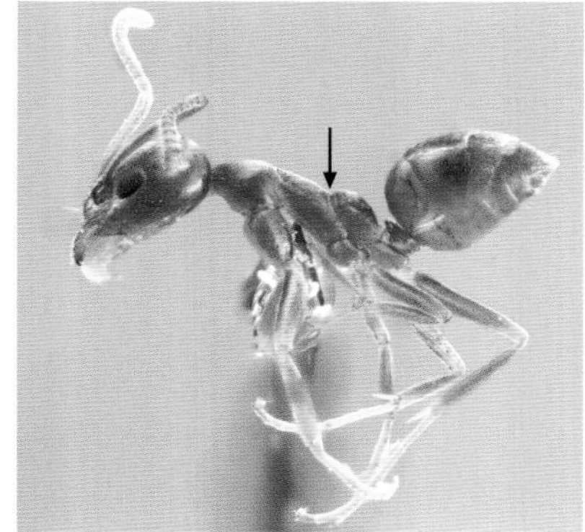

PHOTO 11. *Linepithema humile*

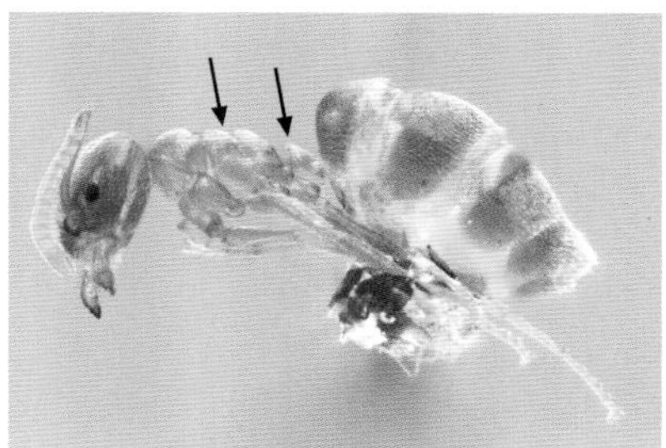

PHOTO 12. *Bothriomyrmex meridionalis*

Key to the species of the genus *Tapinoma*

There are some 100 species in the genus *Tapinoma* distributed throughout all continents. In tropical regions many species are arboreal, establishing close relationships with myrmecophyte plants. There are about ten species in Europe. They are closely related and specific identification is difficult. Certain characters are used in their taxonomy such as the size and shape of the notch on the front edge of the clypeus. The form of the male's genitalia may also be diagnostic. These characters are almost impossible to see in the field and even difficult to judge under a binocular microscope, as differences between species are small.

1 : workers very small, less than 2 mm long. No notch on the front edge of the clypeus (photo 13)........ **2**
1': workers a little bigger, 3–5 mm. The front edge of the clypeus always has a notch (photo 15)........ **3**

2 : completely black body. .... ***Tapinoma pygmaeum* (see page 120)**
2': bicoloured body, brown head and rest of body pale yellow (photo 14). .... ***Tapinoma melanocephalum* (see page 120)**

3 : shallow notch on the front edge of the clypeus, more of a semicircular shape (photo 15). The second segment of funiculus shorter or of equal length to third (photo 17). Workers in nest all more or less same size. .... ***Tapinoma* species of the *erraticum* group (see page 116)**
3': deeper notch on the front edge of the clypeus, of elongated form (photo 16). The second segment of funiculus longer or of equal length to third (photo 18). Workers are more polymorphic, with different sizes in the same nest. .... ***Tapinoma* species of the *nigerrimum-simrothi* group (see page 118)**

PHOTO 13. *Tapinoma pygmaeum*

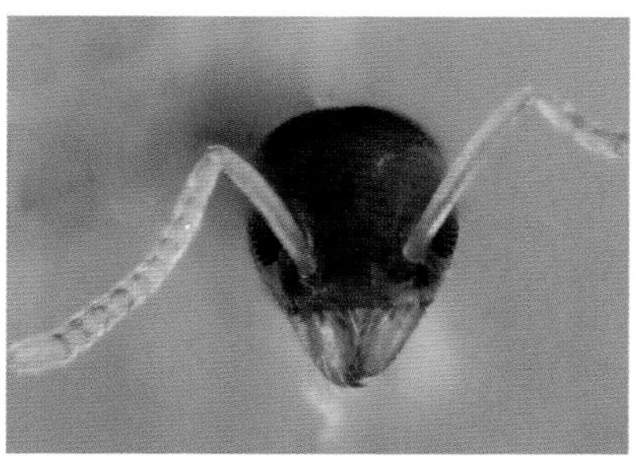

PHOTO 14. *Tapinoma melanocephalum*

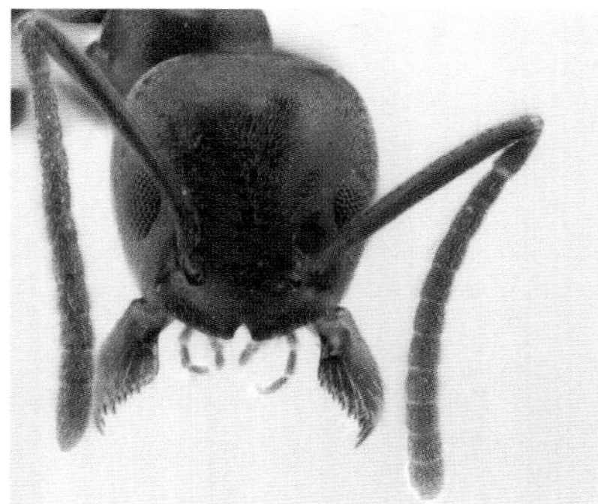

PHOTO 15. *Tapinoma erraticum*

PHOTO 16. *Tapinoma nigerrimum* head

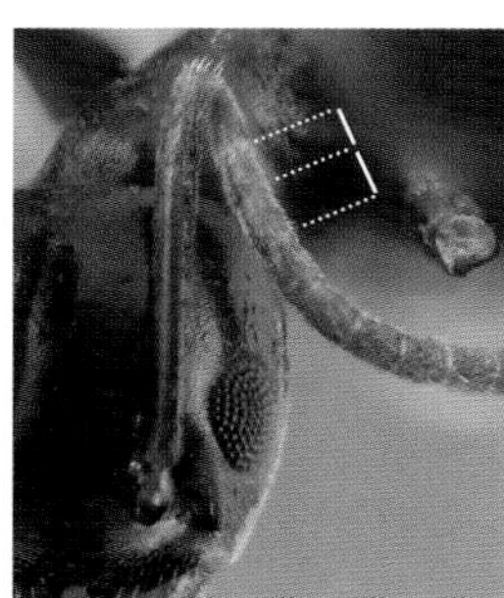

PHOTO 17. *Tapinoma madeirense* funiculus

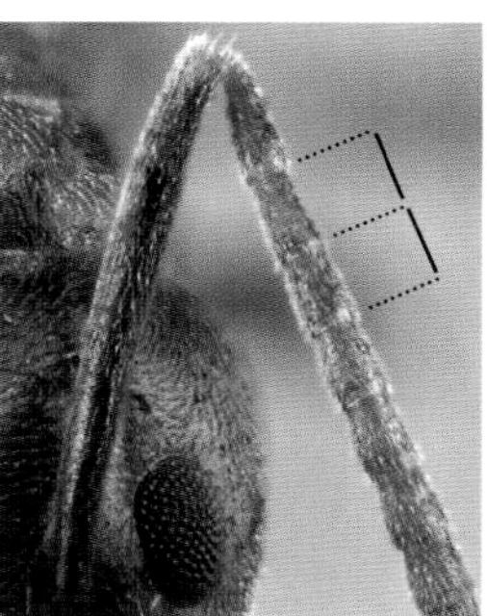

PHOTO 18. *Tapinoma nigerrimum* funiculus

Key to the genera of the subfamily Formicinae

The Formicinae is a very large subfamily including some 50 genera and more than 3,700 described species. In Europe it is the second-most important subfamily after the Myrmicinae, including 156 species of 14 genera.

1 : 11 segments in the antennae. **2**
1': 12 segments in the antennae. **4**

2 : very small ant, less than 2 mm long. A rounded propodeum. **3**
2': bigger. Propodeum with two teeth (photo 19). Petiole narrow at the top, more or less with a wide notch. .... ***Lepisiota* genus (see page 226)**

3 : well-developed eyes. .... ***Plagiolepis* genus (see page 232)**
3': very reduced eyes, with five or six indistinct ommatidia (photo 20). .... ***Acropyga* genus (see page 232)**

4 : sabre-shaped mandibles (photo 21). Body entirely red. .... ***Polyergus* genus (see page 236)**
4': triangular mandibles, masticating surface has many distinct teeth. **5**

5 : antennae attached a distance from the back edge of the clypeus (photo 22). No ocelli. .... ***Campanotus* genus (see key, page 76)**
5': antennae bases very close to the back edge of the clypeus. **6**

6 : top of head evidently indented (photo 23). Long, erect hairs on the pronotum. Very shiny tegument. Uniformly brown body. .... ***Rossomyrmex* genus (see page 242)**
6': not all these characters together. **7**

7 : very long scapes, at least 1½ times the length of the head (photo 24). .... ***Paratrechina* genus (see page 230)**
7': shorter scapes. **8**

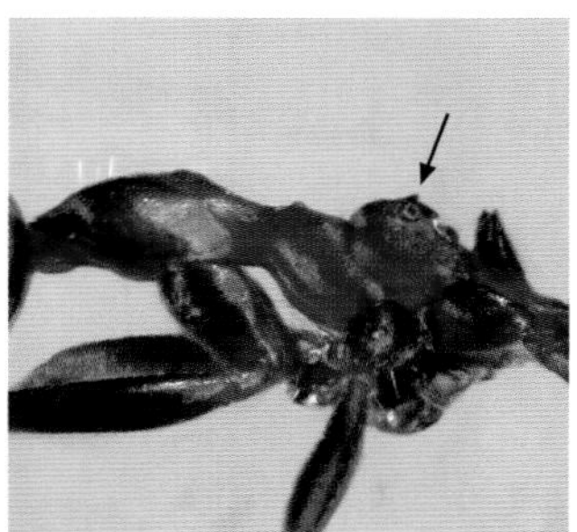

PHOTO 19. *Lepisiota dolabellae*

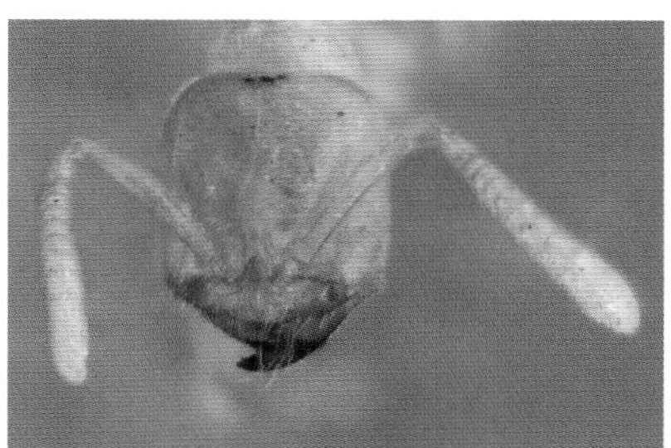

PHOTO 20. *Acropyga* sp.

PHOTO 21. *Polyergus rufescens*

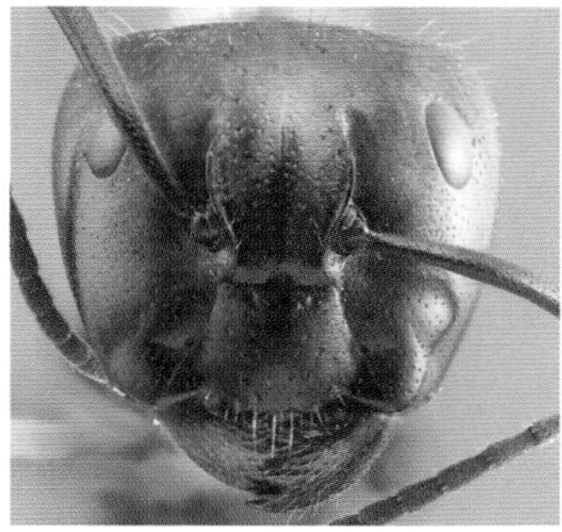

PHOTO 22. *Camponotus vagus*

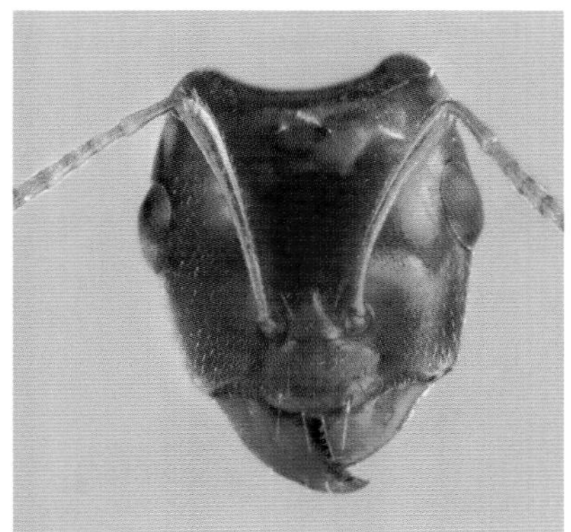

PHOTO 23. *Rossomyrmex minuchae*

PHOTO 24. *Paratrechina longicornis*

8 : eyes positioned in the front half of the head (photo 25), close to the antennae attachment. Body covered in long, straight hairs. .... ***Nylanderia* genus (see page 228)**
8': eyes placed in the upper half of the head.. **9**

9 : ocelli hardly visible in workers (except for *Lasius fuliginosus*, see page 208)........ **10**
9': ocelli readily visible in workers. **11**

10 : very long scape, obviously passing the occiput (photo 26). Very long hairs on the gaster.. ***Prenolepis* genus (see page 238)**
10': shorter scape, hardly passing the occiput (photo 27). Shorter hairs on the gaster...... .... ***Lasius* genus (see key, page 66)**

11 : mandibles have at least eight teeth. Counting from the tip, the third tooth is always smaller (photo 28). **12**
11': mandibles normally with five teeth, of diminishing size from the tip of mandible.... **13**

12 : throughout Europe. Mesosoma with a convex mesonotum. Variable colour, uniformly dark or bicoloured. Sometimes no covering of hair, or sometimes hairs present but finer. .... ***Formica* genus (see key, page 70)**
12': only in the Iberian Peninsula. Mesosoma with a concave mesonotum. Front of body often reddish. Body matt. Much hair cover, short and thick. .... ***Iberoformica* genus (see page 200)**

13 : propodeal spiracle oval-shaped (photo 29). Body always totally black. Size very variable within a colony. Small workers have a very elongated head. .... ***Proformica* genus (see page 240)**
13': propodeal spiracle slit-shaped (photo 30). Body may be entirely black or bicoloured, depending on the species. The size may be variable within a colony. Small workers do not have elongated heads.............................. ***Cataglyphis* genus (see key, page 74)**

PHOTO 25. *Nylanderia jaegerskioeldi*

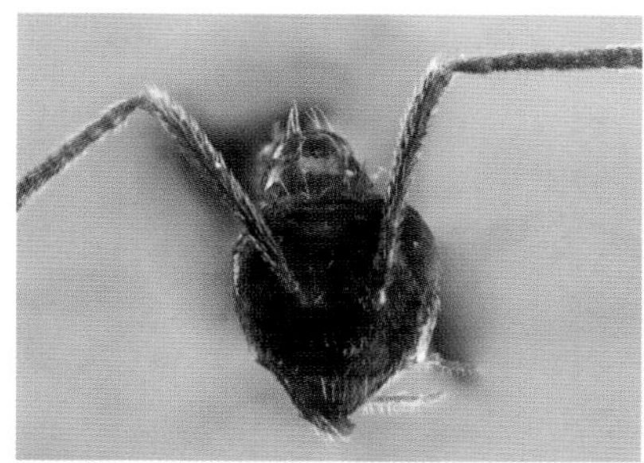

PHOTO 26. *Prenolepis nitens*

PHOTO 27. *Lasius niger*

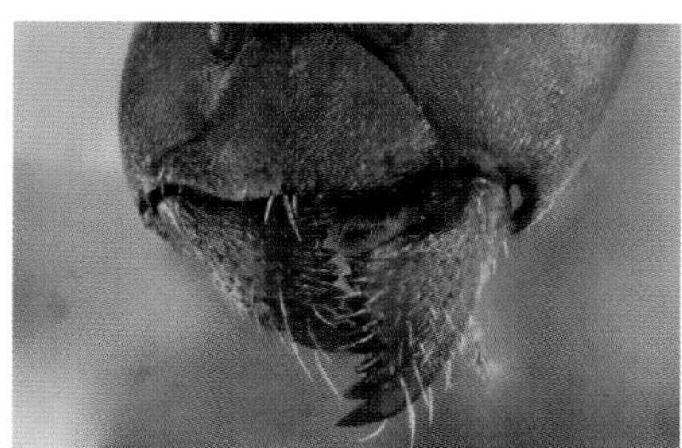

PHOTO 28. *Formica clara*

PHOTO 29. *Proformica* sp.

PHOTO 30. *Cataglyphis nodus*

Key to the identification of the principal *Lasius* species – genus *Lasius* Fabricius, 1804

The classification of the genus *Lasius* has been much revised since the 1990s, leading to the recognising of several 'new' species. There are 35 species in Europe, difficult to identify. The genus *Lasius* is split into five subgenera: *Dendrolasius* (one species), *Austrolasius* (two species), *Cautolasius* (three species), *Chthonolasius* (12 species) and *Lasius* (*sensu stricto* – 17 species). *Lasius* species (*sensu stricto*) are familiar to many people as they are omnipresent in many habitats, especially in urban areas. *Cautolasius* species are also very common, but are rarely seen on the ground surface as they have underground habits; *Austrolasius* and *Chthonolasius* are generally much rarer. *Austrolasius* and *Chthonolasius* species found colonies by temporary social parasitism in colonies of other *Lasius* species.

1 : shiny, black tegument. Hairs short and dispersed. From the front the head is heart-shaped (photo 31).. ***Dendrolasius*** **subgenus (see page 208)**

1': tegument appears more matt. Variable in colour, from pale yellow to black. **2**

2 : body uniform yellow.. **3**

2': body blackish-brown or reddish.. **5**

3: from the front the head is heart-shaped, the occipital edge is concave (photo 32). Mandible bases close together, petiole is quite low and large.................................... .... ***Austrolasius*** **subgenus (see page 202)**

3': a squarer head with straight occipital edge. Petiole is higher, in the form of a thin scale. .... **.4**

4 : the cheeks and generally the underside of the head have erect hairs (photo 33). The petiole scale when seen from the front is higher than it is wide, often with a notched summit.. ***Chthonolasius*** **subgenus (see page 206)**

4': cheeks and underside of head without erect hairs (photo 34). From the front the petiole scale is as high as it is wide................................ ***Cautolasius*** **subgenus (see page 204)**

5 : erect hairs on the scape (photo 35)... **6**

5': no erect hairs on the scape, simply some flattened hairs (photo 36). **9**

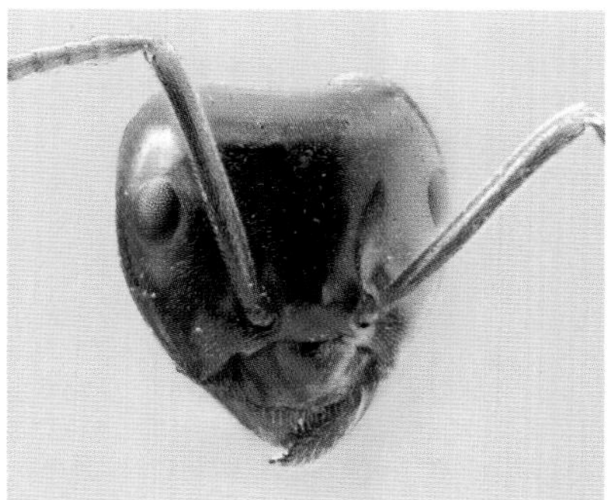
PHOTO 31. *Lasius fuliginosus*

PHOTO 32. *Lasius carniolicus*

PHOTO 33. *Lasius umbratus*

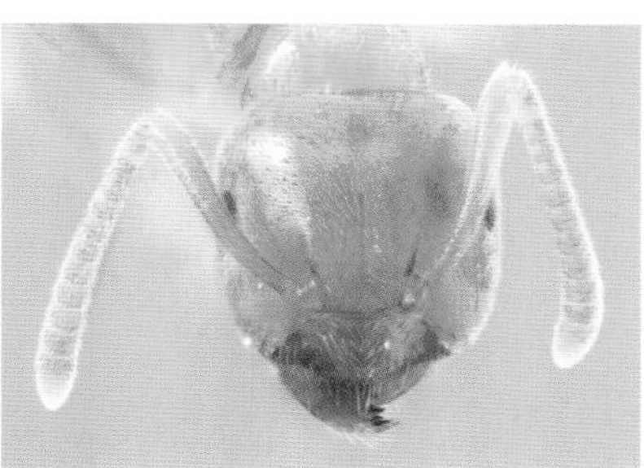
PHOTO 34. *Lasius flavus*

PHOTO 35. *Lasius platythorax*

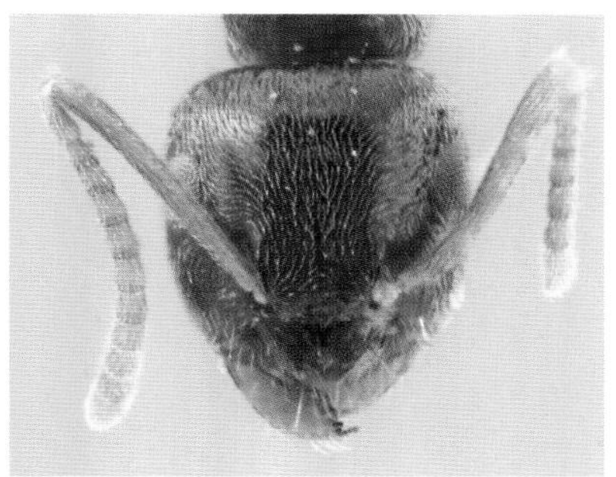
PHOTO 36. *Lasius alienus*

6 : bicoloured species, the reddish mesosoma contrasts with the black head and gaster (photo 37). The scape hairs do not stand perpendicular to the scape surface but are more oblique; they are more abundant on the base of the scape. .... ***Lasius emarginatus*** **(see page 214)**

6': body black, sometimes with brown mesosoma. The hairs stand perpendicular to the scape and occur along its whole length. **7**

7 : densely haired on the clypeus (photo 38), the erect hairs on the scape are relatively short.. ***Lasius niger*** **(see page 220)**

7': sparse hairs on the clypeus (photo 39), the erect hairs on the scape are longer. **8**

8 : the scape is shorter than the head is wide. Clypeus without an obvious ridge. Species present throughout Europe, in forest and marsh habitats. .... ***Lasius platythorax*** **(see page 222)**

8': the scape is longer than the head is wide. Clypeus with a reasonably obvious ridge. Species present in the Iberian Peninsula and southern France. .... ***Lasius*** **species of the *grandis* group (see page 216)**

9 : mandibles with eight teeth. Absence of erect hairs on the scape, but hairs elsewhere quite visible, although small and flattened. .... ***Lasius*** **species of the *alienus* group (see page 210)**

9': mandibles with seven teeth. Absence of erect hairs or other visible hairs on the scape, just the presence of a few very fine, barely visible hairs. **10**

10 : head relatively large. Head and mesosoma paler than the gaster (photo 40). .... ***Lasius brunneus*** **(see page 212)**

10': head not enlarged. Colour a uniform pale to dark brown...................................... **11**

11 : erect hairs only on the occiput, not reaching around the eyes (photo 41). Body a dark colour. Notched top to the scale. .... ***Lasius lasioides*** **(see page 218)**

11': erect hairs on the top of the head reaching as far as eye level (photo 42). Paler colour. .... ***Lasius*** **species of the *turcicus* group (see page 224)**

PHOTO 37. *Lasius emarginatus*

PHOTO 38. *Lasius niger*

PHOTO 39. *Lasius platythorax*

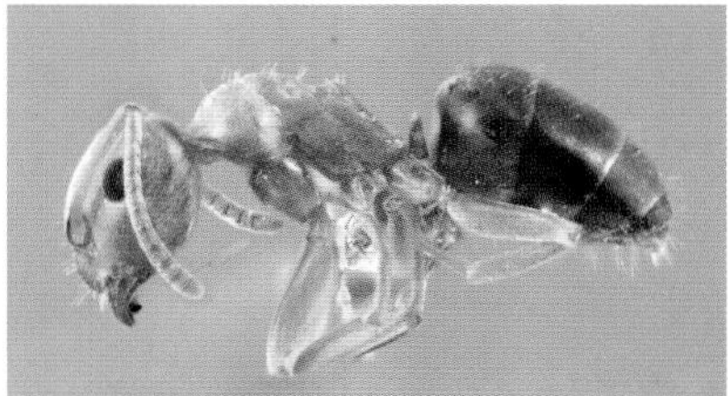

PHOTO 40. *Lasius brunneus*

PHOTO 41. *Lasius lasioides*

PHOTO 42. *Lasius neglectus*

Key to the identification of the principal *Formica* species – genus *Formica* Linnaeus, 1758

With 33 species, the genus *Formica* is one of the most diverse in Europe. The four subgenera, *Coptoformica*, *Formica* (*sensu stricto*), *Raptiformica* and *Serviformica,* are reasonably easy to differentiate. However, identification at species level is much more difficult. The amount of hair covering is a frequently used criterion for differentiating similar species. The seven species of the *Coptoformica* all occur in colder parts of Europe, or at altitude in the south, and construct small domes. The ten *Formica* (*sensu stricto*) species construct large domes that can be as much as 2 m in height. There is only one species in the subgenus *Raptiformica*, an optional slavemaker. The 15 species of *Serviformica* do not build domes; they may be used as hosts by other *Formica* species in situations of social parasitism.

1 : a notch at the occipital edge of the head (photo 43). Always bicoloured, with a red mesosoma. .... ***Coptoformica* subgenus (see page 170)**

1': rounded occipital edge to the head. **2**

2 : notched front edge to the clypeus (photo 44). .. ***Raptiformica* subgenus (see page 180)**

2': front edge of clypeus without a notch. **3**

3 : the frontal triangle is obviously more shiny than the surrounding integument. Always bicoloured with part of the head and gaster black, the reddish mesosoma is more or less spotted with black. A dome-shaped nest, built of small twigs. .... ***Formica* subgenus (sensu stricto), 4**

3': the frontal triangle not more shiny than surrounding tegument. Uniform brown or black-coloured ants, a rarely bicoloured species.. **7**

4 : head entirely red (photo 46) in large workers. .... ***Formica* species of the *truncorum* group (see page 178)**

4': bicoloured head, red cheeks, rest of the head black. **5**

5 : occipital edge of the head without erect hairs (photo 45). .... ***Formica* species of the *rufa* group (see page 176)**

5': occipital edge of the head with numerous erect hairs. **6**

6 : the scape widens in a continuous and regular manner from its base to its tip. The occipital edge of the head with numerous hairs (photo 47). Well-defined black spots on the mesosoma. Tegument of gaster very matt. A lowland species, generally not above 1,000 m. .... ***Formica pratensis* (see page 174)**

6': the scape widens continuously from the base to its middle, then has a constant width to its tip. Fewer hairs at the occipital edge of the head (photo 48). Spots on mesosoma smaller and more diffuse. The tegument of the gaster is slightly shiny. Generally found above 1,000 m altitude. .... ***Formica* species of the *lugubris* group (see page 172)**

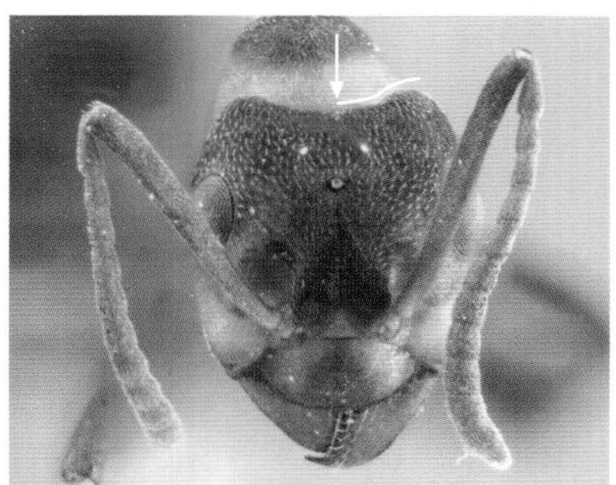
PHOTO 43. *Formica foreli*

PHOTO 44. *Formica sanguinea*

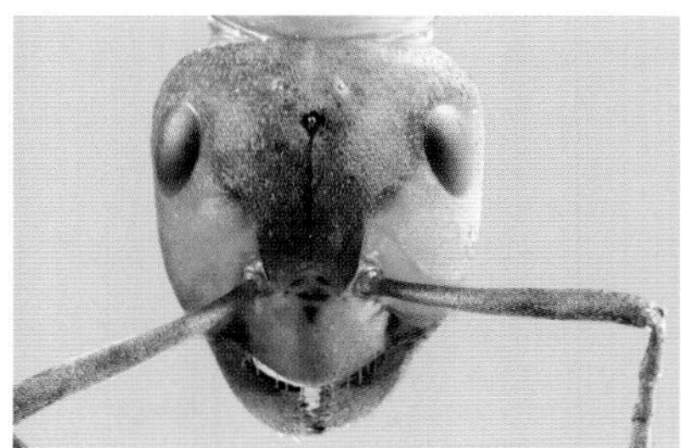
PHOTO 45. *Formica rufa*

PHOTO 46. *Formica truncorum*

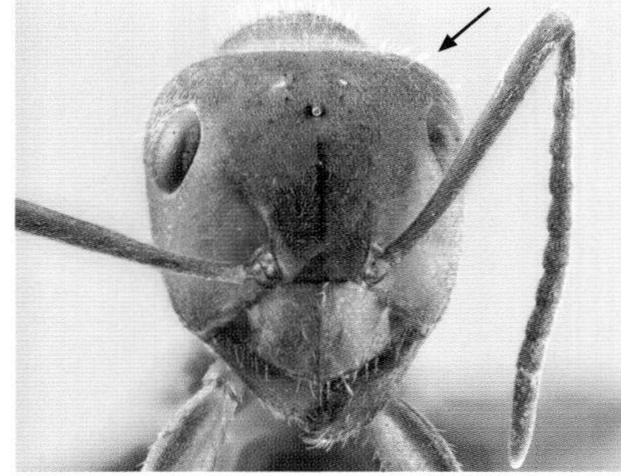
PHOTO 47. *Formica pratensis*

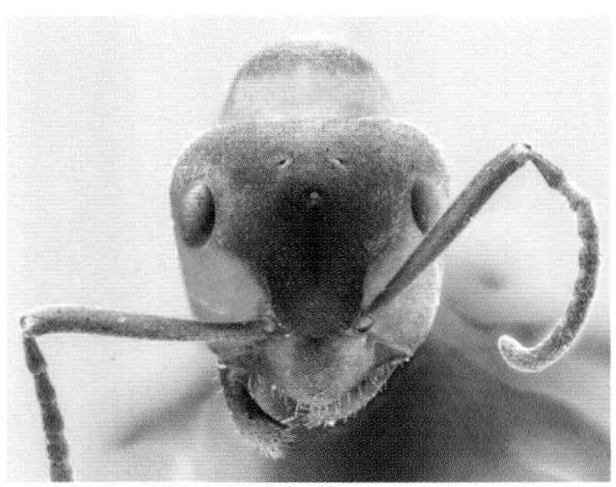
PHOTO 48. *Formica lugubris*

7 : characteristic colour, with black head and pronotum, rest of mesosoma red (photo 49). The scapes are short, their length less than the width of the head. .... ***Formica uralensis* (see page 182)**

7': different colour. Scapes longer, their length more than the width of the head. **8**

8 : Numerous erect hairs on the occipital part of the head and the whole of the mesosoma and gaster (photo 50); very dense, silky hairs give this species a silvery appearance. Dark colour, sometimes mesosoma is paler. .... ***Formica* species of the *cinerea* group (see page 184)**

8': absence of erect hairs on the occipital edge of the head. **9**

9 : dark, shiny body. Rather few hairs, which allows the blackish-brown and shiny tegument to be apparent (photo 51). **10**

9': hairs quite dense, hiding the tegument. Ants without a shiny black aspect. **11**

10 : ants of humid, open, cool habitats, in Northern Europe and mountainous areas. Few hairs on the gaster. .... ***Formica picea* or *F. gagatoides* (see page 196)**

10': ants of wooded habitats, especially in Southern Europe. Hairs on the gaster not so sparse. .... ***Formica gagates* (see page 192)**

11 : no erect hairs on the pronotum, or at most two or three erect hairs. **12**

11': erect hairs on the pronotum. **13**

12 : dark body, mesosoma without reddish patches. .... ***Formica fusca* (see page 190)**

12': mesosoma with at least one reddish patch, sometimes extensive (photo 52)............. .... ***Formica cunicularia* (see page 186)**

13 : obviously bicoloured body, mesosoma with extensive reddish patches (photo 53).... .... ***Formica* species of the *rufibarbis* group (see page 198)**

13': darker, uniformly coloured body. **14**

14 : entirely black ants (photo 54), the gaster can appear quite shiny. Species of Central and Northern Europe, only at altitude in the south. ... ***Formica lemani* (see page 194)**

14': gaster completely matt, or hidden by a thick layer of hairs which give a silvery aspect. Species of Mediterranean habitats and the Iberian Peninsula.................................... .... ***Formica gerardi* or *F. decipiens* (see page 188)**

PHOTO 49. *Formica uralensis*

PHOTO 50. *Formica selysi*

PHOTO 51. *Formica gagates*

PHOTO 52. *Formica cunicularia*

PHOTO 53. *Formica rufibarbis*

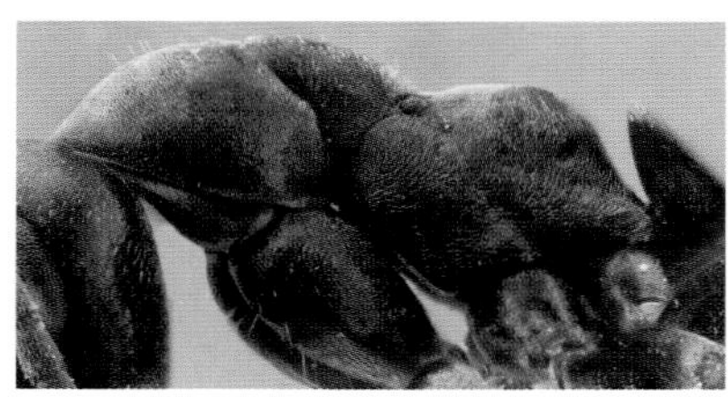
PHOTO 54. *Formica lemani*

Key to the identification of *Cataglyphis* species' groups – genus *Cataglyphis* Foerster, 1850

Cataglyphis species are adapted to arid and semi-desert environments of the Old World (Europe, Asia and North Africa). Of about 100 known species, some 15 occur in the Mediterranean region of the south of Europe. They are diurnal species, predators that hunt in open habitats. They move about very quickly during the hottest part of the day. Some species move with the gaster held high. The maxillary palps are very long, with the fourth segment twice as long as the fifth (photo 55). The groups in this genus have for most part been defined from names of North African and the Middle Eastern species, but species from the latter area do not occur in Europe.

1 : a low petiole, of knotted or ball shape, as high as long when seen in profile.......... **2**
1': thick, scale-shaped petiole, higher than long in profile.. **3**

2 : rounded petiole, top in the form of a ball (photo 56). Workers in the nest very polymorphous, the largest workers are very big. Balkans. .... ***bicolor* group (see page 164)**
2': petiole low and angular (photo 57), its dorsal surface more or less sloping forwards. The gaster is pushed forward when the ant moves. Very small ants, little variation within a nest. Bicoloured or entirely black. Several species in the Iberian Peninsula and Greece. .... ***albicans* group (see page 160)**

3 : when seen in profile, the petiole shape is a small dome, its width decreasing from its base to the top (photo 58). Polymorphic ants, with large workers. Only in the south of the Iberian Peninsula. .... ***altisquamis* group (see page 162)**
3': petiole in the shape of a raised scale (photo 59). Dark body. Workers not very polymorphic. Species occurring in Mediterranean habitats from Spain to Greece. .... ***cursor* group (see page 166)**
3': petiole in the shape of a low scale (photo 60). Dark or bicoloured body. Workers not very polymorphic. Only in south-east Spain................. ***emmae* group (see page 168)**

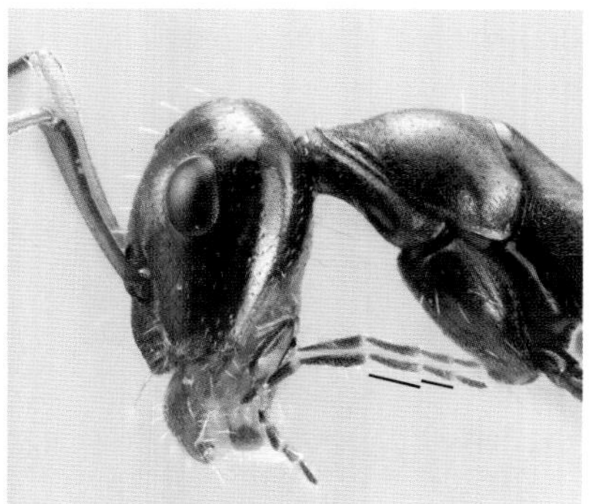

PHOTO 55. *Cataglyphis piliscapa*

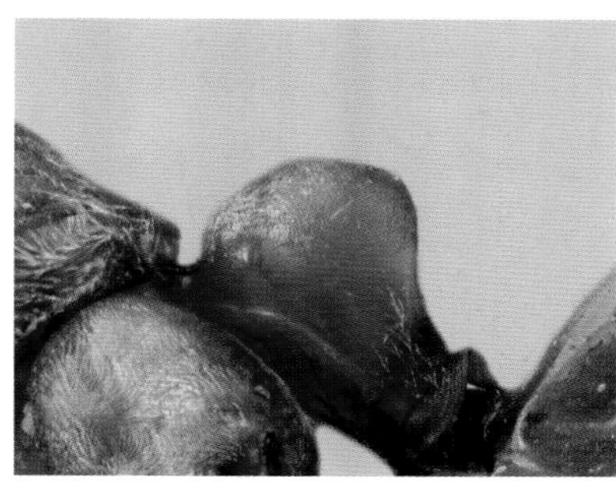

PHOTO 56. *Cataglyphis nodus*

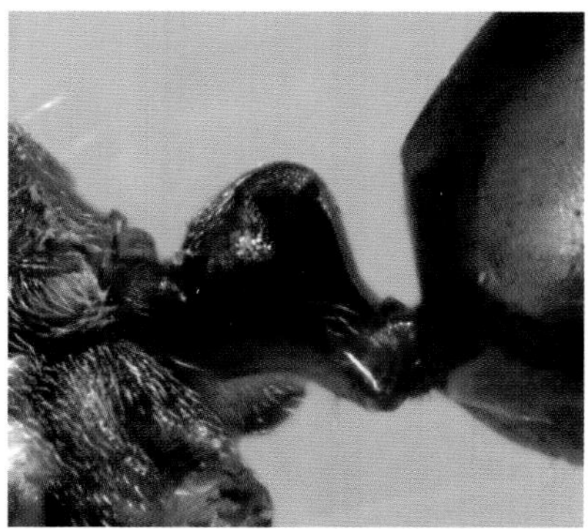

PHOTO 57. *Cataglyphis douwesi*

PHOTO 58. *Cataglyphis humeya*

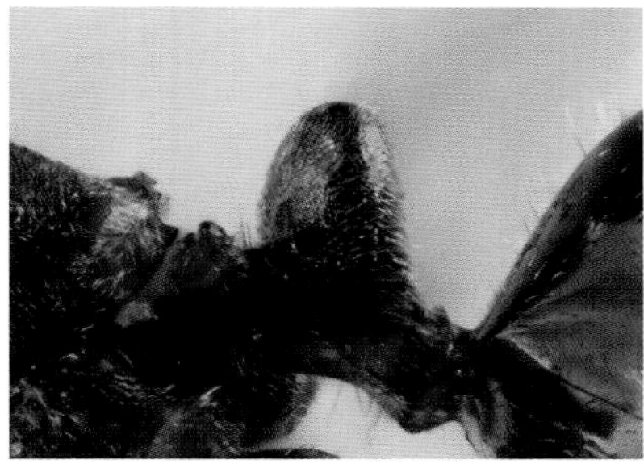

PHOTO 59. *Cataglyphis cursor*

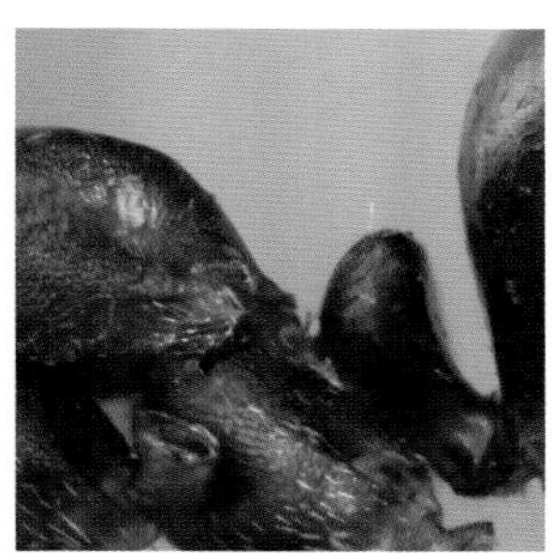

PHOTO 60. *Cataglyphis floricola*

Key to the identification of the principal *Camponotus* species – genus *Camponotus* Mayr, 1861

A very important genus throughout the world, more than 1,000 species described. There are 42 *Camponotus* species in Europe. They are very variable in size, colour and shape, making identification easy. The species are divided among five subgenera: *Colobopsis* (one species), *Camponotus sensu stricto* (three species), *Myrmentoma* (18 species), *Myrmosericus* (three species) and *Tanaemyrmex* (18 species).

1 : workers with a marked dimorphism; the front of major workers' heads are truncated, a very sculpted, reticulated tegument surface (photo 61); minor workers do not have a truncated head, the frontal plates are almost straight. In both types of worker the top of the petiole scale is concave. Workers are bicoloured, red front of body and black gaster. .... ***Camponotus truncatus*** **(see page 132)**

1': large difference in size between workers, with transitional forms between the smallest and the biggest. Sinuous frontal shield an elongated S-shape (photo 62). Rounded top to petiole, never notched.. **2**

2 : clypeus with a longitudinal median ridge, elongated forwards by a subrectangular plate (photo 62). **9**

2': rounded clypeus, without longitudinal ridge. **3**

3 : very matt, black body. Many hairs on the gaster, mesosoma and top of head (photo 64). .... ***Camponotus*** **species of the** ***kiesenwetteri*** **group (see page 136)**

3': fewer hairs. Shiny gaster. **4**

4 : the mesosoma profile marked by a deep notch at the level of the mesopropodeal joint. Concave propodeum (photo 65)... **5**

4': mesosoma profile a continuous line, without a noticeable notch, at most a slight interruption at the level of the joint.. **6**

5 : red front to body. .... ***Camponotus*** **species of the** ***lateralis*** **group (see page 138)**

5': body entirely black. .... ***Camponotus*** **species of the** ***piceus*** **group (see page 140)**

6 : numerous erect hairs, thick on the gaster. Body completely black (photo 67)............ .... ***Camponotus vagus*** **(see page 130)**

6': fewer hairs on the gaster. **7**

PHOTO 61. *Camponotus truncatus* major worker

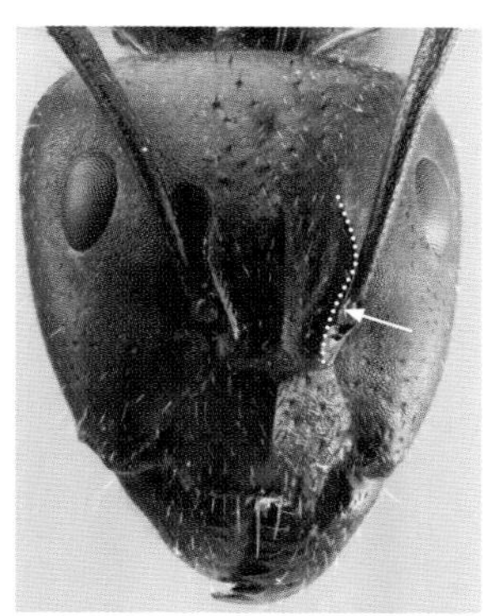
PHOTO 62. *Camponotus aethiops* major worker

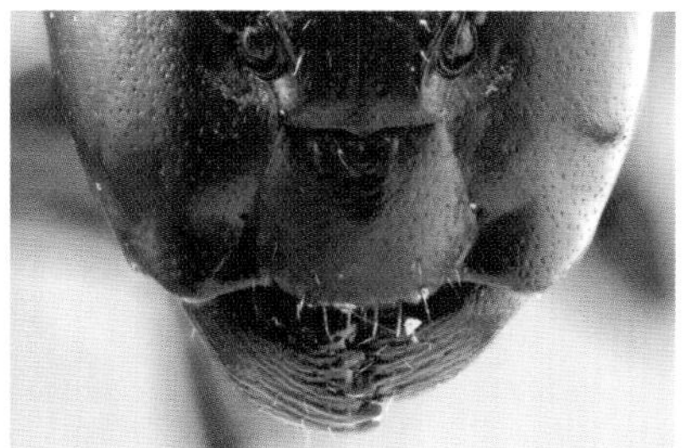
PHOTO 63. *Camponotus vagus* clypeus

PHOTO 64. *Camponotus kiesenwetteri*

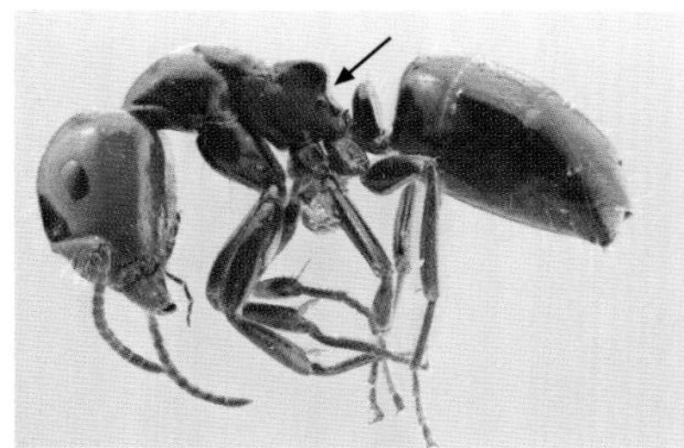
PHOTO 65. *Camponotus lateralis*

PHOTO 66. *Camponotus vagus* major worker

7 : body entirely black. .... ***Camponotus*** **species of the** ***fallax*** **and** ***gestroi*** **groups (see page 134)**
7': reddish mesosoma.. **8**

8 : paler red mesosoma. Top of the first tergite of the gaster often also a reddish colour. Hairs on the gaster are quite short. .... ***Camponotus ligniperda*** **(see page 128)**
8': darker red mesosoma. Top of the first tergite of the gaster is always black. The hairs on the gaster are always longer.................... ***Camponotus herculeanus*** **(see page 126)**

9 : body entirely matt. Thick layer of hairs over the gaster (photo 68). .... ***Myrmosericus*** **subgenus, 10**
9': body generally quite shiny. Gaster usually with sparse hairs .... ***Tanaemyrmex*** **subgenus, 11**

10 : body entirely black. .... ***Camponotus micans*** **(see page 144)**
10': body coloured with orangish areas................. ***Camponotus cruentatus*** **(see page 142)**

11 : mesosoma profile sinuous.. ***Camponotus foreli*** **(see page 148)**
11': mesosoma profile a continuous curve.. **12**

12 : gaster with very numerous erect hairs. ....***Camponotus*** **species of the** ***samius*** **group (see page 154)**
12': gaster with far fewer erect hairs. **13**

13 : hairy cheeks (photo 69). **14**
13': no hairs on cheeks (photo 70). **15**

14 : body entirely black. .... ***Camponotus*** **species of the** ***aethiops*** **group (see page 146)**
14': bicoloured species, mesosoma pale brown to yellow, paler than the gaster. .... ***Camponotus*** **species of the** ***pilicornis*** **group (see page 152)**
15 : no hairs under the head (photo 71). .... ***Camponotus sanctus*** **(see page 156)**
15': erect hairs present under the head (photo 72). **16**

16 : tibia with spines on its inner edge.. .... ***Camponotus*** **species of the** ***sylvaticus*** **group (see page 158)**
16': tibia without spines on its inner edge. .... ***Camponotus nylanderi*** **(see page 150)**

PHOTO 67. *Camponotus fallax*

PHOTO 68. *Camponotus cruentatus*

PHOTO 69. *Camponotus pilicornis*

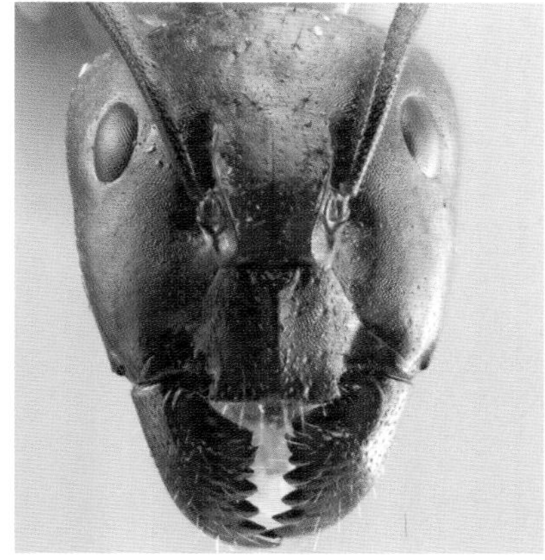
PHOTO 70. *Camponotus sylvaticus*

PHOTO 71. *Camponotus sanctus*

PHOTO 72. *Camponotus sylvaticus*

Key to the genera of the subfamily Myrmicinae

1 : very small ant, equal to or less than 2.5 mm. Pear-shaped head (photo 73). Funiculus of 3–5 segments. .... ***Strumigenys*** **genus (see page 340)**

1': generally bigger. Head not pear-shaped. Funiculus of 9, 10 or 11 segments. **2**

2 : postpetiole attached to the top of the first gaster tergite. Gaster heart-shaped, pointed towards the back, can be lifted to the vertical when the worker is alarmed............. .... ***Crematogaster*** **genus (see key, page 96)**

2': the postpetiole attached differently. **3**

3 : sabre-shaped mandibles (photo 74). .... ***Strongylognathus*** **genus (see page 338)**

3': triangular mandibles. **4**

4 : propodeum without spines (photo 75), rounded or angular propodeum. **5**

4': propodeum with spines (photo 76), very elongated or reduced to simple teeth. **10**

5 : funiculus of nine segments ends in a two-segment club (photo 77). Less than 3 mm. Body yellow or orangish-yellow. **6**

5' funiculus of 10 or 11 segments. **7**

6 : rounded propodeum, smooth sides to mesosoma. Clypeus with one erect median hair. .... ***Solenopsis*** **genus (see page 334)**

6': angular propodeum, mesosoma sides reticulated. Clypeus with two median hairs.... .... ***Carebara*** **genus (see page 334)**

7 : large workers, 5–12 mm. Mandibles with more than ten teeth. **8**

7': small workers, 2–4 mm. Mandibles with four teeth. **9**

8 : uniformly red body, more or less pale. Antennal clubs with five segments. The spurs on all the tibiae are arranged comb-like. .... ***Manica*** **genus (see page 288)**

8': workers in the nest of very variable size, minor workers 3.5 mm, up to 12 mm for major workers. These last have a massive square head and wide mandibles (photo 78). The body often very dark-coloured, a few species have a red front to the body. The spurs on the tibiae II and III are simple. .... ***Messor*** **genus (see key, page 90)**

PHOTO 73. *Strumigenys tenuipilis*

PHOTO 74. *Strongylognathus testaceus*

PHOTO 75. *Messor capitatus*

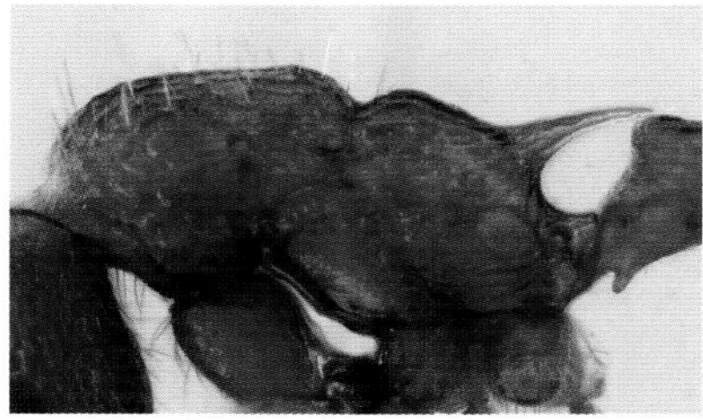

PHOTO 76. *Myrmica scabrinodis*

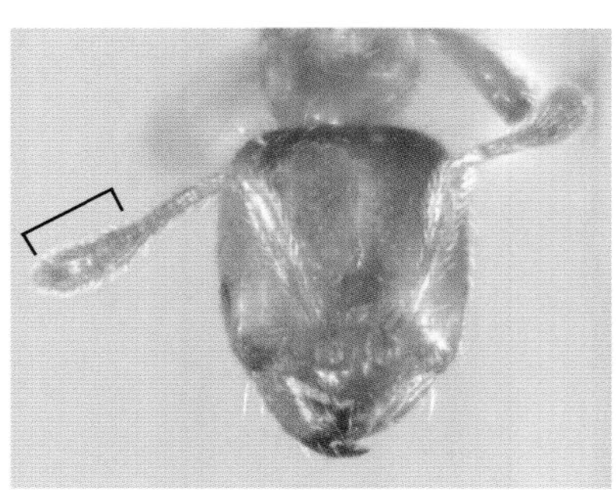

PHOTO 77. *Solenopsis fugax*

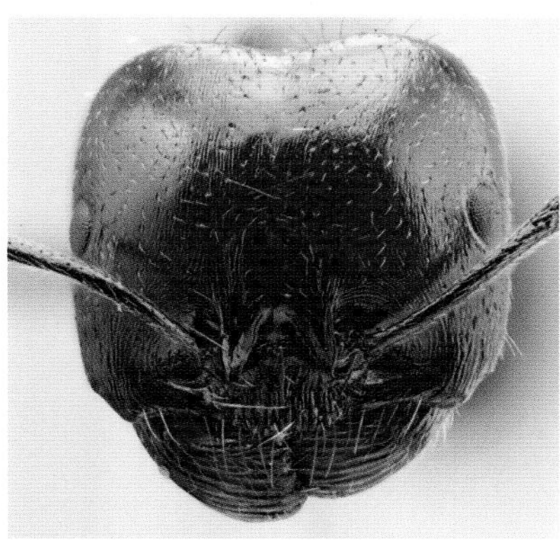

PHOTO 78. *Messor barbarus* major worker

9 : workers small, less than 2.5 mm, more or less all the same size in the nest. No erect hairs under the head. Body entirely shiny black, or yellow. Three segments to the antenna club. .... ***Monomorium* genus (see pages 302–305)**

9': variable size in the nest, the large workers with a wide head. Numerous erect hairs under the head. .... ***Trichomyrmex* genus (see page 398)**

10 : the lateral edges of the pronotum appear angular when worker is seen from above (photo 79a). Small ants 2–4 mm. Generally very dark colour. Very sculpted tegument. The back border of the clypeus rises into a ridge around the antennae bases. **11**

10': the lateral edges of the pronotum appear rounded when the worker is seen from above (photo 79b). Clypeus without an obvious ridge at the base of the antennae. **12**

11 : very characteristic cubic petiole and postpetiole (photo 80). Clypeus with two forward-pointing teeth.. ***Myrmecina* genus (see page 306)**

11': petiole and postpetiole different. Clypeus without teeth. .... ***Tetramorium* genus (see key, page 98)**

12 : seen from above, the postpetiole is much wider than the petiole (photo 81). .... ***Cardiocondyla* genus (see page 266)**

12': postpetiole as wide as or only slightly wider than the petiole................................ **13**

13 : large eyes, placed near to where mandibles join head and elongated in a point towards them (photo 82).. **14**

13': oval or round eyes, distant from where the mandibles join head by at least the length of the eye. **15**

14 : 11 segments to funiculus... ***Goniomma* genus (see page 280)**

14': 10 segments to funiculus.................................... ***Oxyopomyrmex* genus (see page 330)**

15 : underside of the petiole and postpetiole have a very visible tooth or lobe-shaped extension (photo 83). Commensal, parasitic or slavemaking ants......................... **16**

15': underside of postpetiole without an elongation, or one very reduced tooth. **19**

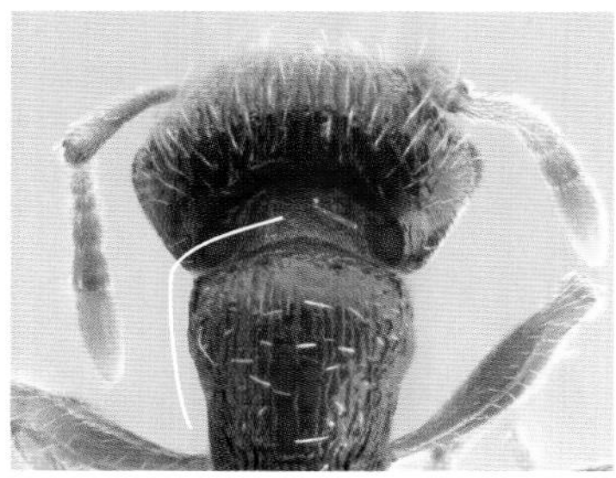

a. *Tetramorium*

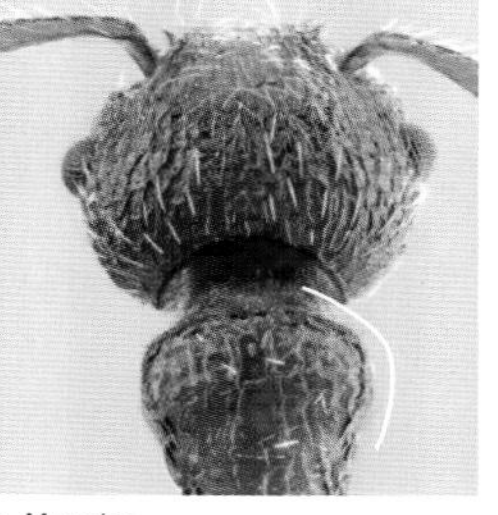

b. *Myrmica*

PHOTOS 79. Dorsal views of pronotum of *Tetramorium* (left) and *Myrmica* (right) workers.

PHOTO 80. Profile of the petiole and postpetiole of a *Myrmecina graminicola* worker.

PHOTO 81. Dorsal view of the petiole and postpetiole of a *Cardiocondyla elegans* worker.

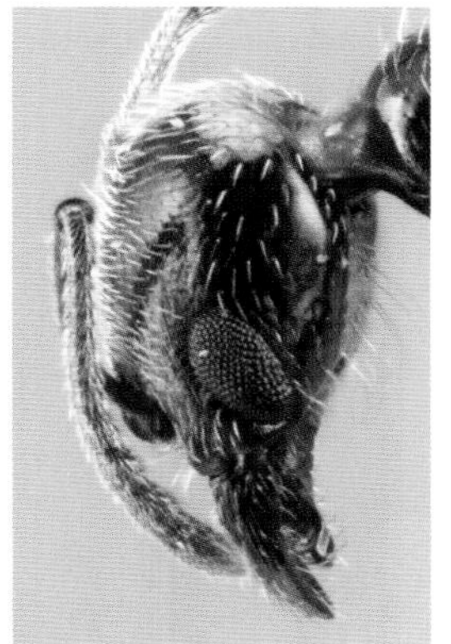

PHOTO 82. *Goniomma hispanicum*

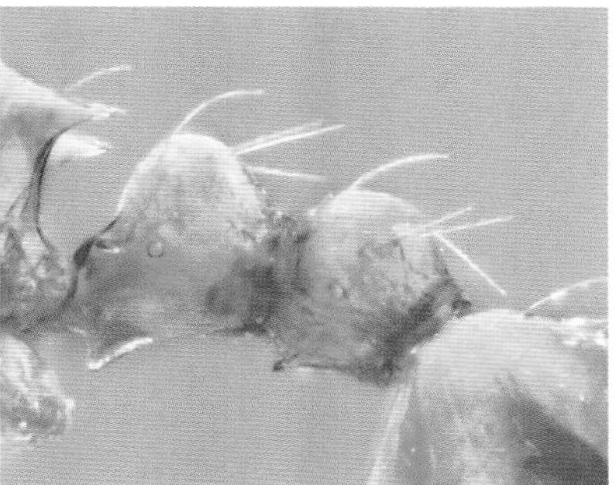

PHOTO 83. Profile of the petiole and postpetiole of a *Chalepoxenus muellerianus* worker.

16 : wide mandibles, without teeth. Large rectangular head (photo 84). .... ***Harpagoxenus*** **genus (see page 282)**

16': mandibles always with teeth. **17**

17 : funiculus with 11 segments. Small yellow workers, 3–4 mm. Slavemaker, with ants of *Temnothorax* species as hosts. Ventral surface of the postpetiole has a blunt tooth. .... ***Chalepoxenus*** **genus (see page 268)**

17': funiculus with 10 segments. **18**

18 : a blade-shaped extension under the petiole (photo 85). Body matt. Parasitises *Temnothorax* species. .... ***Myrmoxenus*** **genus (see page 328)**

18': a tooth-shaped extension under the petiole. Shiny body. Occurs on the surface in domes of *Formica* species. .... ***Formicoxenus*** **genus (see page 278)**

19 : very small eyes, with a diameter less than or equal to the width of the scape (photo 86). Petiole with long, forward-pointing peduncle. .... ***Stenamma*** **genus (see page 336)**

19': bigger eyes, with a diameter greater than the width of the scape. **20**

20 : funiculus with 10 segments. Clypeus without a central ridge. .... ***Leptothorax*** **genus (see page 284)**

20': funiculus with 11 segments (except *Temnothorax flavicornis*, see page 352). **21**

21 : antennal clubs with three segments and a length equal to half that of the funiculus (photo 87). Small size, workers 2–3.5 mm. **22**

21': antennal clubs with four or five segments, or no clubs. Bigger size, workers 4–9 mm. **23**

22 : presence of a characteristic soldier caste with an enormous head, with a notched occipital border. Smooth clypeus, without a median ridge. Minor worker mandibles with more than five teeth. .... ***Pheidole*** **genus (see page 332)**

22': workers of a colony about the same size. Mandibles with five teeth. Clypeus with a median ridge, sometimes incomplete. .... ***Temnothorax*** **genus (see key, page 100)**

23 : the mesosoma profile almost straight, very sculpted tegument, propodeum spines well developed (photo 88). Spurs on tibiae II and III in a comb form. The body colour often reddish, sometimes the head and gaster are duller. .... ***Myrmica*** **genus (see key, page 92)**

23': mesosoma with sinuous profile, tegument far less sculpted, sometimes almost smooth, propodeum spines shorter (photo 89). Spurs on tibiae II and III simple. Body completely black or a more or less pale red. .... ***Aphaenogaster*** **genus (see key, page 86)**

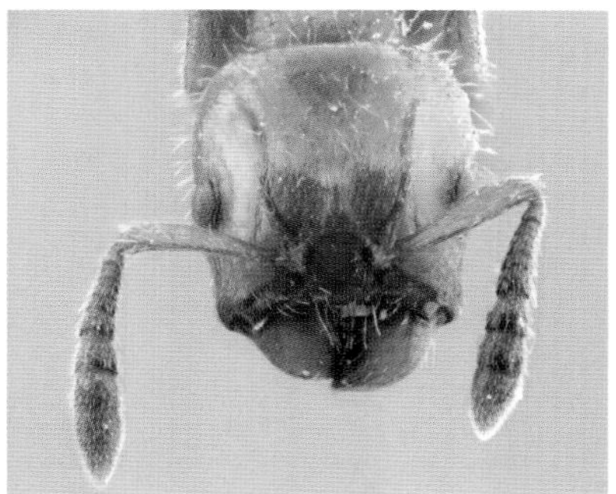
PHOTO 84. *Harpagoxenus sublaevis*

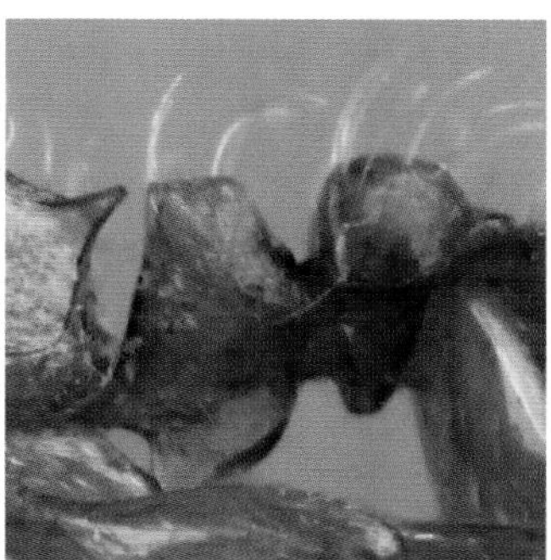
PHOTO 85. The blade-shaped petiole of the genus *Myrmoxenus*.

PHOTO 86. *Stenamma debile*

PHOTO 87. *Pheidole pallidula* minor worker

PHOTO 88. *Myrmica sabuleti*

PHOTO 89. *Aphaenogaster subterranea*

Key to the identification of the principal *Aphaenogaster* species – genus *Aphaenogaster* Mayr, 1863

A very large genus, with more than 200 species in the world. Thirty-eight species are known to occur in Europe. The genus *Aphaenogaster* is related to the *Messor* and *Pheidole* genera, but worker polymorphism is much reduced. Species are generally predatory, present in all habitats, with a maximum diversity in Mediterranean regions. The Balkans, in particular, have been an important area in their speciation.

1 : body totally matt. The tegument of the whole of the head and mesosoma is spotted and covered with thick, stiff hairs. Generally, the gaster is also finely sculpted, but may appear shiny in certain species. **2**

1': body with a shinier aspect. The tegument can be highly sculpted, leaving smooth areas visible between the grooves. Tegument of gaster is smooth. **5**

2 : body entirely yellow (photo 90). Only occurs in Sardinia and Sicily. .... ***Aphaenogaster sardoa* (see page 252)**

2': body black, covered with thick, stiff white hairs. Head quite elongated (photo 91). .... ***testaceopilosa* group, 3**

Note: The species *A. testaceopilosa* (Lucas, 1849) occurs in Algeria; its name has been used for a group of species frequenting the Mediterranean Basin.

3 : antennal clubs with five segments (photo 92). .... ***Aphaenogaster senilis* (see page 248)**

3': antennal clubs with four segments (photo 93) **4**

4 : long propodeum spines, longer than the distance separating their bases (photo 94). .... ***Aphaenogaster iberica* in the Iberian Peninsula or *A. spinosa* in central Italy, Sardinia and Corsica (see page 246)**

4': propodeum spines shorter (photo 95). Numerous species in southern Italy and the Balkans. .... **(see page 250)**

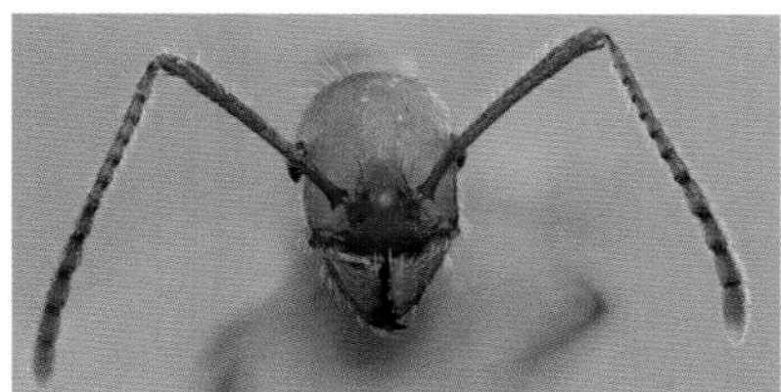

PHOTO 90. *Aphaenogaster sardoa*

PHOTO 91. *Aphaenogaster semipolita*

PHOTO 92. *Aphaenogaster senilis*

PHOTO 93. *Aphaenogaster semipolita*

PHOTO 94. *Aphaenogaster spinosa*

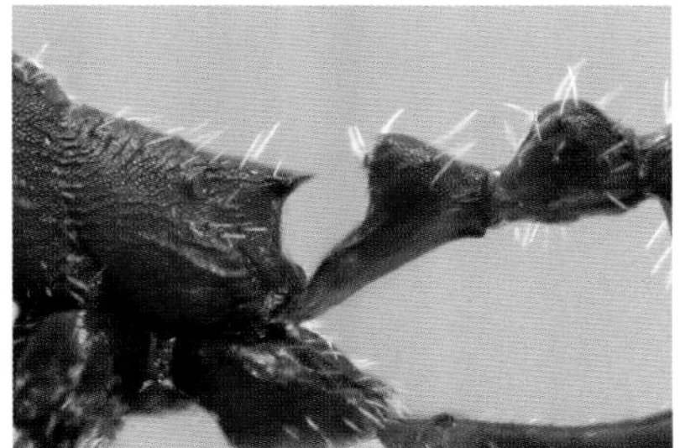

PHOTO 95. *Aphaenogaster balcanica*

5 : very slim body, very long legs, head twice as long as wide (photo 96). Black body.... ....***Aphaenogaster* species of the *cecconii* group (see page 254)**

5': body less elongated. **6**

6 : long scapes, easily passing the top of the head. The central segments of the funiculus longer than they are wide. **7**

6': scapes shorter, hardly passing the head. The central segments of the funiculus as long as they are wide, or slightly longer than wide. **9**

7 : the second funiculus segment less than 1½ times as long as it is wide. The tegument of the head slightly sculpted (photo 97). .... ***Aphaenogaster* of the *subterranea* group (see page 264)**

7': the second funiculus segment more than 1½ times as long as it is wide. **8**

8 : body colour dark (photo 98). ....***Aphaenogaster* of the *gibbosa* group (see page 256)**

8': body colour quite pale, between yellow and orangish (photo 99). .... ***Aphaenogaster* of the *splendida* group (see page 262)**

9 : body colour dark. Head always sculpted (photo 100). .... ***Aphaenogaster* of the *obsidiana* group (see page 258)**

9': body colour pale. Head mainly smooth (photo 101). .... ***Aphaenogaster* of the *pallida* group (see page 260)**

PHOTO 96. *Aphaenogaster cecconii*

PHOTO 97. *Aphaenogaster subterranea*

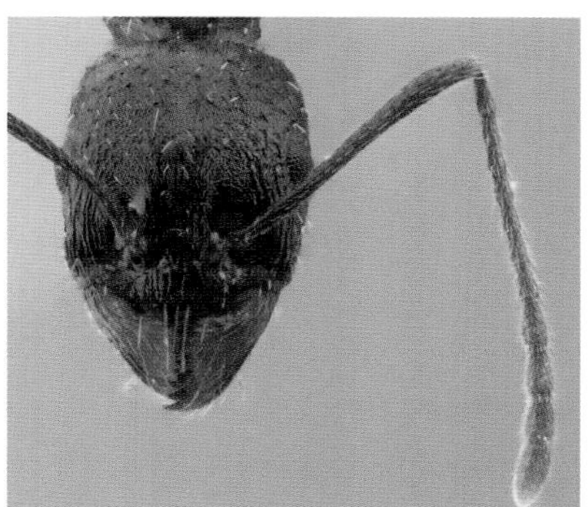

PHOTO 98. *Aphaenogaster gibbosa*

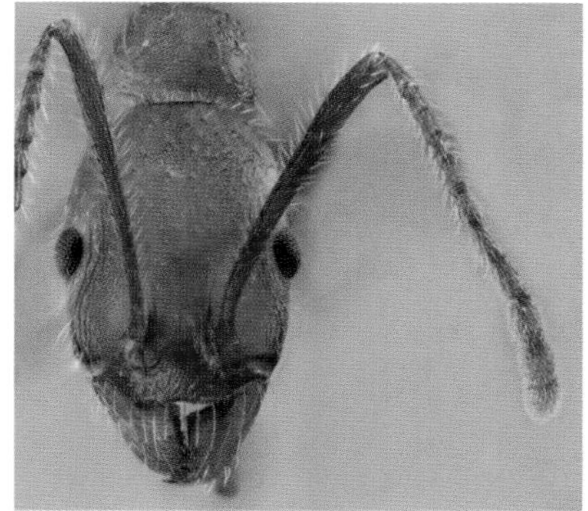

PHOTO 99. *Aphaenogaster splendida*

PHOTO 100. *Aphaenogaster epirotes*

PHOTO 101. *Aphaenogaster dulciniae*

Key to the identification of the principal *Messor* species – genus *Messor* Forel, 1890

There are 19 species of the genus *Messor* in Europe, their identification difficult. They are all granivorous species that occur in open habitats, often rich in grasses. Species in the genus *Messor* are characterised by showing a great variation of individual size within the same colony. The bigger workers have a very big head, enclosing very large mandible muscles. The main occupation of these large workers is the breaking-up of seeds brought to the nest. They are not aggressive but because of the force in their mandibles their bite can be painful.

1 : underside of the head with long, forward-pointing hairs (psammophores) (photo 102). Gaster without or with just a few erect hairs. **2**

1': underside of head with short hairs (photo 103). No hairs on the gaster. **4**

2 : body entirely black (except for ***M. marocanus***, southern Spain)................................. .... ***Messor* species of the *bouvieri* group (see page 292)**

2': body not entirely black, mesosoma partly reddish. Ants absent from Spain. **3**

3 : red head and mesosoma.. ***Messor minor* (see page 296)**

3': dull head, mesosoma reddish with brown spot. .... ***Messor* species of the *wasmanni* group (see page 300)**

4 : hairy over the whole body, especially on the head. In large workers the whole of the head is wrinkled (photo 104)....... ***Messor* species of the *structor* group (see page 298)**

4': less densely haired, especially on the head. In large workers the head surface is more or less smooth (photo 105). **5**

5 : body entirely black. Angular propodeum in large workers (photo 106). .... ***Messor capitatus* (see page 294)**

5': head normally a more or less dark red. Rounded propodeum in large workers (photo 107). .... ***Messor barbarus* (see page 290)**

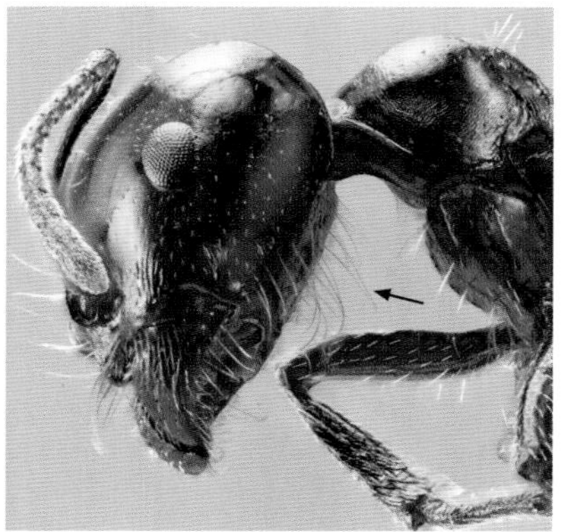
PHOTO 102. *Messor bouvieri*

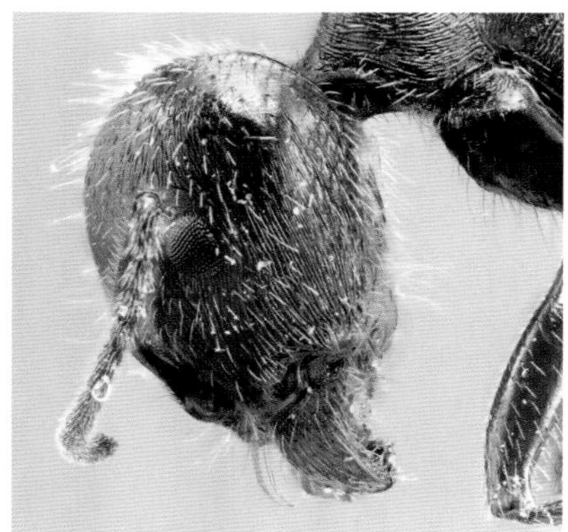
PHOTO 103. *Messor structor*

PHOTO 104. *Messor structor*

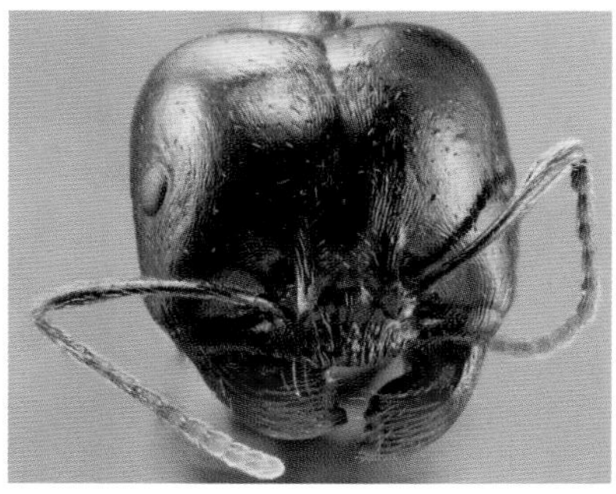
PHOTO 105. *Messor capitatus*

PHOTO 106. *Messor capitatus*

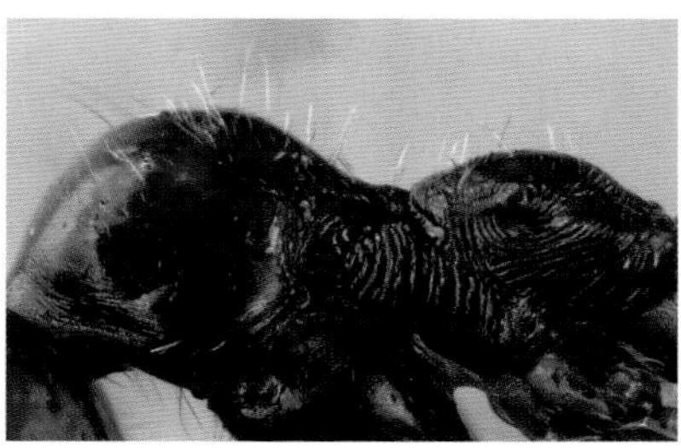
PHOTO 107. *Messor barbarus*

Key to the identification of the principal *Myrmica* species – genus *Myrmica* Latreille, 1804

The genus *Myrmica* forms a morphologically very homogenous group. They are commonly called 'red ants'. Effectively, all species have a more or less pronounced reddish colour (from pale red to dark red, almost black). They measure about 5 mm in length, without any size variation within the same colony. Identification of the 30 or so species that occur in Europe is quite difficult and is based mainly on the shape of the scape base. Some species are obligate parasites occurring in colonies of other species of the genus *Myrmica*; they do not produce workers. These parasitic species are treated on page 326.

1 : the antennal scape is simply curved as its base, without any angular part and without any tooth or lobe-shaped extension (photos 110 and 111). **2**

1': antennal scape angular towards its base, with a vertical tooth-shaped extension, or a lobe-shaped dilation that is underlined by a longitudinal ridge (photos 108 and 109). **6**

2 : antennal scape slightly bent at its base (photo 110). Shiny frontal triangle............... .... ***Myrmica* species of the *rubra* group, 3**

2': antennal scape more strongly bent at its base (photo 111), sometimes with a slight longitudinal ridge but not underlining the dilation. Frontal triangle partly sculpted. **4**

3 : short propodeum spines, with smooth space between them. Petiole entirely smooth (photo 112).. ***Myrmica rubra* (see page 312)**

3': longer propodeum spines, space between them striped transversally. Petiole rough (photo 113)... ***Myrmica ruginodis* (see page 314)**

4 : tegument highly sculpted over the whole body. Frontal triangle almost totally sculpted. Antennal scape strongly arched towards its base.. .... ***Myrmica sulcinodis* (see page 310)**

4': less pronounced sculpting on tegument. Frontal triangle partly smooth at its base. **5**

PHOTO 108. *Myrmica lobicornis*

PHOTO 109. *Myrmica sabuleti*

PHOTO 110. *Myrmica rubra* scape shape

PHOTO 111. *Myrmica sulcinodis* scape shape

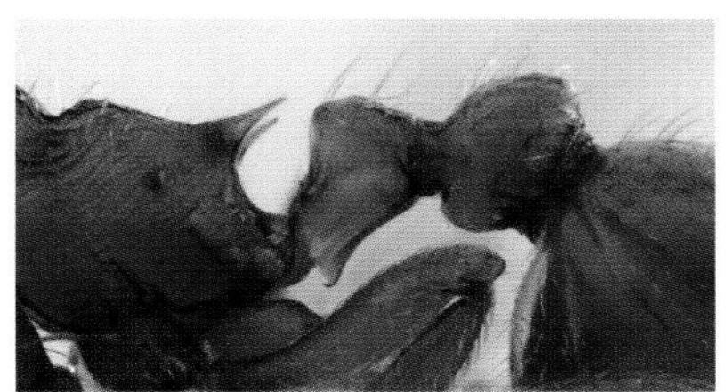

PHOTO 112. *Myrmica rubra* petiole profile

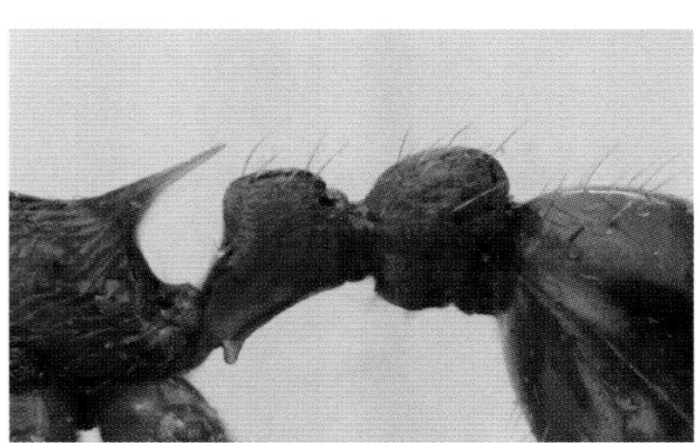

PHOTO 113. *Myrmica lobicornis* petiole profile

5 : scape quite strongly curved at its base, sometimes the trace of a longitudinal ridge along it.. ***Myrmica*** **species of the** ***rugulosa*** **group (see page 316)**

5': scape not so strongly curved, no trace of a longitudinal ridge.................................. .... ***Myrmica*** **species of the** ***bergi*** **group (see page 308)**

6 : the angle in the scape with a vertical lobe-shaped extension (photo 108)................ **7**

6': angle in the scape with a longitudinal ridge, accompanied by a more or less developed, horizontal lobe-shaped dilation (photo 109).. **8**

7 : seen in profile the petiole has a quite angular summit (photo 114). Quite short propodeum spines......................... ***Myrmica*** **species of the** ***lobicornis*** **group (see page 310)**

7': seen in profile the petiole has a rounded summit (photo 115). Propodeum spines long and narrow. .... ***Myrmica*** **species of the** ***schencki*** **group (see page 322)**

8 : seen in profile the dorsal and rear part of the petiole form a simple curve before joining the postpetiole (photo 116).. .... ***Myrmica*** **species of the** ***specioides*** **group (see page 324)**

8': dorsal and rear part of the petiole angular before joining the postpetiole (photo 117). **9**

9 : base of the antennal scape with a horizontal lobe-shaped dilation (photo 118). Top of the petiole slightly rounded when seen in profile. .... ***Myrmica*** **species of the** ***sabuleti*** **group (see page 318)**

9': base of the antennal scape with a longitudinal ridge (photo 119). Truncated top to petiole, angular in profile...... ***Myrmica*** **species of the** ***scabrinodis*** **group (see page 320)**

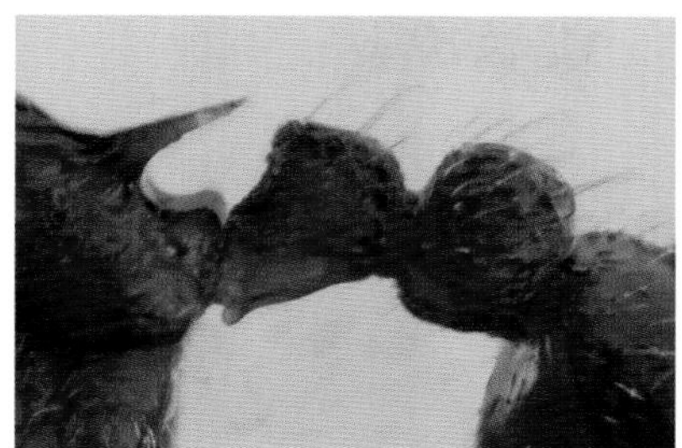

PHOTO 114. *Myrmica lobicornis* petiole profile

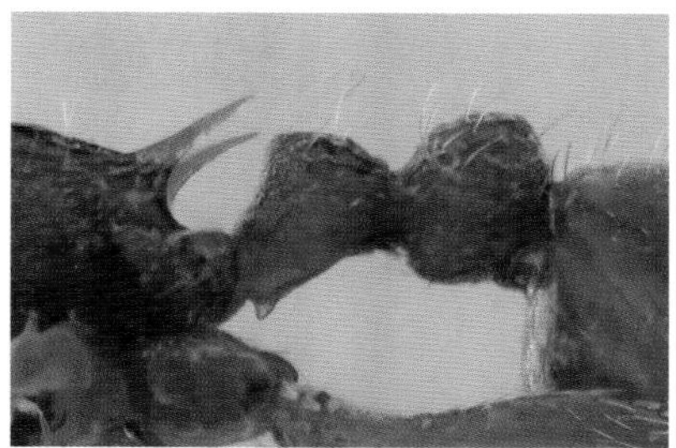

PHOTO 115. *Myrmica schencki* petiole profile

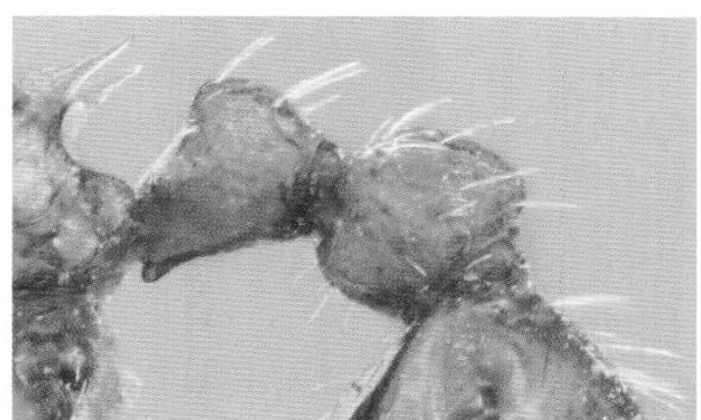

PHOTO 116. *Myrmica specioides* petiole profile

PHOTO 117. *Myrmica spinosior* petiole profile

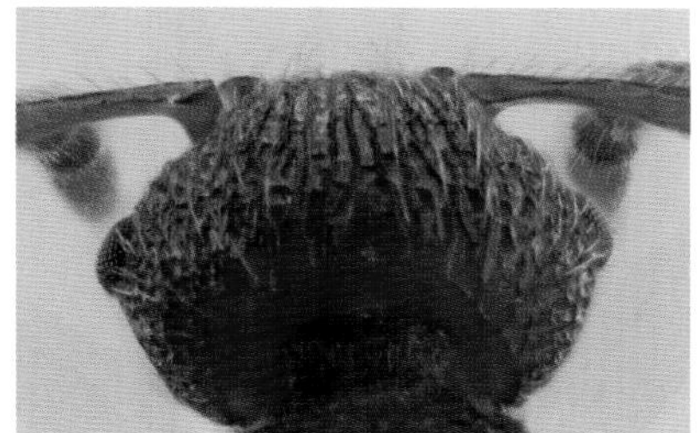

PHOTO 118. *Myrmica sabuleti* scape shape

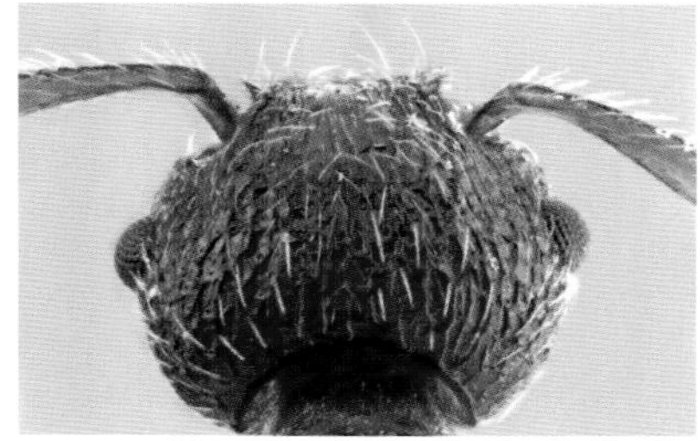

PHOTO 119. *Myrmica scabrinodis* scape shape

Key to the identification of the principal *Crematogaster* species – genus *Crematogaster* Lund, 1831

Crematogaster is a large genus containing nearly 500 described species. It has become more diverse in the tropical and subtropical zones. Only 11 species are known to occur in Europe. Specific determination can be difficult in the southern Balkans, where seven species coexist. The species of this genus are ground-dwelling or tree-dwelling.

1 : under 2.5 mm long. Body entirely pale brown, dotted with slender, long hairs. Seen from above the petiole has parallel sides (photo 120). .... ***Crematogaster sordidula* (see page 276)**

1': more than 3 mm long. Body entirely black or with a red front to the body, fewer hairs. Seen from above the petiole is triangular, widened at the front (photo 121)........... **2**

2 : front of body (head, mesosoma and sometimes the petiole) pale red or a dark red that contrasts with black gaster (photo 122). Throughout Southern Europe. .... ***Crematogaster* species of the *scutellaris* group (see page 272)**

2': body uniform, brown or black. **3**

3 : body completely black or brown. Western Mediterranean Basin, from Spain to Sicily. **4**

3': body entirely brown, or front of body only slightly paler than the gaster (photo 123). Southern Balkans. .... **other *Crematogaster* species (see page 274)**

4 : propodeum spines cylindrical and elongated (photo 124). Mesosoma without longitudinal central ridge. .... ***Crematogaster auberti* (see page 270)**

4': propodeum spines short and triangular (photo 125). Mesosoma with a longitudinal central ridge. .... ***Crematogaster laestrygon* (see page 270)**

PHOTO 120. *Crematogaster sordidula*

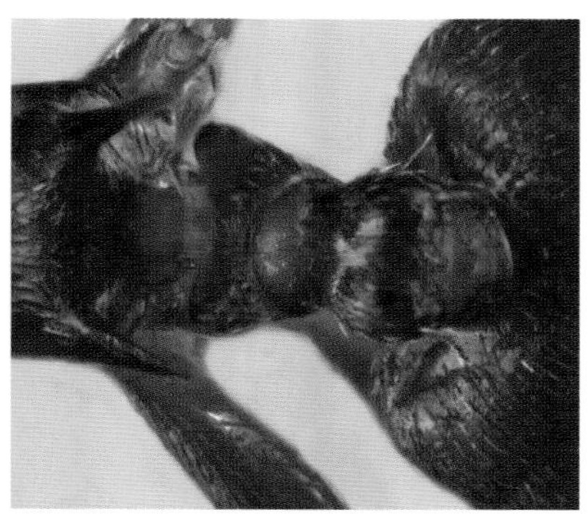
PHOTO 121. *Crematogaster scutellaris*

PHOTO 122. *Crematogaster scutellaris*

PHOTO 123. *Crematogaster ionia*

PHOTO 124. *Crematogaster auberti*

PHOTO 125. *Crematogaster laestrygon*

Key to the identification of the principal *Tetramorium* species – genus *Tetramorium* Mayr, 1855

A very big genus incorporating 600 species. Thirty of these occur in Europe. Identification to species level in *Tetramoriumis* is difficult due to convergent morphology between workers. Certain species are essentially identified from queens and winged males, especially from the males' genitalia. They are a very common species, found in numerous habitats. Can be pale or very dark in colour, with a size of about 3–4 mm. Certain species are obligate parasites of *Tetramorium* colonies and do not produce workers. This is the case of species of the *Anergates* (see page 394) and *Teleutomyrmex* (see page 396) genera.

1 : the head tegument is mainly smooth: the wrinkles are progressively less marked towards the occiput, sometimes the head is completely smooth (photo 126)............ .... **several species groups of the genus *Tetramorium*, including the *semilaeve* group (see page 392)**

1': the head tegument is entirely sculpted, more often than not in the form of longitudinal wrinkles that continue onto the top of the head. **2**

2 : obvious frontal ridges that continue onto the head (photo 127). .... **several species groups, including the *simillimum* group (see page 380)**

2': short frontal ridges that do not continue onto the head. **3**

3 : on the vertex the longitudinal wrinkles stop and are replaced by transverse wrinkles (photo 128).. ***Tetramorium meridionale* (see page 390)**

3': absence of transverse wrinkles on the top of the head.. **4**

4 : totality of petiole and postpetiole sculpted, even on their top (photo 129). .... ***Tetramorium* species of the *chefteki* group (see page 386)**

4': top of petiole and/or postpetiole partly smooth. **5**

5 : spines placed very low on the propodeum (photo 130). Petiole and postpetiole are relatively wide......................... ***Tetramorium* species of the *ferox* group (see page 388)**

5': spines placed higher on the propodeum (photo 131). Petiole and postpetiole narrower. **6**

6 : numerous wrinkles on the head, more than 16 between the frontal ridges. Queens small. .... ***Tetramorium* species of the *biskrense* group (see page 382)**

6': fewer wrinkles, maximum of 16 between the frontal ridges. Queens large. .... ***Tetramorium* species of the *caespitum-impurum* group (see page 384)**

PHOTO 126. *Tetramorium semilaeve*

PHOTO 127. *Tetramorium caldarium* head

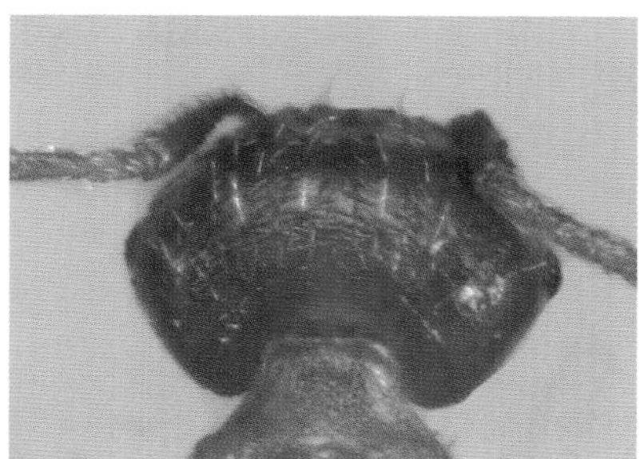

PHOTO 128. *Tetramorium meridionale*

PHOTO 129. *Tetramorium forte* petiole and postpetiole

PHOTO 130. *Tetramorium ferox*

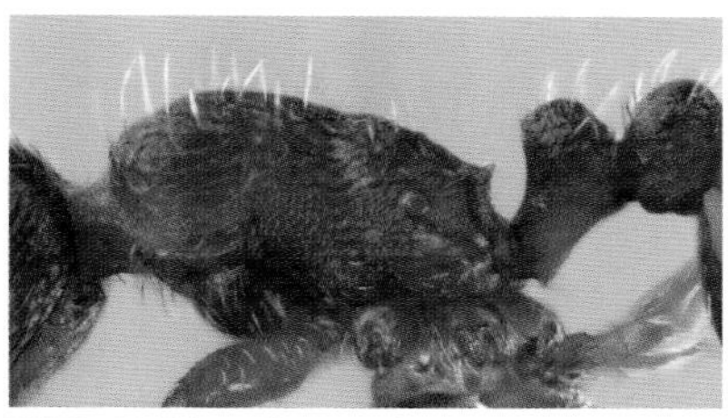

PHOTO 131. *Tetramorium caespitum*

Key to the identification of the principal *Temnothorax* species – genus *Temnothorax* Mayr, 1861

With 80 species occurring in Europe, the genus *Temnothorax* is the most diverse. Small ants (about 3 mm long), identification is often difficult. Although a few species build nests directly in the ground, they are usually specialists in occupying natural cavities. They are often found in small dead branches on the ground or inside cracks in stones. Their small size and small number of individuals in a colony as well as their discreet habits means they are not well known except by experts. Notwithstanding, most species are common.

1 : funiculus with 10 segments............................ ***Temnothorax flavicornis*** **(see page 352)**
1': funiculus with 11 segments.. **2**

2 : big eyes, about one third of the head length (photo 132)..
....***Temnothorax*** **species of the *laurae* group (see page 370)**
2': smaller eyes, about one quarter of the head length (see photo 133)......................... **3**

3 : body mainly pale-coloured, between yellow and pale brown, sometimes the gaster segments are dull. **4**
3': body totally dark, sometimes the mesosoma is brown to reddish. **11**

4 : yellow antennal clubs, like the rest of the antennae (photo 134). **5**
4': antennal clubs dark, rest of the antennae paler... **14**

5 : presence of a furrow in mesopropodeum, more or less marked. **6**
5': no visible mesopropodeum furrow, mesosoma profile a continuous curve........... **10**

6 : very deep mesopropodeum furrow, mesosoma profile very sinuous. Long hairs (photo 136)...................... ***Temnothorax*** **species of the *recedens* group (see page 370)**
6': less obvious mesopropodeum furrow. Short hairs. **7**

7 : darker first sternite (photo 137). **8**
7': first sternite not darker. **9**

8 : dorsal part of the mesosoma totally sculpted. Body colour very pale, propodeum spines wide-based and quite long. Throughout Europe...
....***Temnothorax*** **species of the *nylanderi* group (page 366)**
8': dorsal part of the mesosoma only slightly sculpted, generally smooth and shiny. Body darker, a dull head. Very short propodeum spines. Iberian Peninsula. ....
.... ***Temnothorax gredosi*** **(see page 354)**

PHOTO 132. *Temnothorax laurae*

PHOTO 133. *Temnothorax recedens*

PHOTO 134. *Temnothorax nylanderi*

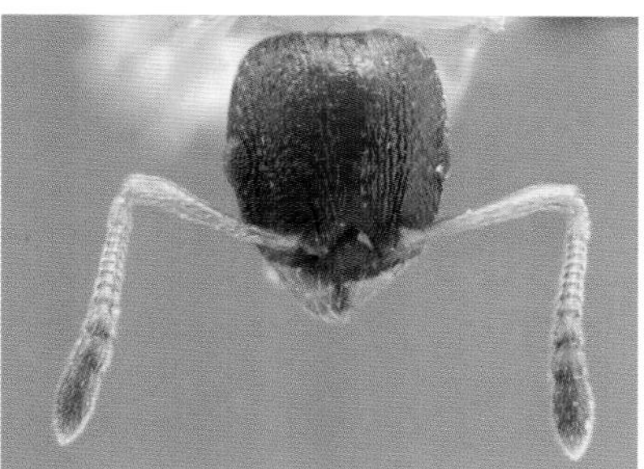
PHOTO 135. *Temnothorax tuberum*

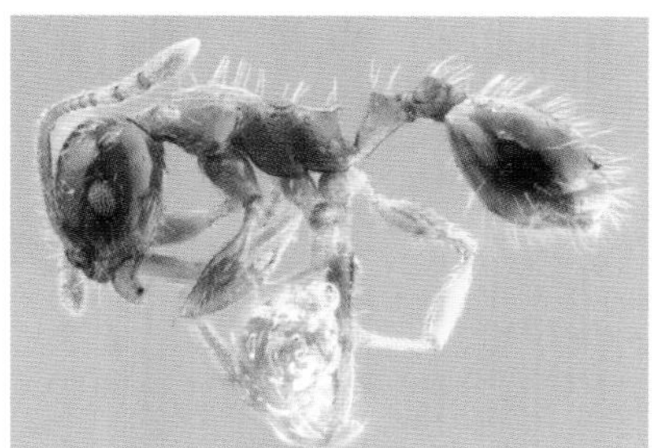
PHOTO 136. *Temnothorax recedens*

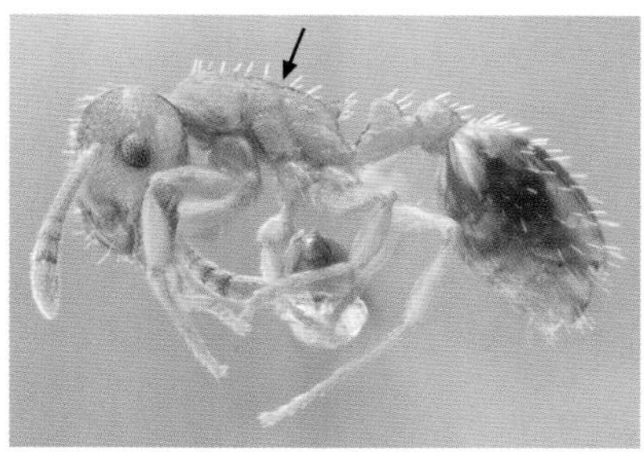
PHOTO 137. *Temnothorax nylanderi*

9 : propodeum spines long, indistinct mesopropodeal groove. .... **Temnothorax species of the lichtensteini group (see page 358)**

9': shorter propodeum spines, obvious mesopropodeal groove. .... ***Temnothorax* species of the *parvulus* group (see page 368)**

10 : petiole triangular seen in profile. Rear end straight. Tree-dwelling ants. .... ***Temnothorax* species of the *corticalis* group (see page 348)**

10': petiole different. The sloping face is concave (photo 139). Body uniform yellow, sometimes the gaster with a slightly duller segment. .... ***Temnothorax* species of the *luteus* group (see page 360)**

10': petiole swollen, its summit very rounded. Pale brown body and quite dark gaster. .... ***Temnothorax clypeatus* (see page 346)**

11 : petiole with a long attachment, joint very round, nearly spherical (photo 140)........ ***Temnothorax* species of the *rottenbergii* group (see page 372)**

11': petiole triangular seen in profile, angular at its top (photo 141). Sculpted side to mesosoma. **12**

11': more rounded petiole seen in profile. **13**

12 : head finely sculpted and whole of mesosoma highly sculpted. .... ***Temnothorax* species of the *angustulus* group (see page 344)**

12': head and front part of pronotum completely smooth. .... ***Temnothorax* species of the *exilis* group (see page 350)**

13 : absence of a mesopropodeal groove, head partly smooth. .... ***Temnothorax* species of the *niger* group (see page 364)**

13': presence of a mesopropodeal groove, head completely sculpted. .... ***Temnothorax* species of the *sordidulus* group (see page 374)**

14 : stepped rear profile to petiole (photo 142). **15**

14': petiole different, either triangular in profile or truncated at its summit (photo 143)...... **17**

15 : gaster largely hidden under the last tergites. .... ***Temnothorax* species of the *tuberum* group (see page 376)**

15': gaster with only one darker band on the rear part of the first tergite. **16**

16 : quite short propodeum spines. Frontal lobes slightly sinuous at the level of the antennae. .... ***Temnothorax* species of the *unifasciatus* group (see page 378)**

16': propodeum spines long and thin. The frontal lobes are wide and angular at the level of the antennae. .... ***Temnothorax interruptus* (see page 356)**

17 : propodeum spines almost non-existent, reduced to tooth-like humps. .... **several species, including *Temnothorax nadigi* (see page 362)**

17': propodeum spines well defined, often long and thin. .... **several species, including *Temnothorax affinis* (see page 342)**

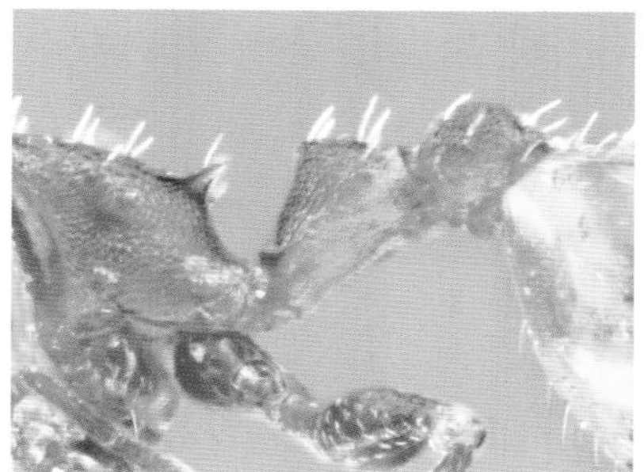

PHOTO 138. *Temnothorax aveli* petiole profile

PHOTO 139. *Temnothorax luteus*

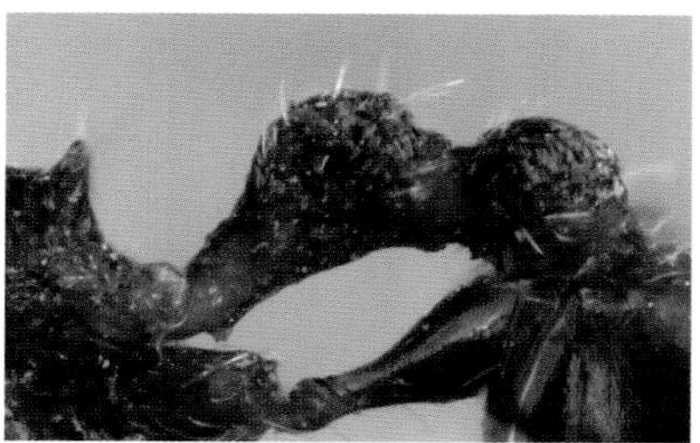

PHOTO 140. *Temnothorax formosus*

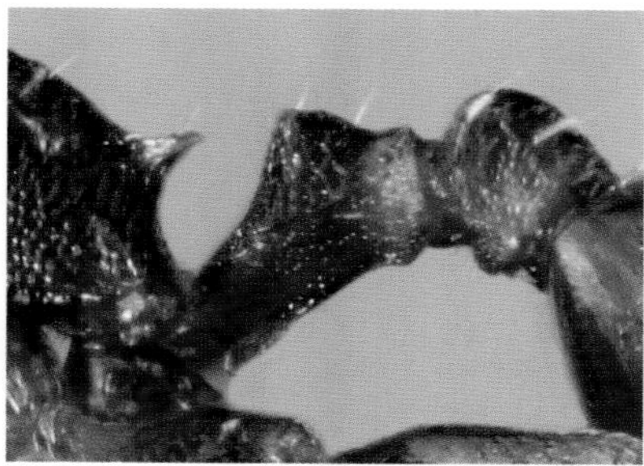

PHOTO 141. *Temnothorax exilis*

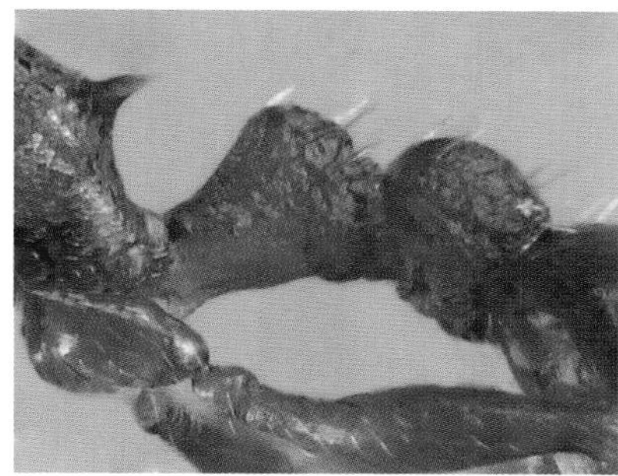

PHOTO 142. *Temnothorax unifasciatus*

PHOTO 143. *Temnothorax nadigi*

Species descriptions

Some descriptions concern a single species, however most present several species together. This is the case for rare genera containing few species and for those groups that include species difficult to identify, and also for groups of species in the same genus. In those containing several species, their names are specified in the 'Identification' section. Some of the rare species are not included in the main text but are cited with that species judged to be the most similar in the 'Possible confusion' section of the species account, even though the two may not be particularly closely related. Their names are followed by the name of the author who first described the species and the date when this occurred. The identification keys allow for finding the relevant description, and it is advised that the reader always consult the 'Identification' and 'Possible confusion' sections to be sure of identifying a species correctly. Species distribution is presented in pink on the maps, or in grey if a map features two or more species. Countries appearing in brown are not considered in the text. The reader will find definitions of terms used to describe an ant's morphology in the section 'Worker morphology', pages 9 and 10, as well as in the glossary, pages 410 and 411.

Opposite:
Formica sanguinea.

Stigmatomma genus Roger, 1859

subfamily Amblyoponinae

Stigmatomma denticulatum worker.

Identification

Size: 4–7 mm. The body is entirely yellowish and cylindrical. The petiole is cubic with a large attachment to the gaster on its lower edge. The very elongated mandibles have many teeth.

This genus of some 60 species has a worldwide distribution. Four species are present in Mediterranean Europe. They differ from each other by the number and shape of the teeth on the mandibles. *Stigmatomma emeryi* (Saunders, 1890) and *S. gaetulicum* (Baroni Urbani, 1978) occur in southern Spain. *Stigmatomma denticulatum* (Roger, 1859) and *S. impressifrons* (Emery, 1869) appear to have a wider distribution, with records from Spain, Italy and the southern Balkans.

Swarming

Distribution

Range of the genus *Stigmatomma*.

Possible confusion

The genus *Stigmatomma* cannot be confused with any other European genus. Species identification is, however, very difficult.

Habitat

Soil-dwelling, occupying different types of habitat with a cool soil.

Where to look

Nests are formed deep in the ground. Workers may be found under stones in cooler habitats that are nonetheless exposed to the sun.

Biology

Colonies are small, 40 individuals on average, with several queens (three maximum). They settle under stones, leaves or leaf-litter. The workers and the queens practise a form of cannibalism by drilling at a vulnerable point into a larva's cuticle and feeding on its haemolymph. However, this does not appear to harm the larvae, which grow into normally formed adults. The workers do not feed the queens by trophallaxis. These species specialise in predating on centipedes.

Mandibles of *Stigmatomma denticulatum*, with teeth along their whole length.

Bothriomyrmex genus Emery, 1869

subfamily Dolichoderinae

Bothriomyrmex meridionalis winged queen and worker.

Identification

Size: 2–3 mm. The body is a more or less pale grey-brown. The front edge of the clypeus is not notched. The petiole has the shape of a flat scale. Contrary to *Tapinoma* spp. which they use as temporary hosts, workers do not give off a rancid butter smell. The queen is quite similar in size and shape to large workers of the genus *Tapinoma* (< 4 mm, and of a purer black than the workers). Of the 20 or so described *Bothriomyrmex* species, four can be found in Europe: *B. meridionalis* (Roger, 1863), *B. corsicus* (Santschi, 1923) and two species restricted to the very south – *B. communistus* (Santschi, 1919), particularly in Eastern Europe, and *B. atlantis* (Forel, 1894) in the south of the Iberian Peninsula. Precise morphometric measurements are needed to distinguish between species. *Bothriomyrmex meridionalis* and *B. atlantis* are pale-coloured with an ill-defined mesopropodeal groove, and the mesosoma's profile is in a continuous straight line, whereas in *B. corsicus* and *B. communistus* the body is darker and the mesopropodeal groove is clearly visible and followed by a domed propodeum.

Possible confusion

The *Tapinoma*, their hosts, resemble them but are a purer black, have a

Swarming

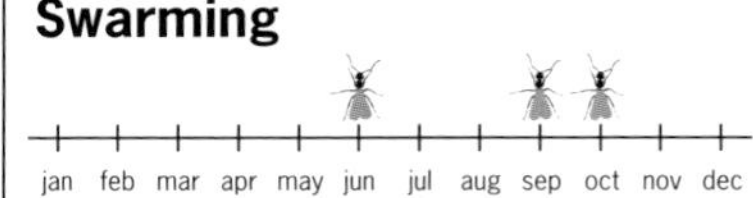

flat petiole (not scale-shaped) as well as a notch in the front of the clypeus. Worker *Linepithema humile* are more slender and have a head clearly longer than it is wide. *Lasius* species are generally bigger, but most obviously they have a circular cloaca edged with hairs; in *Bothriomyrmex* species it is slit-shaped and hairless.

Habitat

The *Bothriomyrmex* species prefer arid habitats: scree, clay soils exposed to the sun, embankments.

> **Where to look**
> Nests are under stones or in open ground. Workers do not leave the nest during the day; to find them the soil needs to be raked in areas rich in *Tapinoma*.

Biology

All *Bothriomyrmex* species are quite rare. They are temporary parasites of *Tapinoma* species. Nests occur at low densities, probably due to the low rate of success of parasitising host colonies. Colonies are monogynous and may contain several thousand workers. Following a nuptial flight, the queen tries to insinuate herself into a *Tapinoma* colony. Once inside she grabs the host queen by the neck with her mandibles and decapitates it. The female then becomes phytogastric. When the first workers emerge the nest contains both species (host and parasite). Once all the original *Tapinoma* workers in the colony have died the *Bothriomyrmex* colony is independent. They feed primarily on Hemiptera honeydew, often placed underground, on roots.

Distribution

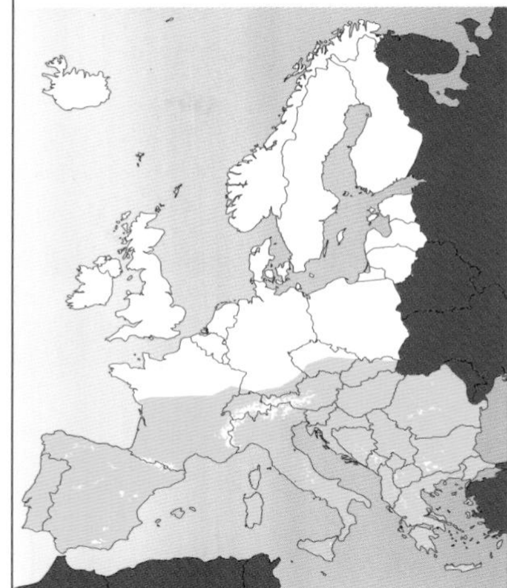

Range of the genus *Bothriomyrmex*.

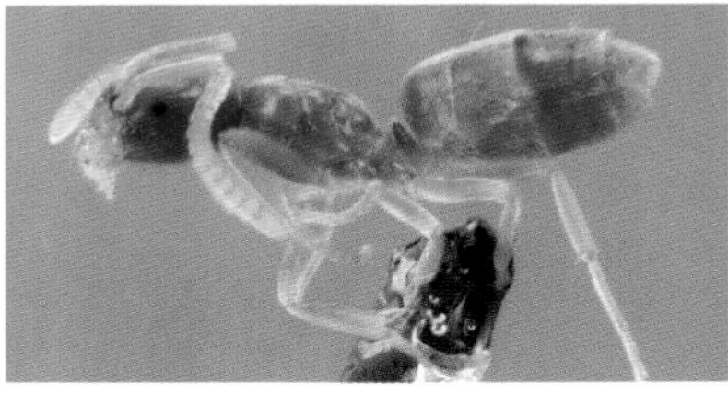

Bothriomyrmex atlantis worker.

Dolichoderus genus Lund, 1831

subfamily Dolichoderinae

Three castes of *Dolichoderus quadripunctatus*, From left to right: a queen, a male and a worker.

Identification

Size: 3–4 mm. The worker has a dark red to brown mesosoma, black head and a black, shiny gaster with four golden lateral spots on the first tergite. The head and mesosoma are finely spotted. *Dolichoderus quadripunctatus* (Linnaeus, 1771) is the only species of this genus in Europe.

Possible confusion

Small workers of *Camponotus truncatus* are similar but their heads are not spotted. Moreover, in *Camponotus* spp. the cloaca is round.

Habitat

Quite a ubiquitous species, but associated with trees. It often occupies areas near permanent sources of humidity (rivers, lakes, etc.).

Where to look

This is essentially a tree-dwelling species. Nests are in hollows in wood and branches, under bark, in acorns and walnuts. It is common on fruit trees, particularly walnut trees, and in oaks. It can be found by beating branches. Workers search for food on trunks, in branches and among ivy.

Biology

Quite a common species, and a few colonies may be present on the same tree. Colonies are

Swarming

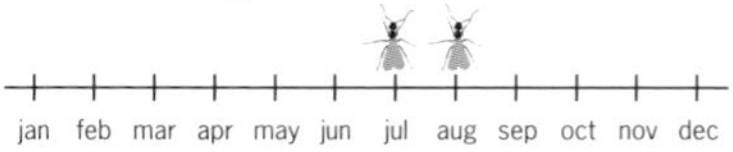

jan feb mar apr may jun jul aug sep oct nov dec

monogynous, with a few dozen workers. They are founded independently. An omnivorous species: harvesters search for any form of sugary substance and capture small arthropods that they bring back to the nest. A relatively unaggressive species that does not flee but rather hides in a crack at the slightest danger.

Distribution

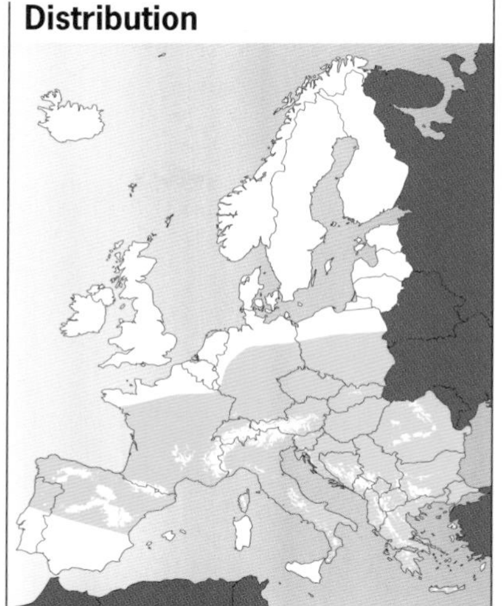

Range of *Dolichoderus quadripunctatus*.

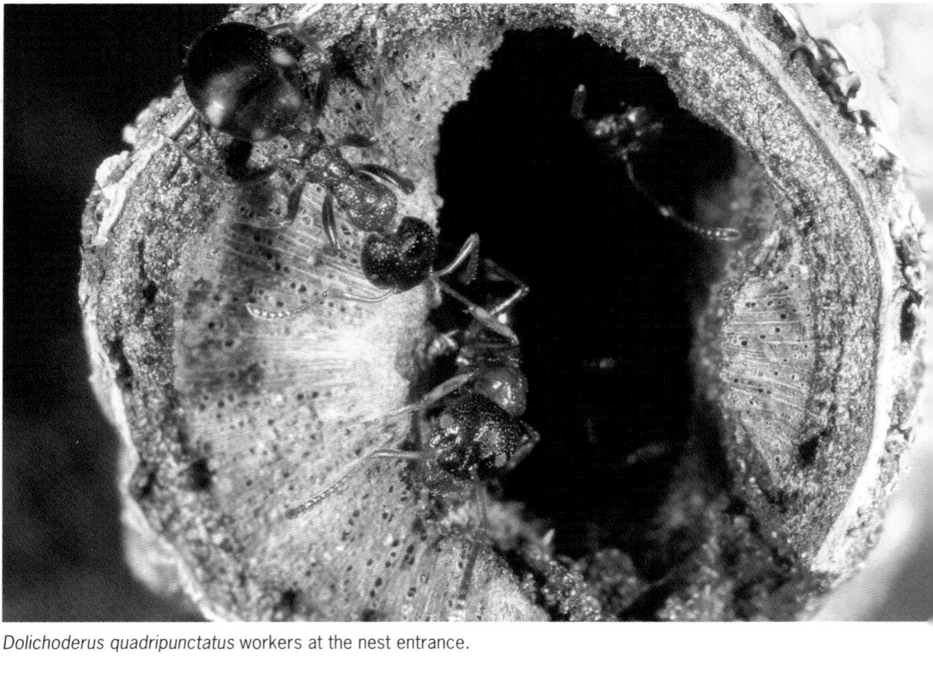

Dolichoderus quadripunctatus workers at the nest entrance.

Linepithema genus Mayr, 1866

subfamily Dolichoderinae

Linepithema humile workers.

Identification

Size: 2–3 mm. A uniform brown body with long antennae. Workers are very active. There is a single species of this genus in Europe: *Linepithema humile* (Mayr, 1868), commonly known as the Argentine ant. Of South American origin, it is considered to be an invasive species in many parts of the world.

Possible confusion

The *Tapinoma* are a blacker colour and have a flatter petiole covered by the gaster's first tergite. *Linepithema humile* can easily be confused with black *Lasius* species, but these latter are a little more thickset, not as slender, and have a circular cloaca with a hairy edge; this is a slit without hairs in *L. humile*. The *Bothriomyrmex* species have much smaller eyes.

Habitat

Generally present in warm and humid, human-created habitats along the Mediterranean coast. Apparently it can only become permanently established along the Mediterranean seaboard, although it may be accidently transported and introduced into large towns. It endures low temperatures with difficulty and is thus never found at altitude.

Where to look

Nests are found under stones, rotting logs on the ground, pieces of plastic, corrugated iron, cardboard, planks, in cracks in concrete structures (especially pavements), rubble, dustbins, drainage systems, water meters and so on. The nests are constantly changing place. They are found on the surface, and are shallow and poorly constructed.

Swarming

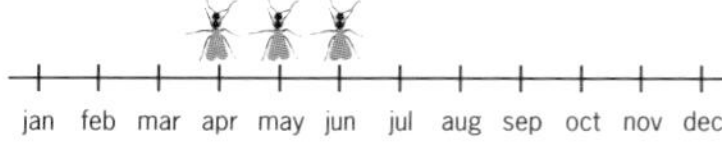

Sexual individuals are present in spring.

Distribution

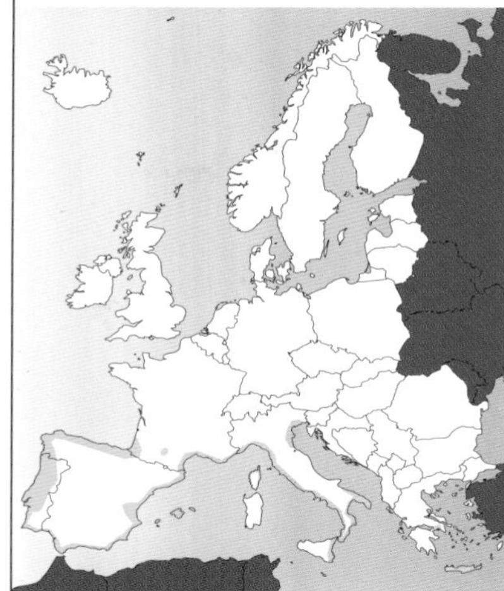

Range of *Linepithema humile*.

Biology

A common species in urban areas along the Mediterranean coast. Nests can be densely distributed locally. A single nest can contain more than a hundred queens and thousands of workers. Even though the queens are winged, there is no nuptial flight. New nests are formed by cloning. This omnivorous species promotes the development of aphid colonies in order to harvest their honeydew. Introduced from South America in the early twentieth century through merchant shipping, it has established itself along the coast from Italy to Portugal. The European population is made up of just two super-colonies. Workers of different nests of the same colony are not aggressive towards each other, even if the nests are very far apart (the largest of the two super-colonies extends for 6,000 km along the coast!). It is a very competitive species. It appears that *Tapinoma* species of the *nigerrimum-simrothi* group limit its expansion and may even cause its regression.

Two *Linepithema humile* queens accompanied by workers.

Liometopum genus Mayr, 1861

subfamily Dolichoderinae

Liometopum microcephalum worker.

Identification

Size: 3.5–7.5 mm. Head and abdomen are black, the mesosoma red. There is a high level of polymorphism among workers. The workers emit a strong odour. The head is heart-shaped with ocelli. *Liometopum microcephalum* (Panzer, 1798) is the only species of this genus in Europe.

Possible confusion

Liometopum microcephalum can be confused with other bicoloured species of the *Lasius*, *Formica* or *Camponotus* genera. The smaller workers, for example, resemble *Lasius emarginatus* in having a red mesosoma and in their behaviour, occurring on trees and searching for honeydew.

Habitat

Open deciduous forests, copses and woodland edges. Warm conditions.

Where to look

Nests are in trees, essentially in oaks. These can be at heights of up to 35 m.

Swarming

jan feb mar apr may jun jul aug sep oct nov dec

Distribution

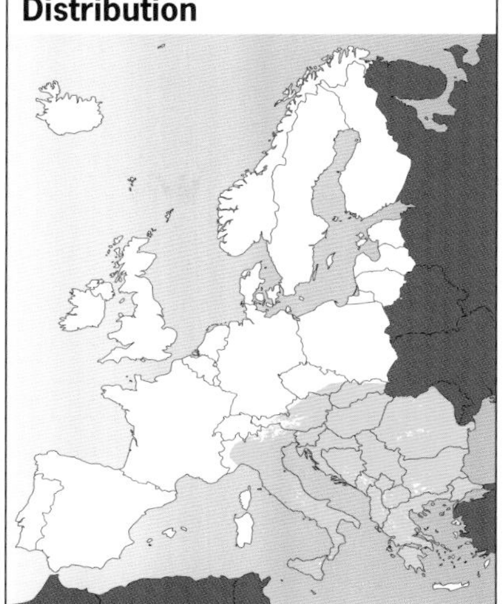

Range of *Liometopum microcephalum*.

Biology

Colonies form in hollows created by other wood-boring insects and do not harm tree trunks. They then protect the tree against harmful organisms such as caterpillars. The workers forage in long processions on the ground and in trees up to 80 m from the nest. The workers take honeydew from aphids and predate a wide variety of invertebrates (insects, spiders, myriapods, worms, etc.). Workers produce a 'paper' from wood fibres to form the outer surface of their nest.

Liometopum microcephalum worker.

Tapinoma of the *erraticum* group

subfamily Dolichoderinae

Identification

Size: 2–3.5 mm. Workers are entirely black and quite shiny. They emit a strong rancid butter smell when handled. The small group of *Tapinoma* species are characterised by a shallow notch in the clypeus. At least four species occur in Europe, however their distinction is difficult and sometimes requires inspection of the males' genitalia. *Tapinoma erraticum* (Latreille, 1798) is the species with the widest distribution. *Tapinoma madeirense* (Forel, 1895) is found in Mediterranean habitats in the south of France and the Iberian Peninsula; *T. subboreale* (Seifert, 2012) occupies the centre of Europe; *T. festae* (Emery, 1925) is reported from Greece. The notch in the clypeus is less well defined in the last three species.

A queen *Tapinoma madeirense* in the middle of workers.

Possible confusion

Workers in *Tapinoma nigerrimum* colonies normally show great variation in size and can reach 5 mm. The notch in the clypeus is more pronounced than in *Tapinoma erraticum*. Ants of the genus *Bothriomyrmex*, temporary parasites of *Tapinoma* spp., are paler than their hosts and have a raised scale-shaped petiole (whereas it is low in *Tapinoma* spp.). The black *Lasius* species (*Lasius* subgenus), although belonging to a different subfamily, are easily confused with *Tapinoma erraticum* but they are less black than this latter species (with a hint of dark brown or less intense black) and have a raised scale-shaped petiole.

Swarming

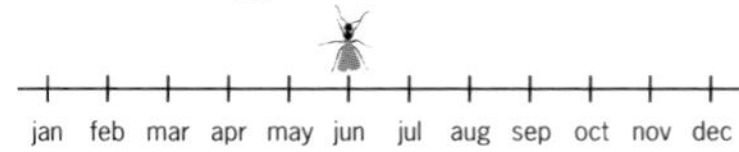

Habitat

Tapinoma erraticum is quite ubiquitous, but with a definite preference for open habitats. In the north or at altitude, it occurs in favourably exposed sites. It appears in a variety of habitats: cultivated areas, gardens, meadows, clearings, garrigue, coastal sites, rocky outcrops and rocky south-facing slopes in mountainous areas, to an altitude of 2,000 m, even on very sloping sites.

Where to look

Nests are built under stones, between stones in walls or consist of a well-formed mound of plant debris and soil pellets in a sunny position. Galleries do not go far into the ground. Workers search for food on the ground, on rocks or in vegetation, moving about quickly in all directions.

Biology

Tapinoma erraticum is widely distributed and very common. Nests may be very densely distributed. Colonies are polygynous and may contain a few thousand workers. The founding can be independent or by cloning, started by a queen and workers from a nearby source nest. This omnivorous species will attack small arthropods and search for honeydew from sap-sucking bugs (especially aphids) that it actively defends.

Distribution

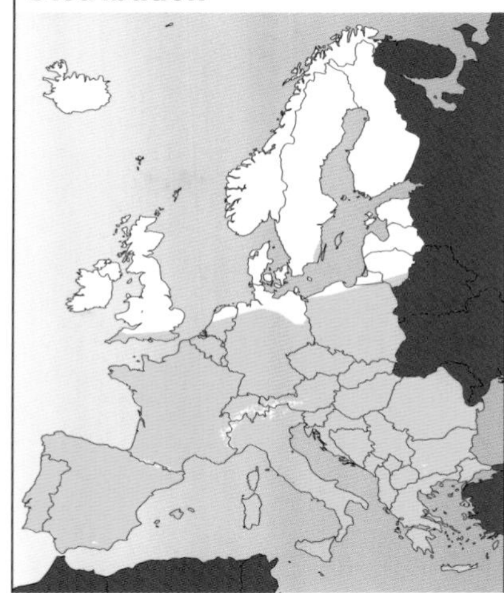

Range of *Tapinoma erraticum.*

Head of a *Tapinoma erraticum* worker showing the clypeus notch.

In *Tapinoma madeirense* the clypeus notch is less pronounced.

Tapinoma of the *nigerrimum-simrothi* group

subfamily Dolichoderinae

Tapinoma nigerrimum colony. The queen can be seen in the foreground.

Different sizes of *Tapinoma nigerrimum* workers.

Identification

Size: 2–5 mm. The workers are shiny black with an ashy aspect due to a covering of fine hairs. Pronounced U-shaped notch on the front edge of the clypeus. The workers emit a strong small of rancid butter when touched. *Tapinoma nigerrimum* (Nylander, 1856) and *T. simrothi* (Krausse, 1911) are identified from male genitalia and difficult-to-measure biometrics. *Tapinoma simrothi* occurs mainly in North Africa, and in Europe only present in the extreme south (southern Spain, Italian islands). Recent research has shown that these species could be classified into several varieties. Some subspecies exhibit invasive behaviour.

Possible confusion

Tapinoma spp. of the *nigerrimum* group have a deeper clypeus notch than other *Tapinoma* species, and the difference in size between workers is much less obvious; there are no workers larger than 5 mm. The *Bothriomyrmex* spp. and black *Lasius* spp. (*Lasius* subgenus) are less black with a raised scale-shaped petiole, whereas the petiole is low in *Tapinoma* species.

Habitat

Open, warm habitats of the Mediterranean zone: humid, clay areas of the sides of rivers, frequently irrigated cultivated areas, coastal dunes, banks,

Swarming

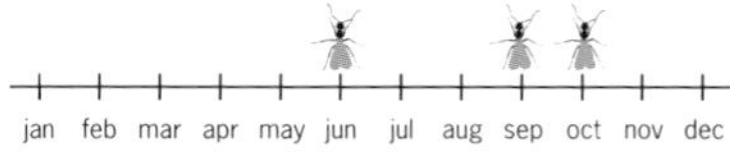

June, then September to October sparingly.

set-aside, uncultivated ground, garrigues, pavements. These species adjust to any soil, wet or very dry. They rarely occur above 1,500 m. Workers search for food on the ground or in low vegetation.

Where to look

Nests are under stones or directly in the ground, sometimes evident from the mound of soil pellets at the base of low plants. Workers are active both day and night. They are permanently searching for food for much of the year. In winter it is sometimes possible to see lone active workers.

Biology

Very common species in the Mediterranean zone. Nests can be densely distributed. Colonies are polygynous and can contain several thousands of workers. Once mated, queens can form a new colony alone or return to the colony to form a new one by cloning with a group of workers. The harvesters in this omnivorous species hunt small insects, search out any sugary substance and feed on the honeydew of bugs that are on aerial parts of plants, as well as on their roots.

Distribution

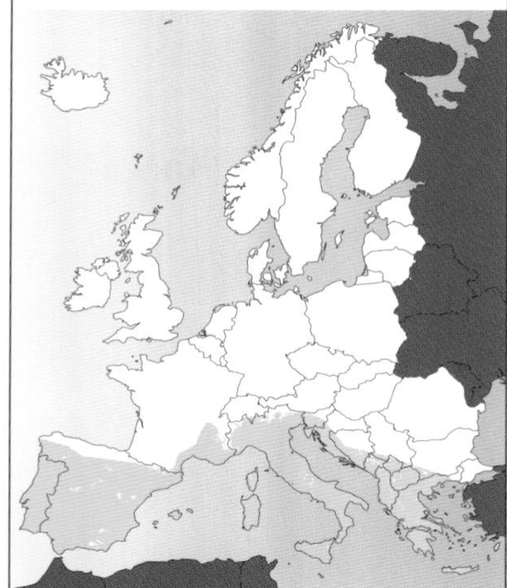

Range of the *Tapinoma* spp. of the *nigerrimum-simrothi* group.

Three *Tapinoma nigerrimum* castes: a queen, a winged male and three workers two of which are carying a white pupa.

Tapinoma pygmaeum Dufour, 1857

subfamily Dolichoderinae

Tapinoma pygmaeum Colony.

Identification

Size: 2 mm. Workers have entirely black bodies. No notch to the clypeus.

Possible confusion

The small size and general appearance are reminiscent of workers of the genus *Plagiolepis*. *Tapinoma pygmaeum* can be distinguished by the funiculus having 11 segments (10 in *Plagiolepis*); a reduced petiole scale, covered by the gaster; and the absence of a hairy fringe around the acidopore. *Tapinoma melanocephalum* (Fabricius, 1793) is a tropical invasive species, introduced throughout the world – its natural distribution is unknown. It can be present in heated buildings such as hospitals, blocks of flats and tropical greenhouses.

Swarming

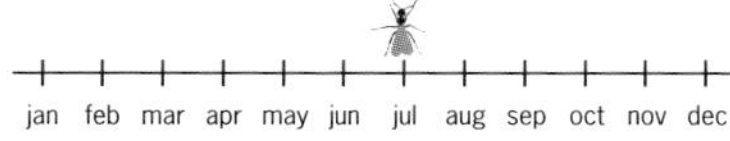

Tapinoma melanocephalum workers in wood.

Habitat

Woodland edges, hedgerows, well-wooded gardens.

Where to look

More often than not, nests are in rotten wood, on the ground or standing. Workers can be found by beating hedgerows or fruit trees. Colonies sometimes form in cracks in roof timbers or wooden fence posts.

Distribution

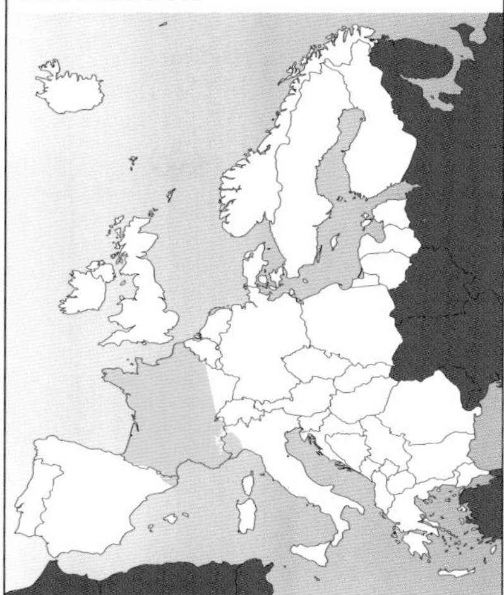

Range of *Tapinoma pygmaeum*.

Biology

A rare species. Colonies have limited numbers, a hundred individuals at most. Colonies are nomadic and can change sites to be nearer to food sources. Workers actively search for sugary liquids. An entire colony can establish itself in a peach stone still on the tree.

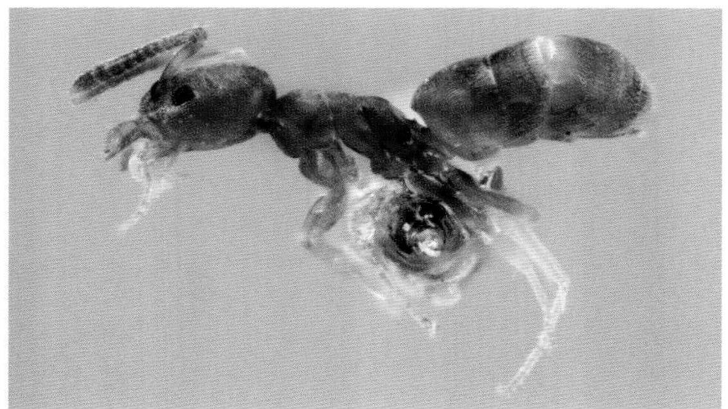

Tapinoma pygmaeum worker.

Technomyrmex genus Mayr, 1872

subfamily Dolichoderinae

Technomyrmex albipes worker with scale insects.

Identification

Size: 2–3.5 mm. Generally workers are black, except those of *Technomyrmex vexatus*, which have a brown mesosoma and an un-notched or only slightly notched clypeus. There are 95 species of *Technomyrmex*, but only one occurs naturally in Europe: *Technomyrmex vexatus* (Santschi, 1919), which is present on Gibraltar and in northern Morocco. Other species of tropical origin have been introduced and can be found in heated buildings and greenhouses: *Technomyrmex albipes* (Smith, 1861), *T. vitiensis* (Mann, 1921) and *T. difficilis* (Forel, 1892).

Possible confusion

The *Tapinoma* species are very similar in colour, the form of the petiole and in their recruitment attitude.

Habitat

Technomyrmex vexatus occurs in the bushy hillsides of Gibraltar.

Swarming

Where to look

Technomyrmex vexatus nests are built under stones. This invasive species usually occurs in heated greenhouses.

Biology

Certain species in this genus are considered as pests worldwide. They have been introduced accidently through global commerce, but at present in Europe they do not occur outside heated buildings. The key to their success is their capacity to reproduce rapidly. Sexual individuals are winged and mate in the air. An inseminated queen will found a new colony independently. She produces workers as well as inter-caste queens that will eventually replace her and then form new colonies through a process called 'budding'. In greenhouses, worker *Technomyrmex* species exploit scale insect colonies. In tropical areas these ants are especially unpopular as their populations can occupy vast zones in different terrestrial ecosystems, and develop anywhere from the ground to the tops of trees. They disrupt pollination.

Technomyrmex difficilis worker.

Distribution

Range of *Technomyrmex vexatus*.

Technomyrmex vitiensis workers.

Aenictus genus Shuckard, 1840

subfamily Dorylinae

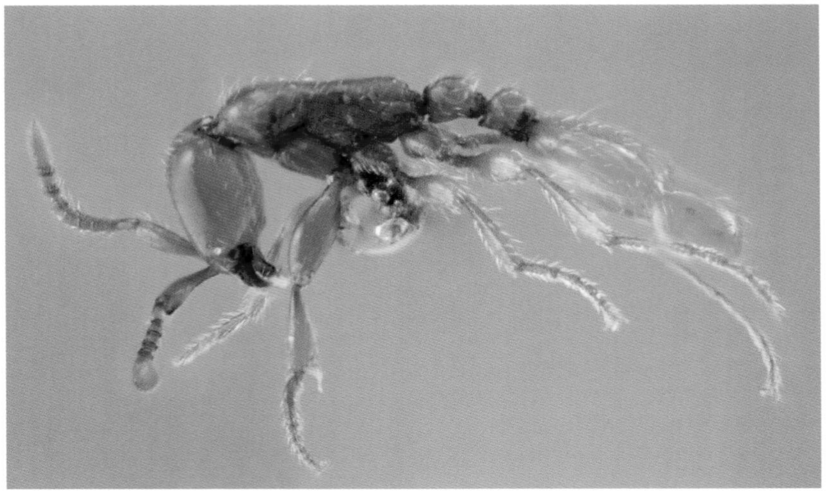

Aenictus rhodiensis worker.

Identification

Size: 3 mm. Workers have completely yellow bodies. They have no eyes. The whole body is covered with hairs. A very important genus containing nearly 200 species, they occur in tropical regions of Africa and Asia. A single species has reached Mediterranean areas of Europe, *Aenictus rhodiensis* (Menozzi, 1936), but it occurs only on some eastern Greek islands.

Possible confusion

Aenictus rhodiensis cannot be confused with any other species of the European fauna.

Habitat

All types of habitat.

Where to look

Under large stones and on the ground.

Biology

A species of army ant; they do not construct permanent nests and colonies are nomadic. Workers move as whole colonies in long processions and also form hunting columns. They search for food mainly underground, among leaf litter or on the ground surface, where they feed on other ants, termites and various arthropods. Queens have a well-developed gaster and move about with help from workers. They are constantly on the move, except when they form a bivouac when the colony comes together in the ground.

Distribution

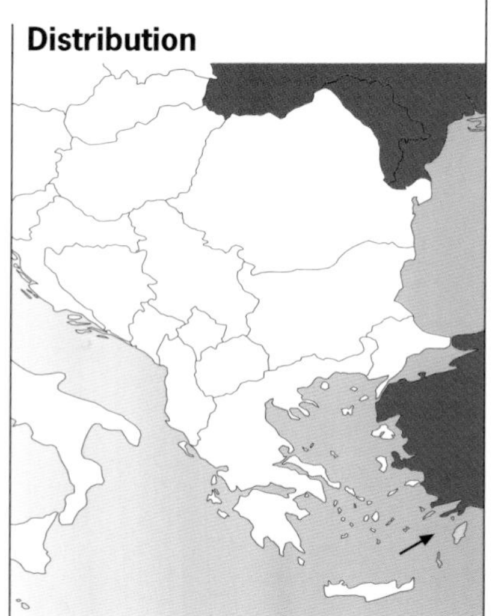

Range of *Aenictus rhodiensis*.

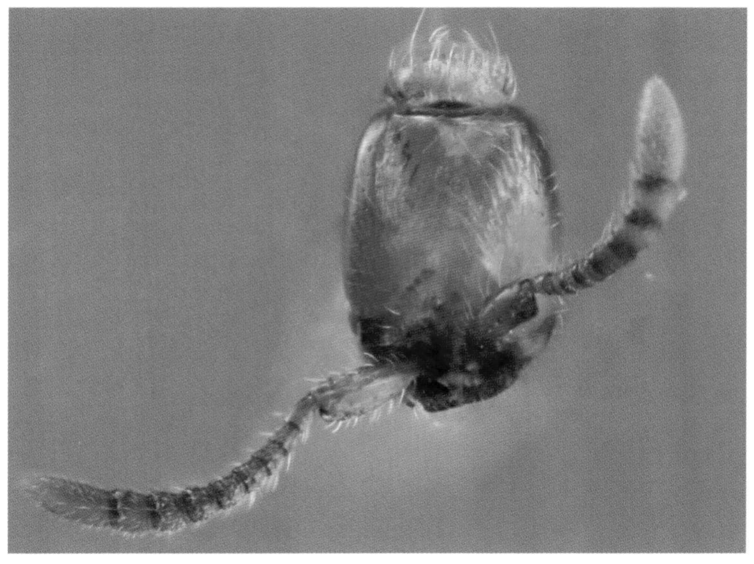

Head of *Aenictus rhodiensis*, an army ant.

Camponotus herculeanus Linnaeus, 1758

subfamily Formicinae – subgenus *Camponotus*

Camponotus herculeanus worker.

Identification

Size: 7–15 mm. The thorax is dark red. The head and first tergite of the gaster are entirely black. Body hairs are yellowish. One of the largest European species.

Possible confusion

There is another species of *Camponotus* also widely distributed throughout Europe: *C. ligniperda*. This latter species has a slightly paler thorax, the front of the first segment of the gaster is brown or orange, and the gaster hairs are more thinly distributed and shorter. Several species of *Camponotus* of the subgenus *Tanaemyrmex* have a body colour similar to that of *C. herculeanus* and *C. ligniperda*, but the clypeus of the two latter species does not have a median ridge.

Swarming

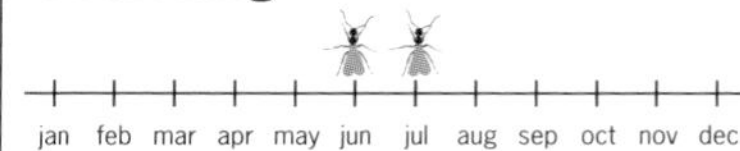

Distribution

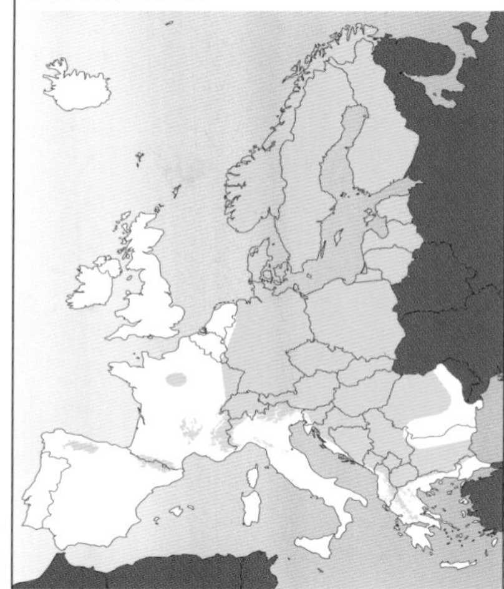

Range of *Camponotus herculeanus*.

Habitat

Conifer and beech forests. A boreal-montane species found only at altitude in Southern Europe.

Where to look

Camponotus herculeanus nests are found in dead wood (either on the ground or standing), or in living trees. Colonies may also occur within the framework of chalets or houses.

Camponotus herculeanus queen.

Biology

Common at altitude or at lower levels in colder regions. Colonies are either monogynous or slightly polygynous and very large, with several thousand workers. Colony founding is independent but often several queens come together to form a new colony (pleometrosis). The species feeds mainly on sugary substances: honeydew, nectar and sap, but also consumes arthropods. Contrary to popular belief, *Camponotus* species are not capable of digesting wood. However, workers will tunnel into wood and form galleries that increase in size as the colony develops.

Camponotus herculeanus worker.

Camponotus ligniperda Latreille, 1802

subfamily Formicinae – subgenus *Camponotus*

Camponotus ligniperda worker.

Identification

Size: 7–15 mm. The thorax and upper surface of the first tergite of the gaster are orange-brown. The head and rest of the gaster are black. The body hairs are yellowish. This is one of the largest European species.

Possible confusion

There are two similar species that can cause confusion, *Camponotus ligniperda* and *C. herculeanus*. In the latter species the thorax is generally darker and the front of the first gaster segment completely black (it is orange or brown in *C. ligniperda*). In *C. ligniperda* the hairs on the gaster are more widely spaced and shorter. Several species of *Camponotus* in the subgenus *Tanaemyrmex* have a similar body colour to that of *C. herculeanus* and *C. ligniperda*, but the clypeus of these two species does not have a median ridge.

Swarming

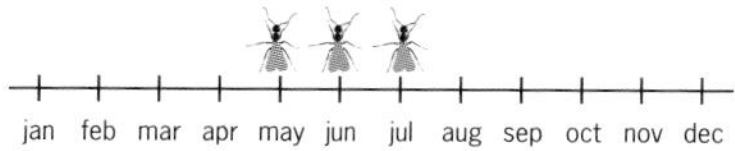

Habitat

Cool, damp forests, forest edges, sometimes box or juniper heath, or rocky slopes and conifer woods on calcareous or sandy substrates. To an altitude of 2,100 m.

Where to look

Nests of *Camponotus ligniperda* are either in dead tree trunks on the ground or in tree stumps, or in the ground under sun-exposed rocks. Workers prefer to search for food in trees, in low vegetation or on dead wood.

Biology

Common at altitude or lower elevations in colder regions. Colonies are monogynous or slightly polygynous and very large, with thousands of workers. Colony founding is independent but several queens regularly come together to found a new colony (pleometrosis). Diet is many based on sugary substances: honeydew, nectar and sap. This species also consumes arthropods. Contrary to popular belief, *Camponotus* species are not capable of digesting wood. However, workers will tunnel into wood and form galleries that increase in size and complexity as the colony develops.

Distribution

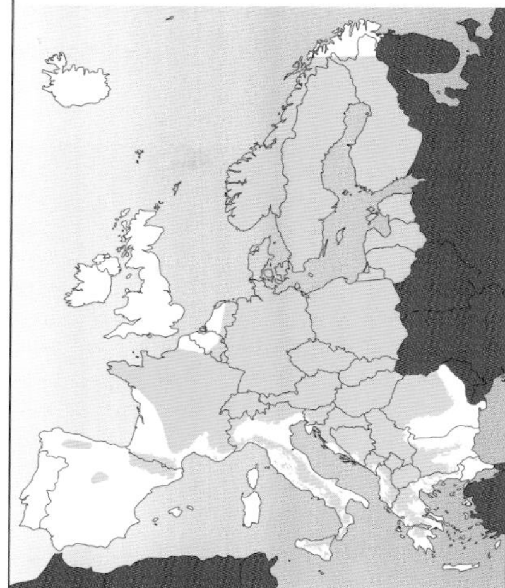

Range of *Camponotus ligniperda.*

Two *Camponotus ligniperda* workers preparing to exchange food (trophallaxis).

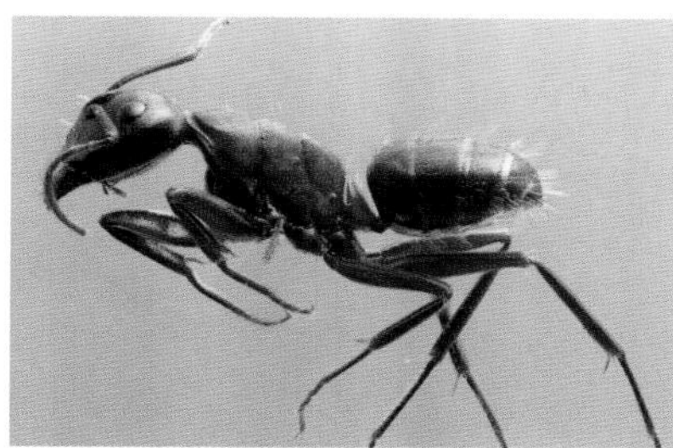

Camponotus ligniperda worker.

Camponotus vagus Scopoli, 1763

subfamily Formicinae – subgenus *Camponotus*

Camponotus vagus worker carrying prey.

Identification

Size: 6–13 mm, with significant variation within a single colony. Large workers have an obviously enlarged head. The body is entirely black, the gaster densely covered in white hairs.

Possible confusion

A recognisable species that is not easy to confuse. In *Camponotus aethiops* the hairs on the gaster are less visible and the clypeus has an obvious median ridge.

Swarming

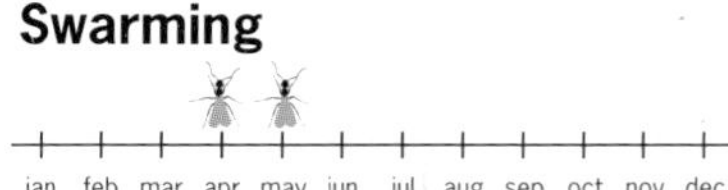

Distribution

Range of *Camponotus vagus*.

Habitat

Wooded areas, particularly with conifers. Sometimes in isolated copses, even isolated trees, including those in gardens. From the seashore to 1,000 m altitude.

Where to look

Nests are found in tree trunks on the ground, in stumps or in tree forks. Several large holes provide nest entrances. A colony is detected by the presence of small mounds of sawdust at the base of the trunk or stump. Workers search for food on the ground, in low vegetation and in trees.

Large *Camponotus vagus* worker cleaning an antenna.

Biology

A reasonably common species. Colonies contain a maximum of 10,000 workers. Colony founding is independent by a single queen. Nests are usually constructed in dead wood but also directly in the ground. However, colony development is dependent on wood. The ants are capable of digging galleries but do not consume lignin. The tiniest trace of fungus in the wood will mean that these ants are not present. They are omnivorous. Workers climb into trees in the vicinity to search for food: insects and sugary substances. Their range extends to a radius of 10 m around the nest.

Camponotus vagus colony in the trunk of a dead pine.

Camponotus truncatus Spinola, 1808

subfamily Formicinae – subgenus *Colobopsis*

Camponotus truncatus workers in a hollow stem.

Identification

Size: 3–5 mm for minor workers, 5–6 mm for major workers. The head and thorax are between orange-brown and dark brown, the gaster is black. There are two pale spots on the sides of the gaster in major workers. The latter are characterised by having a short cylindrical-shaped head. The front of the head appears truncated, in the form of a flat disc.

Note: According to recent research, the genus *Colobopsis* is quite distinct from *Camponotus*, so this species should be named *Colobopsis truncata*.

Possible confusion

Small *Camponotus lateralis* workers are very similar to *C. truncatus* minor workers, however the propodeum is concave in *C. lateralis*. *Dolichoderus quadripunctatus* workers resemble *C. truncatus* minor workers but they have spotted heads and a very angular propodeum.

Swarming

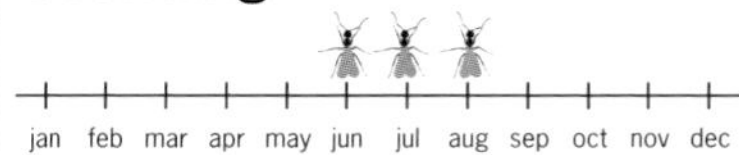

Habitat

A strictly tree-dwelling species, especially on oaks but also on fruit trees, poplars, walnut trees and elms. It is found in all low-altitude habitats where these trees occur.

Where to look

Nests are formed in hollow tree cavities, generally high up, in dead branches or under bark, sometimes in old galls. Workers search for food on the tree. This species can be found by branch-beating.

Biology

A common species that often goes unnoticed since it occurs in the higher parts of trees. Colonies are monogynous and contain up to a hundred workers. It is common for the same colony to occupy several nests simultaneously. Colony founding is independent with a single queen. Workers search for sugary substances and small insects. When in danger they flatten onto the bark.

Distribution

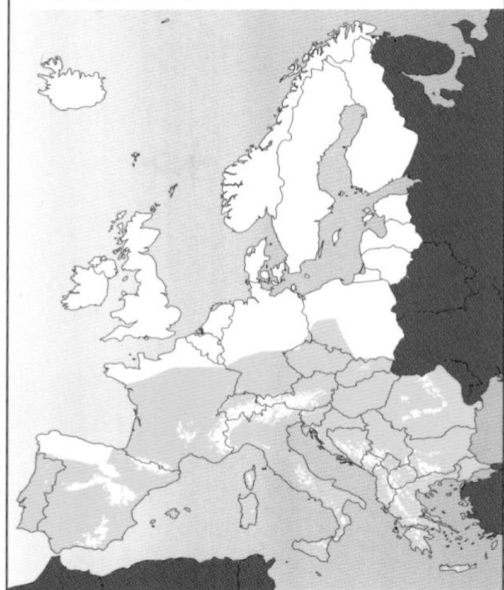

Range of *Camponotus truncatus*.

Camponotus truncatus queen, a major worker and a minor worker.

Camponotus of the ***fallax*** group and ***C. gestroi*** Emery, 1878

subfamily Formicinae – subgenus *Myrmentoma*

Camponotus fallax workers in a hollow stem.

Identification

Size: 5.5–8.5 mm. A black, quite shiny body thinly covered with white hairs. Their legs are brown to reddish. There is no ridge on the clypeus. Two closely related species *Camponotus fallax* (Nylander, 1856) and *C. tergestinus* (Müller, 1921) have incisions in the lower edge of the clypeus. *Camponotus tergestinus* is much hairier than *C. fallax* and only occurs in the Balkans. *Camponotus fallax* is widely distributed throughout Europe. *Camponotus gestroi* (Emery, 1878)

Swarming

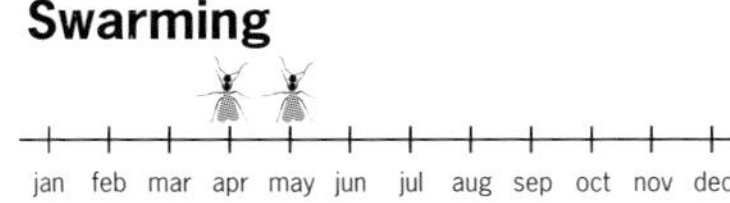

Distribution

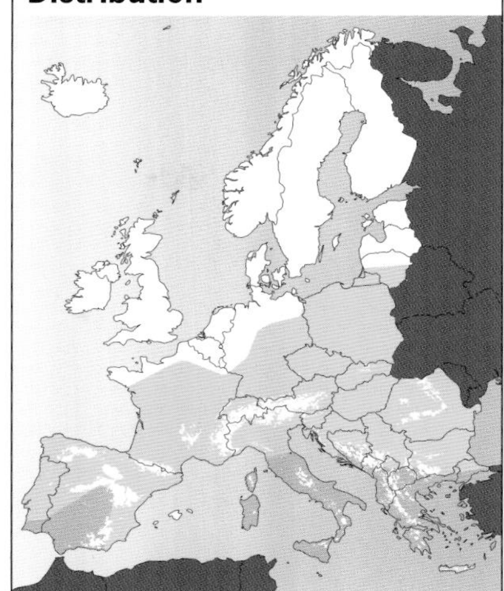

Range of *Camponotus fallax* (pink) and *C. gestroi* (grey).

occurs throughout the Mediterranean zone, from Spain to Greece. It has no notch on the bottom edge of the clypeus.

Possible confusion

Camponotus piceus has a concave propodeum. *Camponotus vagus* has much white hair on the gaster. Other entirely black species of the genus *Camponotus* have an obvious median ridge on the clypeus.

Habitat

Both *Camponotus fallax* and *C. tergestinus* occur in forests and wooded areas, especially those with oak. They rarely occur above 1,000 m. *Camponotus gestroi* occurs more frequently in warm, open areas with a few scattered trees or bushes and a well-developed herbaceous layer.

Where to look

Camponotus fallax and *C. tergestinus* build their nests in dead branches on the ground or in hollow cavities in trees (especially in dead branches or under bark). Workers search for most of their food in trees. *Camponotus gestroi* build their nests in the ground.

Biology

Very secretive species, difficult to find. Colonies are monogynous with a few dozen workers. Independent founding by the queen. Searching for food is done individually. They are omnivorous and the diet includes sugary substances (honeydew, nectar). Workers have very good sight, and will let themselves fall to escape from danger. They move quickly.

Camponotus gestroi worker.

Camponotus of the ***kiesenwetteri*** group

subfamily Formicinae – subgenus *Myrmentoma*

Camponotus kiesenwetteri workers under a stone.

Identification

Size: 5.5–8.5 mm. Workers are dull black and pitted over the whole body. There are several white hairs on the top of the head, on the thorax and the gaster, mixed with other shorter hairs. Erect hairs on the tibiae and femora. In Europe this group occurs only in Greece. It consists of four similar species, distinguished by slight morphological differences: *Camponotus kiesenwetteri* (Roger, 1859) and *C. boghossiana* (Forel, 1911) have a marked mesopropodeal groove, which is only slight in *C. libanicus* (André 1881) and *C. aegaeus* (Emery, 1915).

Swarming

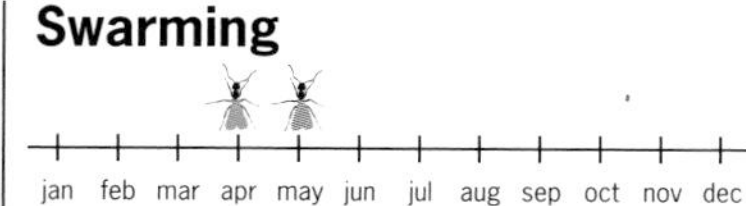

Possible confusion

The body appears similar to that of *Camponotus* species of the *piceus* group; however, in the latter the outer surface is not completely matt – it even appears a little shiny.

Habitat

Various warm, open habitats: garrigue, scrub, clearings, meadows, disused saltpans, calcareous hillsides. A preference for clay soils. Rarely found above 1,000 m.

Where to look

Occurs essentially on the ground. Nests are formed under stones or directly in the ground but also in dead wood. The nest entrance may be a simple hole in the ground without even a pile of soil grains around it, which can make them difficult to find especially as there is little activity at the entrance. A secretive ant that is solitary when foraging, on the ground, in low vegetation and in trees. It can often be found on flowers (Apiaceae, euphorbias, brooms, etc.), where it takes nectar.

Biology

A common species. Nests can be at high densities. Colonies are monogynous with few individuals (a few dozen or a few hundred workers). Colony founding is independent, by a single queen. It is an omnivorous species although workers show a preference for sugary substances: honeydew of Hemiptera and nectar. Sexual individuals are present as early as July, staying in the nest until swarming the following spring.

Distribution

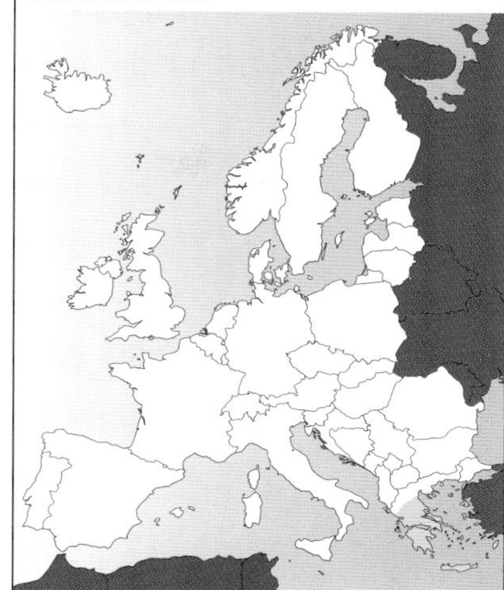

Range of *Camponotus kiesenwetteri*.

Camponotus kiesenwetteri worker.

Camponotus of the *lateralis* group

subfamily Formicinae – subgenus *Myrmentoma*

Camponotus candiotes in the dead branch of a fig.

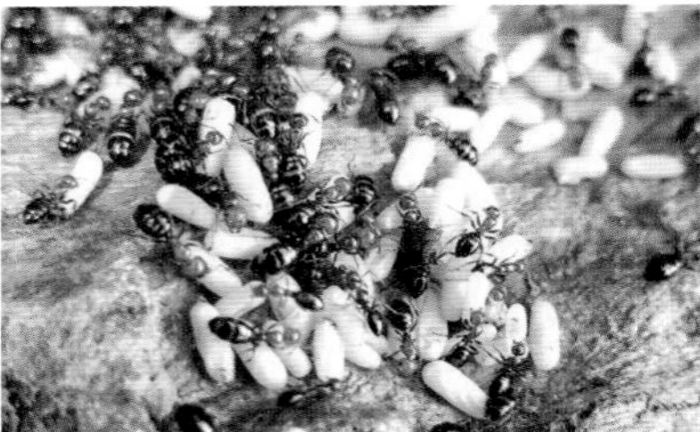

Camponotus lateralis colony.

Identification

Size: 3.3–7 mm, with large variation of individuals within the same colony. The gaster is black, the thorax and sometimes the head are red, with much variation between individuals from pale red to very dark red, almost black. Generally, small workers are darker than bigger ones. The outer surface is very shiny, the propodeum concave. Found in trees more often than not, very common in Southern Europe. Differences between species can be seen in the quantity of hairs and in colour. *Camponotus lateralis* (Olivier, 1791), *C. dalmaticus* (Nylander, 1849) and *C. candiotes* (Emery, 1894), have sparse hairs, the erect hairs thinly spread on the thorax. On the other hand, *Camponotus honaziensis* (Karaman & Aktaç, 2013) has numerous erect hairs on its body. *Camponotus dalmaticus* and *C. candiotes* in the Balkans, *C. figaro* (Collingwood & Yarrow, 1969), which occurs in Spain, are very dark with only the pronotum brown or reddish.

Possible confusion

Camponotus ruber (Emery, 1925), present in the south of the Iberian Peninsula, has a less concave propodeum. *Crematogaster scutellaris* also has a red head but has a petiole in two parts (*Myrmicinae*) and shows little variation in size within the same colony. Small *Camponotus lateralis* workers that are very similar to *Crematogaster scutellaris* often occur at the edges of trails of this last species and can be easily mistaken for them. *Camponotus piceus* is entirely black.

Swarming

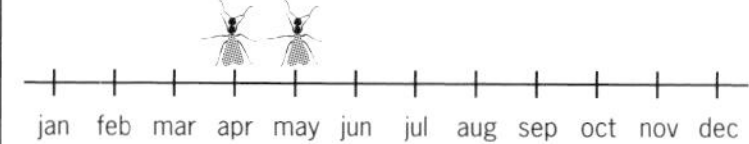

Camponotus ruber worker.

Habitat

Areas that are sufficiently wooded to provide much shade and a relative coolness, even in the height of summer. Holm oak *Quercus ilex* forest is a typical habitat of this species. Does not occur above 1,000 m.

Where to look

Nests are formed under stones, in dead branches on the ground and sometimes in old walls. Workers search for most of their food in trees.

Biology

A common species. Nest density can be high in favourable habitat such as holm oak and cork oak woodland and wooded garrigue. Colonies are monogynous and not populous (a few dozen or a few hundred workers). Independent colony founding, with a single queen. Workers are secretive, searching individually for food. They are omnivorous and often feed on Hemiptera honeydew. *Camponotus lateralis* is a Batesian mimic with *Crematogaster scutellaris*, sometimes following their trails to arrive at a food source. Sexed individuals are present in the nest from July, staying until swarming occurs.

Distribution

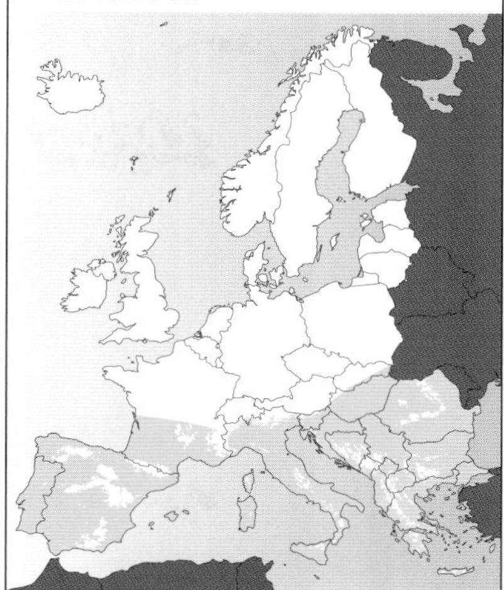

Range of *Camponotus lateralis*.

Camponotus lateralis workers in the company of a *Crematogaster scutellaris* worker (left).

Camponotus of the **piceus** group

subfamily Formicinae – subgenus *Myrmentoma*

Camponotus piceus worker.

Identification

Size: 3.5–7 mm, with marked variation within a colony. The body is shiny black all over. The propodeum is concave. This group is composed of four ground-dwelling species that are quite common in Southern Europe. *Camponotus piceus* (Leach, 1825) is the commonest. *Camponotus spissinodis* (Forel, 1909) is a North African species introduced into Sicily. *Camponotus nitidescens* (Forel, 1889) has been described from the Greek island of Cephalonia. In *Camponotus atricolor* (Nylander, 1849), present from Greece to Romania, the notch at the level of the mesopropodeum is less distinct.

Swarming

jan feb mar apr may jun jul aug sep oct nov dec

Possible confusion

Camponotus lateralis always has red colouring on the head and thorax. Formica ants that are entirely black and shiny (such as *Formica gagates*) have a propodeum of rounded dome form.

Habitat

Various warm, open habitats: garrigue, scrub, clearings, meadows, ancient saltpans, calcareous hillsides. Prefers clay soils. Rarely higher than 1,000 m altitude.

Where to look

These species live entirely on the ground. Nests are under stones or directly in the ground. The nest entrance is a simple hole without any piles of soil around it, which makes it difficult to find, especially as there is generally little activity at the entrance. These are secretive ants that search for food individually, either on the ground or in low vegetation. They are often found on flowers (Apiaceae, euphorbias, broom, etc.), from which they take nectar.

Biology

Common species. Nests may be densely distributed. Colonies are monogynous and have relatively few individuals (a few dozen or hundreds of workers). Colony formation is independent, with a single queen. They are omnivores, but individuals show a preference for sugary substances: Hemiptera honeydew and nectar. Sexual individuals are present in the nest as early as July and remain there until swarming occurs.

Distribution

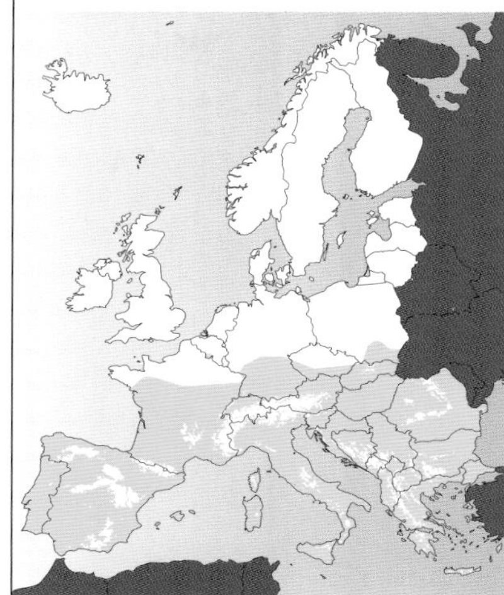

Range of *Camponotus piceus*.

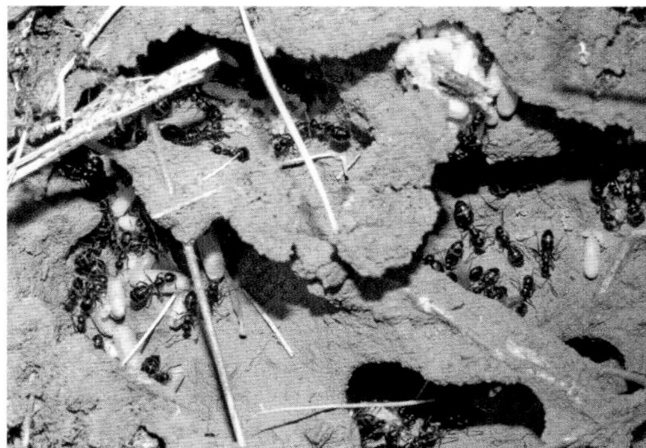

Camponotus piceus colony.

Camponotus cruentatus Latreille, 1802

subfamily Formicinae – subgenus *Myrmosericus*

Camponotus cruentatus worker.

Identification

Size: 6–14 mm, with significant individual variation within a colony. Overall, the body is matt black, with orange to reddish areas on the thorax, legs and front of the gaster. The smallest workers are sometimes totally black. *Camponotus cruentatus* belongs to the subgenus *Mymosericus*, characterised by a very matt body surface and dense hairs covering the body.

Possible confusion

The smallest workers can resemble small *Camponotus sylvaticus* workers, but these latter are less matt and their hairs less dense on the body. Small workers may resemble those of *Aphaenogaster senilis* but are easily distinguished by their lack of a postpetiole.

Habitat

Occurs in warm open habitats: garrigue, scrub, human-made environments and also open holm oak and pine woods. A preference for calcareous soils, in a sunny position, no matter what the gradient.

Where to look

Nests occur under stones. Workers hunt individually, usually on the ground or in low vegetation but also in trees. Food sources with aphids are much favoured during the hottest hours. Workers do not hunt large prey but several may come together to collect a larger item if it is dead.

Biology

A common species within its biotope, with several nests close together. Colonies are

Swarming

Distribution

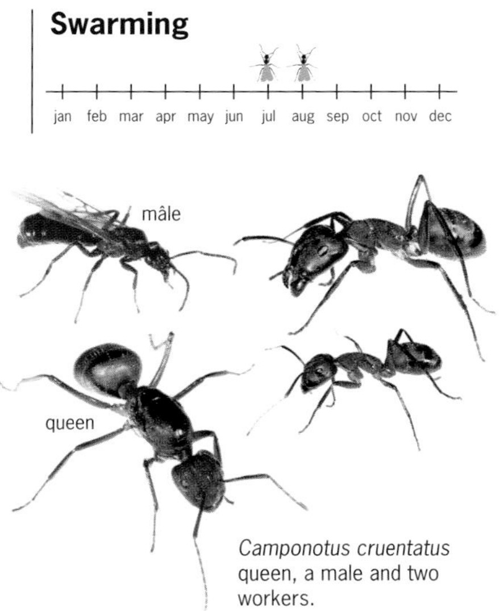

Camponotus cruentatus queen, a male and two workers.

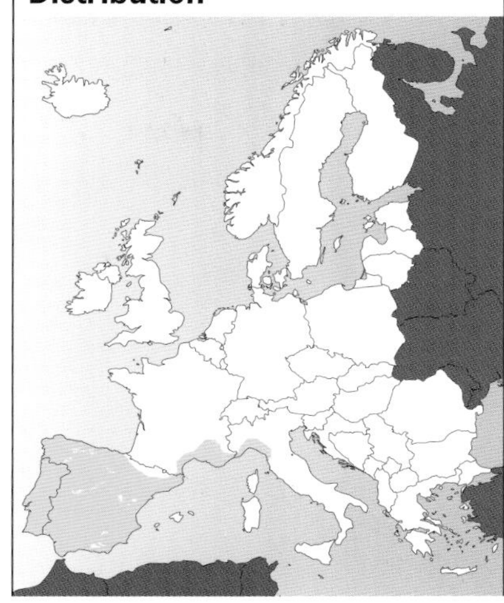

Range of *Camponotus cruentatus*.

monogynous and may contain several thousand workers. Colony founding is independent, by a single queen. They are an omnivorous species, feeding on various small arthropods and collecting their dead bodies. They are present on plants that potentially attract Hemiptera, on whose honeydew they feed: umbellifers, *Pistachia* species, kermes and holm oaks, and so on. Large workers are very aggressive and can have a powerful bite.

Camponotus cruentatus colony with workers of different sizes.

Camponotus micans Nylander, 1856

subfamily Formicinae – subgenus *Myrmosericus*

Camponotus micans worker leaving the nest.

Identification

Size: 5–11 mm. It has a matt aspect. Sparse cover of white hairs on the whole body, thicker on the head and gaster. The surface of the hairs is silvery, especially on the first two tergites of the gaster and pronotum. *Camponotus micans* is found in the extreme south of Europe, in southern Spain and Sicily.

Possible confusion

Camponotus cruentatus is a closely related species also part of the subgenus *Myrmosericus*. It is also matt but differs in having ferrous colouring on the thorax and first tergite. *Camponotus haroi* (Espadaler, 1997) is endemic to Spain and differs in having more diffuse, short and fine hairs.

Swarming

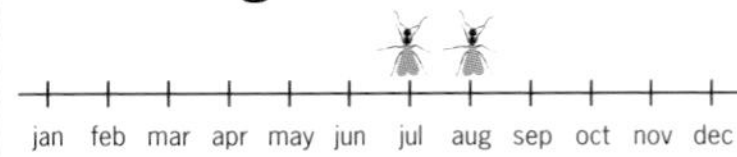

Camponotus aethiops is more shiny and longer. *Camponotus foreli* is a smaller ant, is shiny and has a more sinuous body.

Habitat

Colonies occur in open, sunny areas. Vegetation around nest is short but nearby trees are an important source of food.

Where to look

Nests are in the ground with an entrance at the base of a large root, under small stones exposed to the sun. Workers can be found looking for food during the warmest part of the day.

Biology

Workers hunt in full sun, seeking out prey and sugary substances. Highly active, they enter and leave the nest very quickly, weaving among low plants and hunting individually. During summer heatwaves, workers stay in the nest. As in desert-dwelling species, the largest workers can stock reserves in their gaster. Swarming occurs at the end of the day.

Distribution

Range of *Camponotus micans*.

Camponotus micans worker.

Camponotus micans worker.

Camponotus of the **aethiops** group

subfamily Formicinae – subgenus *Tanaemyrmex*

Camponotus aethiops worker.

Identification

Size: 5–10 mm, with significant individual variation within a colony. Workers are shiny black. Hairs on the gaster are bronze-coloured, cheeks are hairy. The clypeus has an obvious median ridge. *Camponotus aethiops* (Latreille, 1798) is widely distributed throughout Southern Europe.

Possible confusion

Camponotus sannini (Tohmé & Tohmé, 1999), from Greece, is very similar to *C. aethiops* but its body is not as dark. *Camponotus universitatis* (Forel, 1890) is a parasitic species found in *C. aethiops* nests, recognised by a much less shiny body surface, erect hairs on the scapes and a brownish-black colour on some of the body. Worker *Camponotus universitatis* are the size of small *C. aethiops* workers. *Camponotus universitatis* occurs sparsely throughout Southern Europe.

Swarming

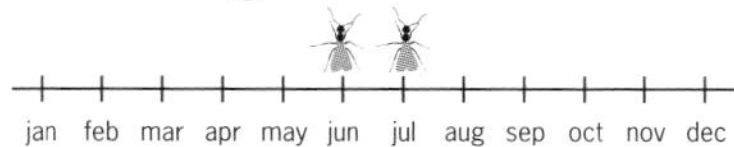

Camponotus foreli is entirely black and terrestrial, as is *C. aethiops*, but has smooth cheeks and a sinuous thorax profile. *Camponotus vagus* has denser, longer white hairs.

Habitat

Camponotus species of the *aethiops* group are xerophile and adapted to various open habitats. They do not occur above an altitude of 1,500 m.

Where to look

Nests are deep in the ground, under stones, and few workers are visible. Workers search food individually, on the ground, in low vegetation and in trees. They are often found in various Apiaceae species, from which they take nectar.

Biology

Camponotus aethiops is a very common species. Nest density can be very high. Colonies are normally monogynous and contain several hundred workers. A single queen founds the colony independently. Workers search mainly for sugary substances: Hemiptera honeydew, nectar, fruits and so on. They also hunt for insects.

Distribution

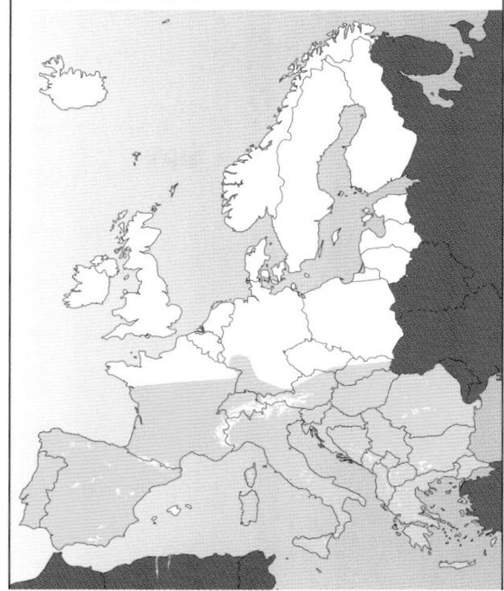

Range of *Camponotus aethiops*.

Camponotus aethiops workers guarding aphids.

Camponotus universitatis worker (arrow) amongst *C. aethiops* workers.

Camponotus of the **foreli** group

subfamily Formicinae – subgenus *Tanaemyrmex*

Camponotus foreli worker hunting for insects.

Identification

Size: 4–8.2 mm. Glossy black body with brown-black appendages. The clypeus is ridged. Sparse hairs on and under the head. The body has a sinuous aspect, with a bend at the level of the mesopropodeal grove. Hairs are thinly spread over the body. The petiole is high and wide. *Camponotus foreli* (Emery, 1981) and *C. amaurus* (Espadaler, 1997) – present only in south-eastern Spain – are the two species found in Europe.

Possible confusion

In *Camponotus aethiops,* workers are larger and more thickset and have a more continuous body outline. *Camponotus* species of the *piceus* group have no ridge on the clypeus.

Swarming

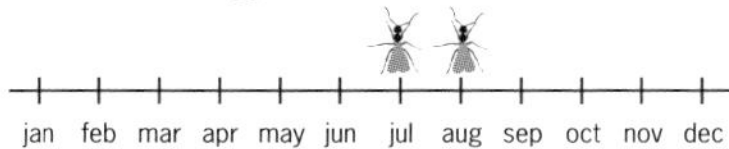

Habitat

Open, arid areas. Very warm terrain with sparse vegetation.

Where to look

Nests are under small stones or with an entry directly into the ground.

Biology

During the spring *Camponotus foreli* is very active throughout the day. In June, workers are also active at night. During July and August the workers do not leave the nest. As in desert ants, the largest workers are capable of storing reserves in their gasters. This species lives alongside others such as *Camponotus cruentatus* and *C. sylvaticus*. The feeding area used by the different colonies overlaps almost completely, but there is no conflict over resource use. Workers search mainly for flower nectar and aphid honeydew. They eat very few arthropods. They also draw nutrients from vertebrate excrement.

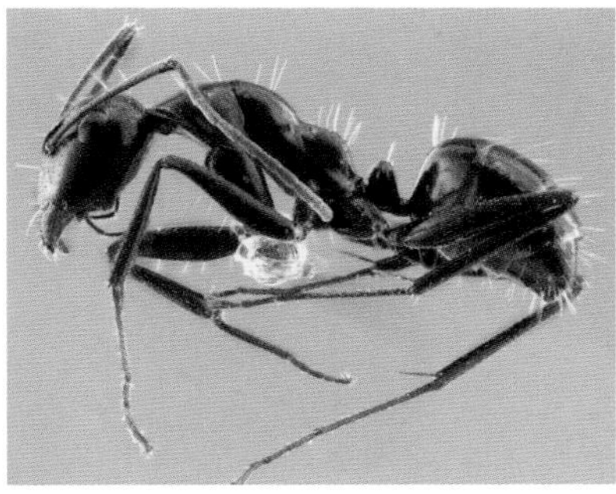

Camponotus foreli worker.

Distribution

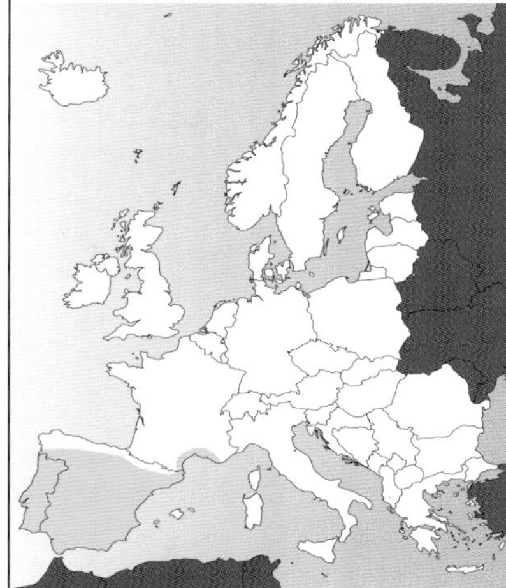

Range of *Camponotus foreli.*

Camponotus foreli worker cleaning its antennae.

Camponotus nylanderi Emery, 1921

subfamily Formicinae – subgenus *Tanaemyrmex*

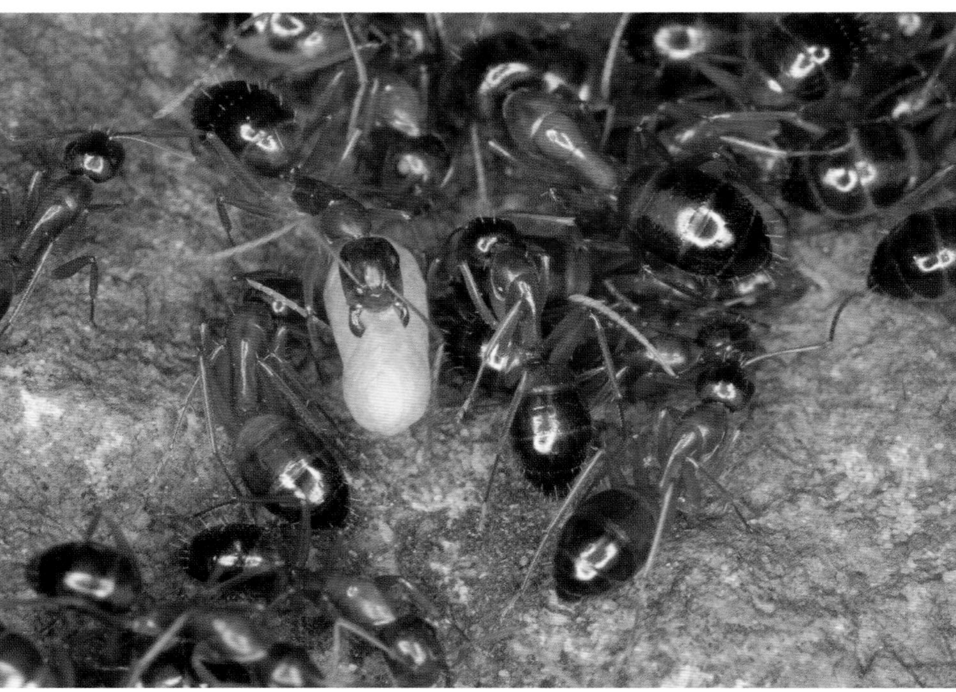

Camponotus nylanderi workers in their nest.

Identification

Size: 5–11 mm. The body is orange-red, the head brownish and the gaster almost completely black except for the base of the first tergite, which is the same colour as the rest of the body. The sparse hairs are erect. Workers' bodies appear thickset and rectangular. The tibiae have no spines on their bottom edge.

Possible confusion

This species, which occurs in Italy, is distinguished from other pale members of the genus *Camponotus* by the absence of spines on the inner edge of the tibia.

Habitat

Open forest, clearings. *Camponotus nylanderi* can be found in city gardens, oak woodland, copses and so forth.

Swarming

jan feb mar apr may jun jul aug sep oct nov dec

Camponotus nylanderi worker.

Distribution

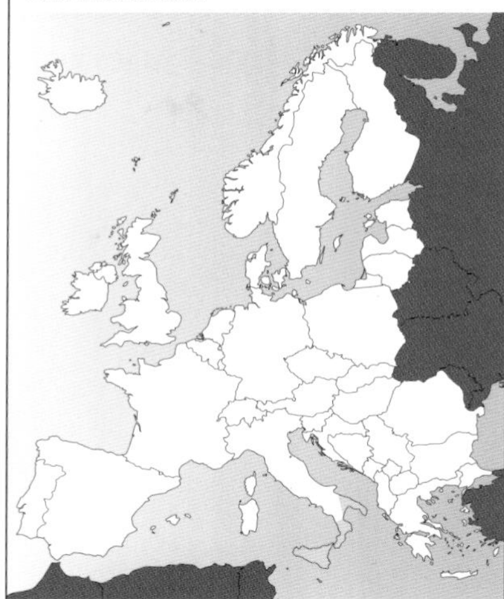

Range of *Camponotus nylanderi*.

Where to look
Nests are formed in the ground with the entrance at the foot of a tree, under stones exposed to the sun or in walls.

Biology

A common species. Density of nests can be quite high. The colonies are mainly monogynous, containing several hundred workers. Colony founding is independent and by a single queen. Workers mainly search for sugary substances: Hemiptera honeydew. They also hunt for arthropods.

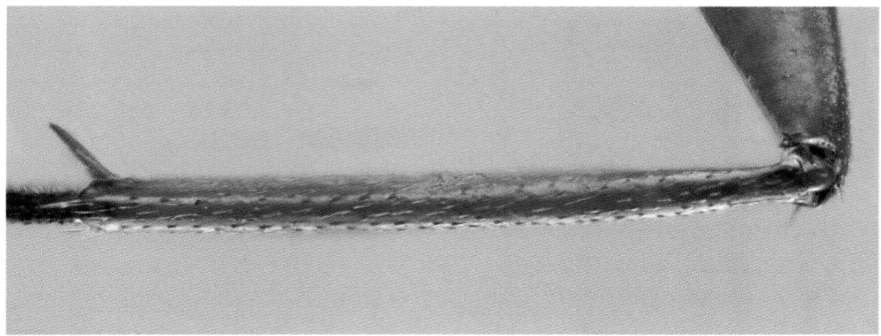

Camponotus nylanderi tibia.

Camponotus of the **pilicornis** group

subfamily Formicinae – subgenus *Tanaemyrmex*

Camponotus pilicornis major worker.

Identification

Size: 7.5–13.5 mm, with significant variation within the colony. Glossy body – yellow in small workers, brownish-yellow in larger workers. Black gaster. The head is generally dark or paler depending on the individual. A few upright hairs on cheeks. Within this *Camponotus* group we find pale species with erect hairs on the cheeks. *Camponotus pilicornis* (Roger, 1859) occurs in Spain and the south of France. Three closely related species, difficult to distinguish, occur in Greece: *Camponotus andrius* (Dalla Torre, 1893), *C. oertzeni* (Forel, 1889) and *C. jaliensis* (Dalla Torre, 1893) – their bodies can be a little darker. *Camponotus barbaricus* (Emery, 1905) originates from North Africa but occurs in Spain and Sicily; it differs from the preceding species by having a longitudinal groove along the tibia.

Swarming

Possible confusion

Other species of pale *Camponotus* do not have any erect hairs on the cheeks (*sylvaticus* and *sanctus* groups).

Habitat

Warm, open areas, especially garrigue. Also found in open woodland. A warmth-loving species of low altitude.

> **Where to look**
> Nests are found under stones. Workers search for food on the ground and in low vegetation. They are most active at nightfall.

Biology

Quite common but secretive species. Colonies are monogynous, with several hundred workers. Colony founding is independent, by a single queen. The new queen does not start laying until the spring. Workers search for food individually, especially at night. They are omnivorous, searching for arthropods, Hemiptera honeydew and bird excrement. During the day, workers are often found on plants searching for aphids or nectar. They are shy and retreat at the slightest sign of danger.

Distribution

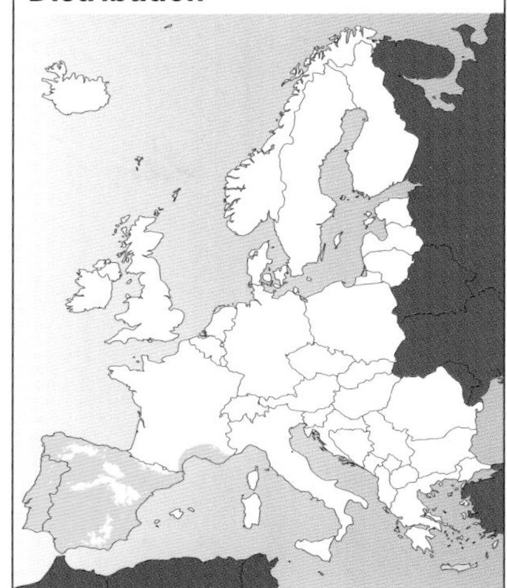

Range of *Camponotus pilicornis* (pink) and *C. jaliensis* (grey).

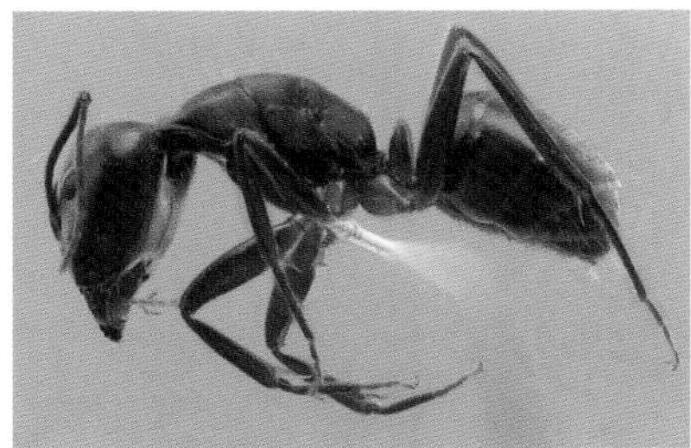

Large *Camponotus barbaricus* worker.

Camponotus jaliensis workers in their nest.

Camponotus of the **samius** group

subfamily Formicinae – subgenus *Tanaemyrmex*

Large *Camponotus ionius* worker.

Identification

Size: 5–11 mm. Workers are a glossy black with pale brown femora and funicula. The gaster is densely covered in long hairs. Long hairs over the whole body. Body colour can tend towards reddish-brown. There are four related species: *Camponotus samius* (Forel, 1889), *C. ionius* (Emery, 1920), *C. festai* (Emery 1894) and *C. laconicus* (Emery, 1920). They occur in Greece and the southern Balkans.

Possible confusion

The *Camponotus* species of the *Tanaemyrmex* are distinguished by the presence of dense, long hairs over the whole body.

Habitat

In Mediterranean-type habitats. Never above 500 m altitude.

Where to look

Nests are under stones or directly in the ground, in olive groves, pine woods or in areas of maquis.

Swarming

jan feb mar apr may jun jul aug sep oct nov dec

Head of small *Camponotus ionius* worker.

Distribution

Range of *Camponotus ionius*.

Biology

Quite a common species. Nest density can be high. Colonies are monogynous, with several hundred workers. Founding is independent, by a single queen.

Workers forage for small insects on rocks, and for honeydew and nectar on plants. When disturbed they lift their gaster (especially smaller individuals).

Small *Camponotus ionius* worker.

Camponotus sanctus Forel, 1904

subfamily Formicinae – subgenus *Tanaemyrmex*

Camponotus sanctus worker.

Identification

Size: 5–15.5 mm. The clypeus is ridged. No erect hairs on the head. The underside of head without hairs, or sometimes one or two. In small workers the head is a little duller. Present in Greece (the Dodecanese).

Possible confusion

A very large ant distinguished from other pale *Camponotus* species (*pilicornis* and *sylvaticus* groups) by absence of hairs on cheeks or under the head.

Habitat

Mediterranean habitats. No higher

Swarming

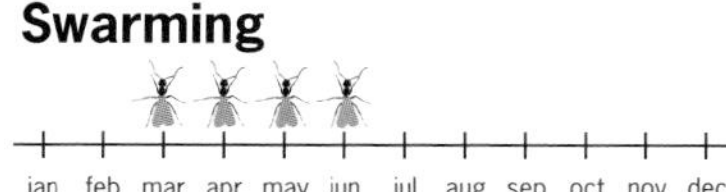

than 550 m altitude. Adapts to any type of soil, from sandy soils of pine woods to marls.

Where to look

Nests found in open habitats and open forest.

Biology

Quite common but secretive. Colonies are monogynous, with several hundred workers. Founding is independent, by a single queen. Workers forage individually, often at night; they hunt small prey individually (arthropods) and take Hemiptera honeydew. During the day they may be found on plants, foraging for aphids or nectar. They are shy, hiding at the slightest danger.

Distribution

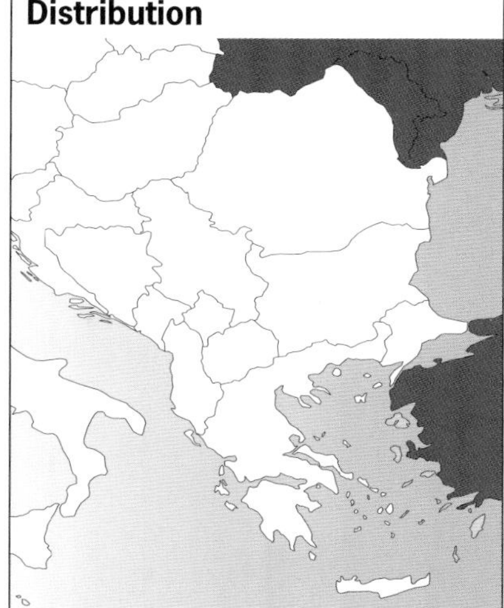

Range of *Camponotus sanctus*.

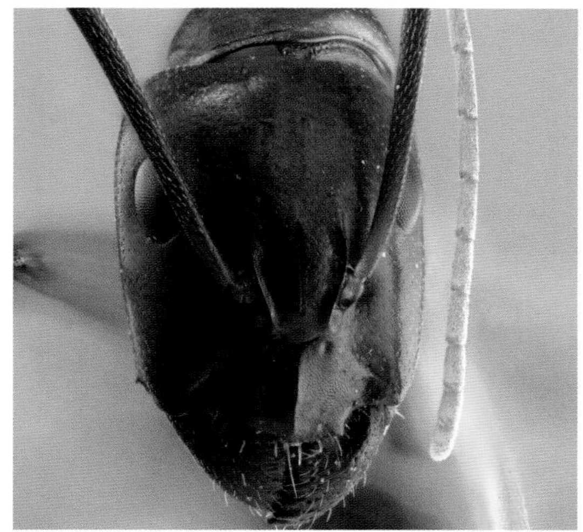

Head of *Camponotus sanctus* worker.

Camponotus of the ***sylvaticus*** group

subfamily Formicinae – subgenus *Tanaemyrmex*

Camponotus sylvaticus worker.

Identification

Size: 5–11 mm, with significant variation within a colony. No erect hairs on the cheeks, but some under the head. There are two species in this group: *Camponotus sylvaticus* (Olivier, 1792) in Spain and France, and *Camponotus baldaccii* (Emery, 1908) in Crete. Small *Camponotus sylvaticus* workers are very dark, almost entirely black, whereas large workers have a very dark head and gaster but more or less dark orange-red mesosoma, depending on nest and biotope. Both small and large *Camponotus baldaccii* workers are very pale.

Possible confusion

Camponotus species of the *pilicornis* group have hairy cheeks. In *Camponotus ligniperda* and *C. herculeanus* there is no obvious median ridge on the clypeus, and both species are absent from warm habitats of the Mediterranean zone.

Swarming

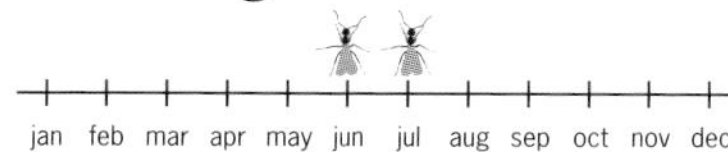

Habitat

Warm, open habitats, especially garrigue. Also found in open woodland. A lowland, warmth-loving species. As much at home on calcareous soils as siliceous rock.

Where to look

Nests are under stones. Workers forage on the ground or in low vegetation.

Biology

Common. Nests can occur at high densities. Colonies are monogynous, with several hundred workers. Founding is independent, by a single queen. Workers forage for small insects on rocks and for honeydew and nectar on plants. When alarmed they lift their gaster (especially the smaller individuals).

Distribution

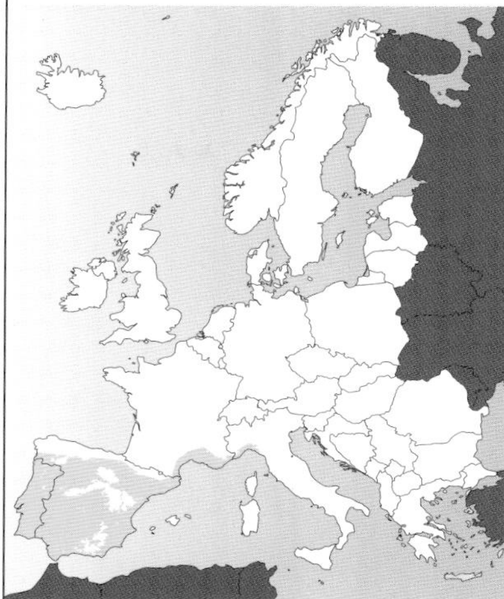

Range of *Camponotus sylvaticus* (pink) and *C. baldaccii* (grey).

Camponotus baldaccii small worker.

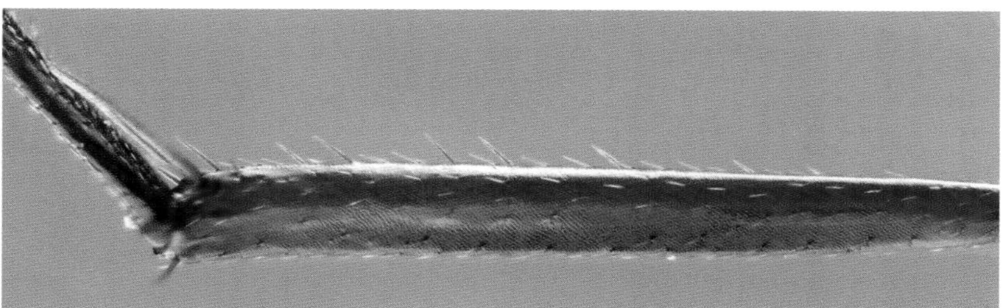

Spines on tibia of *Camponotus sylvaticus*.

Cataglyphis of the *albicans* group

subfamily Formicinae

Cataglyphis rosenhaueri worker hunting for food.

Identification

Size: less than 9 mm. The body is either uniformly coloured black or strikingly bicoloured with a red front. The petiole is low and angular in shape. Legs are long to cope with the heat when moving. These species are similar to *Cataglyphis albicans* (Roger, 1859), which is frequent in North Africa. Four species occur on the Iberian Peninsula. Three are entirely black: *Cataglyphis iberica* (Emery, 1906), present in northern and central Spain; *C. douwesi* (De Haro & Collingwood, 2000), on the Atlantic coast in the south of the peninsula, in the Cadiz area; and *C. gadeai* (De Haro & Collingwood, 2003), in the south-east of the peninsula. The main differences are found on the parts of the male's genitalia. *C. rosenhaueri* (Santschi, 1924), which occurs in Spain, is bicoloured. Another bicoloured species can be found on Greek islands: *C. viaticoides* (André, 1881).

Swarming

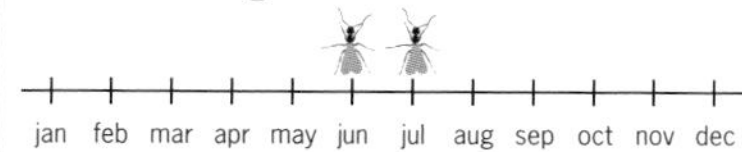

Possible confusion

These species can be distinguished from other *Cataglyphis* by petiole shape.

Habitat

Arid, open areas with a Mediterranean influence. Dry grassland, rocky or grass ridges, scrub, dirt tracks and paths, edges of cultivated areas, green urban areas.

Where to look

Nests are in the ground, opening via a simple hole, generally surrounded by a small dome of soil pellets. Nests may go quite deep underground, up to 50 cm. These species are adapted to desert climates and are most active during the hottest part of the day.

Biology

When on the move, workers may lift their gasters to an angle of 90°. Colonies are monogynous. Nests are polydomous, with workers from secondary nests obliged to return regularly to the queen in order to refresh their colonial odour. These species feed primarily on dead insects but also capture small live insects.

Distribution

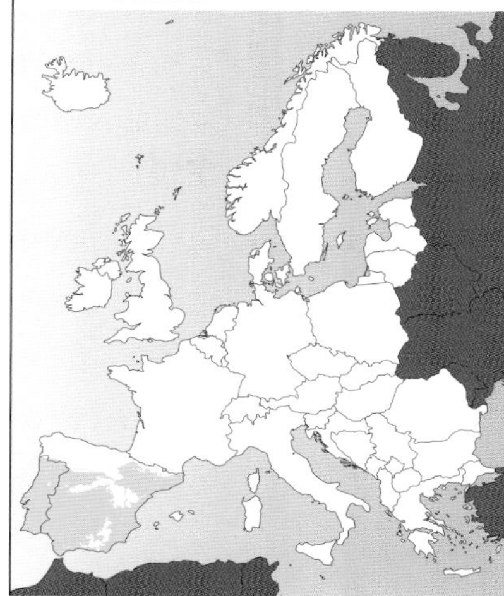

Range of *Cataglyphis iberica* (pink) and *C. viaticoides* (grey).

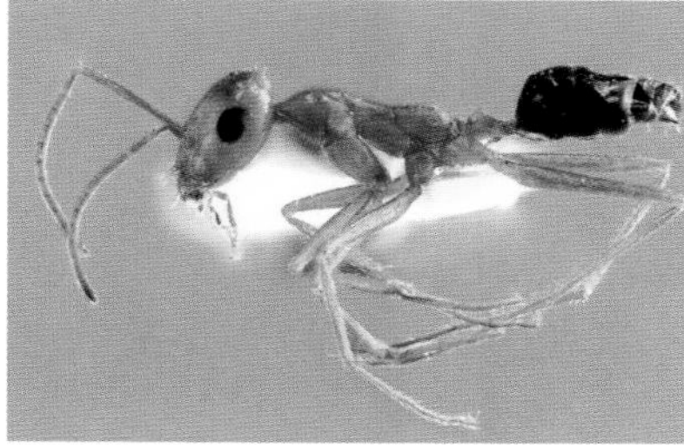

Cataglyphis viaticoides worker.

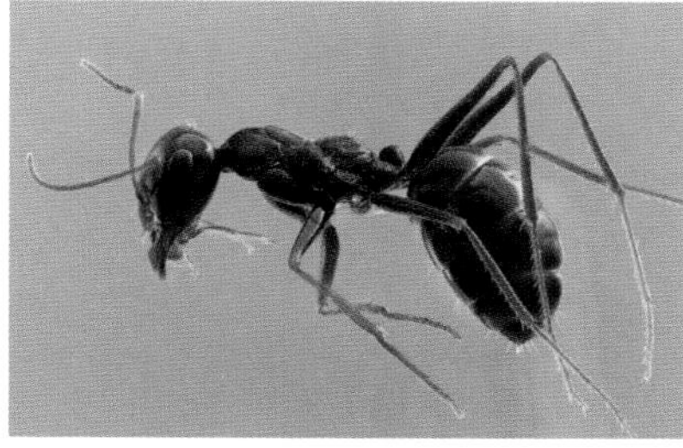

Cataglyphis iberica worker.

Cataglyphis of the *altisquamis* group

subfamily Formicinae

Cataglyphis hispanica workers in a nest.

Identification

Size: 6–9 mm. Matt black or bicoloured body. There is a very marked polymorphism of workers. The head's tegument is finely reticulated. The cover of silvery hairs gives a silky appearance. Many yellowish-white hairs. In Europe this group only occurs in the south of Spain. There are three species: *Cataglyphis velox* (Santschi, 1929), *C. hispanica* (Emery, 1906) and *C. humeya* (Tinaut, 1991). These differ in their body colour (front of body red in *C. velox*, body mainly dark in the other two species), and hair density (hairs almost absent in *C. velox*, dense in *C. hispanica*, less so in *C. humeya*). They also have a

Swarming

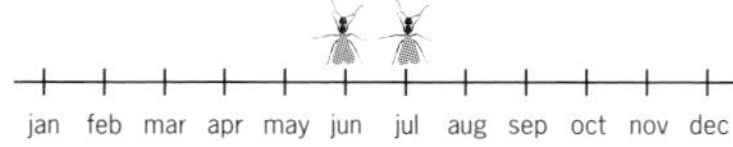

Cataglyphis humeya worker.

different distribution: *Cataglyphis velox* in Andalusia, *C. hispanica* in Extremadura and Castillo, and *C. humeya* in the Murcia region.

Possible confusion

This group can be distinguished from other *Cataglyphis* species by petiole shape.

Habitat

Oak woodlands of the Mediterranean zone.

Where to look

Nests occur in the ground or under stones with a simple entrance hole surrounded by material.

Biology

These species hunt small arthropods on the ground during the hottest part of the day. The gaster is not raised when on the move. Workers bring back stones, vegetation, broken stems and other items that they place in front of the nest entrance in order to protect the nest from high temperatures.

Distribution

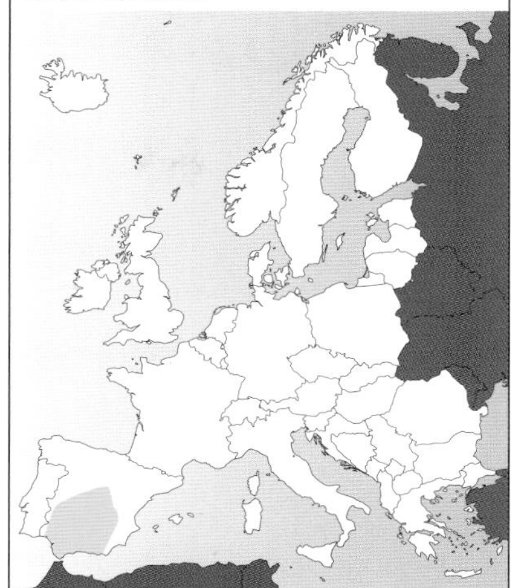

Range of *Cataglyphis velox*.

Social carrying in *Cataglyphis velox*.

Cataglyphis of the ***bicolor*** group

subfamily Formicinae

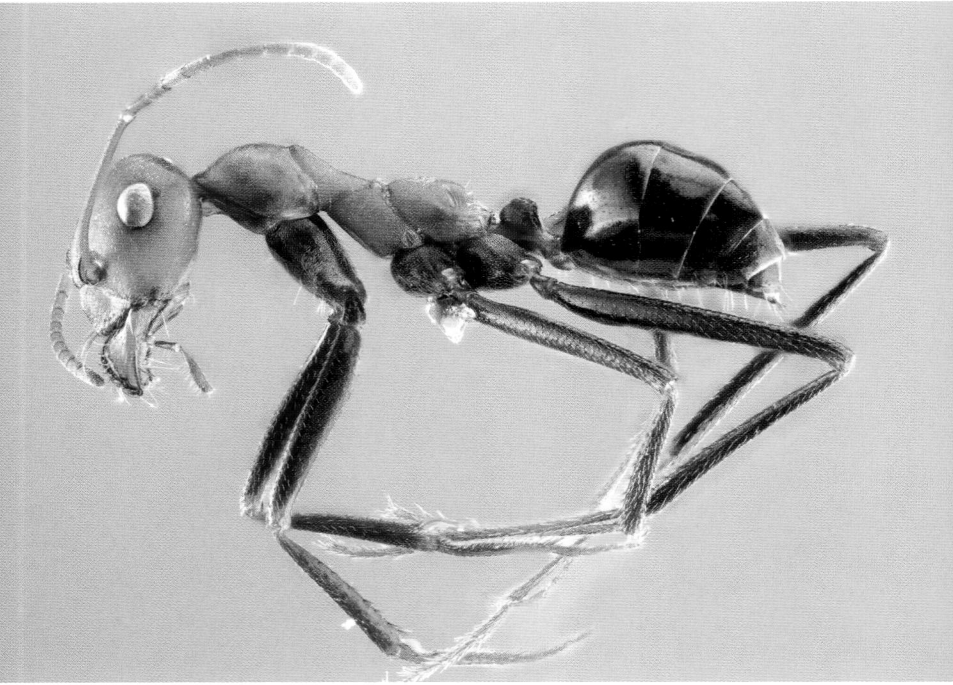

Cataglyphis nodus worker.

Identification

Size: 6–12 mm. Reddish head and mesosoma. Smaller ants may be brownish. Many closely related species exist in North Africa and the Middle East, but *Cataglyphis nodus* (Brullé, 1833) is the only representative of the group in Europe, only in the Balkans.

Possible confusion

Cataglyphis species of the *altisquamus* group are also big but are only present in southern Spain.

Habitat

Hot, open habitats.

Swarming

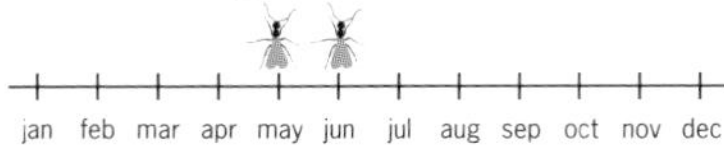

Distribution

Range of *Cataglyphis nodus*.

Where to look

Mainly in areas with sparse, low vegetation, as on tracks and paths. Nests in the ground.

Biology

Cataglyphis nodus digs its nest to a depth of 35–40 cm. It consists of a few interconnected galleries and generally has a single entrance, occasionally two, in the form of a 1.5 cm-long slit surrounded by earth. In excavating the tunnels and chambers, the workers form a crater around the nest entrance. This species feeds solely on insects, hunted by the workers during the hottest part of the day. On the ground, workers move with their gaster held erect and may travel more than 20 m from their nest: they often move in a jerky fashion, examining their surroundings and changing direction while looking for insects among plants and dead material.

Cataglyphis nodus.

Cataglyphis of the *cursor* group

subfamily Formicinae

Cataglyphis cursor workers communicating.

Identification

Size: 5–7.5 mm, with little individual size difference within a colony. Body entirely black, sometimes reddish on the head and quite glossy. Long legs. Petiole is scale-shaped. There are four species of *Cataglyphis* of the *cursor* group in Europe: *Cataglyphis cursor* (Fonscolombe, 1846), *C. piliscapa* (Forel, 1901), *C. aenescens* (Nylander, 1849) and *C. italica* (Emery, 1906). Species are differentiated by the extent of hairs on their bodies. They also each have a distinct distribution: *Cataglyphis piliscapa* occurs in Spain and the south of France, west of the Rhone; *C. cursor* occurs in south-eastern France, east of the Rhone; *C. italica* in southern Italy; and *C. aenescens* over a wide area in the Balkans.

Possible confusion

These species can be distinguished from other *Cataglyphis* species by petiole shape.

Swarming

jan feb mar apr may jun jul aug sep oct nov dec

Distribution

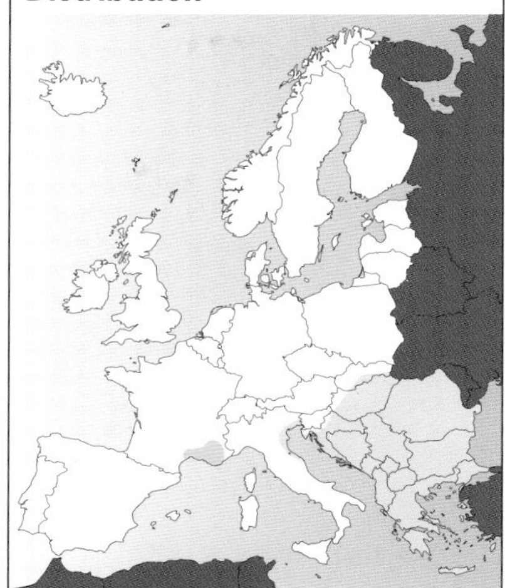

Range of *Cataglyphis cursor* (pink) and *C. aenescens* (grey).

Habitat

Well-exposed hot, open areas of Mediterranean influence: garrigue, dry grassland, rocky or grassy ridges, areas of gravel or sand, scrub, earthen tracks and paths, edges of cultivated areas, unkempt green urban areas. These species prefer lower altitudes, present to 1700 m on Mediterranean hillsides.

Where to look

Nests in the ground, with a single entrance hole often surrounded by soil pellets. Nests can descend a long way.

Biology

Common species in the Mediterranean zone. Nests may reach high densities. Colonies are monogynous, containing a few hundred workers. Nest founding occurs through fission: males come to the nest to fertilise future queens that then leave their original colony to form another nest a few metres or tens of metres away. Female dispersion is thus limited. Only males are able to fly and disperse over long distances. These species feed mainly on dead insects but also catch small live insects. Workers move about very quickly, lifting their gasters; they hunt on the ground. These species are adapted to desert conditions, with peak activity occurring during the hottest part of the day.

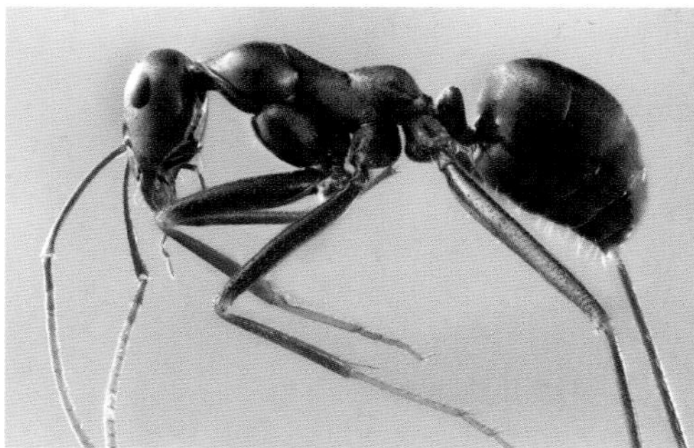

Cataglyphis aenescens worker.

Cataglyphis of the *emmae* group

subfamily Formicinae

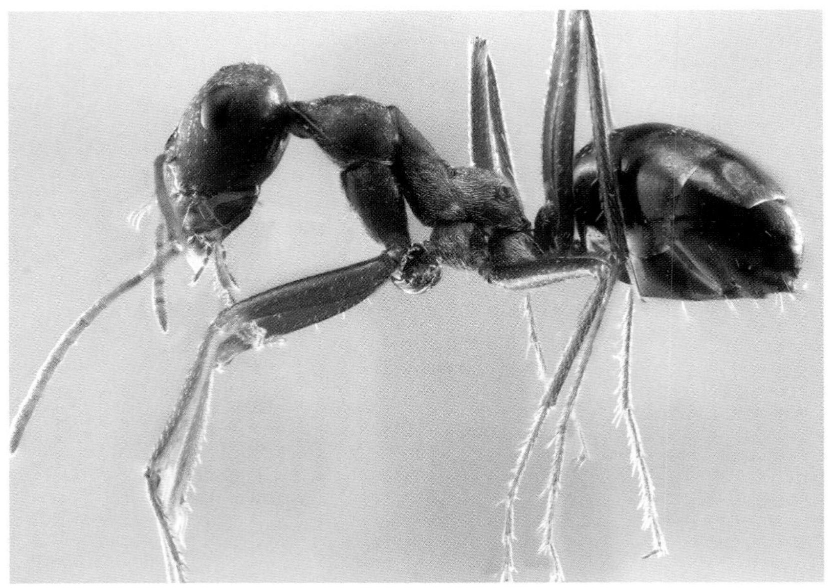

Cataglyphis floricola worker.

Identification

Size: 4.5–7.5 mm. The body is either entirely black or bicoloured with red head and mesosoma and black gaster. The petiole is rounded, in scale form, and wider than thick when seen from above. Two species are present in Europe in a very limited area in south-west Spain between Huelva and Cadiz. *Cataglyphis floricola* (Tinaut, 1993) has a dark body. *Cataglyphis tartessica* (Amor & Ortega, 2014) has an obviously red front half to its body.

Possible confusion

These two species can be confused with members of the *albicans* group. They are distinguished by petiole shape.

Habitat

These species occur in open sandy areas, with very many nests in

Swarming

jan feb mar apr may jun jul aug sep oct nov dec

Head of *Cataglyphis floricola* worker.

their territory. In scrub, heath and edges of crops.

Where to look

Nest can go down to a depth of 60 cm. The entrance hole is 0.5–1 cm in diameter. A perfectly conical mound of soil is made up of material excavated from galleries and chambers.

Biology

The monogynous colonies can contain up to 1,200 workers. It is the smallest workers that leave the colony at the hottest time of day.

Distribution

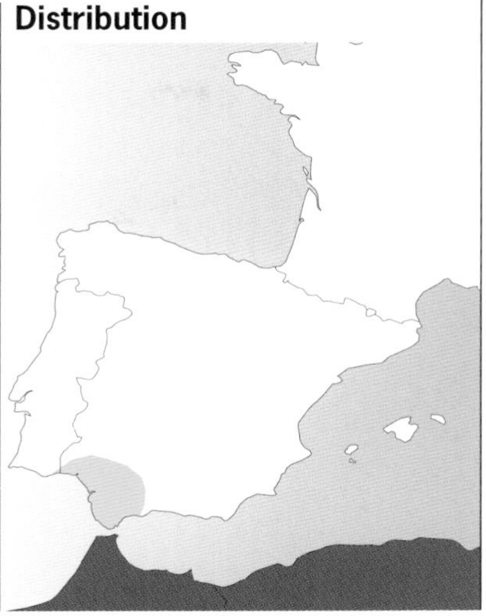

Range of *Cataglyphis floricola* and *C. tartessica*.

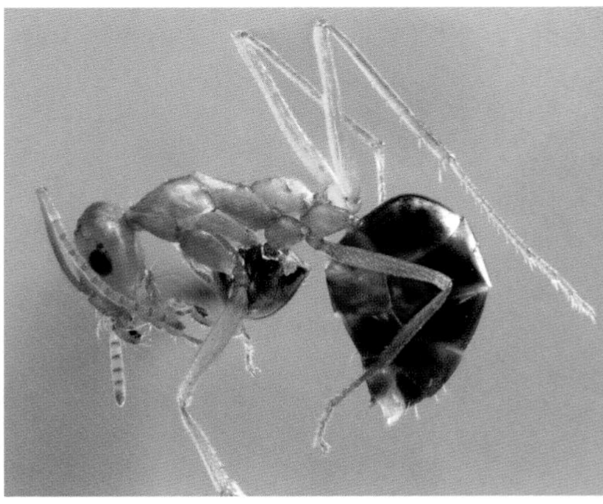

Cataglyphis tartessica worker.

Workers hunt up to 20 m from the nest. *Cataglyphis* species such as these need important protein resources. These ants are aggressive towards all forms of competition.

Coptoformica subgenus Müller, 1923

(*Formica* genus) subfamily Formicinae

Formica pressilabris worker.

Identification

Size: 4–7.5 mm. Bicoloured workers with reddish mesosoma, sometimes spotted with brown, dark brown to almost black gaster, dark head sometimes with more or less pale areas. The occipital edge of the head is notched. The *Coptoformica* are a group of species from colder parts of Europe present at low altitudes in the north and only at high altitudes in the south. Separating the seven species known in Europe is difficult, based mainly on differences in the amount of hairs. *Formica exsecta* (Nylander, 1846) is the most widespread. *Formica bruni* (Kutter, 1967), *F. pressilabris* (Nylander, 1846) and *F. foreli* (Bondroit, 1918) have also been recorded from most European countries. *Formica forsslundi* (Lohmander, 1949), *F. suecica* (Adlerz, 1902) and *F. fennica* (Seifert, 2000) are present only in Northern Europe.

Possible confusion

This group is distinguished from other *Formica* groups by having a concave edge to the occiput.

Swarming

jan feb mar apr may jun jul aug sep oct nov dec

Habitat

Coptoformica species occupy subalpine and boreal-mountainous meadows, forest clearings and edges, dry and sunny alpine meadows, heaths and dried up marshes, peat bogs; generally at an altitude of 800 to 1,200 m.

Where to look

Nests form small, 5–30 cm high domes made of plant debris, small branches and sometimes pebbles. Workers look for food on the ground or in vegetation.

Biology

Nests need to receive a good deal of heat from the sun for optimum development. This dependence is addressed by nests occurring in sites with little or no shade from trees. Nest density can be high. Colonies are either monogynous or polygynous. Colony founding occurs through temporary social parasitism within a colony of *Formica fusca* or *F. lemani*. They are mainly carnivorous. There can be as many as 4,000 workers in a colony. Mating may occur during a nuptial flight or in the nest.

Distribution

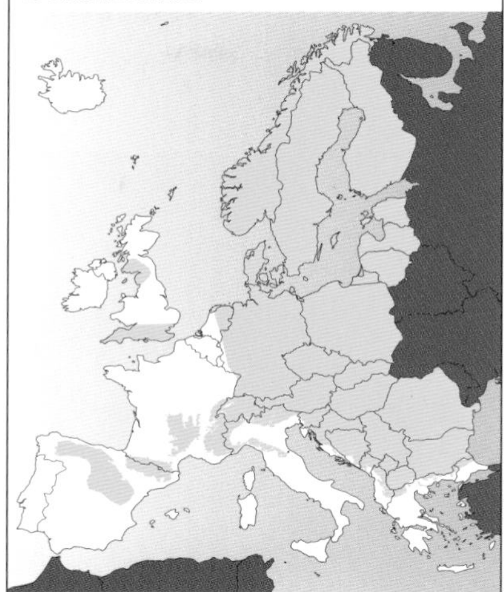

Range of the subgenus *Coptoformica*.

Formica exsecta workers.

Domes of small twigs over *Formica exsecta* nests.

Formica of the ***lugubris*** group

subfamily Formicinae – subgenus *Formica*

Formica lugubris colony.

Identification

Size: 4–9 mm. Dark, almost black gaster, head and mesosoma blotched with dark brown. Hairs on the occiput. Blurred edges to the dark blotches on the head and mesosoma. *Formica lugubris* (Zetterstedt, 1838), *F. paralugubris* (Seifert, 1996) and F. *aquilonia* (Yarrow, 1955) are very similar species. Differences concern the density and length of hairs. *Formica paralugubris* appears to be restricted to the Alpine arc, whereas *F. lugubris* is widely distributed in Europe (in the south it is restricted to high altitudes). *Formica aquilonia* has a more northerly distribution.

Possible confusion

In *Formica pratensis* the markings on the head and mesosoma are darker with a better defined edge. *Formica rufa* and *F. polyctena* have no erect hairs on the occiput. *Formica truncorum* and *F. sanguine* have workers with entirely reddish or orangish head and mesosoma.

Habitat

Mountain forests, forest edges and peat bogs. To an altitude of 2,000 m.

Swarming

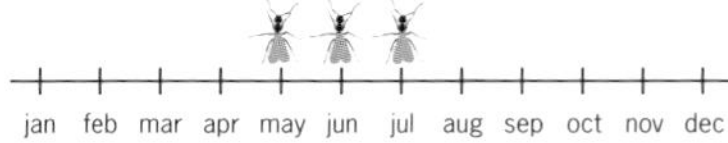

Where to look

Nests of conifer needles form domes up to 1.5 m high. Workers hunt for food on the ground or in trees.

Biology

Very common species in mountainous areas. Nests may occur at a high density. Colonies are monogynous or polygynous and may contain tens of thousands of workers. Colony founding may occur through adoption in a colony of the same species or by temporary parasitism in a colony of a species from the subgenus *Serviformica*. They are omnivores. Aphid honeydew is an important resource. Workers also hunt small invertebrates. They form obvious and well-defined trails. They are one of the host species of the wood-eating ant *Formicoxenus nitidulus*.

Distribution

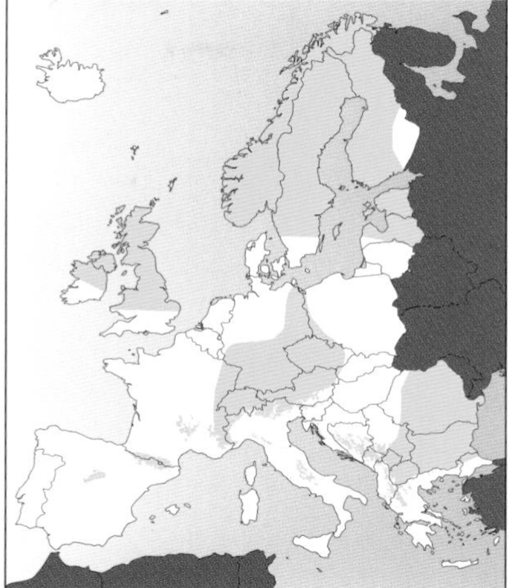

Range of *Formica lugubris*.

Formica lugubris workers around a prey item.

Three castes of *Formica lugubris*. From left to right: a queen, a male and a worker.

Formica pratensis Retzius, 1783

subfamily Formicinae – subgenus *Formica*

Formica pratensis worker.

Identification

Size: 4–9 mm. Dark, nearly black gaster, reddish head and mesosoma spotted with dark brown. Many hairs on the occiput. The markings on the head and mesosoma are very dark with a clear-cut edge.

Possible confusion

This species could be confused with one of those of the *lugubris* group. In that group the dark markings on the head and mesosoma are paler and have a diffuse edge, and they have fewer hairs. The gaster also appears more shiny. *Formica rufa* and *F. polyctena* have no erect hairs on the occiput. *Formica truncorum* and *F. sanguinea* have workers with completely reddish or orangish head and mesosoma.

Formica pratensis worker.

Swarming

jan feb mar apr may jun jul aug sep oct nov dec

Habitat

Essentially in open habitats: forest edges, clearings, heather moors, lightly grazed meadows, ditches, field edges. Rarely found above 1,500 m.

Where to look

Nests comprise domes made of conifer needles or plant debris and small stones, often with good exposure to the sun. These domes are often small and hard to find if surrounding vegetation is high. Workers search for food on the ground and on the trunks of trees.

Biology

A common species. Nests usually occur at a lower density than those of other dome-building *Formica* species. Colonies are monogynous or slightly polygynous and normally have a single dome. Even though they may have several thousand workers, nests are less populous than those of *Formica rufa* and *F. polyctena*. Newly fertilised queens founding a new colony may become temporary social parasites by using *Serviformica* species. They are omnivorous. Aphid honeydew is an important resource. Workers also hunt for small invertebrates. It is one of the host species of the xenobiotic ant *Formicoxenus nitidulus*.

Distribution

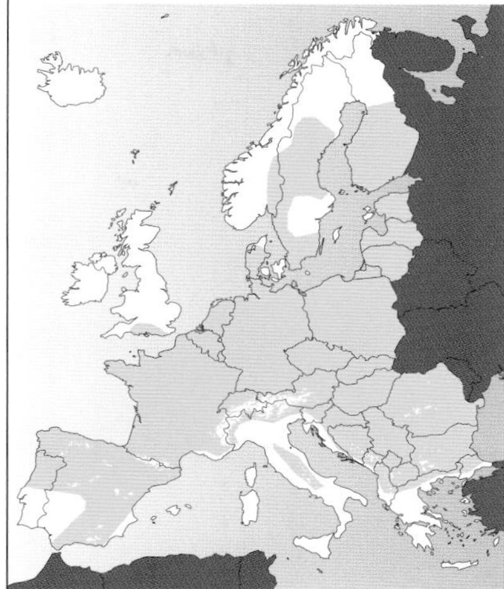

Range of *Formica pratensis*.

Formica pratensis workers around a berry.

Formica of the *rufa* group

subfamily Formicinae – subgenus *Formica*

Formica rufa worker.

Identification

Size: 4–9 mm. Dark, nearly black gaster, the head and mesosoma spotted with dark brown. No hairs on the occiput. There are two very closely related species that in fact often hybridise: *Formica rufa* (Linnaeus, 1758) and *F. polyctena* (Foerster, 1850). The latter species differs only in having fewer hairs, in particular there are none on the pronotum. Both species are very common.

Possible confusion

The head and pronotum of *Formica uralensis* are entirely black. *Formica pratensis*, *F. lugubris*, *F. paralugubris*, *F. aquilonia*, *F. frontalis* and *F. trunorum* have erect hairs on the occipital part of the head.

Swarming

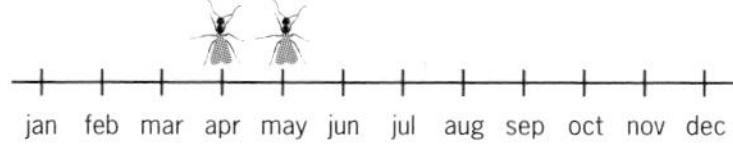

Formica dusmeti has an entirely red head. *Formica sanguinea* has a notched clypeus.

Habitat

Lowland forest. Absent from Mediterranean forest. Does not occur above 1,500 m.

Where to look

Nests form big domes (up to 2 m in height) made of conifer needles. Workers hunt for food on the ground or in trees.

Biology

Extremely common species. Nests can occur at a very high density. Colonies are monogynous or polygynous, sometimes consisting of several domes connected by trails. They are the species with the most populous colonies, which may contain more than 100,000 workers. The newly fertilised queen can either get herself adopted by a colony of the same species, or found a new colony through temporary social parasitism by using a species of the subgenus *Serviformica* (generally *F. fusca*) as a host. Omnivorous. At least half of the energy input for the colony is provided by tree aphid honeydew (especially those on conifers). Workers hunt for invertebrates and play a role in pest control – in some regions they are an excellent ally in the fight against processionary moth caterpillars. Workers create well-defined trails and collaborate with each other to carry large items back to the nest. They are host species of the xenobiotic ant *Formicoxenus nitidulus*.

Distribution

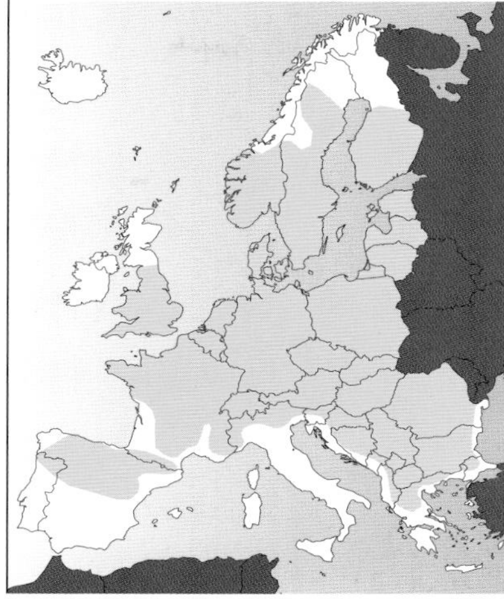

Range of *Formic rufa*.

Formica rufa dome of twigs.

Formica of the **truncorum** group

subfamily Formicinae – subgenus *Formica*

Formica truncorum worker.

Identification

Size: 3.5–9 mm, with great variation within the colony. Small workers have a dark, almost black gaster and reddish head and mesosoma with dark brown spotting. Larger workers have a uniform orangish head and mesosoma. They have many erect hairs over the whole body, except for *Formica dusmeti*. The group comprises three species: *Formica truncorum* (Fabricius, 1804) occurs in the Alps, Central and Northern Europe; *F. dusmeti* (Emery, 1909) and *F. frontalis* (Santschi, 1919) are found in the Iberian Peninsula.

Possible confusion

Formica sanguinea has a notch on the upper edge of the clypeus. In other bicoloured *Formica* species, workers' heads and/or mesosoma are spotted with brown and have fewer hairs.

Swarming

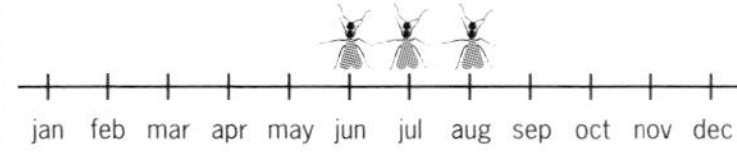

Habitat

Open habitats: forest edges, clearings, peat bogs, heather moors, or on sandy soils.

Where to look

Nests form domes of conifer needles. These domes, similar to those of *Formica rufa*, are situated to receive maximum sun. Nests can also occur in the ground (rock crevices), under stones or in tree stumps. Workers hunt for food on the ground or on tree trunks.

Biology

Colonies are monogynous or polygynous and contain several thousand workers. The newly fertilised queen will found a new colony through temporary social parasitism by using a species of the subgenus *Serviformica* (*Formica fusca*, etc.) as a host. They are omnivorous, feeding mainly on aphid honeydew and also small invertebrates. Workers can often be found on the trunks of trees such as spruces or pines, searching for aphids. It is a host species of the xenobiotic ant *Formicoxenus nitidulus*.

Distribution

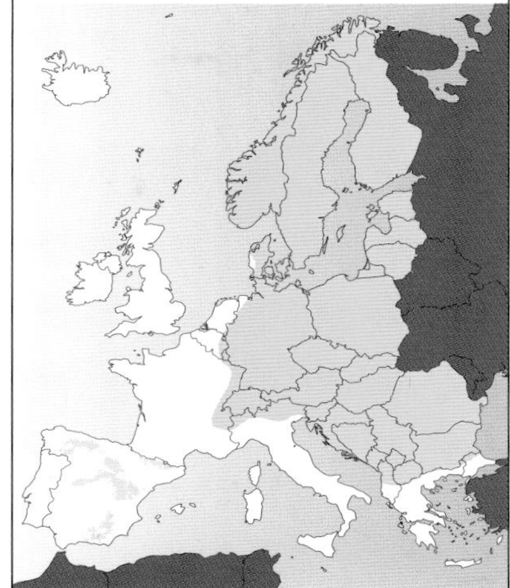

Range of *Formica truncorum* (pink) and *F. frontalis* (grey).

Formica truncorum workers.

Formica truncorum worker.

***Raptiformica* subgenus** (*Formica* genus)

subfamily Formicinae

Formica sanguinea workers in the company of *F. fusca* workers.

Identification

Size: 4–9 mm. Dark, almost black gaster, pale reddish mesosoma, reddish head darker than the mesosoma. Notch in front edge of the clypeus.

Possible confusion

Formica sanguinea (Latreille, 1798) is the only species of *Formica* with a notched clypeus. The other bicoloured *Formica* species normally have a darker head (except large workers of the *truncorum*) and do not have a notched clypeus.

Habitat

This species occurs in a diverse range of biotopes, generally open ones: sunny meadows, alpine meadows, sandy areas, forest edges, clearings, heather moors, peat bogs and so on. To an

Swarming

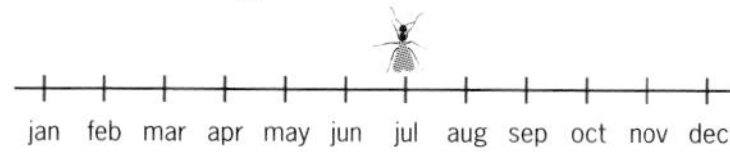

altitude of 1,800 m. Absent from dry Mediterranean habitats.

Where to look

Nests are built in old tree stumps or in the ground, under stones. Sometimes they are topped with an irregular, low pile of twigs. Workers search for food on the ground or in low vegetation.

Biology

A common species. Colonies are monogynous or polygynous and can contain several thousand workers. Newly fertilised queens can found a new colony through temporary social parasitism by entering into a nest of a species of the subgenus *Serviformica*. They can equally return to their nest of origin or move into another *Formica sanguinea* nest; or independently found a new nest with other queens. *Formica sanguinea* feeds mainly on small invertebrates and aphid honeydew. It is a facultative slavemaker that regularly undertakes raids into *Serviformica* nests (particularly those of *Formica cunicularia*, *F. fusca*, *F. lemani* and *F. rufibarbis*) in order to steal their pupae. It is possible to find colonies without host workers.

Distribution

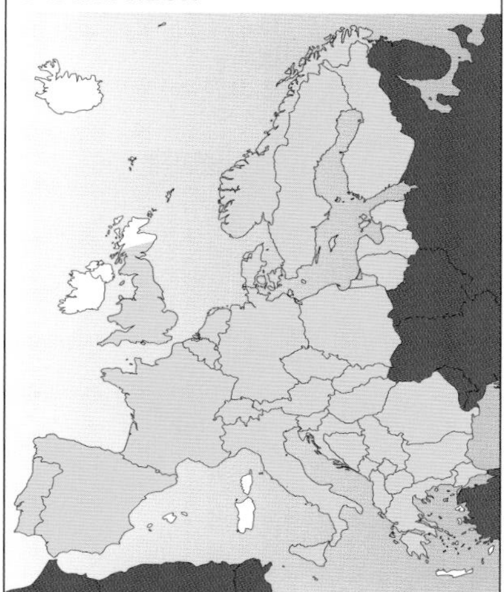

Range of *Formica sanguinea*.

Formica sanguinea worker and queen.

Formica sanguinea worker in a flower.

Formica uralensis Ruzsky, 1895

subfamily Formicinae

Formica uralensis worker.

Identification

Size: 4.5–8 mm. *Formica uralensis* workers have a completely black head and pronotum.

Possible confusion

Formica uralensis has a combination of characters that is unique for a *Formica* species. It has a short scape, a characteristic colouration different from that of other *Formica* (of the subgenus *Formica*) and like *uralensis* constructs twig domes. It differs from *Formica rufa*, *F. polyctena*, *F. pratensis*, *F. truncorum* and *F. lugubris* by having a completely black head.

Habitat

A boreal-mountainous species. Found mainly in peat bogs and other wetlands. In Europe its distribution overlaps that of *Formica picea*.

Swarming

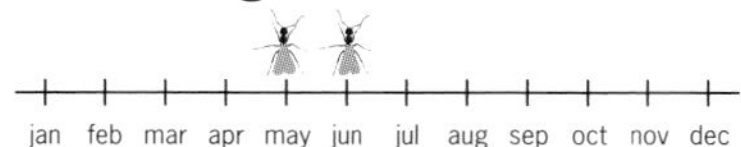

Where to look
Mainly in open, sunny habitats. The nests, built of plant debris or conifer needles, are dome-shaped, similar to those of *Coptoformica* species, and well exposed to the sun. In well-vegetated habitats, nests are constructed on the top of grass tufts in order to have maximum sun exposure. Workers search for food on the ground, in vegetation or in trees (conifers, birches, etc.).

Biology
The colony is always founded by temporary social parasitism of *Formica picea*. Colonies are either monogynous or polygynous (sometimes with more than 300 queens), and may contain several hundred workers. In cases of high polygyny, multiplication of the colony may occur through splitting. Omnivores that feed principally on aphid honeydew but also some small invertebrates. Workers may often be found hunting for aphids on trunks of trees: spruce, pines, silver birch and so on.

Distribution

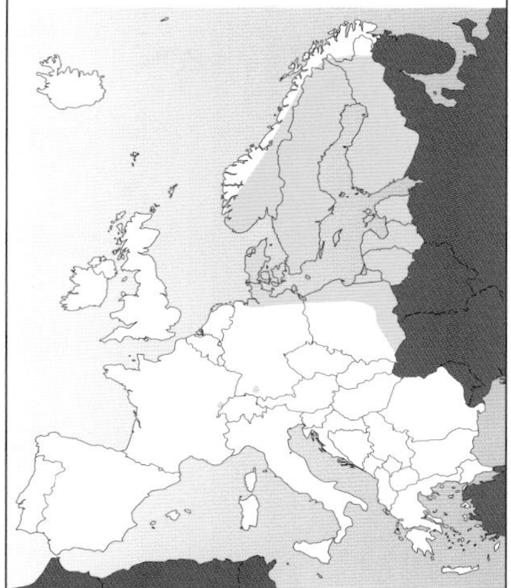

Range of *Formica uralensis*.

Formica uralensis worker.

Formica uralensis workers on a nest dome.

Formica of the *cinerea* group

subfamily Formicinae – subgenus *Serviformica*

Formica selysi worker.

Identification

Size: 4.5–6.5 mm. Entire body thickly covered with hairs, even under the head, giving species of this group a shiny, silver appearance. The cuticle is blackish. Numerous erect hairs on the occiput. There are four species of this group present in Europe: *Formica cinerea* (Mayr, 1853), *F. selysi* (Bondroit, 1918), *F. fuscocinerea* (Forel, 1874) and *F. corsica* (Seifert, 2002). All species of the *cinerea* group can be distinguished from other *Serviformica* species in that they have erect hairs on the occiput. The species differ in the amount and distribution of body hairs. *Formica corsica* is endemic to Corsica. *Formica fuscocinerea* is present around the Alpine arc. *Formica selysi* is mainly found in the western half of Europe, whereas *F. cinerea* is above all present in Eastern Europe.

Swarming

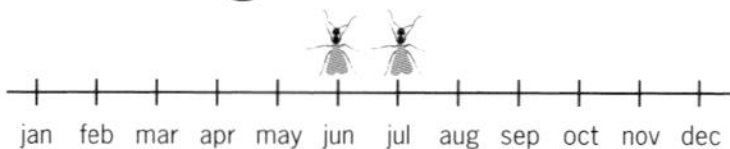

Possible confusion

Formica decipiens is present in the Iberian Peninsula and the Pyrenees. It also has much hair, giving it a silvery appearance, but it does not have erect hairs on the occiput.

Habitat

Open areas with short vegetation, on the edges of water bodies, from sea level to 2,500 m. Some species can be found in towns, especially on pavements and the like.

Where to look

Nests occur in the ground, under stones, on the edges of streams.

Biology

A common species in the right habitat. Nests can occur at a high density. Colonies are monogynous or polygynous, with many hundreds of workers. They are omnivorous, feeding on Hemipteran honeydew and various arthropods (including other ants). These species are very aggressive. *Formica selysi* is especially well adapted to flooding: colonies can easily survive two days under water and workers are capable of digging through 20 cm of any sand and gravel that may be deposited in front of the nest entrance.

Distribution

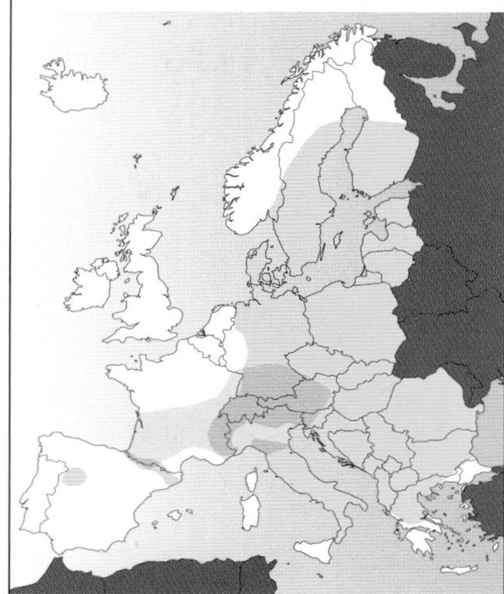

Range of *Formica cinerea* (pink) and *F. selysi* (grey).

Formica fuscocinerea worker.

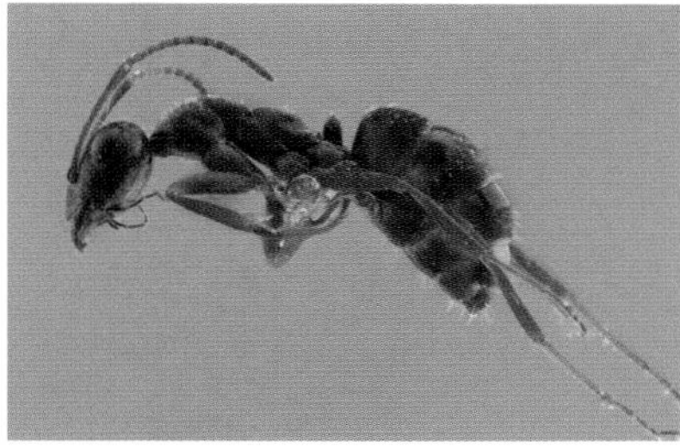

Formica cinerea worker.

Formica cunicularia Latreille, 1798

subfamily Formicinae – subgenus *Serviformica*

Formica cunicularia worker.

Identification

Size: 4–7 mm. Overall a matt dark brown with some paler, orangish colouring on the mesosoma and cheeks. Some forms sometimes appear entirely black, but looking through a microscope always shows there to be a reddish zone on the sides of the mesosoma and on the cheeks. No erect hairs on the pronotum.

Possible confusion

Formica pyrenaea (Bondroit, 1918), very rare and endemic to the Pyrenees, differs from *F. cunicularia* in having a thicker petiole. *Formica rufibarbis* and *F. clara* have erect hairs on the pronotum. The dark forms of *Formica cunicularia* always have a small reddish patch on the cheeks which distinguishes them from *F. fusca*.

Habitat

Various open habitats, generally well exposed to the sun: meadows,

Swarming

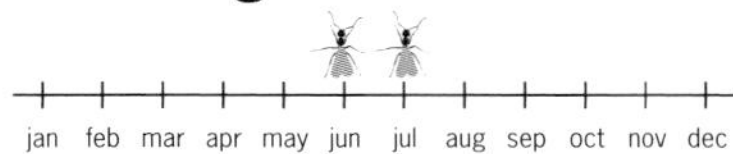

calcareous hillsides, grassy ridges, sparsely vegetated slopes, banks, scrub, sandy soils, heaths, as well as many man-made habitats such as town flowerbeds, tracks and paths, and so forth. As much at home at sea level as in mountainous areas, to an altitude of 1,800 m.

Where to look

Nests are in the ground, under a stone or pavement slab, where each one forms a small mound of earth. Workers search for food on the ground, in the grass layer or sometimes on tree trunks.

Biology

A common species. Colonies are either monogynous or polygynous and may have as many as a thousand workers. Founding is independent and generally by a single, isolated queen, more rarely by several queens together. This species is omnivorous, favouring honeydew and various arthropods. *Formica cunicularia* is often found on tree trunks as well as on various grasses, where it searches for aphids. It is used for slaves by the slavemaker species *Polyergus rufescens* and *Formica sanguinea*.

Distribution

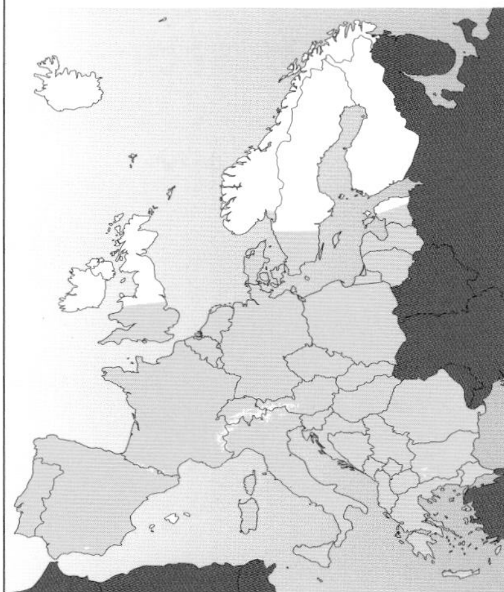

Range of *Formica cunicularia*.

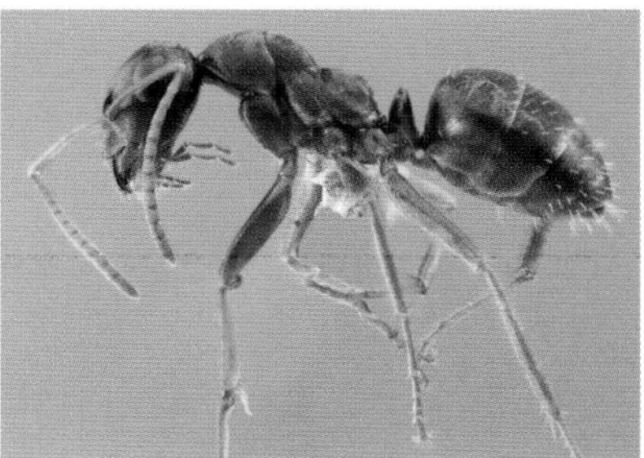

Formica cunicularia worker.

Formica cunicularia workers carrying a pupa.

Formica decipiens Bondroit, 1918 and *F. gerardi* Bondroit, 1917

subfamily Formicinae – subgenus *Serviformica*

Formica decipiens worker.

Identification

Size: 4–7 mm. Workers are a dark colour. No erect hairs on the occiput. A few hairs on the pronotum. *Formica decipiens* has dense hair over the rest of the body, giving it a silvery appearance, reminiscent of species of the *cinerea* group. On the other hand, *Formica gerardi* has shorter hairs, thus revealing a very matt body, different from other *Formica* species. These two species occur on the Iberian Peninsula and in the French Pyrenees.

Possible confusion

These species have erect hairs on the pronotum which differentiates them from *Formica fusca* and

Swarming

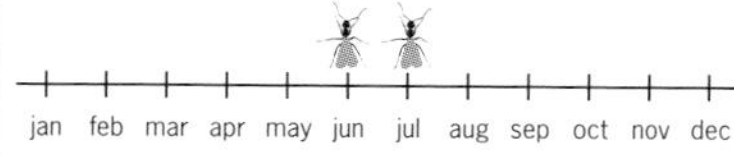

Formica decipiens worker.

Distribution

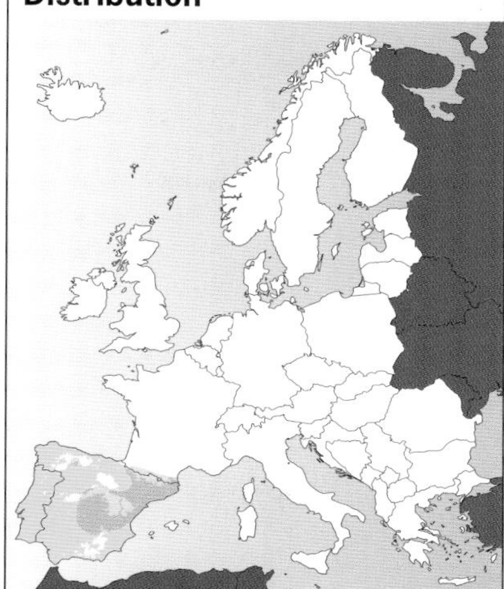

Range of *Formica gerardi* (pink) and *F. decipiens* (grey).

F. cunicularia. *Formica lemani* does not have such dense hairs as *F. decipiens* and the surface of the gaster is shinier than that of *F. gerardi*.

Habitat

Formica decipiens is found near rivers and scree. *Formica gerardi* occupies shaded areas at forest edges.

> **Where to look**
> Nests are in the ground or under a stone; occasionally at the foot of a large dead tree trunk on the ground.

Biology

Colonies are monogynous. Workers hunt various arthropods

Formica gerardi workers hidden under leaves.

and also look for aphid honeydew or the nectar of low plants or bushes. *Formica decipiens* can be found at higher altitudes (up to 1,500 m) than *F. gerardi*.

Formica fusca Linnaeus, 1758

subfamily Formicinae – subgenus *Serviformica*

Formica fusca worker leaving the nest.

Identification

Size: 4.5–7.5 mm. Entirely black with an only slightly shiny aspect due to having quite dense hairs. No erect hairs on the pronotum (occasionally one or two). A common and widespread species in Europe.

Possible confusion

Formica lemani has more hairs on the pronotum (> 2 hairs). *Formica gagates*, *F. picea* and *F. gagatoides* have less dense hairs on the gaster (thus a shinier gaster). *Formica selysi* has hairs on the hind edge of the head and a more silvery look due to denser hairs, particularly on the gaster. *Formica fuscocinerea* and *F. cinerea* have hairs on the hind edge of the head. In *Formica cunicularia*, even in the darkest

Swarming

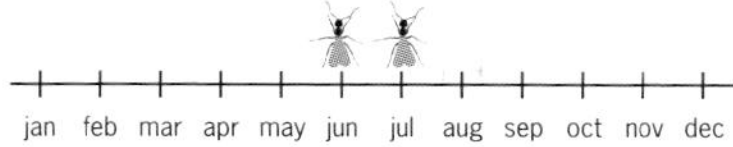

forms there is always a reddish area on the mesosoma and on the cheeks.

Habitat

An omnipresent species within its range: woodland floors, meadows, urban areas and so on. Occurs from sea level to 2,000 m.

Where to look

Nests are built under stones or sometimes in rotten wood on the ground or under the bark of dead branches. Workers hunt for food on the ground and in vegetation.

Biology

A very common species. Nest density within an occupied area is normally high. Colonies are polygynous and may contain as many as a few thousand workers. Founding is either independent or results from adoption in another colony. An omnivorous species that feeds particularly on aphid honeydew and various invertebrates. Workers protect aphid colonies on plants, defending them from predators and their being exploited by other ants. It is a host species of the slavemakers *Formica sanguinea* and *Polyergus rufescens*, and of temporary parasites (species of the *Coptoformica* and *Formica* subgenera).

Distribution

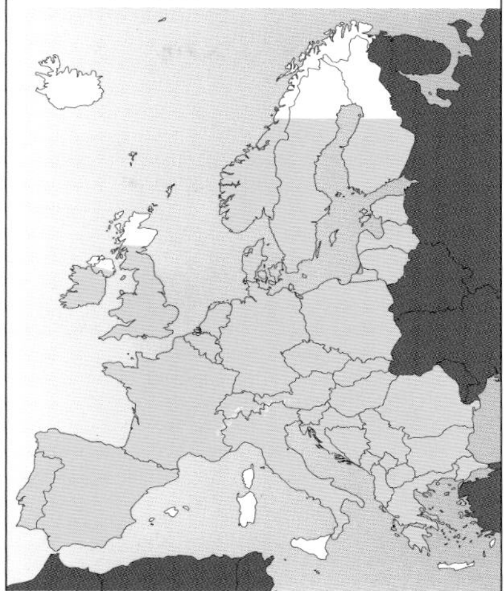

Range of *Formica fusca*.

Formica fusca worker.

Formica gagates Latreille, 1798

subfamily Formicinae – subgenus *Serviformica*

Formica gagates worker bringing prey back to the nest.

Trophallaxis between two *Formica gagates* workers.

Identification

Size: 5–7 mm. Body entirely shiny black. A few erect hairs on the pronotum. Longish hairs over the whole body. Quite dense hairs which nonetheless allow the shininess of the body surface to be seen.

Swarming

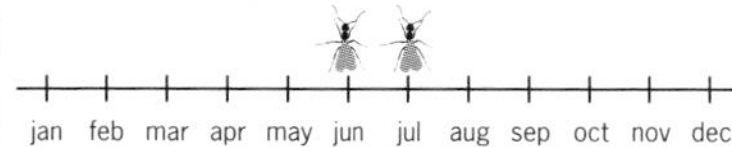

Distribution

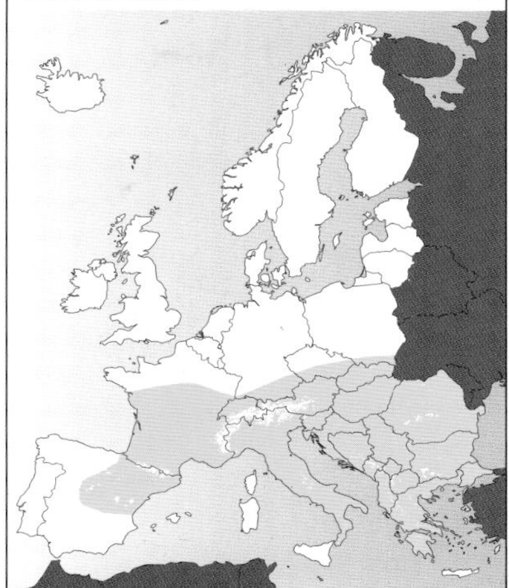

Range of *Formica gagates*.

Possible confusion

There are three species of *Formica* ants with shiny black bodies in Europe. *Formica gagates* is the only southern species that occurs in wooded habitats; the other two (*F. gagatoides* and *F. picea*) occur in the colder parts of Europe, living in peat bogs and other wetland habitats. In *F. gagates* the hairs on the gaster are denser. *Camponotus piceus* is also black and shiny but has a concave propodeum.

Habitat

Wooded habitats, particularly oak woods, from lowlands to the colline zone (around 800 m).

Where to look

Nests are in the ground, under stones. Workers search for food in leaf litter and low vegetation.

Biology

A common species. Nests contain a high number of individuals. Omnivorous on various arthropods and Hemiptera honeydew.

Formica gagates worker guarding aphids.

Formica lemani Bondroit, 1917

subfamily Formicinae – subgenus *Serviformica*

Formica lemani colony.

Identification

Size: 4.5–6.5 mm. Entirely black, only slightly glossy appearance due to quite dense covering of hairs. A few erect hairs on the pronotum.

Possible confusion

A very common species in mountainous areas and in lowlands in Northern Europe.

Habitat

All habitat types at altitude, from 500 m to higher than 2,500 m (optimum is above 1,500 m). It gradually replaces *Formica fusca* with altitude. These two closely related species can coexist in the same area.

Swarming

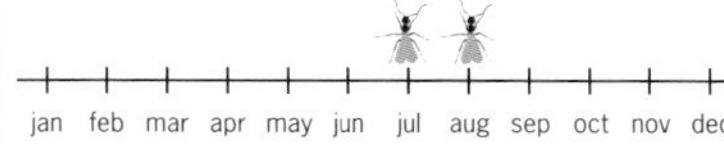

Distribution

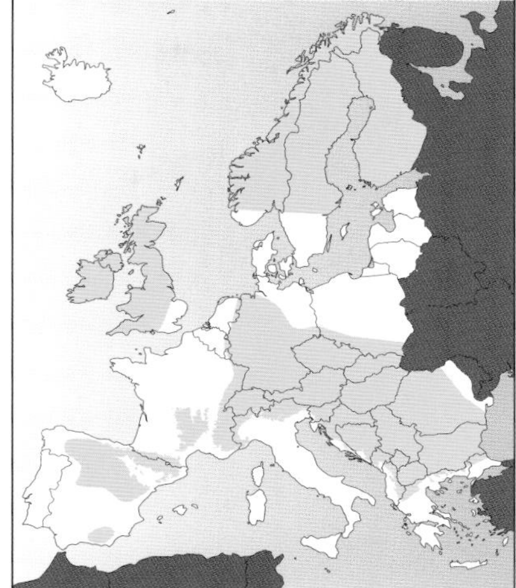

Range of *Formica lemani*.

Where to look

Nests are usually situated under stones but also directly in the ground, in cracks in shale, under bark, under moss and in dead wood. Workers search for food on the ground and in vegetation.

Biology

A common species at altitude. Nests can occur at a high density. Colonies are polygynous, with several hundred workers. Founding is independent or by adoption in another colony. An omnivorous species that feeds mainly on aphid honeydew and various invertebrates. Workers guard aphid colonies on plants, defending them from predation and their being exploited by other ants. It is a host of the slavemaker species *Formica sanguinea* and *Polyergus rufescens*, and temporary parasite species (true members of the subgenera *Coptoformica* and *Formica*).

Formica lemani worker on a flower.

Formica picea Nylander, 1846 and ***F. gagatoides*** Ruzsky, 1904

subfamily Formicinae – subgenus *Serviformica*

Formica picea workers and queen.

Identification

Size: 4–5.5 mm. Entirely black, shiny body. Long hairs over the whole body. The hairs are not dense, so the glossy body surface is visible. *Formica picea* (Nylander, 1846) and *F. gagatoides* (Ruzsky, 1904) are two closely related species that occupy the cooler parts of Europe. *Formica picea* is quite widely distributed, whereas *F. gagatoides* occurs only in Scandinavia. *Formica picea* has a few erect hairs on the pronotum; *F. gagatoides* has no erect hairs.

Possible confusion

Formica gagates is the only other black *Formica* species to have such a glossy appearance, but it does not occur in open, wet and cold habitats. Hairs are sparser on the

Swarming

jan feb mar apr may jun jul aug sep oct nov dec

gaster in *Formica gagates*. *Camponotus piceus* is just as black and shiny but is also absent from those habitats occupied by *Formica picea*.

Habitat

Open, wet and generally cool habitats: peat bogs, damp meadows at altitude, heather moors. Occurs at more than 2,000 m altitude.

Where to look

Nests are generally in sphagnum, grass tussocks or clumps of moss, sometimes against a stone. They are visible due to the accumulation of plant debris on their top, forming a flattish cone a little less than 10 cm in diameter.

Biology

Colonies are polygynous and rarely have more than a few hundred workers. Founding is independent or by adoption in another colony. They mainly feed on sugary substances, especially Hemiptera honeydew. Workers also hunt insects. *Formica picea* is sometimes used as a host by the slavemaker *Formica sanguinea*, and for founding by *F. truncorum* and *F. uralensis*.

Distribution

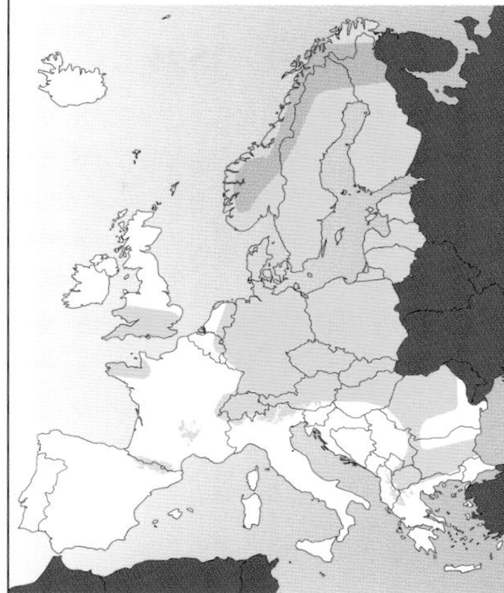

Range of *Formica picea* (pink) and *F. gagatoides* (grey).

Habitat occupied by *Formica picea*.

Formica of the ***rufibarbis*** group

subfamily Formicinae – subgenus *Serviformica*

Formica rufibarbis worker.

Identification

Size: 4.5–7.5 mm, with quite significant differences between individuals of the same colony. Dark, almost black gaster. Dark brown head often with paler, orangish patches. Mesosoma is generally orangish, sometimes brown. The general colour of the head and mesosoma varies between colonies and between individuals of the same colony, the smaller individuals being darker. There are erect hairs on the pronotum. *Formica rufibarbis* (Fabricius, 1793) and *F. clara* (Forel, 1886) are two closely related species that can be separated by the covering of hairs–denser in *F. rubibarbis*.

Possible confusion

Some individual *Formica clara* could be confused with *F. cunicularia* but the latter species is

Swarming

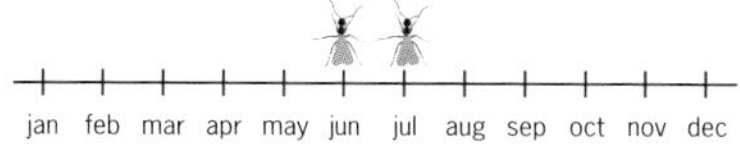

generally darker. Bicoloured species of the true subgenus *Formica* are usually larger with high, domed nests. Species of the subgenus *Coptoformica* have an obvious notch at the back of the head.

Habitat

Various open habitats, generally well exposed to the sun: meadows, calcareous hillsides, grassy ridges, less vegetated slopes, banks, scrub, sandy soils and also man-made habitats such as gardens, town flower borders, edges of cultivated ground, derelict railway lines and so on. Occurs in lowlands as much as mountainous areas, to an altitude of 2,000 m.

Where to look

Nests are in the ground or under stones. Workers sometimes collect plant debris around the nest entrance. They search for food on the ground and in vegetation, sometimes in trees.

Distribution

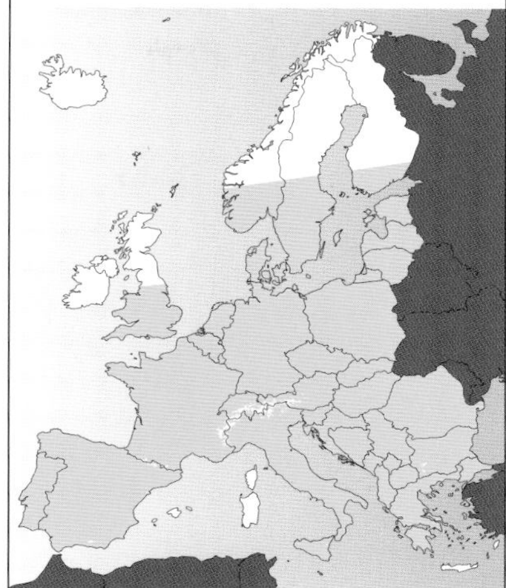

Range of *Formica rufibarbis*.

Formica rufibarbis workers attending sap-sucking Hemiptera.

Biology

A very common species. Nest density can be extremely high. Colonies are monogynous or polygynous and have several hundred workers. They are omnivores, feeding on Hemiptera honeydew and various arthropods. Workers can often be seen on the trunks of trees and on plants in the search for aphids. They are host species of slavemakers *Polyergus rufescens* and *Formica sanguinea*, and of the temporary parasite *F. rufa*.

Iberoformica genus Tinaut, 1990

subfamily Formicinae

Iberoformica subrufa worker.

Identification

Size: 5–6 mm. A monomorphic species. A dark reddish-brown colour, the mesosoma more or less dark. They are redder at altitude. Concave mesonotum. Erect, thick, short white hairs over the whole body. *Iberoformica subrufa* (Roger, 1859) is the only species in the genus.

Possible confusion

Workers are distinguished from those of the genus *Formica* by their concave mesonotum.

Habitat

Prefers holm oak or cork oak forests. *Iberoformica subrufa* inhabits degraded forests with sparsely vegetated and sunny open spaces. Present in south-eastern Spain and Andalusia, from the coast to mountainous areas (1,300 m) and in the eastern French Pyrenees, on rocky coasts. A warmth-seeking species.

Where to look

Many sites, including walls of disused cultivated terraces.

Swarming

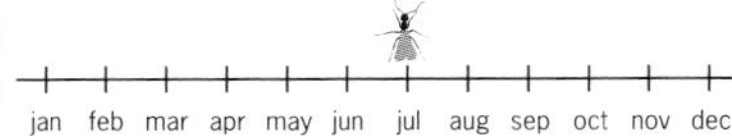

Distribution

Range of *Iberoformica subrufa*.

Iberoformica subrufa worker's head.

Biology

To resist high temperatures, workers are able to lift their gaster over the thorax. Moving rapidly on their long legs when in the open is another adaptation to the heat. Colonies are monogynous. The species feeds on arthropod corpses and sometimes seeds. It will also take nectar and the sap of certain plants: euphorbias, pines, holm oak and box.

Iberoformica subrufa queen after mating, looking for a hiding place.

***Austrolasius* subgenus** Faber, 1967 (*Lasius* genus) subfamily Formicinae

Lasius carniolicus worker seen in profile.

Identification

Size: 3.5–4.5 mm. Entirely yellow. The mandible bases are close together. The petiole is relatively low and thick for a *Lasius*. There are two species within this subgenus in Europe: *Lasius carniolicus* (Mayr, 1861), widely distributed from Spain to Siberia, and *L. reginae* (Faber, 1967), which only occurs in Central Europe. The two species can be separated by the presence or absence of hairs; *Lasius reginae* has no erect hairs on the scapes or the tibiae.

Possible confusion

Lasius species of the *Cautolasius* and *Chthonolasius* subgenera have a more highly placed petiole and the head is not heart-shaped when seen from the front.

Habitat

Various environments, generally warm: dry grasslands, dry and open forests, heath, forest edges. From sea level to the uplands.

Swarming

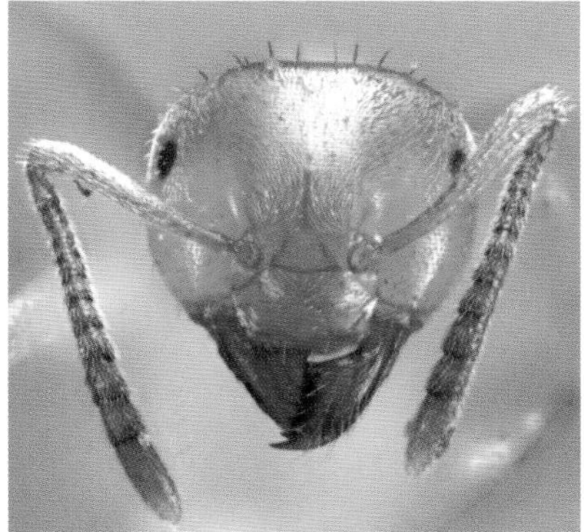

Head of *Lasius carniolicus* seen from the front.

Where to look

Nests are in the ground, often forming a small dome of soil. Workers are rarely visible above ground. They tend to live and search for food underground and are thus secretive.

Biology

Due to their soil-dwelling habits it is difficult to know if the species is really rare or if it simply goes unnoticed. Colonies are monogynous and very populous. Founding occurs through temporary social parasitism. After the nuptial flight, the new queen penetrates a colony of another *Lasius* species (subgenera *Lasius* or *Cautolasius*) and takes the place of the resident queen. When all the host workers have died, the colony is independent. This species feeds mainly by exploiting root aphids.

Distribution

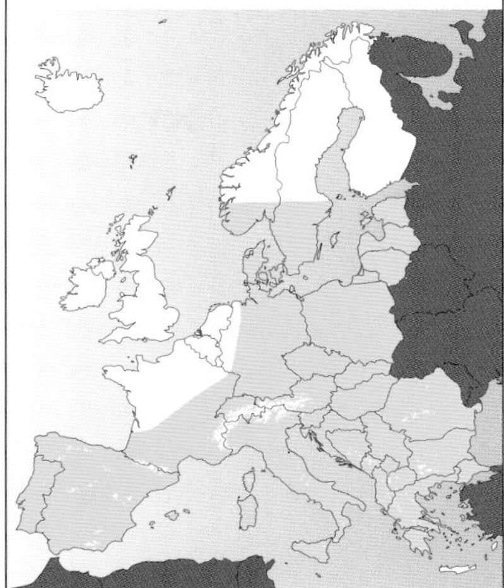

Range of the subgenus *Austrolasius*.

Dorsal view of the gaster of *Lasius carniolicus*.

Cautolasius subgenus Wilson, 1955

(genus *Lasius*) subfamily Formicinae

Lasius flavus colony. A male (black, winged) can be seen at the bottom of the image.

Identification

Size: 1.8–4.5 mm. Body entirely yellow. Large individuals of *Lasius flavus* have a darker head. There are three species in this subgenus that occur in Europe. *Lasius flavus* (Fabricius, 1781) is a widespread species; workers are polymorphous, large individuals have a brownish head. *Lasius myops* (Forel, 1894) and *L. myrmidon* (Mei, 1998) are the two other *Cautolasius* species in Europe. They have a southerly distribution and are very similar to *L. flavus* but can be distinguished by having smaller eyes, the absence of large individuals with dark heads in the colony and their preference for hotter environments. *Lasius myrmidon* has been found only in Greece.

Possible confusion

Species of the subgenus *Austrolasius* have a more heart-shaped head, a thicker and not so high petiole.

Swarming

Species of the subgenus *Chthonolasius* have erect hairs under the head and often on their cheeks.

Habitat

A widely distributed species that occurs in urban as well as natural habitats; cultivated areas, roadside verges, forest, woodland edge and so on, to an altitude of 2,500 m. *Lasius myops* shows a preference for warmer habitats.

Where to look

Usually, a nest's presence is given away on the surface by a mound of earth in the centre of a tuft of grass or simply between plant stems. Nests may also occur under stones, especially in Mediterranean habitats, or in old tree trunks. Workers are rarely seen above ground. They are secretive, living and hunting mainly in the soil.

Distribution

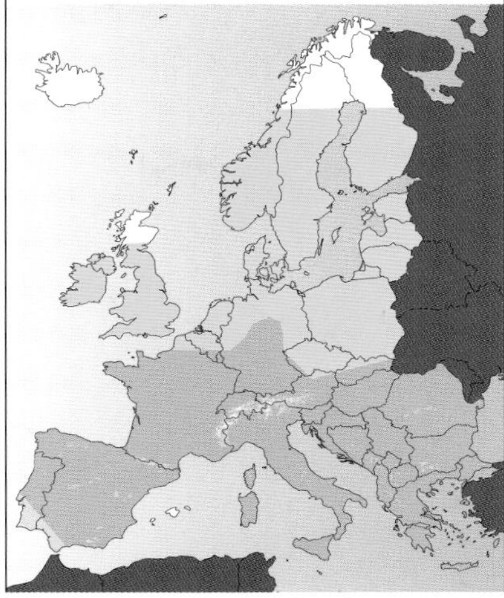

Range of *Lasius flavus* (pink) and *L. myops* (grey).

External view of a *Lasius flavus* nest.

Biology

Lasius flavus nest density may be very high, particularly in northern meadows. Colonies are either monogynous or slightly polygynous. They are very populous, often containing several tens of thousands of workers. Founding generally occurs independently, with several associated queens. This species feeds mainly on honeydew from aphids whose colonies are situated on the roots of herbaceous plants occurring around or in the ant's nest (a mound of soil). Nests may be frequented by a small myrmecophilous beetle (*Claviger testaceus*), which depends on the ants for protection.

Chthonolasius subgenus Ruzsky, 1912

(*Lasius* genus) subfamily Formicinae

Chthonolasius sp. worker.

Identification

Size: 3.2–5.5 mm. Entirely yellow. They have erect hairs on the underside of the head and often on their cheeks. There are at least 12 species of *Chthonolasius* in Europe. Identification of these species is very difficult and based especially on the shape of the petiole scale and amount of hair covering. Three of these species occur only in the Balkans and eastern Europe: *Lasius balcanicus* (Seifert, 1988), *L. nitidigaster* (Seifert, 1996) and *L. viehmeyeri* (Emery, 1922). The nine other species are widely distributed across Europe: *Lasius bicornis* (Foerster, 1850), *L. citrinus* (Emery 1922), *L. distinguendus* (Emery, 1916), *L. jensi* (Seifert, 1982), *L. meridionalis* (Bondroit, 1920), *L. mixtus* (Nylander, 1846), *L. rabaudi* (Bondroit, 1917), *L. sabularum* (Bondroit, 1918) and *L. umbratus* (Nylander, 1846).

Possible confusion

Species of the subgenus *Austrolasius* have a long head and a low, thick

Swarming

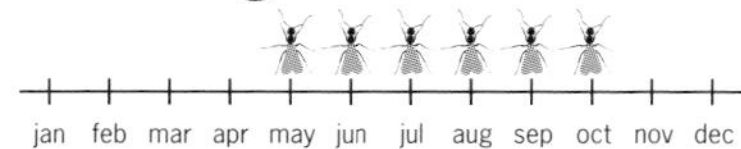

petiole. Species of the subgenus *Cautolasius* have no erect hairs under the head or on their cheeks.

Habitat

Species of the subgenus *Cautolasius* are widely distributed. They are found equally in lowlands and in mountainous areas.

Where to look

All species live in tunnels in the ground, which often means they are difficult to find. Their nests are in the ground, sometimes found under stones or small domes of soil that may be formed. Sometimes they are in roots, tree stumps or dead wood. Workers are rarely seen on the surface. They live and search for food in the ground, remaining secretive. It is only during swarming that they are active above ground.

Biology

All species of the subgenus *Chthonolasius* found colonies by temporary social parasitism. After the nuptial flight, the new queen penetrates the nest of another *Lasius* species (*Lasius* or *Cautolasius* subgenera) to take the place of the resident queen. At that time it is possible to find mixed nests with, for example, black ants (host species) and yellow ants (parasite species). Once all host workers have died, the *Chthonolasius* colony is independent. These species feed mainly on the honeydew of aphids reared on roots, and also small soil arthropods. The nest walls are built of a sort of paper held in shape by the presence of filaments of an *Ascomycota* fungus.

Distribution

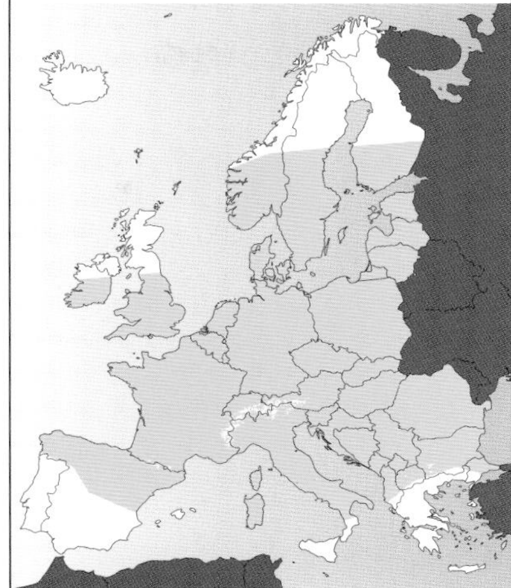

Range of *Lasius umbratus*.

Lasius umbratus winged female.

Dendrolasius subgenus Ruzsky, 1912

(*Lasius* genus) subfamily Formicinae

Lasius fuliginosus worker.

Identification

Size: 3.5–5 mm. The entire body is shiny black. An obviously concave occiput. The head is very wide compared to the mesosoma. *Lasius fuliginosus* (Latreille, 1798) is the only member of this subgenus to occur in Europe.

Possible confusion

Little risk of confusion; other species of *Lasius* are paler and/or less shiny and generally smaller. *Camponotus piceus* and certain shiny, black *Formica* species do not have such a wide head and do not form tracks to food sources.

Habitat

Wooded habitats: forests, copses, parks and sometimes gardens. Absent from low-lying Mediterranean forests; occurs to an altitude of 1,700m.

Where to look

Nests are generally in the centre of a standing, hollow tree trunk. Sometimes also in the ground, at the foot of a tree.

Swarming

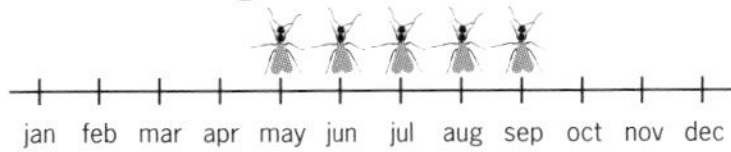

Workers form long, very visible trails leading to their food sources, on the ground and on trees.

Biology

Lasius fuliginosus is a common species. Colonies are generally monogynous, but sometimes polygynous with many individuals, containing as many as several hundreds of thousands of workers. Founding occurs by temporary social parasitism in a colony of a *Chthonolasius* species (particularly *Lasius umbratus*, *L. mixtus*, *L. sabularum*, *L. bicornis* or *L. jensi*). This species feeds principally on aphid or scale insect honeydew. Workers can form sizeable columns between the nest and the food source (aphid colony). The workers produce a 'paper' from wood fibres, which is used in the construction of the nest walls. A fungi is maintained within this 'paper', whose filaments reinforce the structure.

Distribution

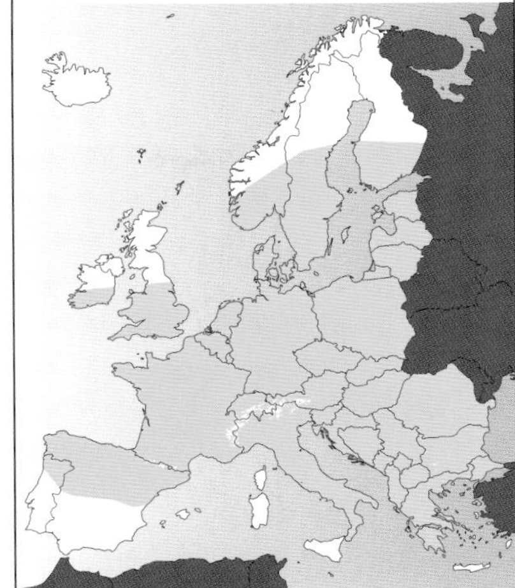

Range of *Lasius fuliginosus*.

Lasius fuliginosus winged queen.

Three *Lasius fuliginosus* castes. From left to right: a queen, a male and three workers.

Lasius of the *alienus* group

subfamily Formicinae – subgenus *Lasius*

Lasius of the *alienus* group worker protecting aphids.

Identification

Size: 2.5–4.5 mm. Body entirely brown-black. No erect hairs on the scapes. Each mandible has at least eight teeth. This group contains four very similar species: *Lasius alienus* (Foerster, 1850), *L. paralienus* (Seifert, 1992), *L. piliferus* (Seifert, 1992) and *L. psammophilus* (Seifert, 1992). These species are differentiated by the density of hairs on the clypeus and the rest of the body. *Lasius piliferus* occurs in Spain and the south of France; the other species are widespread in Europe.

Possible confusion

Lasius niger and allies (*L. platythorax*, *L. cinereus* and *L. grandis*) have erect hairs on their scapes. *Lasius karpinisi* has a reddish mesosoma that contrasts with the brown of the head and

Swarming

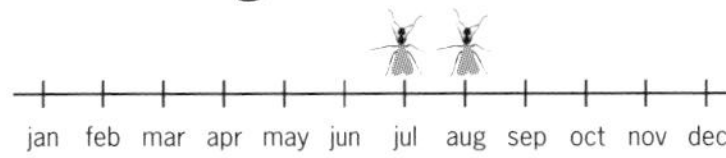

gaster. In *Lasius neglectus* and *L. lasioides* the hairs on the scape are all but invisible and each mandible has seven teeth.

Habitat

Open or partially open habitats: essentially sunny grasslands regardless of the amount of plant cover but with scattered trees. Rarely above 1,500 m altitude.

Where to look

Nests are under stones, sometimes directly in the ground – in which case there may be a mound of soil. Workers search for food on the ground or on plants.

Biology

Common species. Nest density may be very high, which may make them the dominant ant species of warm grasslands. Colonies may be polygynous and may have several thousand workers. They are omnivores but mainly feed on sugary substances. These species can be seen on various herbaceous plants and sometimes on trees on which they search for Hemiptera or extrafloral nectaries. They may also use root-dwelling aphids. They are parasitised by ants of the subgenus *Chthonolasius*, which uses them to form its own colonies by temporary social parasitism. Nests may be frequented by a small beetle *Claviger testaceus* that lives on the ant's broods. *Lasius alienus* is not aggressive, rarely biting if the nest is disturbed.

Distribution

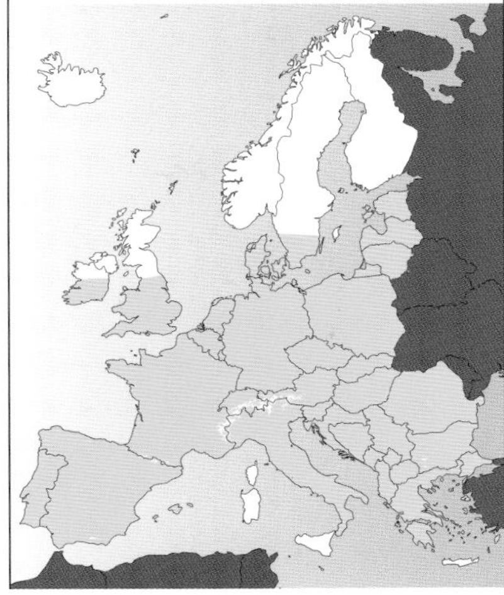

Range of *Lasius alienus*.

Lasius piliferus worker.

Lasius brunneus Latreille, 1798

subfamily Formicinae – subgenus *Lasius*

Lasius brunneus workers attending aphids.

Identification

Size: 2.5–4.5 mm. A bicoloured ant. The clearly brown-black gaster is darker than the rest of the body. The head is slightly darker than the mesosoma, which is pale brown to yellowish. There are no erect hairs on the scapes and the hairs of the scapes lie flat on the cuticle.

Possible confusion

Lasius brunneus shows characters that mean confusion with another species of *Lasius* is unlikely. *Lasius lasioides*, common, shares the same character of typically having hairs on the scapes lying against the cuticle but its body is entirely brownish-black. *Lasius emarginatus* is the only other species of obviously bicoloured *Lasius* but its mesosoma is clearly orange-red and its scape hairs are inclined. *Nylanderia jaegerskioeldi* is smaller and very hairy.

Habitat

A species that occurs in most habitats but depends on the presence of trees: forests, woodland edge, open areas with isolated trees, urban areas with trees. Occurs to 1,500 m altitude.

Swarming

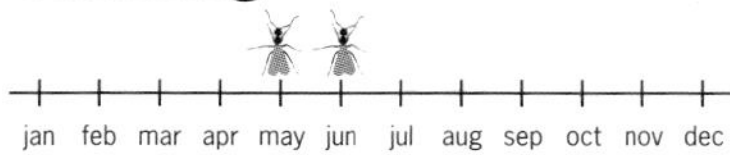

Where to look

Nests occur mainly in dead wood or in hollow cavities of live trees. They are also sometimes found under stones, in leaf litter or in house walls. Workers search for food on the ground and on trees and other plants.

Distribution

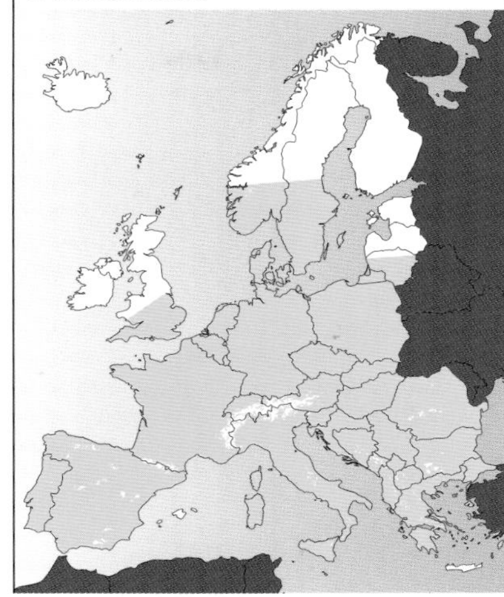

Range of *Lasius brunneus*.

Biology

A common species. Colonies are generally monogynous, with several thousand workers. They are omnivorous, with a preference for sugary substances. The species is often found on live tree trunks and various herbaceous plants in search of aphids and shield bugs.

Lasius brunneus worker carrying a cocoon.

Lasius emarginatus Olivier, 1792

subfamily Formicinae – subgenus *Lasius*

Lasius emarginatus worker.

Identification

Size: 2.5–5 mm. A bicoloured ant with a brown-black head and gaster and orangy-red mesosoma. It has obviously inclined hairs on the scapes and tibiae. A very closely related species occurs in the Balkans, *Lasius illyricus* (Zimmermann, 1935), but this latter species is less hairy on the scapes. *Lasius karpinisi* (Seifert, 1992) occurs in Greece and has a colouration similar to that of *L. emarginatus* but can be recognised by the absence of erect hairs on the scape.

Possible confusion

The obviously bicoloured aspect of *Lasius emarginatus* and its erect, inclined hairs on the scapes allows for an easy separation from other species in the genus *Lasius*.

Swarming

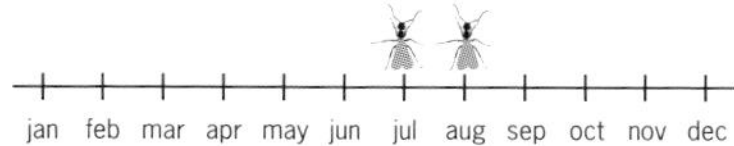

Habitat

Urban areas and villages: inside houses, old walls, green spaces, greenhouses. In the north, in natural habitats the species occupies naturally warm sites: cliffs and the like. It is far more widespread in the south: grasslands, woodland edges, forests. It rarely occurs above 1,500 m.

Where to look

Nests are usually built in natural cavities, hollows in old walls, stone buildings and rock faces, dead wood and the hollow trunks of live trees. Workers search for food on the ground, on walls and rocks as well as on plants. They often form trails to food sources.

Biology

A very common species. Colonies are monogynous and contain several thousand workers. Founding is independent, usually by a single queen. An omnivore, although it feeds essentially on Hemiptera honeydew. It often forms trails from the colony to aphids or scale insects on vegetation. It is an aggressive species, biting if the nest is interfered with.

Distribution

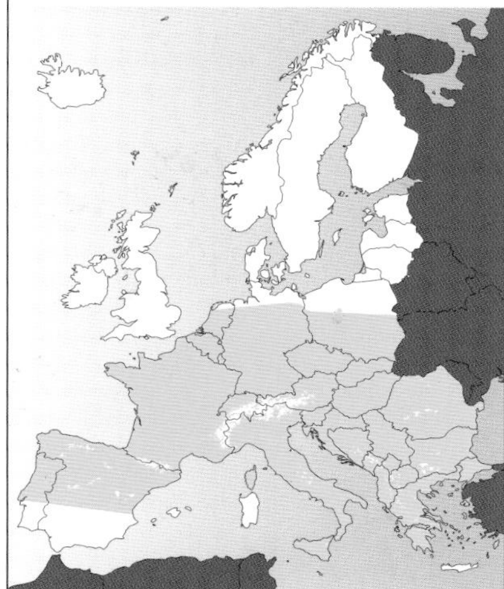

Range of *Lasius emarginatus*.

Lasius emarginatus worker.

Lasius emarginatus workers in the centre of a brood.

Lasius of the **grandis** group

subfamily Formicinae – subgenus *Lasius*

Lasius cinereus worker.

Identification

Size: 2.5–5 mm. The body is generally dark but populations with paler individuals exist. There are many long, erect hairs on the scapes. The hairs on the clypeus are not very dense. This group is more diverse in the west of the Mediterranean Basin. It is represented by three species: *Lasius grandis* (Forel, 1909) in the Iberian Peninsula and the south of France and the west Mediterranean islands; *L. cinereus* (Seifert, 1992) also in the Iberian Peninsula and the south of France, distinguished by a paler and very matt mesosoma; *L. balearicus* (Talavera, Espadaler & Vila, 2014) described from Majorca in the Balearic islands.

Possible confusion

These *Lasius* species can be confused with *L. niger* and *L. platythorax*.

Swarming

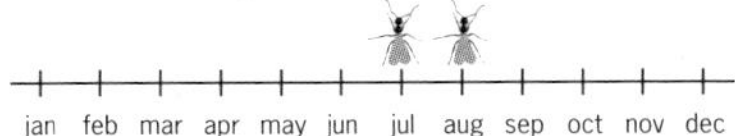

Lasius grandis worker.

Habitat

Widespread species, found to an altitude of 1,500 m. *Lasius cinereus* prefers very dry areas with little vegetation; it is the most drought-resistant *Lasius*.

Where to look

Nests are generally in the form of a small dome of earth and mineral particles. They may also be found under stones, in walls or directly in the ground, with a simple hole as an entrance. Workers search for food on the ground or on trees and other vegetation.

Distribution

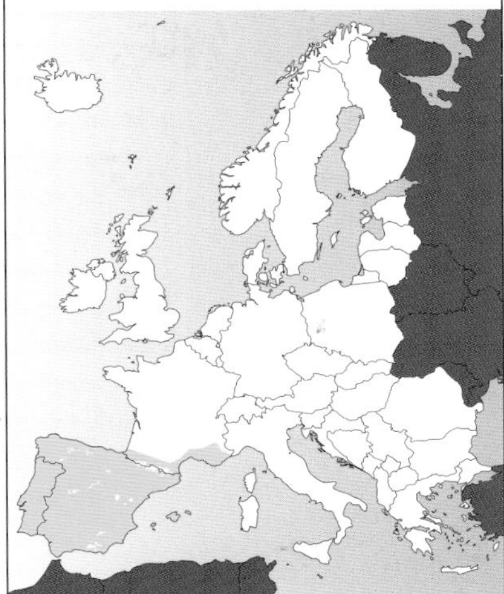

Range of *Lasius* species of the *grandis* group.

Lasius cinereus workers soliciting aphids in order to obtain honeydew.

Biology

Very common species in the west Mediterranean region. Nest density can be very high. Colonies are monogynous, with several thousand workers. Founding is independent, with several queens associating. As soon as the first workers emerge they kill all the queens but one. Omnivorous species. *Lasius* species of the *grandis* group actively search for aphid honeydew in the herbaceous layer. They protect any aphid and scale bug colonies they find. They also feed from extrafloral nectaries.

Lasius lasioides Emery, 1869

subfamily Formicinae – subgenus *Lasius*

Lasius lasioides worker.

Identification

Size: 2.5–4.5 mm. Entire body brown. No erect hairs on the scapes and the hair cover on the scapes, which is difficult to see, lies on the cuticle.

Possible confusion

This species is widely distributed throughout the Mediterranean zone. It can be distinguished from *Lasius brunneus*, which has similar habits, by its having an entirely dark body and a narrower head. Species of the *turcicus* group have a paler body and more hairs on the sides of the head.

Habitat

A species very much dependent on the presence of trees: forest, woodland edge, open habitats with isolated trees and urban areas with trees. Only found in the Mediterranean region.

Swarming

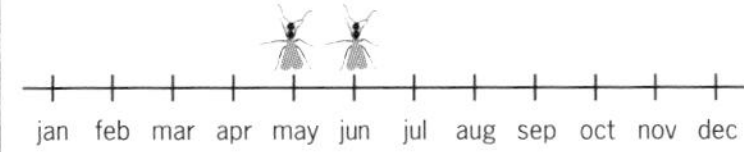

Lasius lasioides worker.

Where to look

Nests are nearly always in dead wood or in the hollow cavities of living trees. They can occasionally be found under stones or in plant litter. Workers search for their food on the ground and on trees and other plants.

Biology

Quite common species in Southern Europe. Colonies are generally monogynous, with several thousand workers. An omnivore with a preference for sugary substances. The species can commonly be seen on the trunks of trees as well as various herbaceous plant species in its search for aphids or scale bugs.

Distribution

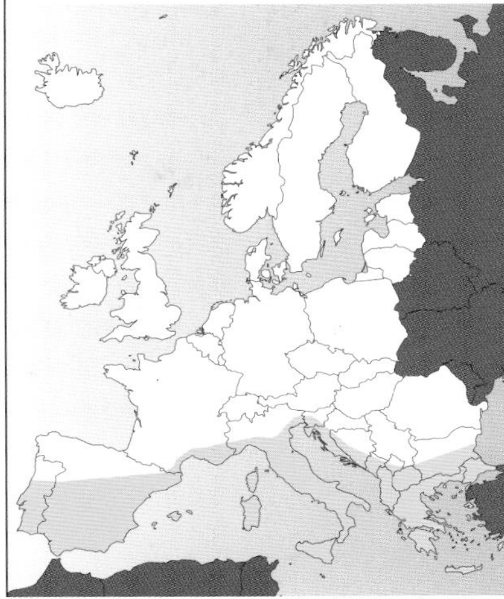

Range of *Lasius lasioides*.

Lasius lasioides workers on a woodland floor.

Lasius niger Linnaeus, 1758

subfamily Formicinae – subgenus *Lasius*

Lasius niger worker.

Identification

Size: 2.5–5 mm. The body is mainly black, sometimes with a hint of brown on the mesosoma. The scapes have numerous erect hairs. Dense hairs on the clypeus.

Possible confusion

Several species of *Lasius* have a morphology similar to that of *L. niger*: *L. platythorax* and species in the *grandis* group have obviously less dense hairs on the clypeus than *L. niger*. *Lasius cinereus* has a paler mesosoma with a very matt tegument.

Habitat

Urban areas, parks, gardens, other human-modified habitats and cultivated areas. In natural habitats it has a preference for meadows. To 1,500 m in altitude.

Where to look

Nests are usually formed of a small mound of soil and mineral particles. They can also be encountered under stones, under flower pots, in cracks in pavements or directly in the ground, their opening being a simple hole. Workers hunt for food on the ground or on plants.

Swarming

jan feb mar apr may jun jul aug sep oct nov dec

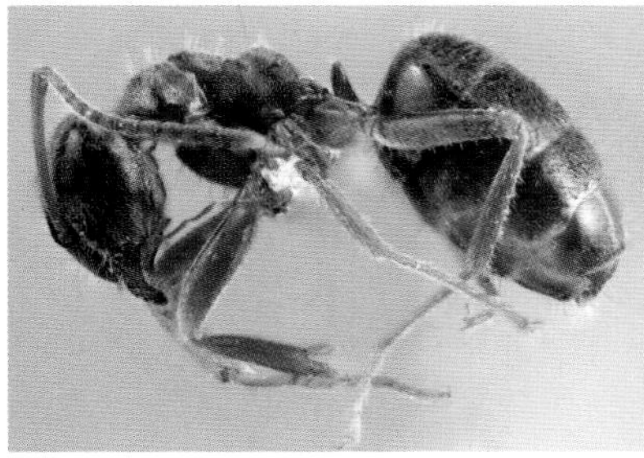

Lasius niger worker.

Distribution

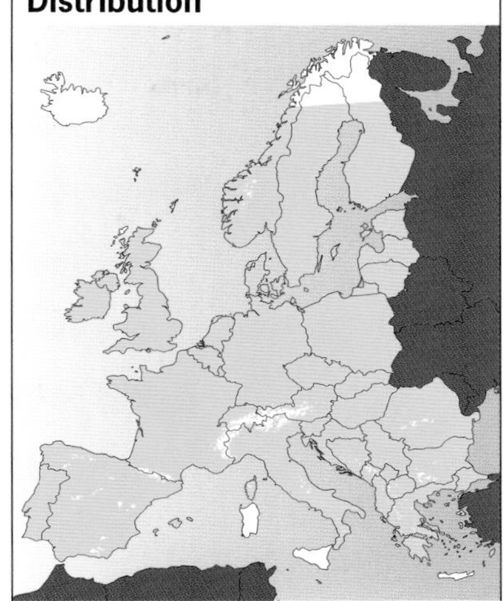

Range of *Lasius niger*.

Biology

A very common species, except in the Mediterranean region where it appears to be replaced by *Lasius grandis* and *L. cinereus*. Nest density can be very high, especially in urban and cultivated areas. Colonies are monogynous and contain many thousands of workers. Founding is independent by the association of several queens. Once the first workers have emerged they kill all queens except one, the most prolific. An omnivorous species, it actively searches for aphid honeydew on trees, bushes and herbaceous plants. It protects the aphid and scale insect colonies it finds. It also takes extrafloral nectar. A very aggressive species which bites if the nest is disturbed.

Lasius niger worker.

Lasius platythorax Seifert, 1991

subfamily Formicinae – subgenus *Lasius*

Winged *Lasius platythorax* female preparing for her nuptial flight.

Identification

Size: 2.5–5 mm. The body is mainly black, occasionally paler on the mesosoma. The scapes have numerous erect hairs. Smooth areas of the tegument appear through the sparse hairs on the clypeus.

Possible confusion

In most of Europe, *Lasius niger* is the only species that can be confused with *L. platythorax*. The main difference is the density of hair covering on the clypeus, which is much denser in *L. niger*. There are also differences in the ecological requirements of the two species. In the west of the Mediterranean Basin, species of the *grandis* group also have sparse hairs on the clypeus but the scapes are longer.

Habitat

Wooded environments, woodland edges; wetlands, marshes and peat bogs.

Swarming

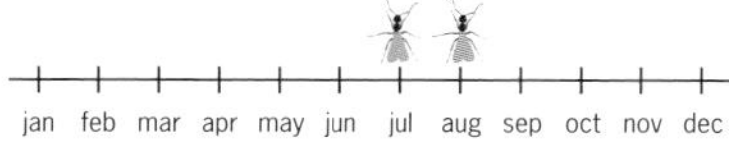

Where to look

In forests, nests are generally constructed in tree stumps or dead branches on the ground. *Lasius platythorax* does not build a dome of earth as *L. niger* does. Workers search for food on the ground or on plants.

Distribution

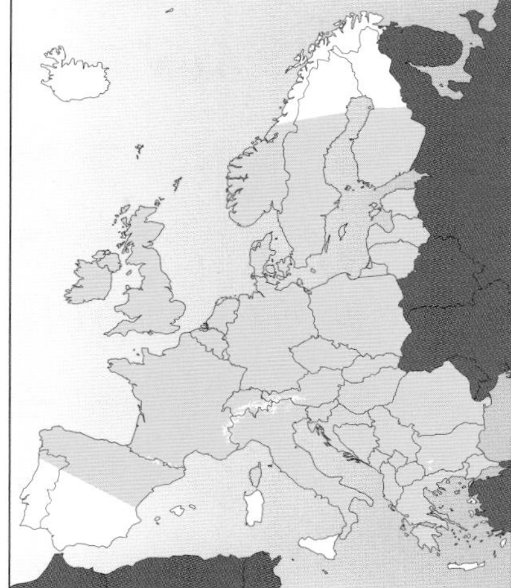

Range of *Lasius platythorax*.

Biology

A very common species throughout Europe, although less frequent in the Mediterranean zone. Colonies are monogynous, with several thousand workers. Founding is independent by the association of several queens. Once the first workers emerge they kill all queens but one, the most fertile. An omnivorous species. This species actively searches for aphid honeydew on trees, bushes and herbaceous plants. It protects aphid and scale bug colonies. It is as aggressive as *Lasius niger*. It is possible to find dipteran larvae such as species of the genus *Microdon* in *Lasius platythorax* nests; Microdon larvae eat the young ants.

Lasius platythorax workers.

Lasius platythorax workers communicating using their antennae.

Lasius of the ***turcicus*** group

subfamily Formicinae – subgenus *Lasius*

Lasius neglectus worker tending a larva.

Identification

Size: 2.5–3.5 mm. Body uniform brown to pale brown. No erect hairs on the scapes, hairs on the body difficult to distinguish. Each mandible generally has less than eight teeth. This group is of eastern origin. *Lasius turcicus* (Santschi, 1921) occurs in the south-east of the Balkans. *Lasius austriacus* (Schlick-Steiner, 2003) has been described from Austria. *Lasius neglectus* (Van Loon, Boomsma & Andrasfalvy, 1990) is an invasive species that has been noted in several European countries and which can become very abundant locally.

Possible confusion

The other species of *Lasius* can be distinguished by the character of the hairs, as presented in the species key.

Habitat

Lasius neglectus can be found in all natural and urban habitats. On the Mediterranean coast it enters into competition with *Linepithema humile*. Elsewhere in Europe it is rarer and more or less associated with urban habitats.

Swarming

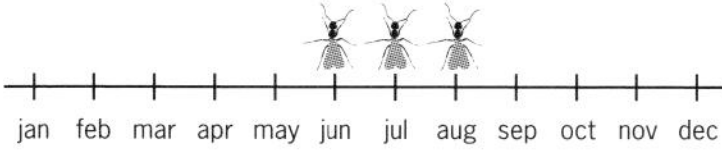

Sexual individuals in the nest June to August.

Where to look

Nests occur in the ground, under stones, in dead wood, under paving slabs, under asphalt or in walls. Workers forage for food on the ground or on plants.

Biology

Lasius neglectus colonies are very polygynous and have several thousand workers. The species can form super-colonies containing hundreds of queens and many hundreds of thousands of workers. They then become dominant, with a high nest density. The new queens stay in their natal nest or found a new colony by budding. The rapid increase in frequency of the species appears to be related mainly to their accidental transportation due to human activity. Apparently there is no nuptial flight but queens are physically capable of flight and in laboratory conditions capable of founding a new colony independently. It is possible that natural habitats with little human interference may be colonised in the same way. An omnivorous species, it exploits all available food sources. It is particularly attracted by Hemiptera honeydew, the producers of which it defends effectively.

Distribution

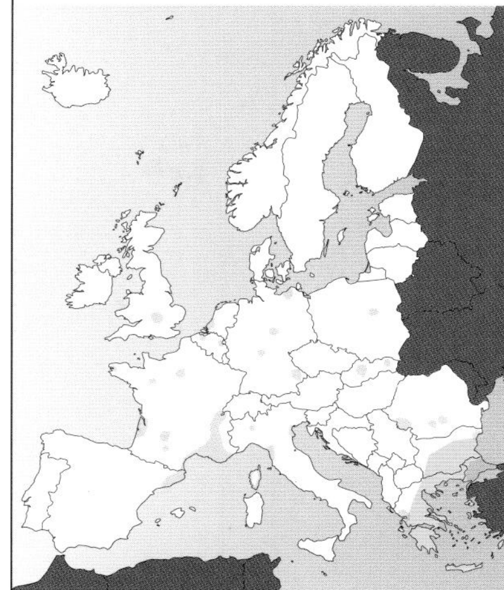

Range of *Lasius turcicus* (pink) and *L. neglectus* (grey).

Lasius turcicus workers, with gasters filled with honeydew.

***Lepisiota* genus** Santschi, 1926

subfamily Formicinae

Lepisiota frauenfeldi workers on a tree.

Identification

Size: 2–3 mm. A shiny mesosoma which can be red with blackish tints or entirely black. All appendages are very long. There are spines on the propodeum. There are some 80 species in the genus, distributed mainly in tropical and subtropical parts of Africa and Asia. Only six species have been identified in the Mediterranean Basin. *Lepisiota nigra* (Dalla Torre, 1893) and *L. splendens* (Karavaiev, 1912) have entirely black bodies; *L. nigra* occurs in various countries from Spain to Greece, whereas *L. splendens* exists only in Greece and the south of Bulgaria. *Lepisiota melas* (Emery, 1915), present in Greece, has a few red spots on the mesosoma, and the other species have a mainly red mesosoma: *L. frauenfeldi* (Mayr, 1855) occurs in the south of Italy, Sicily, Andalusia and in the Balkans; *L. dolabellae* (Forel, 1911) and *L. caucasica* (Santschi, 1917) occur only in Greece.

Possible confusion

Workers of certain species of this genus can be confused with

Swarming

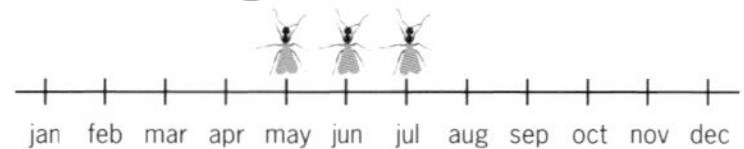

Five *Lepisiota nigra* queens with workers moving to another nest.

workers of the genus *Paratrechina* or small *Proformica* workers.

Habitat

In irrigated crops, gardens and wasteland and in open habitats (open hillsides and the like).

Where to look

Nests are 50 cm deep in the ground where it is humid. The nest entrance is in the form of a small hole or crack. Stones nearby may be used as solariums. Workers form harvesting columns as they forage on trees for food.

Biology

Quite a common species. Workers are very agile and active. They need quite a high level of humidity throughout the year, which they find in the soil. In winter, colonies form into balls under a stone. At the time of founding, colonies are monogynous; later they can adopt other queens. There may be as many as 50,000 workers in one colony. *Lepisiota niger* regularly changes site, when the whole colony moves a few metres in the middle of the day.

Distribution

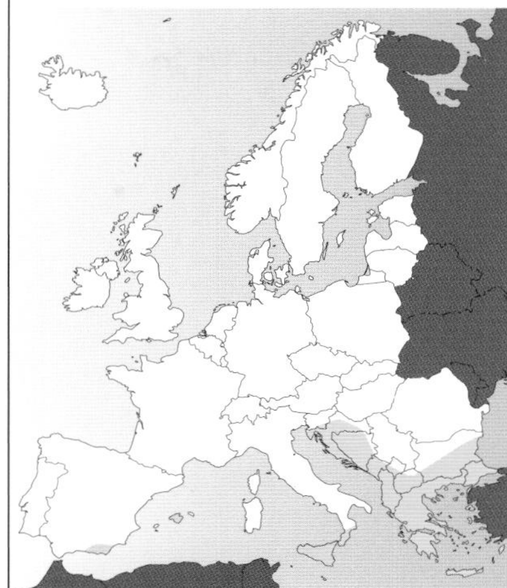

Range of the genus *Lepisiota*.

Lepisiota nigra worker.

Nylanderia genus Emery, 1906

subfamily Formicinae

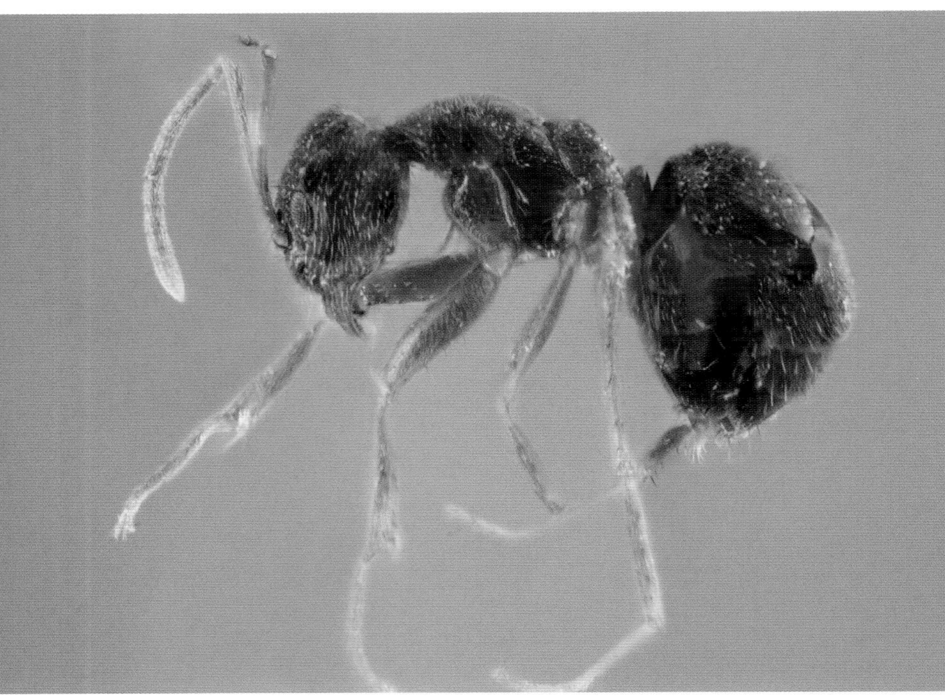

Nylanderia jaegerskioeldi worker.

Identification

Size: 2–3 mm. Quite pale brown body. Very hairy, with thick hairs over the whole body. A vast genus containing more than 100 species of mainly tropical distribution. Two species, probably introduced, are found in Southern Europe in human-made habitats: *Nylanderia jaegerskioeldi* (Mayr, 1904) and *N. vividula* (Nylander, 1846), which is smaller with an entirely pale brown body.

Possible confusion

Separated from *Paratrechina longicornis* by having shorter antennae, and from *Lasius* species by the hairs on its body.

Swarming

jan feb mar apr may jun jul aug sep oct nov dec

Nylanderia vividula queen.

Distribution

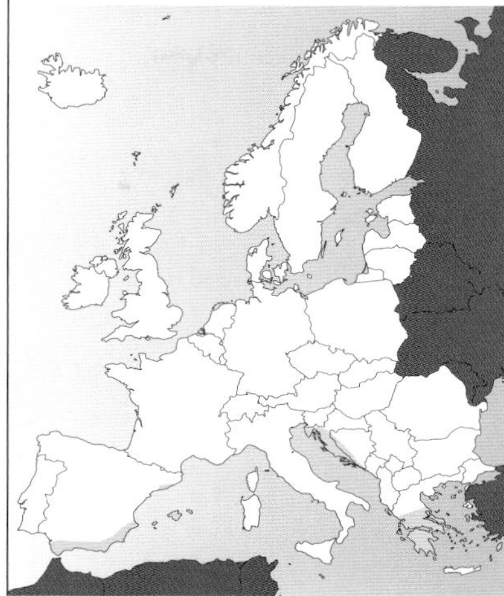
Range of the genus *Nylanderia*.

Habitat

On lawns, near pavements in towns and in public gardens. Sites must be humid or regularly watered.

Where to look

Workers form colonies on the ground or in trees. Nests are under rocks or in decomposing wood.

Biology

Colonies contain a queen and between a few dozen or a few hundred workers. Nests are temporary; the colony relocates regularly. They are active mainly at night. Broods of sexual individuals are produced in the spring. On the ground, workers move in a jerky fashion, by small circular movements, until they find a food source. Once a food source has been found, several more workers are quickly recruited. They exploit the honeydew of aphids on trees. They can be scavengers or predatory on various arthropods.

Nylanderia jaegerskioeldi worker feeding on a liquid.

***Paratrechina* genus** Motschoulsky, 1863

subfamily Formicinae

Paratrechina longicornis worker.

Identification

Size: 2.5–3 mm. Blackish-brown. An elongated thorax, often paler. This genus is distinguished by having very long antennae. *Paratrechina longicornis* (Latreille, 1802) is the only species of the genus present in Europe.

Possible confusion

Species of the genus *Nylanderia* were considered part of the genus *Paratrechina* in the past. They also have thick, erect hairs over the whole body but the antennae are shorter.

Habitat

Human-made environments: pavements, parks and gardens, hotels, restaurants and buildings on the Andalusian coast. Port towns in the Mediterranean Basin. In the rest of Europe *Paratrechina longicornis* can be found in heated greenhouses and other buildings.

Swarming

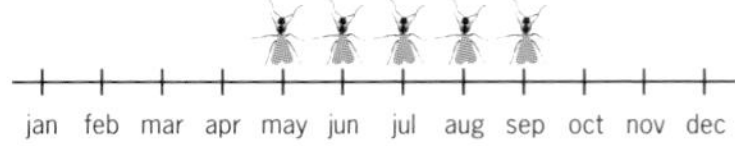

Distribution

Paratrechina longicornis worker.

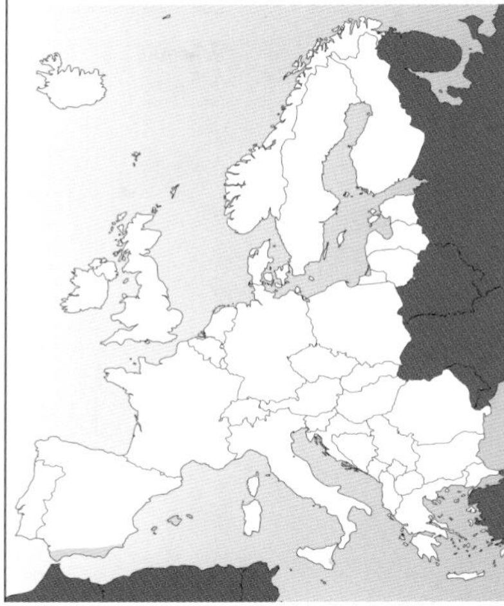
Range of *Paratrechina longicornis*.

Where to look

Nests are under pavements, concrete slabs, etc. Workers forage for food in rubbish bins.

Biology

Paratrechina longicornis is a cosmopolitan, tropical species and considered one of the most invasive ant species in the world. It arrives in ports and towns from boats and quickly becomes resident if the climate is favourable. Plant importation is another means of dissemination. The species is highly polygynous. The production of sexual individuals is continuous, as long as temperatures permit. Mating occurs in the nest (intranidal) without a nuptial flight. This ant rears aphids and scale bugs, from which it takes honeydew. Recruiting of other workers is very rapid. Due to its erratic, jerky movements it is given the name 'the crazy black ant'. It moves very quickly on its long legs.

Paratrechina longicornis workers.

Plagiolepis genus Mayr, 1861 and *Acropyga* genus Roger, 1862 subfamily Formicinae

Plagiolepis sp. workers.

Identification

Size: 1.5–2.5 mm. Black body, sometimes slightly beige in *Plagiolepis* and yellowish in *Acropyga*. There are some 60 species of the genus *Plagiolepis* distributed in temperate and tropical areas of Africa and Asia. At least nine species occur in Europe, of which four are parasitic – they are considered on page 234. The main characteristics that separate *Plagiolepis* species are the size of parts of the funiculus and hair density on the gaster. In the *Plagiolepis pygmaea* (Latreille, 1798), widely distributed across Europe, and *P. karawajewi* (Radchenko, 1989), recorded from Greece, the third segment of the funiculus is short, almost the same length as the second. In the other species, *Plagiolepis taurica* (Santschi, 1920) (= *P. vindobonensis* [Lomnicki, 1925]) from Central and Southern Europe, *P. pallescens* (Forel, 1889), from the Balkans and *P. schmitzii* (Forel, 1895) from the south of the Iberian Peninsula, the third segment of the funiculus is longer and has a rectangular shape. There are dense hairs on the gaster of *Plagiolepis schmitzii*, which are less dense in *P. taurica* and *P. pallescens*. *Acropyga palearctica* (Menozzi, 1936) is endemic to Greece, in pine woods. This species lives underground, only surfacing during nuptial flights. The eyes are very small and composed of just a few ommatidia.

Possible confusion

Plagiolepis and *Acropyga* species are the only Formicinae that are under 3 mm. Ants of the genus *Plagiolepis* can be confused with *Tapinoma pygmaeum* workers, but are mainly distinguished by the number of parts in the antennae.

Habitat

Plagiolepis species occupy dry forest in the south of Europe, also dykes, sides of tracks and unused ground with undisturbed soils found to an altitude of 1,500 m.

Swarming

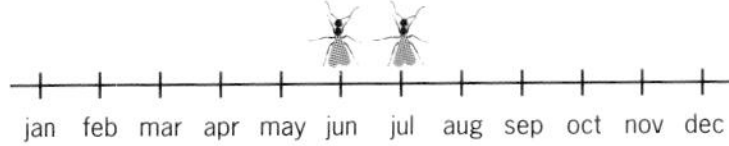

Plagiolepis pallescens worker.

Where to look

Plagiolepis nests occur under stones or in rock crevices, more rarely directly in the ground or in dead wood. Workers forage individually on rocks, low vegetation or in the ground litter. They are one of the first ant species to be active after winter.

Biology

Plagiolepis species are common, particularly in Mediterranean forests where nest density can be high (as many as four or five nests per square metre). Colonies are polygynous and contain several thousand workers. Founding can be independent or by budding. A single colony may form several satellite nests that come together at the end of summer to pass the winter. These omnivorous ants forage for small arthropods and especially favour sugary substances (aphid honeydew, nectar). Some workers store liquids in their crops and have distended gasters. They can be parasitised by red mites which appear large compared to these small ants.

Distribution

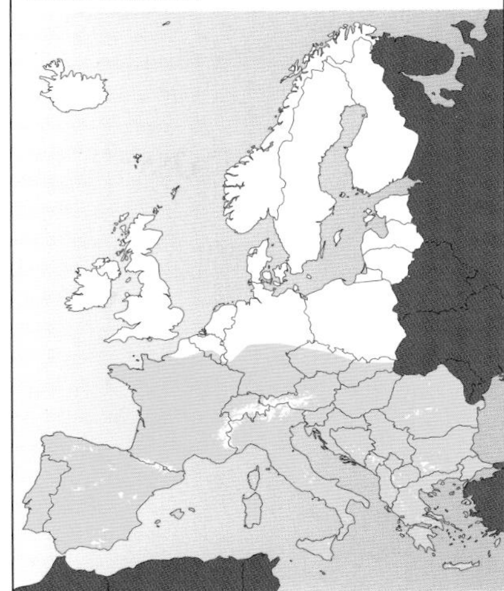

Range of *Plagiolepis* species.

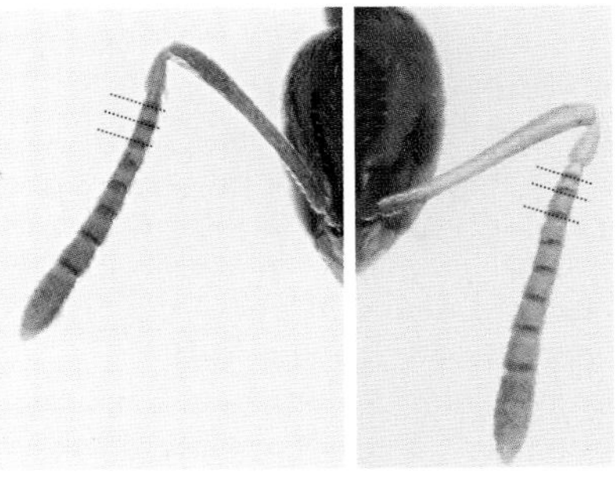

Comparison of the funiculus section sizes in *Plagiolepis taurica* (left) and *P. pygmaea* (right).

Parasite **Plagiolepis** species

subfamily Formicinae

Plagiolepis xene (arrowed) in a *P. pygmaea* colony.

Identification

Parasite species produce few or no workers. Males and queens are very similar in shape, size and colour: 1.2–1.6 mm, with a brown body. Males of certain species are wingless. *Plagiolepis xene* (Staercke, 1936) appears to be the most widespread parasitic species in Europe. *Plagiolepis delaugerrei* (Casevitz-Weulersse, 2014) only occurs on Corsica, where it parasitises *P. taurica*; it has no teeth on the mandibles. *Plagiolepis ampeloni* (Faber, 1969) occurs in Austria, and parasitises *P. taurica*. *Plagiolepis grassei* (Le Masne, 1956) occurs in the south of France and the Iberian Peninsula, where it is very rare. The queens of this latter species are slightly larger (1.9 mm), and it is different

Swarming

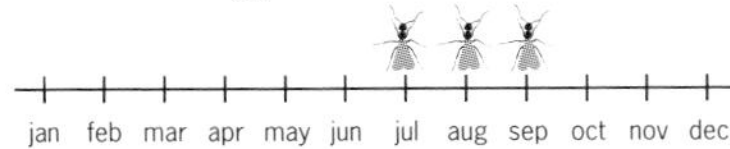

from the others in that it can produce workers.

Possible confusion

Queens are hardly any bigger than the host workers, which makes them hard to find in the field. Under a magnifying glass they are easily recognised, as the thorax is wider than that of host workers.

Habitat

They are found in the same habitat as their hosts (*Plagiolepis pygmaea* and *P. taurica*).

Where to look
In *Plagiolepis* nests.

Biology

Rare species that parasitise other members of the genus *Plagiolepis*. Nest density is low. Parasitised nests can contain several dozen parasite queens. Queens only produce sexual offspring (except for *Plagiolepis grassei*) and do not kill the host queens. Thus, the host workers care for the brood and adults of the parasite species. The queens are less active than the host workers and sometimes lie alongside host queens. Winged males and queens can be found throughout the summer in *Plagiolepis* nests.

Distribution

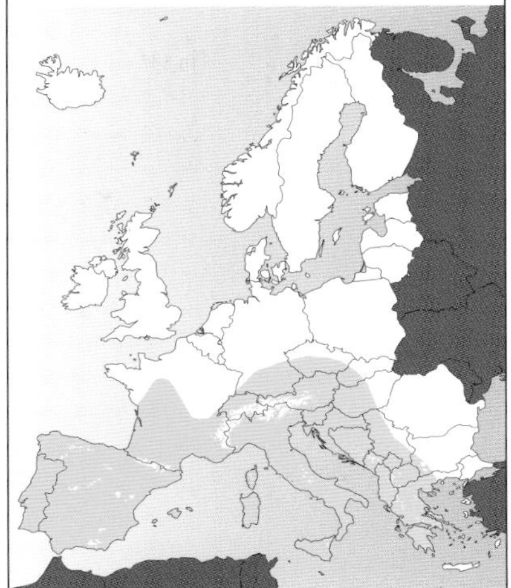

Range of parasite *Plagiolepis* species.

Two *Plagiolepis xene* queens.

Polyergus genus Latreille, 1804

subfamily Formicinae

Polyergus rufescens worker.

Identification

Size: 5–7 mm. This large ant is entirely a uniform orange-red and very active. Its mandibles are sabre-shaped. Only one species from this genus occurs in Europe: *Polyergus rufescens* (Latreille, 1798).

Possible confusion

Polyergus rufescens cannot be confused with any other species.

Habitat

Polyergus rufescens is found in the same habitats as its hosts (species in the subgenus *Serviformica*), at all altitudes.

Where to look

Nests occur directly in the ground or under a stone. In the nest, *Polyergus rufescens* workers mix with the host workers (subgenus *Serviformica*) and

Swarming

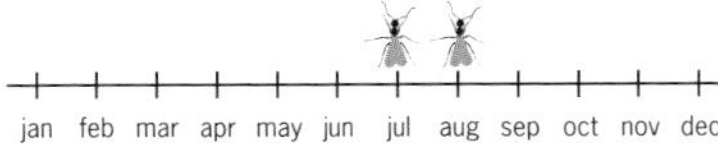

are readily distinguished because they are entirely orange. During a raid, when workers hope to provide the colony with host workers, is the easiest time to find *Polyergus* workers outside the nest. These raids are easily detected if the observer is lucky enough to encounter one, as they involve hundreds of workers moving in the same direction en masse.

Biology

Polyergus rufescens is a rare slavemaker species that parasitises *Formica* species of the subgenus *Serviformica* and particularly *F. fusca*, *F. rufibarbis* and *F. cunicularia*. Nests are usually widely separated and at a low density. Colonies are monogynous and may contain as many as a thousand workers. Once mated, the new queen tries to introduce herself into a *Serviformica* colony. If she is successful, she quickly kills the host queen or queens by piercing their heads with her sabre-shaped mandibles. Next she rubs herself against the dead queen and licks her intensively in order to acquire her odour. These actions are essential as they allow the parasite queen to be definitively accepted by the host workers. The *Polyergus* workers do not occupy themselves with the brood and are fed via trophallaxis by host workers. Their main activity is to make raids in order to provide the colony with host pupae. Raids normally take place in summer during the late afternoon. A large proportion of the *Polyergus* workers of a nest participate in the raid. They may aim for *Serviformica* colonies up to 100 m from the nest.

Distribution

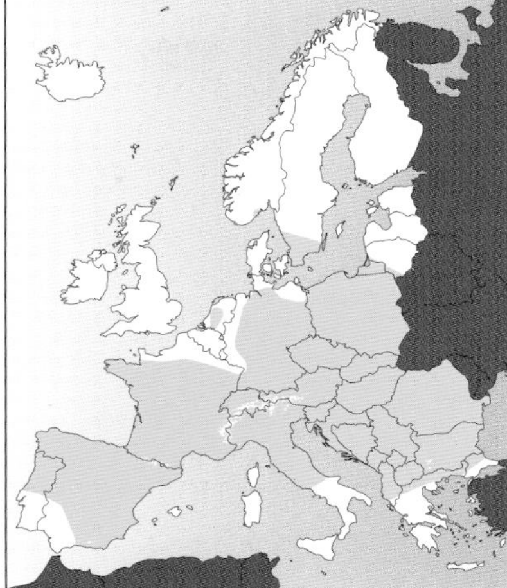

Range of *Polyergus rufescens*.

Polyergus rufescens workers with *Formica cunicularia* workers.

Prenolepis genus Mayr, 1861

subfamily Formicinae

Prenolepis nitens worker.

Identification

Size: 3–3.8 mm. The head and mesosoma are brownish-red. The vertex and gaster are dark brown. There are numerous erect hairs on the scapes, legs and gaster. The body is shiny. The deep depression in the mesosoma is comparable to that in *Lasius* species. Very long scapes. A large, heart-shaped gaster. *Prenolepis nitens* (Mayr, 1853) is the only species of the genus present in Europe.

Swarming

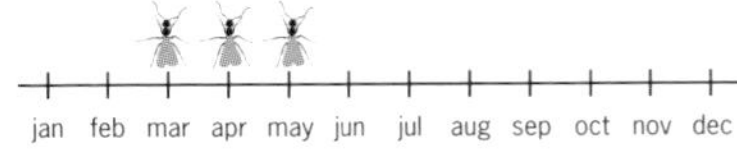

Possible confusion

This species can be confused with species of *Lasius*, *Lepisiota* or *Nylanderia*, from which it can be distinguished by using the characters given in the key.

Habitat

Forest edges and copses. Open habitats.

Where to look

Nests are in the ground, under stones, in tree roots or hollows in rotten wood – places where they are sheltered from frost and can find moisture.

Biology

Prenolepis nitens is considered to be associated with humans. It is susceptible to hard winter weather. Colonies can be very populous. Workers eat fruit, flower nectar, honeydew and elaiosomes of seeds. Some workers perform the function of 'honeypots', storing reserves in their gaster which dilates to become spherical and partly transparent due to the stretching on the inter-segment membranes. Sexual individuals emerge in late summer to pass the winter in the nest; they swarm in the spring.

Distribution

Range of *Prenolepis nitens*.

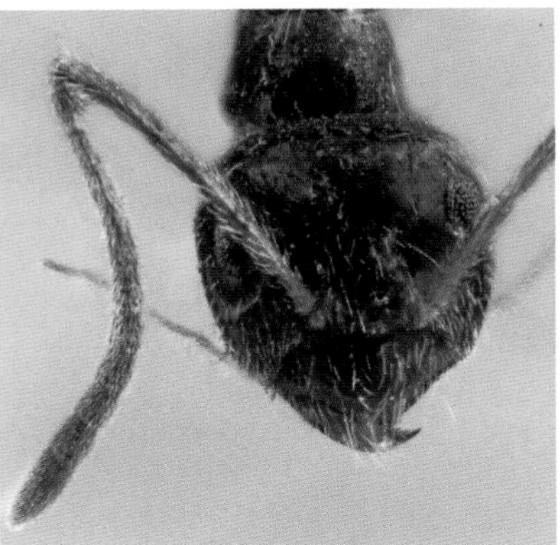

Head of *Prenolepis nitens* worker.

Proformica genus Ruzsky, 1902

subfamily Formicinae

Proformica sp. minor worker.

Proformica sp. major worker 'honey pot'.

Identification

Size: 3–7 mm, with much variation within the same nest. Body with a graceful aspect, totally black and quite shiny. Taxonomy of the *Proformica* is still quite confused and identification risky until a revised taxonomy of the genus exists. Actually, the genus occurs in two different zones in Europe: one in the East (Greece, Bulgaria, Romania, etc.); the second in the West (Portugal, Spain and the south of France). In the eastern zone at least five species have been recorded: *Proformica nitida* (Kuznetsov-Ugamsky, 1923), *P. oculatissima* (Forel, 1886) known only from a male, *P. striaticeps* (Forel, 1911), *P. korbi* (Emery, 1909) and *P. kobachidzei* (Arnol'di, 1968). In Western Europe there are at least three species: *Proformica ferreri* (Bondroit, 1918) and *P. longiseta* (Collingwood, 1978) in Spain, and *P. nasuta* (Nylander, 1856) described from the south of France.

Possible confusion

Species of the genus *Cataglyphis* have similar habits and general aspect but are obviously bigger. Small *Proformica* workers could be confused with *Tapinoma* and *Lepisiota* species which are found in the same habitats, but the latter do not have an elongated head. *Camponotus piceus* has a concave propodeum.

Swarming

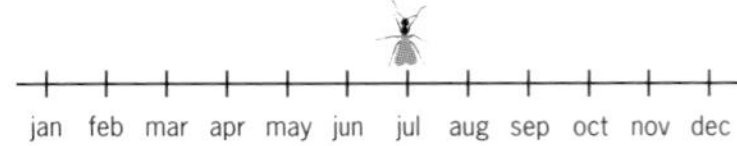

Habitat

Warm, open habitats, well exposed and of Mediterranean influence. Steppe-like habitats, garrigue, rocky or grassy ridges, gravel pits, tracks and unmade footpaths. From lowlands to mountainous areas.

Where to look

Nests are directly in the ground, the entrance being a simple hole, sometimes under a stone. The nest goes deep into the soil by a more or less vertical tunnel. Workers forage on the ground and are most active during the hottest part of the day.

Biology

Not very common. Usually forming small, isolated populations. Nest density can be very high locally, however. Colonies are polygynous and contain a few hundred workers. Foraging workers are generally small, often with a very elongated head. Large workers may assume the role of 'honeypots'; they stay in the nest and stock liquid food in their very inflated gasters.

Distribution

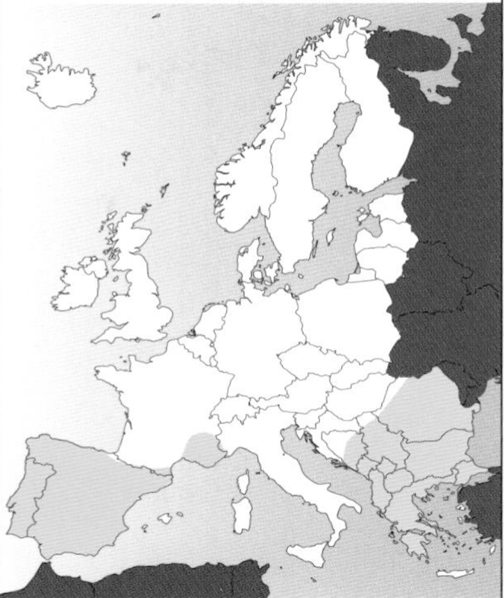

Range of *the* genus *Proformica*.

Different castes of a *Proformica* sp. colony: a queen (left), a male (right) and two workers (centre). The worker above has the role of a 'honeypot' – its gaster is extended as it is filled with liquid food.

Rossomyrmex genus Arnol'di, 1928

subfamily Formicinae

Rossomyrmex minuchae worker.

Identification

Size: 5–7 mm. Entirely brown body, shiny tegument. Long, erect hairs on the body. Occipital part of the head very concave. There are only four species in this genus worldwide, one of which occurs in the Sierra de Nevada in Andalusia: *Rossomyrmex minuchae* (Tinaut, 1981).

Possible confusion

Rossomyrmex minuchae cannot be confused with any other species.

Habitat

Between 1,800 and 2,200 m in the Andalusian sierras. Localised in arid areas; open, short grassland and other steppe-like habitats at altitude.

Where to look

In *Proformica* nests.

Biology

Rossomyrmex minuchae is a rare slavemaker species that only

Swarming

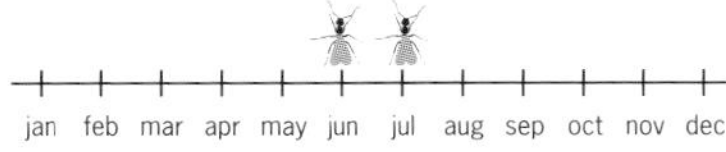

Proformica longiseta colony, potential host of *Rossomyrmex minuchae.*

parasitises *Proformica longiseta* colonies. A *Rossomyrmex* colony is monogynous, usually with less than 200 workers. Generally in a nest there are five times as many host workers as parasite workers. Once fertilised by a single male, the *Rossomyrmex minuchae* queen searches for a *Proformica longiseta* nest. In order to stop the invasion, *Proformica* workers close the nest entrance with earth. Once the *Rossomyrmex* queen penetrates the nest, she kills the host queens with her mandibles but does not touch the workers. The parasite queen lays her eggs, which are tended by the

Distribution

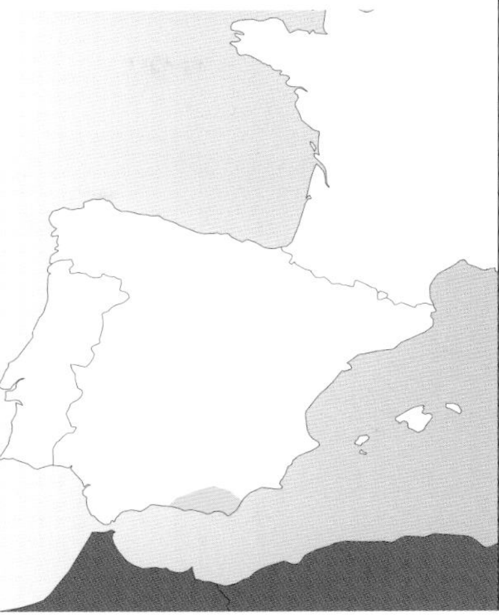

Range of *Rossomyrmex minuchae.*

The Sierra de Nevada (Spain) biotope, home to *Rossomyrmex minuchae.*

Proformica workers. The raids made by the *Rossomyrmex* workers on a nearby host colony may occur over two or three days.

Leptanilla genus Emery, 1870

subfamily Leptanillinae

Leptanilla revelierii worker.

Identification

A very small ant (1.2 mm) which lives underground and is blind. Body totally pale yellow. The tegument is shiny and very finely spotted. Mandibles have four teeth. Of the 45 species of the genus *Leptanilla*, seven occur in Europe. Some are only known from males or small numbers of workers; data are too fragmented to make an identification key of European species. *Leptanilla revelierii* (Emery, 1870) recorded from Corsica may be present in the south of France; *L. doderoi* (Emery, 1915) is recorded from Sardinia; *L. poggii* (Mei, 1995) is recorded from the island of Pantelleria in the south of Italy; and four species have been recorded in Spain: *L. charonea* (López, Martínez & Barandica, 1994); *L. plutonia* (López et al., 1994); *L. zaballosi* (López et al., 1994); *L. ortunoi* (López et al., 1994).

Possible confusion

Workers can be confused with small *Solenopsis* workers.

Swarming

Leptanilla revelierii worker.

Distribution

Range of the genus *Leptanilla*.

Habitat

Colonies have been found on the banks of temporary water courses with damp soil.

Where to look

Under large stones or directly in the ground.

Biology

These ants live underground and are very hard to find. They are nomadic, without a fixed nest. *Leptanillinae* feed on small arthropods, foraging individually or in groups. Queens have very extended gasters (an enormous abdomen, similar to egg-laying termites). Another characteristic of this genus is that queens drink the haemolymph (the 'blood') of their own larvae, which they then secrete through pores in the gaster. The queen's ovaries are then activated and she can start laying again between two migrations of the colony. *Leptanilla* males stridulate using a grooved structure situated on the fourth tergite.

Habitat used by *Leptanilla revelierii* in Corsica (France).

Aphaenogaster spinosa Emery, 1878 and ***A. iberica*** Emery, 1908

subfamily Myrmicinae

Aphaenogaster spinosa worker.

Identification

Size: 5–6 mm. Matt, black wrinkled head and thorax with a few fine hairs. An elongated head. These two species are recognised by the presence of very large spines on the propodeum. *Aphaenogaster spinosa* occurs in central Italy, Corsica and Sardinia; *A. iberica* occurs in the Iberian Peninsula.

Possible confusion

Numerous species of *Aphaenogaster* of the *testaceopilosa* group are easily confused with each other.

Habitat

Open habitats exposed to the sun: maquis, garrigue, fields with little bush cover, urban areas, scrub and so on. Warmth-loving species. Present from sea level to mountains.

Swarming

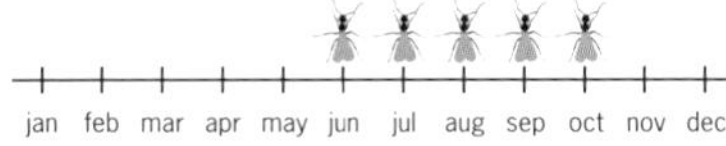

Sexual individuals occur in the nest from June to October.

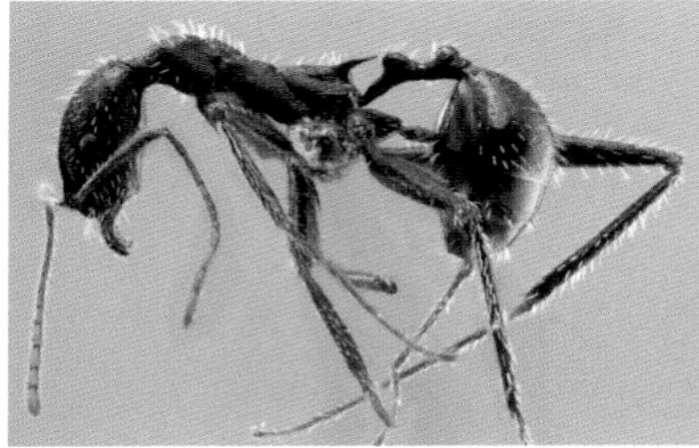

Aphaenogaster iberica worker.

Where to look
Nests are under stones in well-drained soils.

Biology

Nest density can be high. Nests are monogynous and very populous. There is no nuptial flight but mating occurs near the nest. Once mated, the new queen returns to the nest. A little later she leaves the nest with a group of workers and brood to form a new colony (multiplication by budding). They are omnivores and also feed their larvae with flower petals. Workers have a small crop, which limits the stocking of liquid food. Larvae feed directly on food brought back to the nest, without trophallaxis.

Distribution

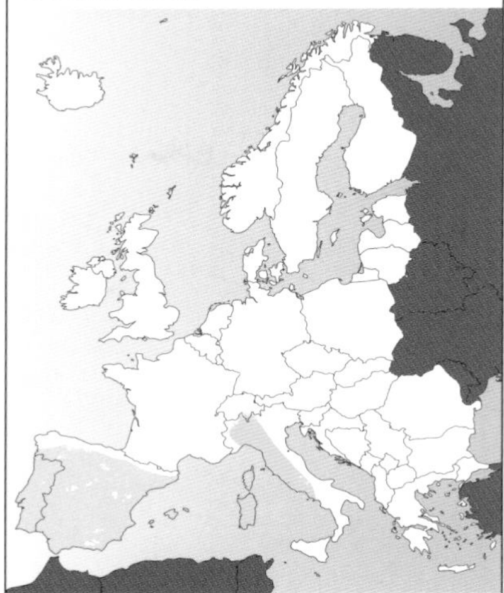

Range of *Aphaenogaster spinosa* (pink) and *A. iberica* (grey).

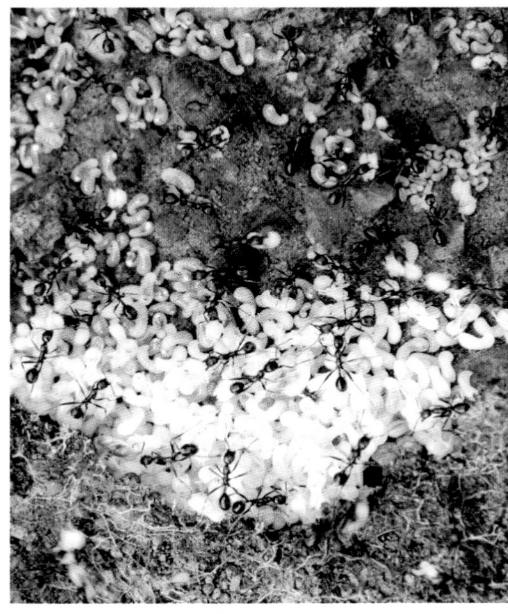

Aphaenogaster spinosa colony.

Aphaenogaster senilis Mayr, 1853

subfamily Myrmicinae

Aphaenogaster senilis colony.

Identification

Size: 6.5–7.5 mm. Very matt, black body, with thick white hairs. Thin, erect spines on the propodeum, very reduced in *Aphaenogaster gemella*. Five parts to the antennal club. *Aphaenogaster senilis* (Mayr, 1853) is quite common in Spain and along the coast of Mediterranean France as well as in southern Sardinia. *Aphaenogaster gemella* (Roger, 1862) is a related species that was introduced in the Balearic islands but has apparently disappeared since.

Possible confusion

Aphaenogaster gibbosa is smaller, less matt and the body is not covered with sparse, long white hairs. *Aphaenogaster iberica* has longer spines. The numerous species of *Aphaenogaster* of the *testaceopilosa* group are easily confused with each other.

Swarming

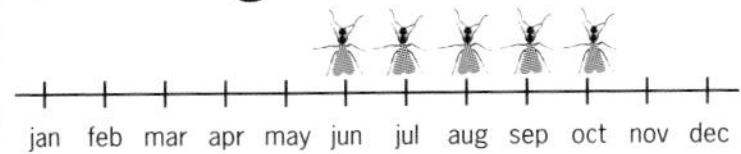

Distribution

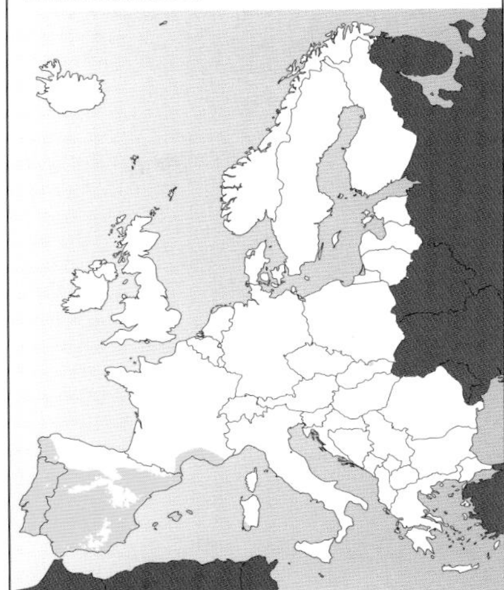
Range of *Aphaenogaster senilis*.

Habitat

Open habitats, well exposed, nearly flat, near the Mediterranean coast, and on the sides of sandy tracks and at the base of tamarisks. Colonies can occur in urban conditions. Normally at low altitudes, but as high as 600 m.

Where to look

Nests are directly in the ground or under stones. Rubble, asphalt debris, rubbish tips are all used. Workers forage on the ground.

Biology

Colonies are monogynous and very populous. Winged females have atrophied wings. Once mated, the new queen returns to the nest. She leaves a little while later with a group of workers and part of the brood in order to found a new colony (multiplication by budding). A varied diet. This species also feeds its larvae with flower petals. Workers have a very small crop, which only allows them to store small quantities of liquid food. Larvae feed directly on food placed near them. Sexual individuals are present in the nest from June to October.

Aphaenogaster senilis worker.

Aphaenogaster senilis worker.

Other species of ***Aphaenogaster*** of the ***testaceopilosa*** group

subfamily Myrmicinae

Aphaenogaster semipolita worker.

Identification

Size: 5–7 mm. Workers are a matt brown or black colour. The thorax is wrinkled with some fine sparse hairs. An elongated head. The propodeum spine is variable. The diversification of a group of the genus *Aphaenogaster* related to the North African *A. testaceopilosa* (Lucas, 1849) is centred on southern Italy and the Balkans. All these species are quite similar, distinguished by variations in the form of the tegument and body part proportions. These species have relatively restricted distributions: *Aphaenogaster inermita* (Bolton, 1995) in southern Calabria (extreme south of Italy) and on Malta; *A. melitensis* (Santschi, 1933) on Malta; *A. balcanica* (Emery, 1898) in the Balkans; *A. simonelli* (Emery, 1894) and *A. balcanicoides* (Boer, 2013) in Crete; *A. semipolita* (Nylander, 1856) in Sicily; *A. campana* (Emery, 1878) in the south of Italy; *A. picena* (Baroni Urbani, 1971) on the Dalmatian coast; *A. sporadis* (Santschi, 1933) on the eastern Greek islands; and

Swarming

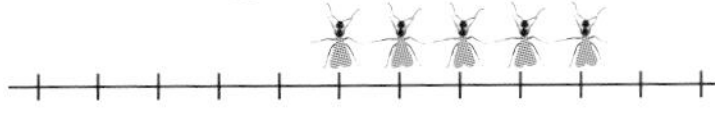

Sexual individuals are present in the nest from June to October.

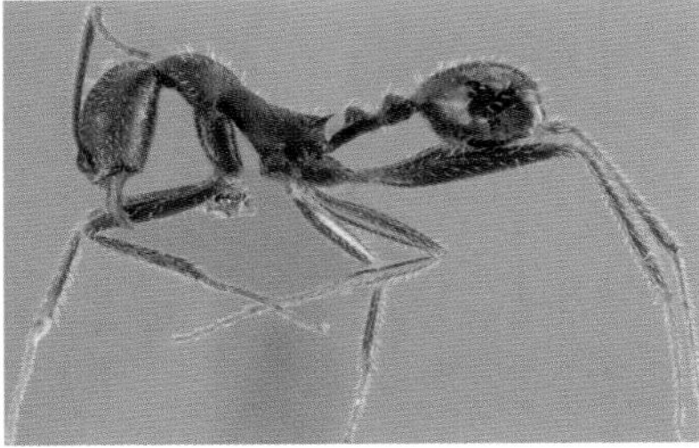

Aphaenogaster balcanica worker.

Distribution

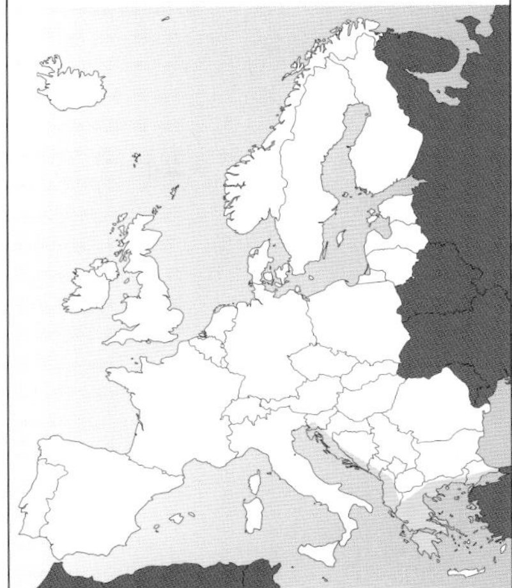

Range of *Aphaenogaster balcanica*.

A. karpathica (Boer, 2013) on the Greek island of Karpathos.

Possible confusion

Numerous species of *Aphaenogaster* of this group can easily be confused with one another.

Habitat

Open habitats, sunny sites: maquis, garrigue, fields with scattered bushes and urban areas. Heat-loving species.

Where to look

Nests in the ground, usually under a stone.

Aphaenogaster simonelli workers bringing an olive stone into their nest.

Biology

Common species. Workers forage individually on the ground, in plants and at the bottom of trees and shrubs. They move slowly in an uncertain manner, except when disturbed. They do not hesitate in capturing small individuals of *Messor* species near their nest entrance. Varied diet, to a great extent composed of small arthropods.

Aphaenogaster sardoa Mayr, 1853

subfamily Myrmicinae

Aphaenogaster sardoa worker.

Identification

Size: 5–6 mm. A quite large, almost spherical petiole. Scapes are longer than the occiput. There are very small, traversal stripes at the base of the gaster, and the rest of the body is slightly spotted. The propodeum is angular, with short spines. The head and mesosoma are a slightly rusty yellow. An elongated head. The mandibles, tibia and tarsi are yellowish. Contrary to other groups all castes are yellowish.

Possible confusion

There are no closely related species, which limits possible confusion. The tegument is matt, including most of the gaster. Other species of pale *Aphaenogaster* have at the least a shiny gaster.

Habitat

Cork oak forests, pines and maquis. Small clearings, woodland rides without full sun. From lowlands to the uplands.

Swarming

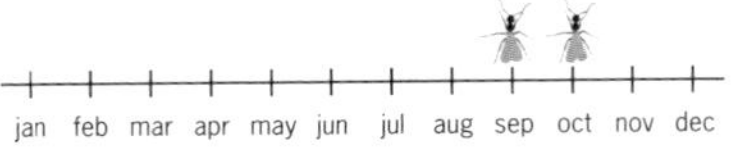

Reproduction of sexual individuals occurs in September and October.

Distribution

Range of *Aphaenogaster sardoa*.

Head of *Aphaenogaster sardoa* worker.

Aphaenogaster sardoa worker.

Where to look

Nests are under small stones. Colonies are near the surface.

Biology

Quite a common species. Colonies are monogynous, with small numbers. There is no nuptial flight but mating occurs near the nest. They are omnivores. Larvae feed directly on food brought to the nest, without trophallaxis. Workers have only a small social crop, which limits the amount of liquids they can carry.

Aphaenogaster of the ***cecconii*** group

subfamily Myrmicinae

Aphaenogaster cecconii worker carrying a rove beetle.

Identification

Size: 7 mm. Species with a very elongated body. From dark brown to black. The occipital part of the head is very slender. Three closely related species are found on Greek islands: *Aphaenogaster cecconii* (Emery, 1894) is present in Crete; *A. jolantae* (Borowiec & Salatan, 2014) on Rhodes; and *A. olympica* (Borowiec & Salatan, 2014) on Karpathos.

Swarming

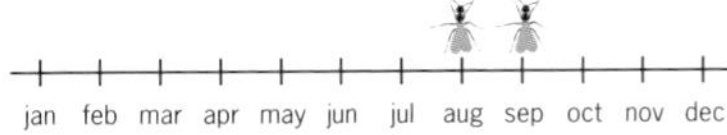

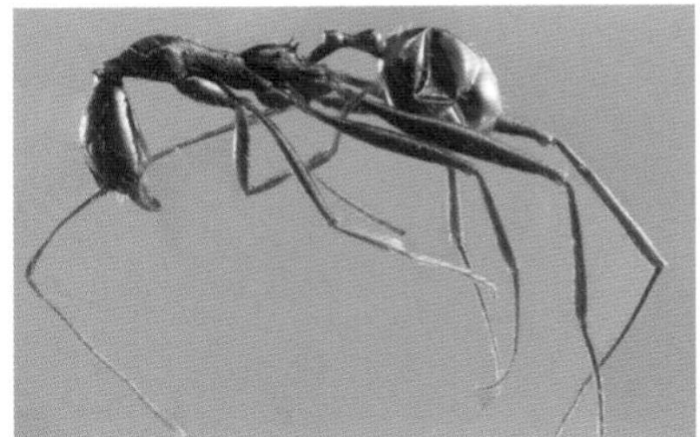

Aphaenogaster cecconii worker.

Distribution

Range of *Aphaenogaster cecconii.*

Possible confusion

This species could be confused with other black *Aphaenogaster* species.

Habitat

Shaded, rocky places, canyons, old walls in ruins but also in towns.

Where to look

Rock faces, cave entrances, large porous limestone rocks, old walls, ruins.

Aphaenogaster cecconii worker at the nest entrance.

Biology

Aphaenogaster cecconii is a common species on Crete. Workers forage over a small area around the nest entrance. They carry seeds and small plant parts as well as insects to the nest. When disturbed, these ants play dead or quickly retreat to the nest where they rest immobile. Sexual individuals are present in the nest from June to October.

Aphaenogaster of the *gibbosa* group

subfamily Myrmicinae

Aphaenogaster gibbosa worker.

Identification

Size: 3.5–6 mm. Body a matt dark black, legs and antennae are paler, slightly reddish. The head is streaked. The propodeum spines are small and slender. There are three species in the group: *Aphaenogaster gibbosa* (Latreille, 1798), widely distributed in Southern Europe, from Iberia to Greece; *A. italica* (Bondroit, 1918) in the north of Italy and south of Switzerland; and *A. striativentris* (Forel, 1895) in Andalusia. *Aphaenogaster striativentris* shows a polymorphism recalling that of *Messor* species.

Possible confusion

Aphaenogaster striativentris could be confused with species of *Messor* of the *structor* group, but in these latter species there are no propodeum spines. *Aphaenogaster senilis* is bigger, more matt and the body is covered in long, thick

Swarming

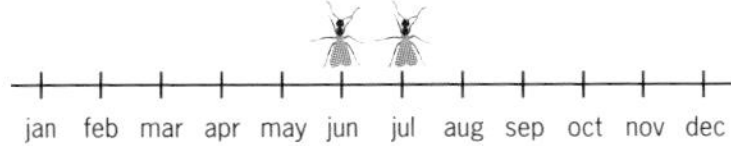

Distribution

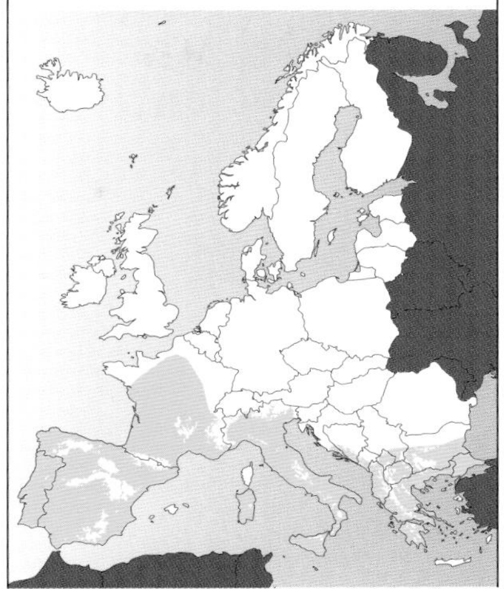

Range of *Aphaenogaster* species of the *gibbosa* group.

white hairs. *Messor* species have no spines on the propodeum and show a greater variation in size of workers within the same nest.

Habitat

Very dry habitats on open limestone plateaus with few trees and little shade. A typical garrigue species. Always on relatively flat areas, to an altitude of 1,000 m.

Where to look

Nests are under calcareous stones. Workers forage on the ground individually.

Aphaenogaster gibbosa queen (upper left) and two workers.

Biology

Uncommon species that can be locally abundant. Colonies are monogynous and contain several hundred workers. Founding is independent, by a single queen. They are omnivores, with a preference for insect prey. Workers have a very small crop, allowing them to stock only small quantities of liquids.

Aphaenogaster gibbosa workers.

Aphaenogaster of the *obsidiana* group

subfamily Myrmicinae

Aphaenogaster epirotes worker.

Identification

Size: 4.5–5.5 mm. The scapes finish at the level of the edge of the occiput. The parts of the funiculus are as wide as they are long. The head has slight reticulated sculpting, and head and thorax are brownish black. All appendages are yellowish, sometimes pale. The propodeum spines are long and narrow. There are numerous erect hairs over the whole body. There are two very similar species from the Balkans in this group: *Aphaenogaster obsidiana* (Mayr, 1861) and *A. epirotes* (Emery, 1895), which has fewer hairs and smaller spines.

Swarming

jan feb mar apr may jun jul aug sep oct nov dec

Distribution

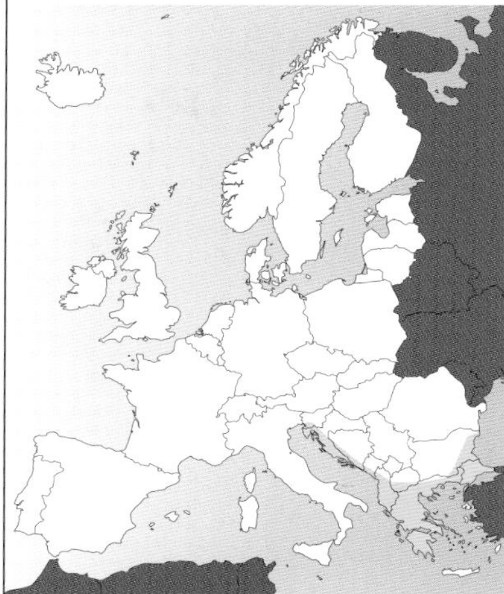

Range of *Aphaenogaster epirotes*.

Possible confusion

Aphaenogaster species of the *gibbosa* group have a longer scape and the tegument is less sculpted. *Aphaenogaster subterranean* is less deeply sculpted with fewer and yellowish hairs and a less humped pronotum. *Aphaenogaster muelleriana* is paler with a reticulated body.

Habitat

Various woodland habitats: beech and oak woods, and coastal conifer woods.

Where to look

Nests are under stones. In wetter habitats nests may be in tree trunks or branches on the ground.

Biology

Uncommon species. Colonies are monogynous. Founding is independent. The species search for dead arthropods in the ground litter. Workers move slowly and independently. They are not aggressive.

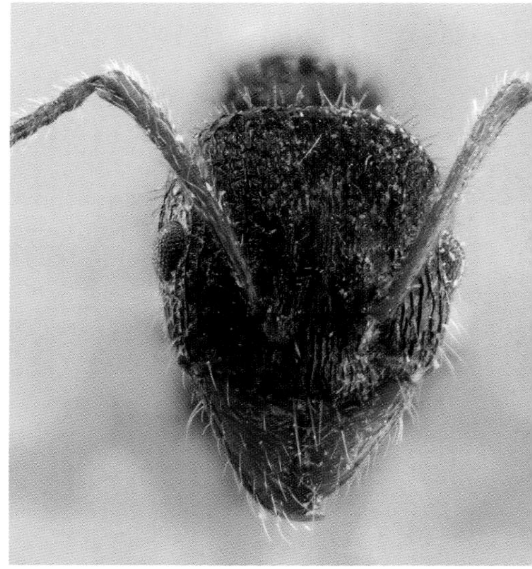

Aphaenogaster epirotes worker.

Aphaenogaster of the *pallida* group

subfamily Myrmicinae

Aphaenogaster dulciniae worker.

Identification

Size: 4–5 mm. The body is pale. The parts of the funiculus are as wide as they are long. The forehead, vertex and sides of the head are only lightly sculpted, with large, smooth, shiny areas. There are six species in this group in Europe, distributed in the Mediterranean region: *Aphaenogaster pallida* (Nylander, 1849), without spines on the propodeum, present in the south of Italy and Sicily; *A. dulciniae* (Emery, 1924) occurs on the Iberian Peninsula and along the Mediterranean coast in France as far as the Gulf of Genoa in Italy. Four other species occur in the Balkans: *Aphaenogaster finzii* (Müller, 1921) in the west of the Balkans and continental Greece; *A. subterraneoides* (Emery, 1881) in the western Greek islands; *A. lesbica* (Forel, 1913), which has a not entirely smooth but only

Swarming

Aphaenogaster dulciniae worker.

Distribution

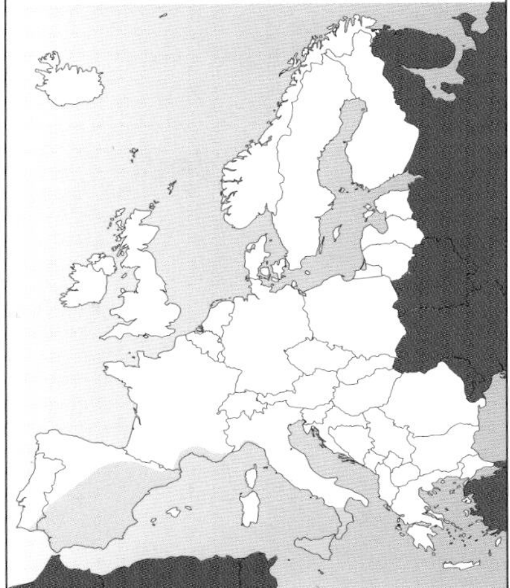

Range of *Aphaenogaster pallida* (pink) and *A. dulciniae* (grey).

slightly sculpted head, and occurs in the eastern Greek islands; and *A. sangiorgii* (Emery, 1901), described from the island of Cephalonia.

Possible confusion

These species are easily confused with other pale *Aphaenogaster* species.

Habitat

Ubiquitous species (open or dense forests, garrigue, gardens, etc.).

> **Where to look**
> Nests are under small stones or directly in the ground.

Biology

Uncommon species. Nests are not fixed, colonies often moving to another site. The colony contains several hundred workers and is monogynous. Larvae are fed on arthropod corpses as well as trophic eggs laid by workers. These species are not aggressive; they prefer trying to escape carrying their brood.

Aphaenogaster subterraneoides worker (Crete).

Aphaenogaster of the ***splendida*** group

subfamily Myrmicinae

Aphaenogaster rugosoferruginea worker carrying a petal to the nest to feed larvae.

Identification

Size: 4–6 mm. Body from pale brown to reddish and bright yellow. The scapes are very long, easily passing the occiput. Short, triangular spines. The ovoid head is marked with well-spaced longitudinal stripes. The mesosoma is only slightly sculpted, the gaster smooth. The head is much longer than it is wide. The pronotum is very arched at the rear. This group assembles *Aphaenogaster* species that are often common but with secretive habits, thus rarely collected in the field. The different species are identified by variations of the sculpting of the tegument. *Aphaenogaster splendida* (Roger, 1859) has been recorded from several Mediterranean countries. *Aphaenogaster muelleriana* (Wolf, 1915) and *A. ovaticeps* (Emery,

Swarming

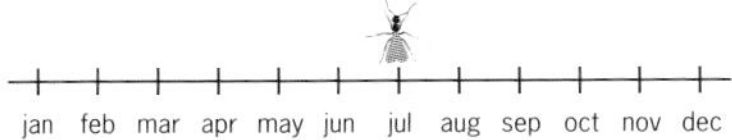

Distribution

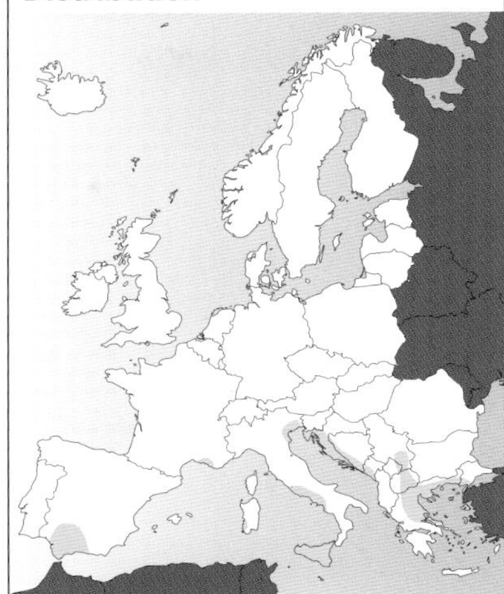

Range of *Aphaenogaster splendida*.

1898) occur in the Balkans. *Aphaenogaster rugosoferruginea* (Forel, 1889) occurs in Crete. *Aphaenogaster cardenai* (Espadaler, 1981) is recorded from Andalusia.

Possible confusion

These species are easily confused with other pale-bodied *Aphaenogaster* species.

Habitat

These species are found in a wide variety of habitats, occasionally close to human habitation. They prefer shade and cool places. They may occur on the coast, in stone embankments near the sea.

Where to look

Nests are built in the ground, under well-anchored stones or even flower pots and in cracks.

Biology

Uncommon species. Workers forage individually in the evening, hunting small, soft-bodied insects such as aphids, which they grasp with their mandibles. Winged individuals fly in the evening and are often attracted by lights.

Aphaenogaster splendida worker.

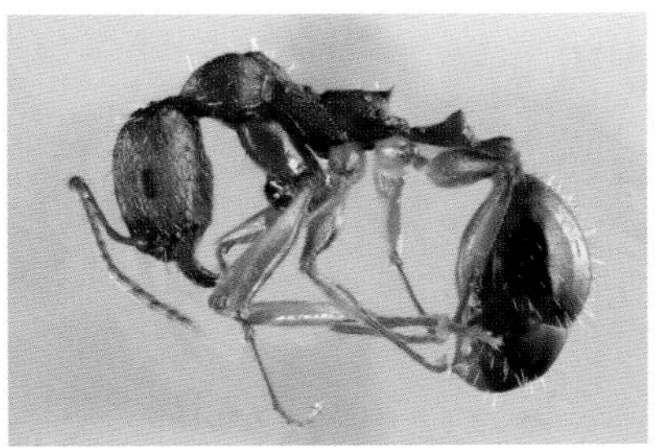

Aphaenogaster rugosoferruginea worker.

Aphaenogaster of the *subterranea* group

subfamily Myrmicinae

Aphaenogaster subterranea worker.

Identification

Size: 3–5 mm. Body orange to dark brown. Scapes are long and pass the occiput. Head as a sculpted tegument. The gaster is shiny and darker. The propodeum is humped and armed with small, pointed spines. There are four species in this group, of which one, *Aphaenogaster subterranea* (Latreille, 1798), is quite common in Central and Southern Europe. The other species have a more restricted distribution: *Aphaenogaster sicula* (Emery, 1908) occurs on Sicily; *Aphaenogaster graeca* (Schulz, 1994) in the north of Greece; and *Aphaenogaster festae* (Emery, 1915) on the eastern Greek islands.

Swarming

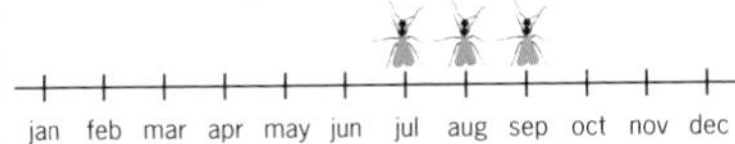

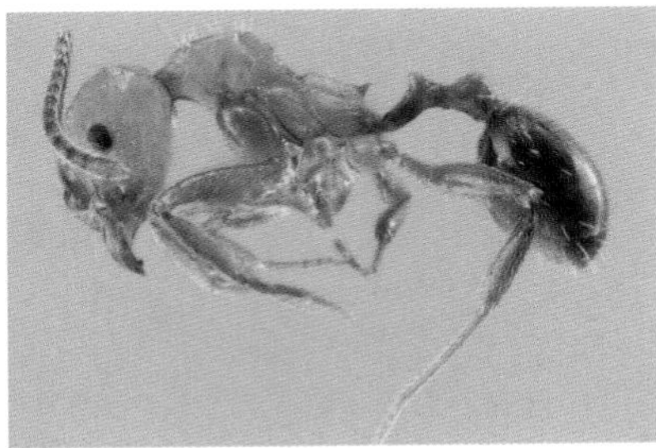

Possible confusion

Aphaenogaster species of the *pallida* group have a much less sculpted head and their scapes are shorter.

Habitat

Various woodland habitats: beech, oak and conifer woods as well as Mediterranean forests. To an altitude of 1,000 m.

Where to look

Nests are generally under stones. In wetter habitats they may be in trunks or branches on the ground. Workers forage in the ground litter.

Biology

These are common species. Nest density is generally high. Colonies are monogynous and very populous. Founding is independent. *Aphaenogaster* *subterranea* is insectivorous and also feeds petals to its larvae. Workers move slowly.

Distribution

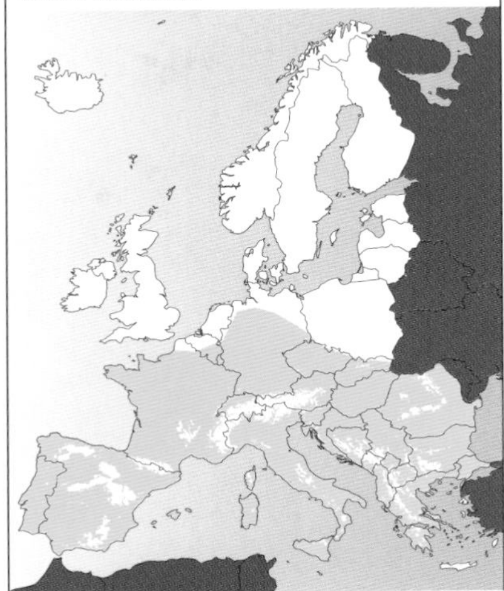

Range of *Aphaenogaster subterranea*.

Aphaenogaster sicula worker.

Cardiocondyla genus Emery, 1869

subfamily Myrmicinae

Cardiocondyla elegans workers, winged queens and a non-winged orange male.

Identification

Size: 2–4 mm. The postpetiole is very large, twice that of the petiole. A generally elongated form. Workers are very lively and move about rapidly. The diverse genus *Cardiocondyla*, distributed throughout the world, contains 70 species. Seven of these are found in Europe. Identification is difficult, based on biometrics and close observation of tegument sculpture. *Cardiocondyla elegans* (Emery, 1869) and *C. nigra* (Forel, 1905) are widely distributed in the Mediterranean region. *Cardiocondyla batesii* (Forel, 1894) is limited to the west of the Mediterranean Basin, whereas *C. bulgarica* (Forel, 1892) and *C. stambuloffi* (Forel, 1892) occur in the Balkans. Two species of tropical origin have become cosmopolitan and can be found in various parts of the Mediterranean Basin: *Cardiocondyla emeryi* (Forel, 1881) and *C. mauritanica* (Forel, 1890).

Possible confusion

Temnothorax species have a narrower postpetiole. *Ponerinae* species have a similar aspect but move more slowly and occur in different habitats.

Swarming

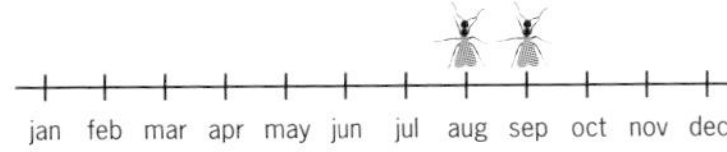

No nuptial flight in the strict sense. Mating occurs in the nest in late summer and autumn.

Habitat

Generally on river banks, gravel and sand banks, within the bed of the watercourse. Also found on flood plains on clay soils. Does not occur at altitude.

Where to look

Nests are established directly in sand where their entrance, a simple hole, is very difficult to detect. Workers forage individually on the ground, on sand, stones or plants. By using a sweep net, it is possible to find workers on grasses or sedges along river banks. They are most active during the hottest part of the day.

Biology

Locally, nest density may be as high as one per square metre. Colonies are monogynous, with about two hundred workers. Males are ergatoid, the majority staying and mating in their original nests. Contrarily to most ant species, male *Cardiocondyla elegans* are capable of mating several times, and they do so throughout the mating season. Living in river beds, colonies are very exposed to flooding. The nest is constructed in such a way that it is relatively impermeable. However, many colonies perish during the winter. They are omnivores, showing a preference for small insect prey.

Distribution

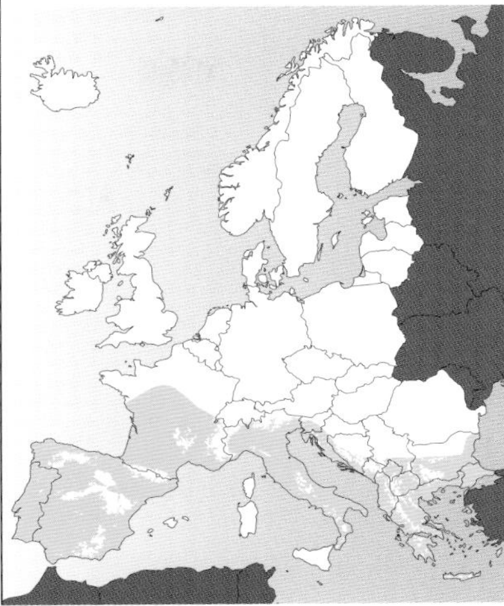

Range of *Cardiocondyla elegans*.

Cardiocondyla mauritanica worker.

Chalepoxenus genus Menozzi, 1923

subfamily Myrmicinae

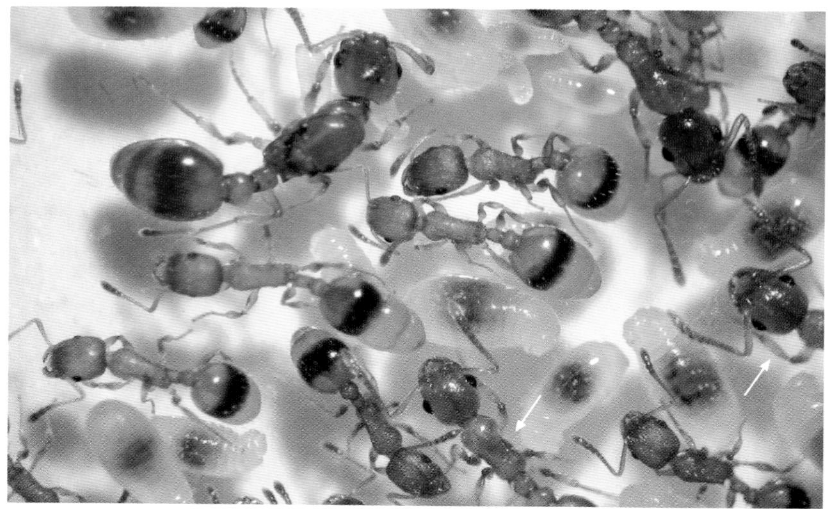

The workers of the slavemaker species *Chalepoxenus muellerianus* (arrowed) are easily distinguished from their hosts, *Temnothorax unifasciatus* here, by their larger size. The *Chalepoxenus muellerianus* queen is visible in the top left of the image.

Identification

Size: 2.5–3.5 mm; queen: 4mm. Body beige to pale brown. Two very similar species of *Chalepoxenus* occur in Europe. They can be differentiated by the amount of hairs: *Chalepoxenus muellerianus* (Finzi, 1922) has raised hairs on the legs, whilst *C. kutteri* (Cagniant, 1973) does not. **Note:** A recent revision based on genetic studies has placed the genus *Chalepoxenus* within the genus *Temnothorax*. So, these species should now be *Temnothorax muellerianus* (Finzi, 1922) and *Temnothorax kutteri* (Cagniant, 1973).

Possible confusion

The *Chalepoxenus* species are distinguished from their hosts (species of the genus *Temnothorax*) by the presence of a spine under the postpetiole, and other social parasite species of the genus *Temnothorax* by their larger size.

Habitat

Same habitats as their respective hosts.

Swarming

jan feb mar apr may jun jul aug sep oct nov dec

The slavemaker species *Chalepoxenus muellerianus*: a winged female (left) and a worker (right).

Where to look

In the nests of their respective hosts.

Distribution

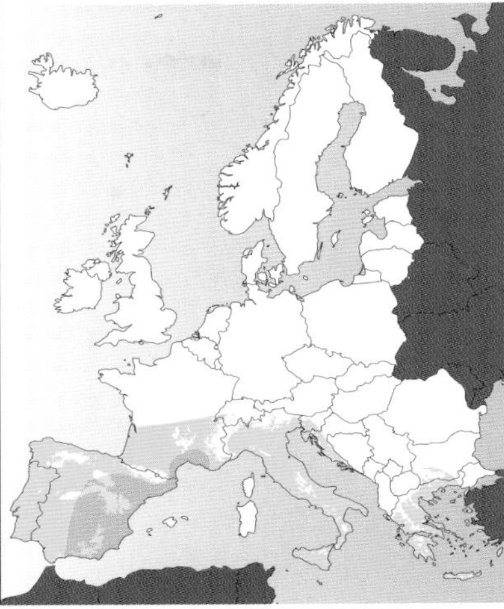

Range of *Chalepoxenus muellerianus* (pink) and *C. kutteri* (grey).

Chalepoxenus muellerianus worker.

Biology

Quite rare species. They are social parasites of *Temnothorax* species. Both species that occur in Europe are slavemakers; *Chalepoxenus muellerianus* is one of the commonest species of slavemaker ants. In areas where they are present, a high proportion of host nests may be parasitised (up to 50%). Colonies are monogynous, with a few dozen parasite workers, normally with far more host workers. When founding occurs the parasite queen attacks a host nest, from which she ejects or kills the workers and queen; she only conserves the brood in order to form her own colony. Raids take place in summer, but are difficult to observe in the wild. *Chalepoxenus muellerianus* uses some 12 different species as hosts, *Temnothorax unifasciatus* and *T. recedens* being the most frequent. *Chalepoxenus kutteri* also exploits several different species, *Temnothorax luteus* most often.

Crematogaster auberti Emery, 1869 and *C. laestrygon* Emery, 1869

subfamily Myrmicinae

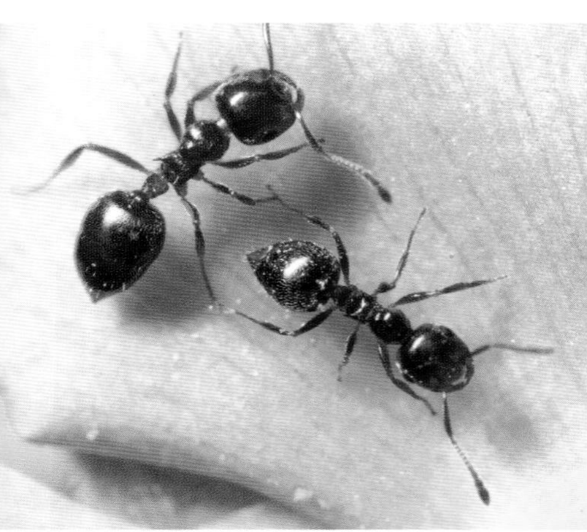

Crematogaster auberti workers.

Crematogaster laestrygon worker.

Identification

Size: 3–4 mm. Body entirely shiny brown or black. The gaster is heart-shaped and raised over the head when the individual is agitated. *Crematogaster auberti* (Emery, 1869) and *C. laestrygon* (Emery, 1869) are two ground-dwelling species frequently found in the western part of the Mediterranean Basin. *Crematogaster auberti* is distributed throughout Spain and the very south of France. *Crematogaster laestrygon* occurs in Sicily. *Crematogaster fuentei* (Menozzi, 1922), a species described from Spain in 1922, has not been found since; its spines are very short, different from those of *C. auberti* which are well developed.

Possible confusion

Crematogaster sordidula is obviously much smaller. *Crematogaster scutellaris* has a reddish head and front to the mesosoma.

Where to look

Nests are directly in the ground. Workers come together under stones and rest immobile during the day. They forage for food mainly during the night.

Habitat

Dry, open habitats. To an altitude of 1,000 m.

Biology

Very common species, especially in garrigue habitats. Colonies are

Swarming

jan feb mar apr may jun jul aug sep oct nov dec

Distribution

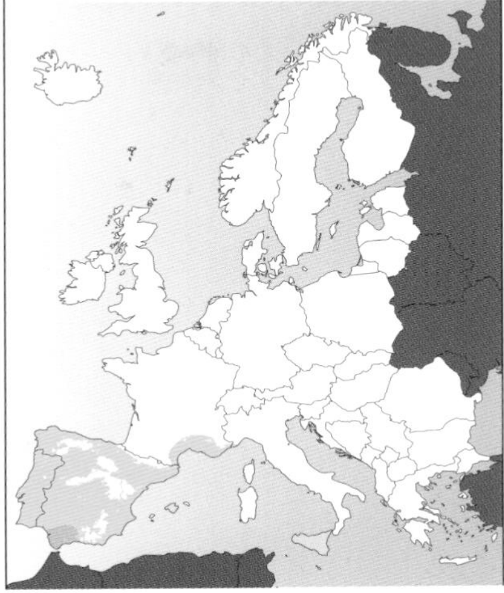
Ranges of *Crematogaster auberti* (pink) and *C. laestrygon* (grey).

Three *Crematogaster auberti* castes. From top to bottom: a queen, two workers and a male.

monogynous with several hundred workers. Founding is independent. They are omnivorous. Workers search for sugary substances on plants and from underground aphids, and hunt small arthropods. They may form tracks to their food sources.

Crematogaster auberti colony.

Crematogaster of the *scutellaris* group

subfamily Myrmicinae

Crematogaster scutellaris worker emitting an alarm pheromone.

Identification

Size: 3–5 mm. Black body with head and often front of mesosoma red, contrasting with dark gaster. The gaster is heart-shaped and raised over the head when the individual is agitated. This group contains two tree-dwelling species which are very common in southern Europe. *Crematogaster scutellaris* (Olivier, 1792) occurs in the west of the Mediterranean Basin, as far as Italy. It is replaced in the Balkans by *Crematogaster schmidti* (Mayr, 1853). *Crematogaster gordani* (Karaman, 2008) is a very yellow species closely related to *C. schmidti* described from Montenegro.

Possible confusion

Camponotus lateralis has a similar shape and colour and often occurs near *Crematogaster scutellaris* trails. However, it does not have a postpetiole (*Formicinae*).

Habitat

Various habitat types, as long as there are trees. Generally, nearly always near wooded areas but also in habitats with just a few isolated trees. To an altitude of 1,200 m.

Where to look

Nests are nearly always in wood: dead branches, tree cavities, felled trunks, vine stocks, fruit trees and under bark. Sometimes in walls between stones. Workers form long, very visible trails, on the ground, in vegetation, in trees and on rocks.

Biology

Colonies are monogynous, containing several thousand individuals. Founding is

Swarming

The three castes of *Crematogaster scutellaris*. From top to bottom: a queen, a male and two workers.

independent. They are omnivores. Workers particularly exploit abundant and reliable food sources: aphid and scale bug honeydew, floral nectar and all forms of dead animal matter. In spring, colonies proliferate and occupy several satellite nests that help to feed the brood. It is possible to see workers carrying part of a brood from one nest to another along connecting trails. Satellite nests are deserted in the autumn. Workers produce a

Distribution

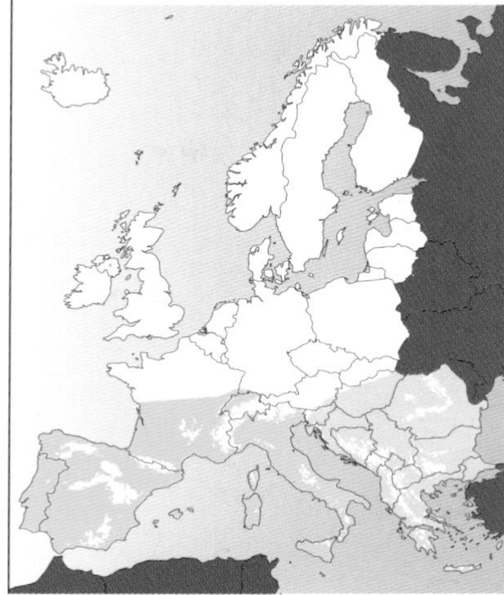

Range of *Crematogaster scutellaris* (pink) and *C. schmidti* (grey).

Crematogaster scutellaris colony in a dead tree.

'paper' from diverse materials, which serves to build lodges within the nest. They are highly aggressive.

Other species in the *Crematogaster* genus

subfamily Myrmicinae

Antennae contact between *Crematogaster ionia* workers.

Entrance to a *Crematogaster ionia* nest.

Identification

Size: 4 mm. Dark head, and mesosoma and petiole are brown to dark brown. A heart-shaped gaster which is raised over the head when an individual is disturbed. Here we present four species that occur in the southern Balkans, all with a quite uniformly coloured body; head and mesosoma sometimes slightly lighter, but any contrast is less obvious than in species in the *scutellaris* group (see page 272).

Crematogaster lorteti (Forel, 1910) is the only species to have very short spines; the top of the head is slightly concave. *Crematogaster erectepilosa* (Salata & Borowiec, 2015) has numerous erect hairs on the gaster, its distribution restricted to the eastern Greek islands. *Crematogaster ionia* (Forel, 1911) is more widely spread in Mediterranean habitats from Croatia to Greece; the front of the body is brown, whereas the gaster is black. *Crematogaster montenigrina* (Karaman, 2008), entirely dark, has been described from Montenegro.

Possible confusion

Crematogaster species of the *scutellaris* group have an obviously red front part of the body, which the species on this page do not.

Habitat

These species establish themselves

Swarming

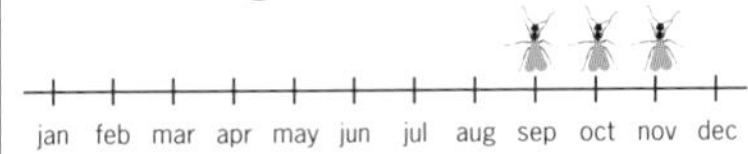

Crematogaster ionia worker.

in dry situations, in stony or rocky places with isolated trees, generally pines, which serve as food stores. They use stones that are either in stone walls or on the ground. They will also use low plants or bushes such as wild olive trees situated near a wall or pile of stones.

Where to look

Nests are under stones in conifer woods in Mediterranean habitats.

Biology

Colonies are monogynous and may contain several hundred

Distribution

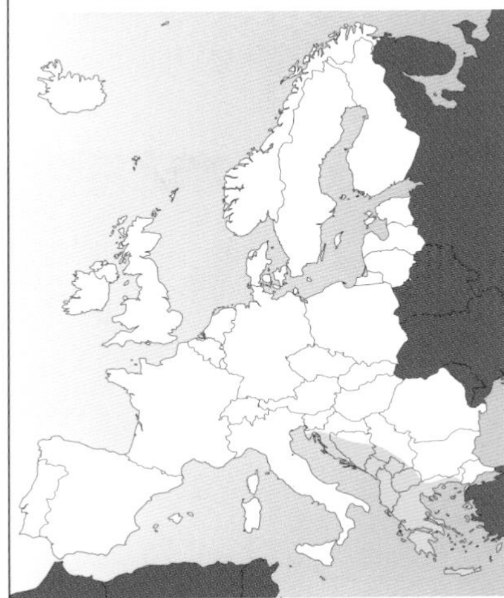

Range of *Crematogaster ionia*.

individuals. Founding is independent. Workers will forage on trees for sugary substances and small arthropods, which they capture or find dead. Aggressive, they lift their gaster when threatened and emit a volatile substance that either alerts their fellow workers or attracts them when a new and abundant food source has been found.

Crematogaster ionia worker.

Crematogaster sordidula Nylander, 1849

subfamily Myrmicinae – subgenus *Orthocrema*

Crematogaster sordidula worker.

Identification

Size: 2–3 mm. Body uniform pale brown to dark. Heart-shaped gaster.

Possible confusion

Other species of *Crematogaster* are bigger. Species of *Plagiolepis* do not have a heart-shaped gaster and there is just one part to the petiole (Formicidae).

Crematogaster sordidula workers carrying larvae.

Swarming

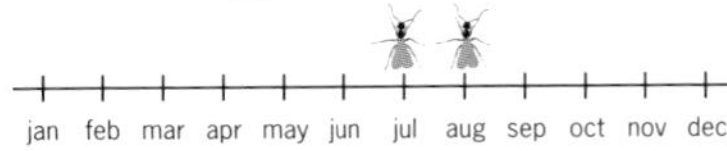

Habitat

Diverse habitats, generally in a sunny position: woodland edges, wooded garrigue, etc. To an altitude of 900 m. Prefers flatter, permeable sites with good drainage.

Where to look

Nests are in the ground, to a depth of 50 cm in the soil. During hot periods workers stay at the bottom of the nest. Therefore, this species is easier to find in the spring when a good proportion of the colony is at the surface, under stones. Founding may occur in dead wood. Workers search for food on the ground, on stones and in low vegetation at nightfall when temperatures are lower. They may form discreet trails.

Distribution

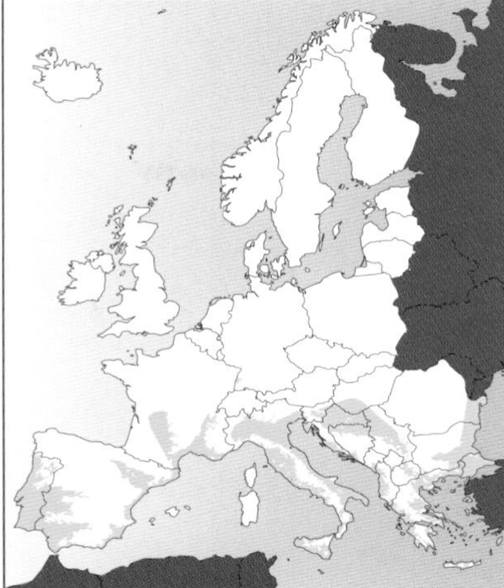

Range of *Crematogaster sordidula.*

Biology

A common but unobtrusive species. Colonies are highly polygynous and have several thousand workers. They are omnivorous, feeding on arthropods and sugary substances found on plants in proximity to the nest. It is very likely that this species also exploits root-living aphids.

Crematogaster sordidula workers.

Formicoxenus genus Mayr, 1855

subfamily Myrmicinae

Formicoxenus nitidulus worker (bottom right) in the company of a *Formica pratensis* worker.

Identification

Size: 3 mm. Uniform shiny, orange-red body. Eleven segments to the antennae. Males are wingless and ergatoid, and are distinguished from workers by having 12 antenna segments and the presence of ocelli on the head. There is just one species in Europe: *Formicoxenus nitidulus* (Nylander, 1846).

Possible confusion

Leptothorax species have a quite similar aspect and can be found in the same type of habitat. However, they are less shiny and have a darker head and gaster.

Habitat

Same as their host species.

Where to look

Nests are in the domes of red ants (of the genus *Formica* in the subgenus *Formica, sensu stricto*), particularly

Swarming

Colony multiplication occurs in August.

F. rufa, F. polyctena, F. lugubris, F. pratensis and *F. truncorum*, either on top of the dome, under it, or under the stone on which the dome is built. Isolated workers can be found on the dome surface, when the sun is shining directly on the nest. Late summer is the best time for finding these species, when they are swarming, when workers and sexual individuals run over the dome surface.

Distribution

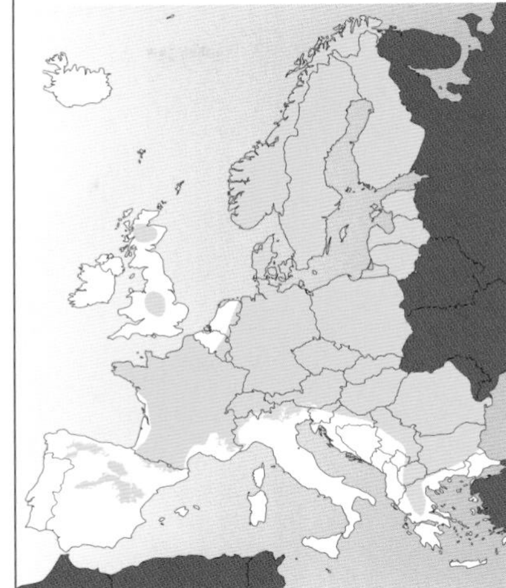

Range of *Formicoxenus nitidulus.*

Biology

Formicoxenus nitidulus is a xenobiotic species, building its nest in the interior of the nest of a *Formica* species of the *Formica* subgenus *sensu stricto*. It is probably quite common but is difficult to find. Several colonies can install themselves in a single *Formica* dome. They are polygynous, with 100 to 500 workers. Founding can be independent or newly mated queens return to the nest and then proceed to colonise the dome by budding. They install themselves in mature *Formica* nests. There is little interaction with the host species. *Formicoxenus nitidulus* squat down or even climb over *Formica* workers when trying to avoid their attention.

Wingless male *Formicoxenus nitidulus.*

Goniomma genus Emery, 1895

subfamily Myrmicinae

Goniomma hispanicum worker.

Identification

Size: 3.5–4.5 mm. Body entirely black with a slight hint of brown, especially on the legs. The head is striped longitudinally and has hairs flattened in the direction of the median line. The eye is characteristically shaped – a rounded comma with the point towards the bottom. The genus *Goniomma* is endemic to the Mediterranean Basin. So far only eight species have been described, one restricted to North Africa. Seven of the species occur on the Iberian Peninsula, and two of these also occur in the south of France. According to the position of the eyes on the head, there are two distinct groups of species: *Goniomma blanci* (André, 1881) and *G. kugleri* (Espadaler, 1986) which have eyes very close to the zone of mandible insertion, whereas in *G. hispanicum* (André, 1883), *G. decipiens* (Espadaler, 1997), *G. baeticum* (Reyes, Espadaler & Rodriguez, 1987), *G. collingwoodi* (Espadaler, 1997) and *G. compressisquama* (Tinaut, 1995) the eyes are farther from the area of mandible insertion.

Swarming

Goniomma blanci worker.

Possible confusion

Species in the genus *Oxyopomyrmex* also have comma-shaped eyes but they are smaller than in *Goniomma* species and they have 11 segments to the antenna compared to 12 in *Goniomma* species.

Habitat

Open, flat, warm areas: dunes and coastal mudflats, sides of lakes and large rivers, gravel pits, sandy areas and open garrigue. Lowland species.

Where to look

Nests are built directly in the ground and generally difficult to find. After periods of rain, as with many ant species, the entrance is sometimes surrounded by a heap of material resulting from nest cleaning; they are then easier to find. Workers forage on the ground.

Distribution

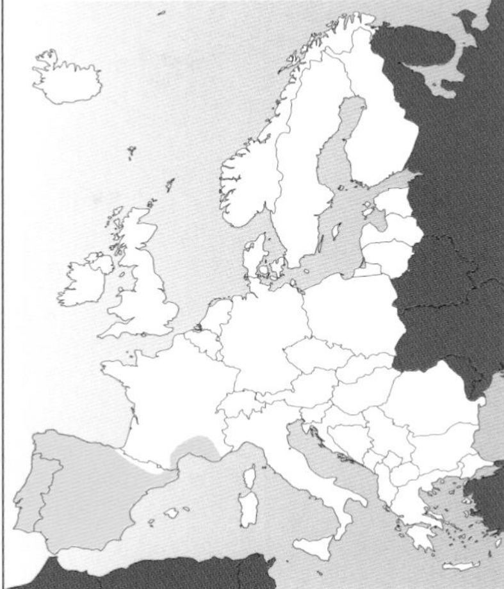

Range of the genus *Goniomma*.

Goniomma hispanicum workers at the nest entrance.

Biology

This species is granivorous. Nests have grain 'lofts' near their surface, where harvested seeds are stored.

***Harpagoxenus* genus** Forel, 1893

subfamily Myrmicinae

Harpagoxenus sublaevis worker.

Identification

Size: 3.5–4.5 mm. Head and mesosoma yellow to brown, gaster partially black. Mandibles are wide and without teeth. In Western Europe most queens are wingless and resemble workers. Only a small proportion is winged. A single species occurs in Europe: *Harpagoxenus sublaevis* (Nylander, 1849).

Possible confusion

As *Harpagoxenus sublaevis* is a parasite of *Leptothorax* species, it can be confused with them in the nest. It is distinguished by its large size and paler colour.

Habitat

Harpagoxenus sublaevis occupies the same habitats as its *Leptothorax* hosts. It appears to be more frequent in mountainous areas. The biotope must have a high concentration of *Leptothorax* nests.

Where to look

In *Leptothorax* nests.

Swarming

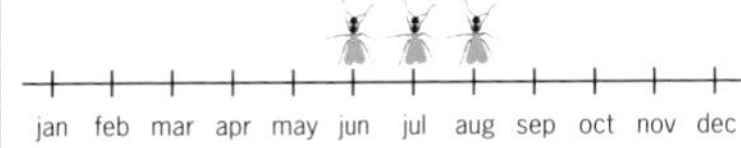

Harpagoxenus sublaevis worker.

Distribution

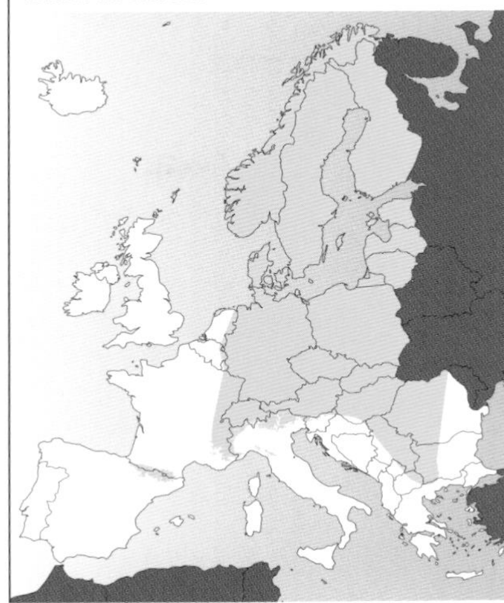

Range of *Harpagoxenus sublaevis*.

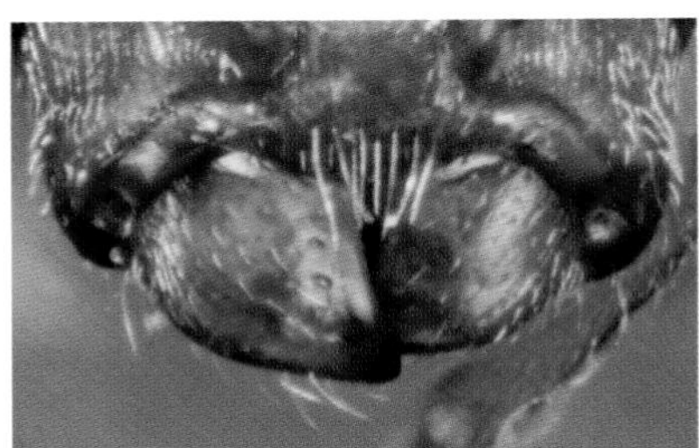

Mandibles of *Harpagoxenus sublaevis* worker.

Biology

Harpagoxenus sublaevis is a slavemaker species, its hosts being *Leptothorax* species (*L. acervorum* and *L. muscorum*). It is rare. Colonies are monogynous, with a few dozen workers as well as the host workers. The new queen kills or expels the workers and queen of a *Leptothorax* colony and appropriates their brood. To this end she emits pheromones that cause conflict among host workers. Colony founding is more likely to be successful if the *Leptothorax* colony contains few workers. Workers that emerge from the host brood care for the parasite queen's brood. In order to maintain a large enough number of host ants in the colony, *Harpagoxenus sublaevis* workers make raids during which they rob nearby *Leptothorax* nests of pupae and larvae. These workers are specialised in making these raids and perform no other task within the colony. Their mandible's shape and the muscles that power them allow them to easily cut off the appendages of any rebellious workers during these raids. All everyday tasks within the colony are performed by the host workers.

Leptothorax genus Mayr, 1855

subfamily Myrmicinae

Leptothorax acervorum worker.

Identification

Size: 3–4 mm. Head and gaster dark brown. Mesosoma reddish. Antennae have 11 segments. Six *Leptothorax* species are found in Europe, three of which are parasite species (see page 286). *Leptothorax acervorum* (Fabricius, 1793) is the most frequent species; common in northern and central Europe, it is found in all southern mountain ranges as well as in lowlands. *Leptothorax muscorum* (Nylander, 1846) and *L. gredleri* (Mayr, 1855) are closely related species, difficult to differentiate: they are distinguished from *L. acervorum* by their smaller size and absence of erect hairs on their tibiae.

Possible confusion

Workers of species in the genus *Leptothorax* can be confused with those of the genus *Temnothorax* but this last group have antennae with 12 segments (except *Temnothorax flavicornis*, see page 352).

Habitat

A very widespread species which prefers cool, damp situations. They are equally found in open (meadows, peat bogs, etc.) and closed (forest) habitats. They occur over a very wide range of altitudes, from sea level to 3,000 m but prefer mountainous areas.

Swarming

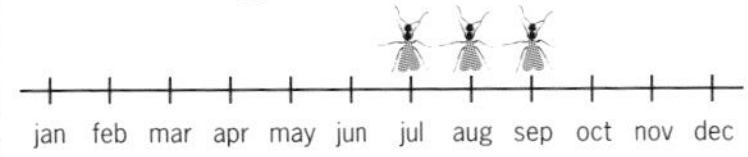

Where to look

Nests are generally in dead wood or under the bark of dead tree parts near the ground: branches and trunks, stumps, but also between pieces of conifer bark at the foot of living trees and in stumps colonised by red ants (genus *Formica*, subgenus *Formica sensu stricto*). Nests may also occur under stones or moss. Workers forage on the ground, on dead wood and among low vegetation.

Distribution

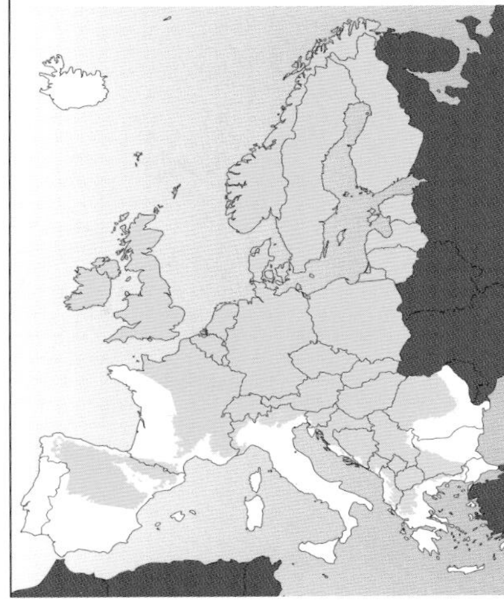

Range of *Leptothorax* species.

Leptothorax muscorum workers in the nest, under a stone.

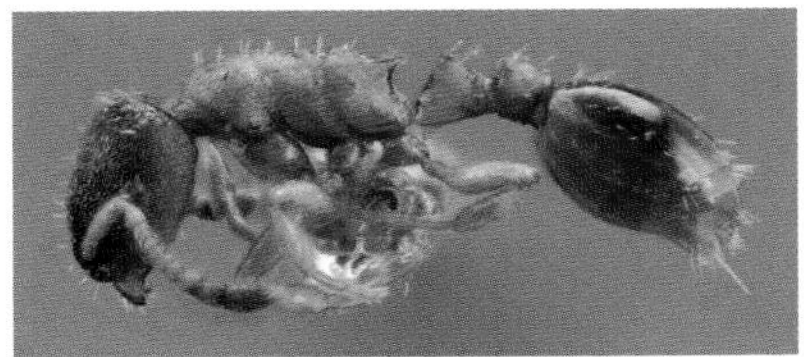

Leptothorax gredleri worker.

Biology

Very common species, except in hot, dry regions (for example, absent from the Mediterranean coast). Nest density may be as high as one per square metre. Colonies are monogynous or polygynous, rarely with more than 200 workers. Founding can be independent or a newly mated queen joins an existing colony. Polygynous colonies can multiply by budding. Omnivorous species. *Leptothorax acervorum* is one of the most cold-resistant ants: it can support extreme temperatures, as low as – 40°C, due to the accumulation of glycerol in the bodies of larvae and adults, which retards ice crystal development. *Leptothorax acervorum* is the principal host species of the slavemaker *Harpagoxenus sublaevis*.

Parasitic species of the **Leptothorax genus** Mayr, 1885 subfamily Myrmicinae

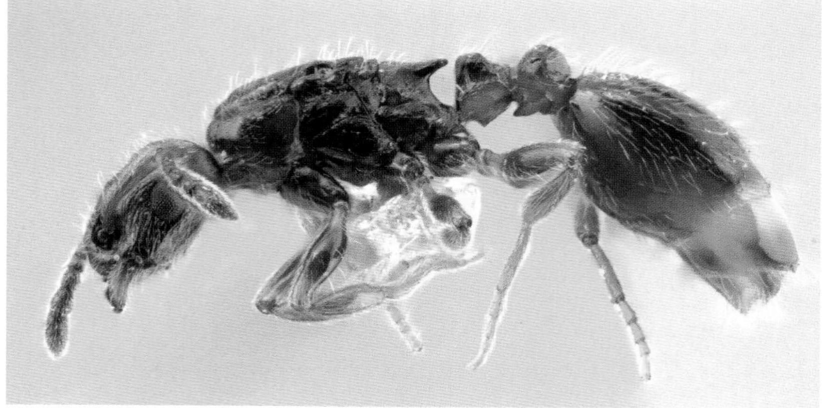

Leptothorax pacis queen.

Identification

Size of queen: 4 mm. There are three species of parasitic *Leptothorax*: *L. pacis* (Kutter, 1945), *L. goesswaldi* (Kutter, 1967) and *L. kutteri* (Buschinger, 1966). *Leptothorax pacis* is distinguished from the two other species by a more marked growth under the postpetiole, and *L. kutteri* has shorter and less dense hairs compared to the other two species. These species are inquilines which do not produce workers.

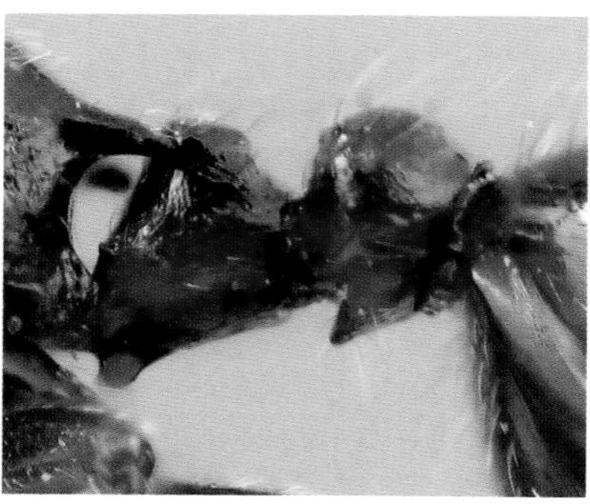

Postpetiole of *Leptothorax pacis* with a well-marked ventral growth.

Possible confusion

They can be distinguished from *Leptothorax acervorum* queens by their smaller size and a bigger growth on the postpetiole.

Habitat

Nests are in dead wood or under the bark of dead wood, near the ground. Conifers offer conditions

Swarming

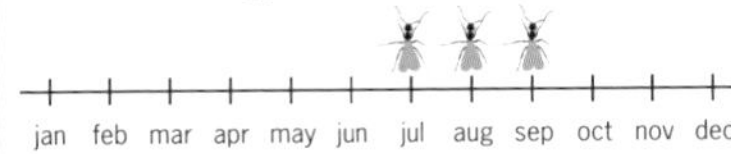

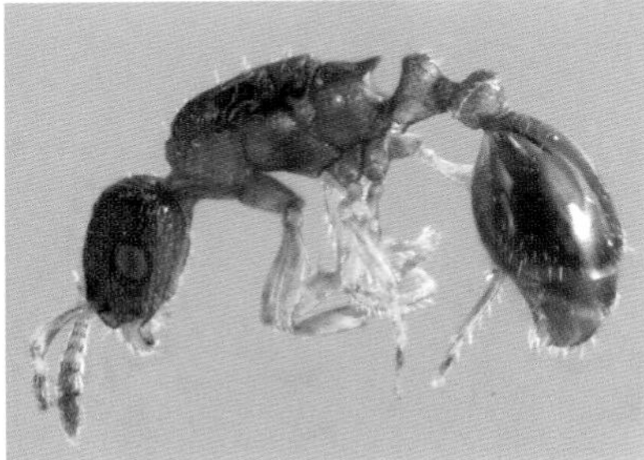

Leptothorax kutteri queen.

that correspond most closely to the species' needs.

Where to look

In the nests of *Leptothorax acervorum*: branches and trunks on the ground, stumps, between large pieces of conifer bark and at the foot of living trees. Nests can also occur under stones or moss.

Biology

These parasitic species are very rare. *Leptothorax acervorum* is widely distributed throughout the Palearctic region and many species of parasitic ant use it as a host. Parasitic *Leptothorax* species are termed 'inquilines' as the queen only produces sexual individuals – males and future queens – and normally no workers. The new queen has to try to be accepted by the *Leptothorax acervorum* colony, where the host workers rear her brood. Contrary to *Leptothorax kutteri* and *L. pacis*, the *L. goesswaldi* queen eliminates host queens.

Distribution

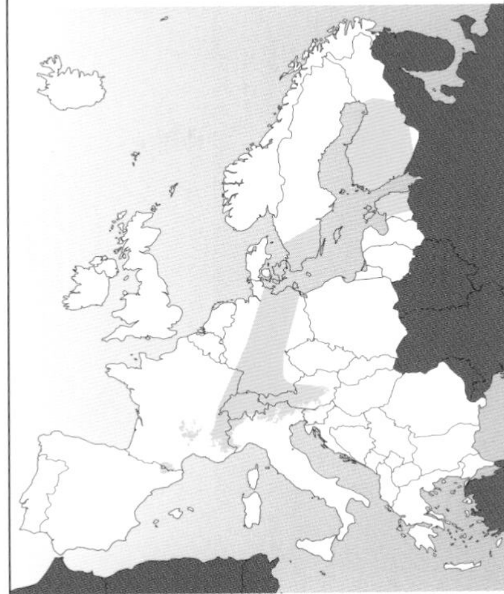

Range of parasitic species of *Leptothorax*.

Leptothorax pacis queen (top) with a *Leptothorax acervorum* worker (bottom).

Manica genus Jurine, 1807

subfamily Myrmicinae

Manica rubida worker.

Identification

Size: 5–9 mm. Entirely reddish body, sometimes browner depending on the biotope. The first gaster segment is slightly darker. The wide mandibles have many small, pointed teeth. There are no spines on the propodeum. A single species occurs in Europe: *Manica rubida* (Latreille, 1802).

Possible confusion

The smallest *Manica rubida* individuals resemble *Myrmica* species but can be distinguished by their lack of propodeal spines.

Habitat

Open habitats at altitude: meadows, forest edges and tracks, embankments, gravel pits and sandy areas of river beds. Between 900 and 2,000 m altitude.

Swarming

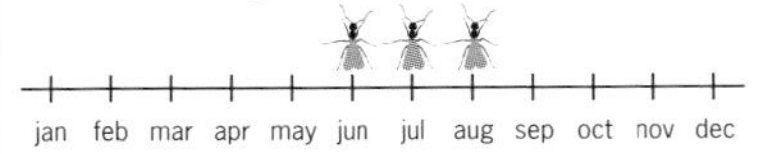

Manica rubida worker.

Distribution

Range of *Manica rubida*.

Where to look

Nests are under stones or directly in the ground. The entrance is normally surrounded by grains of sand or soil all more or less of the same size. Workers forage individually, on the ground or in low vegetation.

Biology

A common species at high altitudes. Colonies are monogynous or oligogynous (a few queens but not occurring together), with a maximum of a thousand workers. Founding is independent by several queens that come together under a stone. During the mating period queens have to exit the colony to find food, as their reserves are not sufficient to feed the first brood. An omnivorous species. It can be aggressive, with a painful sting.

Manica rubida worker.

Messor barbarus Linné, 1767

subfamily Myrmicinae

Messor barbatus major worker.

Identification

Size: 4–12 mm. Great variation within the same colony. The largest workers have a disproportionately large head, armed with strong mandibles.

Messor barbarus worker in profile, showing the rounded propodeum.

An entirely smooth and shiny body. Both the mesosoma and gaster are black, and the head varies between pale and very dark red, almost black, but always with a slight hint of reddish colour. The propodeum is rounded.

Possible confusion

Messor capitatus has no signs of reddish colour on the head and has an angular propodeum. *Messor bouvieri* is entirely black and never longer than 8 mm. *Messor minor* workers are never longer than 8 mm and have some red on the mesosoma.

Swarming

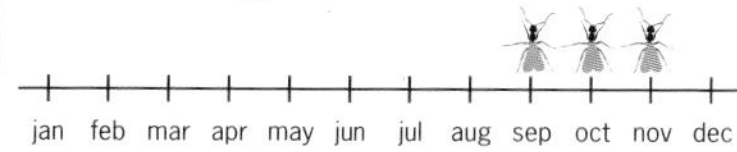

Habitat

Very warm, open habitats: garrigue, vineyards, tracks and paths. Also in urban areas: gardens, parks, etc. and pavements. Prefers flat environments. A lowland species that does not occur at altitude.

Where to look

This species occurs in Spain and along the French Mediterranean coast. Nests are directly in the ground or under a large stone. As in all *Messor* species, when the colony is active the nest entrance sides are covered in seeds and/or grains of soil. Workers form very visible trails to food sources.

Biology

A very common species on Mediterranean coasts. Nest density may be very high. Nests are very populous, containing several thousand workers. Founding is independent. A granivorous species. As in all *Messor* species, they build stores at the surface of nests to stock harvested seeds. They create trails of varying importance according to the significance of the food source and season, sometimes creating veritable motorways due to the amount of worker traffic. With their strong mandibles, the largest workers break seeds into pieces which are reduced to a sort of paste through mastication. Whenever it rains, the remains of the store are taken to the surface and arranged around the main nest entrance.

Distribution

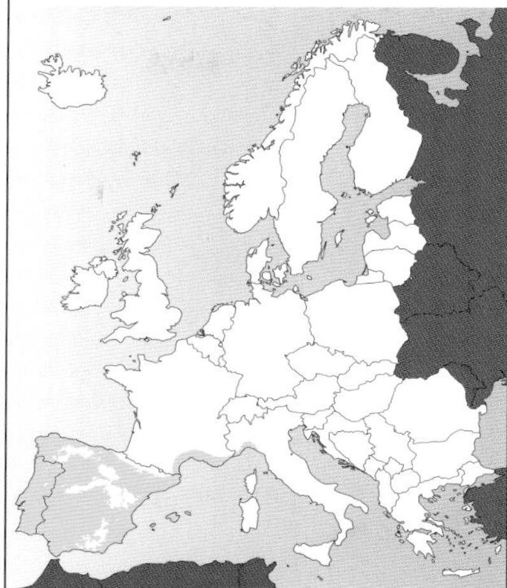

Range of *Messor barbarus*.

The extreme size difference between *Messor barbarus* workers of the same colony is also expressed in their colour. Major workers (left) generally have a paler head than minor workers.

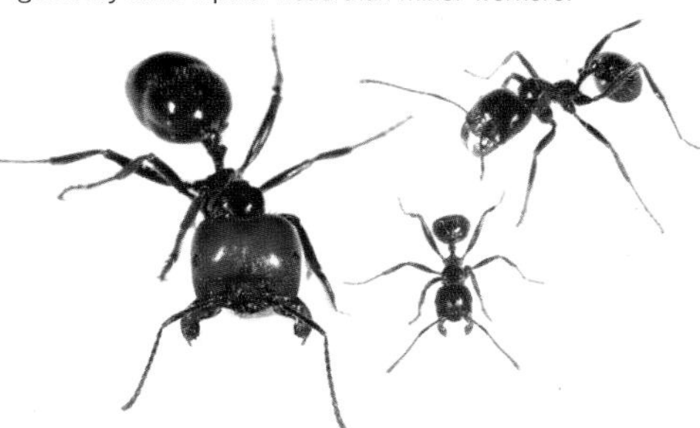

Messor of the *bouvieri* group

subfamily Myrmicinae

Messor bouvieri worker.

Identification

Size: 3–8 mm, with great variation between individuals of the same colony for certain species, but very little for others. Black and shiny body, except *Messor marocanus* which has a reddish mesosoma. Workers are equipped with a psammophore (long, curved hairs under the head that help to keep seeds between the mandibles). This group brings together a large diversity of species from the south of Spain. *Messor bouvieri* (Bondroit, 1918) is the most widespread, from the south of Spain to the Gulf of Genoa and Sicily; its gaster has no hairs. *Messor sanctus* (Emery, 1921) is a North African species recorded from Pantelleria island to the south of Sicily. The other species in the group occur only in the south of Spain: *Messor lusitanicus* is the only one with spines on the propodeum; *M. marocanus* (Santschi, 1927) has a reddish mesosoma; the other species are characterised by having erect hairs on the gaster. In *Messor timidus* (Espadaler, 1997) the workers are polymorphic, whereas in *M. hispanicus* (Santschi, 1919) and *M. celiae* (Reyes, 1985) all members of the colony are of the same size.

Swarming

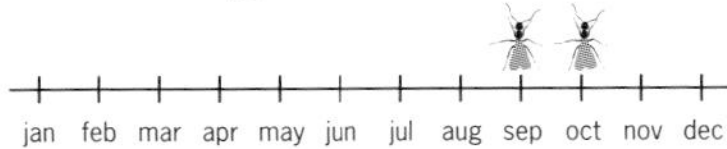

Distribution

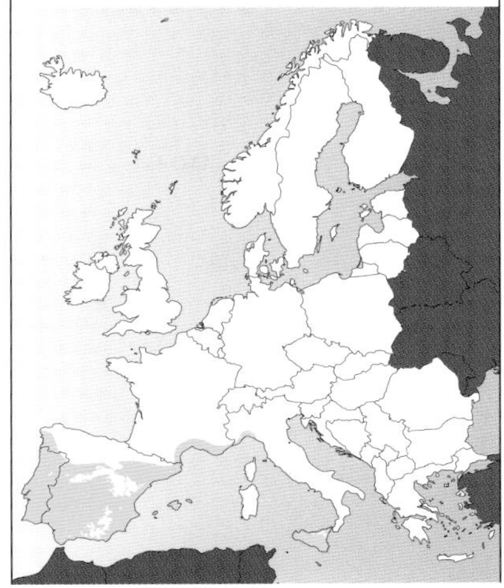

Range of *Messor bouvieri*.

Possible confusion

Messor lobicornis (Forel, 1894) can also be found in the south of Spain; it can be separated from species of the *bouvieri* group by having a lobe-shaped enlargement at the base of the scape.

Habitat

Open and very warm habitats: garrigue, well-exposed hillsides, embankments, the upper parts of beaches and sometimes the sides of lakes. Lowland species.

Messor bouvieri major worker (left) and minor worker (right).

Where to look

Nests are built directly in the ground. Entry can be direct or from under a stone. Workers form tracks leading to food sources.

Biology

Common species in the Mediterranean area. Nest density can be very high. Colonies are populous, with several thousand workers. Founding is independent by a single queen. The species are granivorous but workers sometimes bring back arthropod corpses to the nest. As in all *Messor* species, they build stores at the top of a nest to stock collected seeds.

Messor bouvieri workers at the nest entrance.

Messor capitatus Latreille, 1798

subfamily Myrmicinae

Messor capitatus major worker.

Identification

Size: 4–12 mm, with much variation within the same colony. The largest workers have a disproportionately large head armed with strong mandibles. The body is entirely shiny black. The propodeum is angular.

Possible confusion

Messor bouvieri workers are never longer than 8 mm; they have a rounded propodeum and a hairless gaster. *Messor barbarus* has a rounded propodeum and the larger workers normally have a reddish-coloured head.

Habitat

Open and well-exposed habitats: garrigue, scrub, vineyards, hillsides, embankments, tracks and paths. Prefers flat areas. More a lowland species but can occur as high as 1,000 m altitude.

Where to look

Nests are built directly in the ground or under a large stone. As with all species of the genus *Messor*, whenever the ants are active the sides of the nest entrance are lined with seeds and/or grains of sand. Workers form very visible trails to food sources.

Swarming

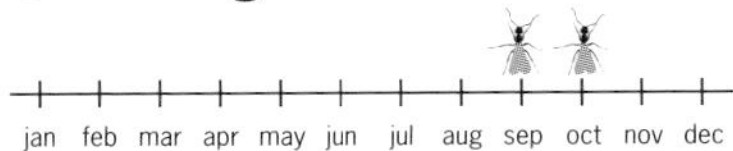

Messor capitatus worker in profile, showing the angular propodeum.

Distribution

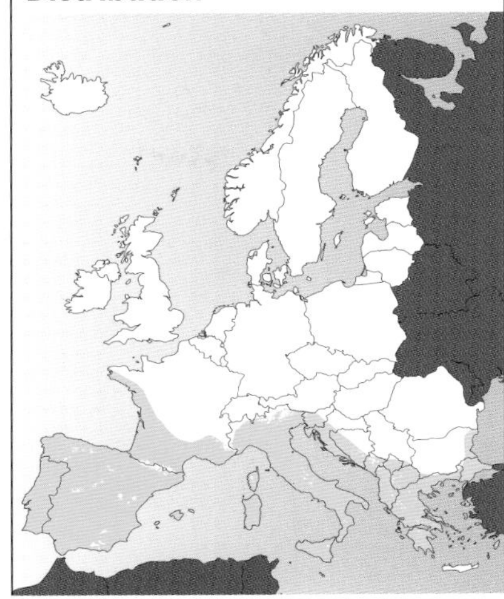

Range of *Messor capitatus*.

Biology

Quite a common species, widely distributed across most of Southern Europe. Colonies are monogynous and very populous, with thousands of workers. Founding is independent. A granivorous species. As in all *Messor* species, it builds seed stores on the nest surface. Trail size varies according to the size of the food source and the season. The large workers, with their impressive mandibles, reduce seeds into small pieces that are transformed into a paste by mastication.

In *Messor capitatus*, as with all members of the genus *Messor*, there is much variation in size between workers of the same colony.

Messor minor (André, 1881)

subfamily Myrmicinae

Messor minor worker.

Identification

Size: 3.5–8 mm, with much variation within the same colony. The gaster is black. The head, mesosoma and petiole are entirely red in all individuals. Workers have a psammophore (long, curved hairs under the head that help to keep seeds held in the mandibles).

This species occurs in Corsica, Sicily and mainland Italy.

Possible confusion

Messor wasmanni has a black head and gaster, and dark red mesosoma. The largest *Messor barbarus* workers can be 12 mm long and do not have a psammophore.

Swarming

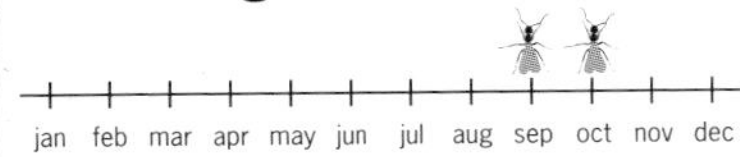

Habitat

Open and very warm habitats: well-exposed hillsides, embankments, dunes, beeches, trails and tracks.

Where to look

Nests are in the ground. The entry opens directly onto the exterior, not under a stone. Small mounds of a few centimetres are constructed on more humid ground. Workers form long trails.

Biology

Can be locally abundant on the coast. Nests are very populous. Founding is independent, by a single queen. A granivorous species. As in all species of the genus *Messor*, *M. minor* builds stores on the surface in order to stock harvested seeds.

Distribution

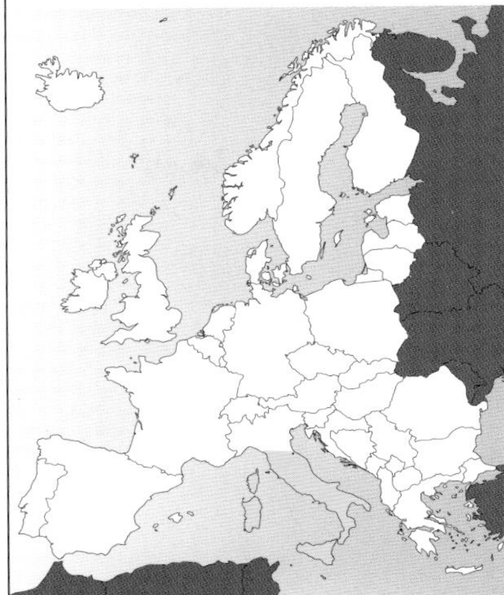

Range of *Messor minor*.

Messor minor worker carrying a seed.

Messor minor workers.

Messor of the **structor** group

subfamily Myrmicinae

Messor structor worker.

Identification

Size: 4–10 mm, with much variation within the same colony. The body is entirely hairy and brown, sometimes pale. The head is striped, except in the smallest individuals. The *structor* group contains very similar species which are difficult to differentiate. The reference species for the group is *Messor structor* (Latreille, 1798); this has different populations within Europe which, according to certain authors, may be distinct species. Three closely related species are known from Greece: *Messor alexandri* (Tohmé & Tohmé, 1981) with a reddish body front, recorded from Greek islands close to Turkey; *M. hellenius* (Agosti & Collingwood, 1987) with a less sculpted body; and *M. orinentalis* (Emery, 1898).

Possible confusion

Messor oertzeni (Forel, 1910), which is quite widespread in the Balkans, does not belong to the *structor* group but shows a similar morphology. The front of the body

Swarming

jan feb mar apr may jun jul aug sep oct nov dec

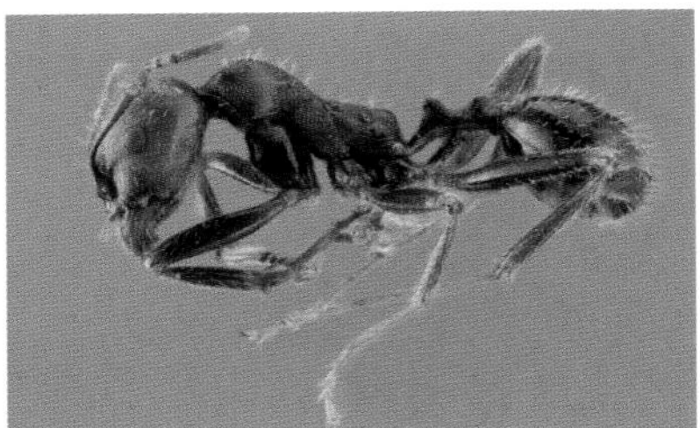
Messor oertzeni worker.

is reddish, and the scape base is enlarged to form a sort of lobe.

Distribution

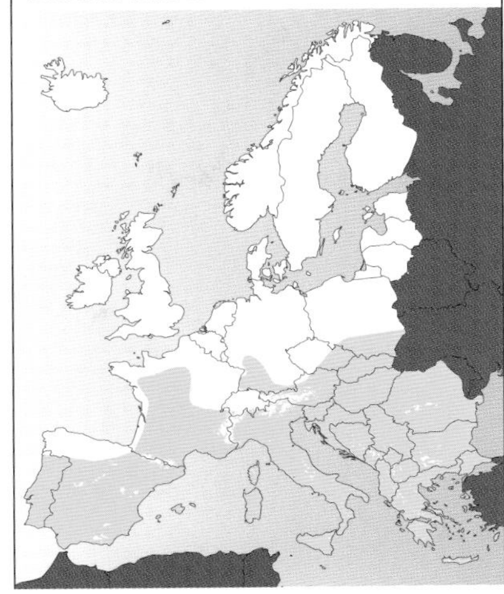
Range of *Messor structor*.

Habitat

Quite open habitats, generally well exposed to the sun but with some moisture: walls, stream banks, meadows, gardens, tracks, roadsides, etc. More of a lowland species, occurring up to 1,300 m.

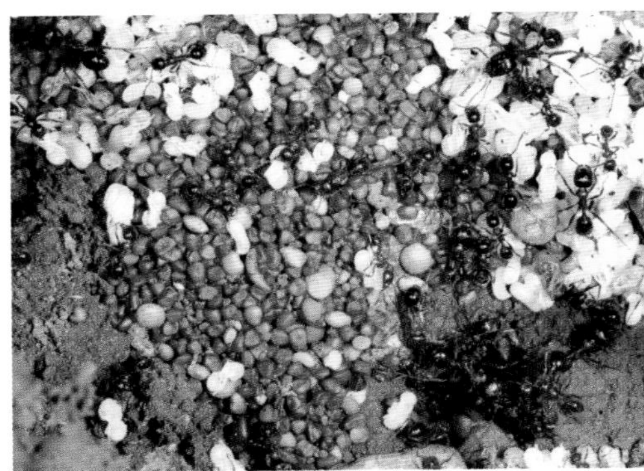
Messor structor colony, showing harvested seeds.

Where to look

Nests are built directly in the ground, under stones. They are secretive. Contrary to other *Messor* species, workers of this group do not create obvious trails.

Biology

Common species. Nest density can be high. Colonies are generally polygynous, with up to a thousand workers. Founding is independent or by budding. The species mainly feeds on seeds but workers regularly bring back arthropod corpses to the nest. As in all *Messor* species, they build surface stores for harvested seeds.

Messor of the ***wasmanni*** group

subfamily Myrmicinae

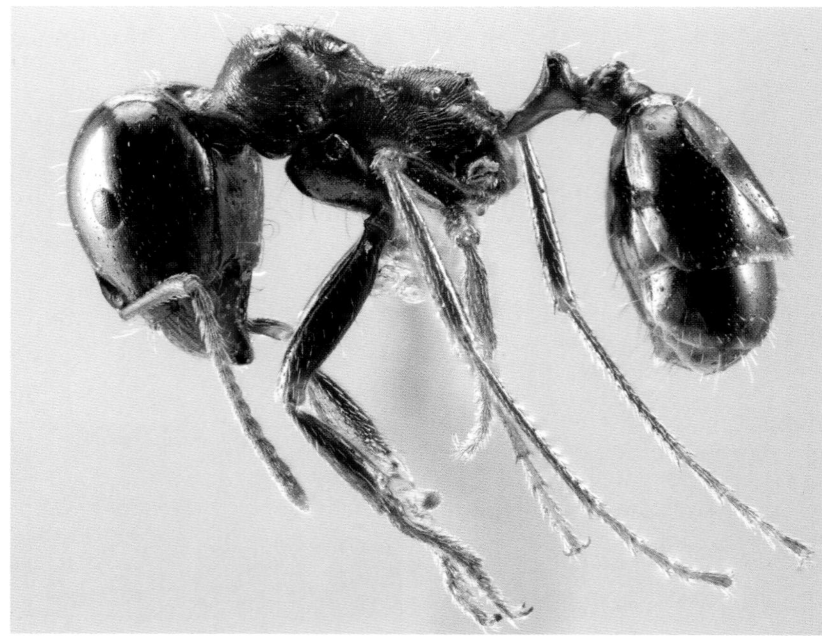

Large *Messor wasmanni* worker.

Identification

Size: 4–10 mm. Black body, glossy on the head and gaster. The mesosoma is either dark red or dark brown. The workers show a progressive polymorphism. Workers have a psammophore allowing the retention of seeds between the mandibles. This group contains several closely related species that are differentiated by the amount of hairs. *Messor meridionalis* (André, 1883) and *M. caducus* (Victor, 1839) have been recorded from the Balkans. *Messor wasmanni* (Krausse, 1910) is also present in the Balkans and on Corsica, on the Italian Peninsula, and in Sardinia and Sicily.

Possible confusion

The front of the body of *Messor minor* is red. Dark *Messor wasmanni* workers can be confused with those of *M. bouvieri*.

Swarming

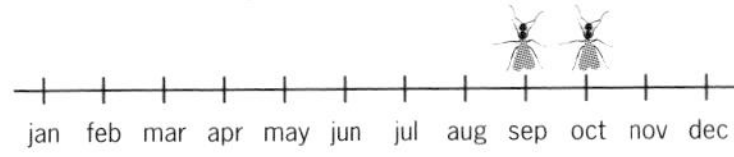

Habitat

These species prefer very warm, open habitats.

Where to look

Mainly in dry meadows, dirt tracks and non-asphalted pavements. Mounds of rejected seed waste, looking like blond hair, are left on the surface near the nest.

Biology

Messor wasmanni is monogynous and colonies are very populous. Workers can be seen in processions in the morning or late afternoon, when it is cooler, transporting seeds. Workers form distinctive motorways, leaving no vegetation on the trail. Colonies dig their nest deep into the ground. All ground vegetation is removed from around the nest. Nuptial flights are often performed after light rain, as in *Messor capitatus*, and around midday.

Distribution

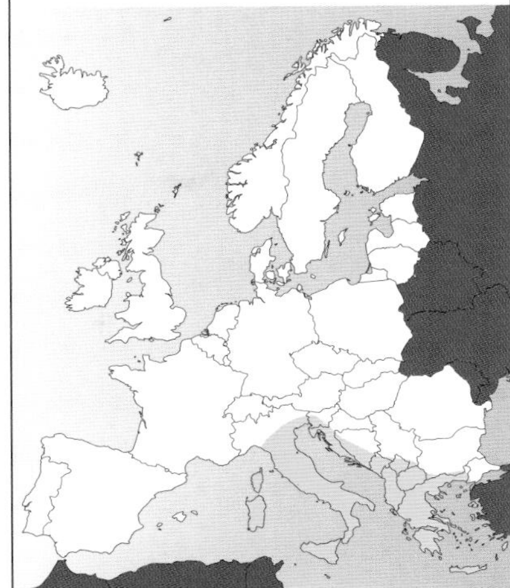

Range of *Messor wasmanni*.

Messor wasmanni worker.

Three *Messor wasmanni* castes. From left to right: two workers, a male and a queen.

Monomorium of the *monomorium* group

Mayr, 1855 subfamily Myrmicinae

Monomorium creticum colony.

Identification

Size: 1.4–1.8 mm. Body is black or yellow. The tegument is entirely smooth and shiny. Four species of this group occur in Europe. Two of them have a totally black body: *Monomorium carbonarium* (F. Smith, 1858), which is considered an invasive species on the Atlantic seaboard, and *M. monomorium* (Bolton, 1987), originally from the Mediterranean Basin, which has become an invasive species on some Pacific islands. Two other species are yellow: *Monomorium andrei* (Saunders, 1890) on Gibraltar, entirely yellow with a slightly darker vertex and gaster; and *M. exiguum* (Forel, 1894), which have 11 segments to their antennae, recorded from the Balearic Islands.

Possible confusion

Monomorium creticum (Emery, 1895) is present on Crete and *M. algiricum* (Bernard, 1955) from the south of Spain are not closely related to *M. monomorium* but they also have a smooth, shiny tegument; they are bigger and their

Swarming

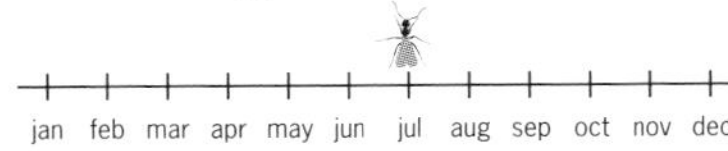

Distribution

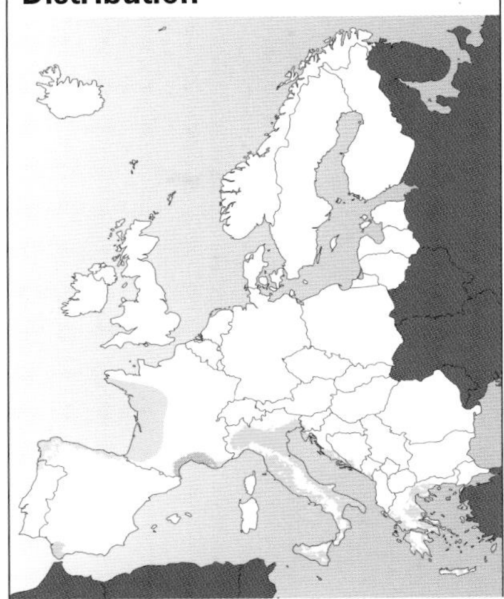
Range of *Monomorium monomorium* (pink) and *M. carbonarium* (grey).

Monomorium monomorium worker.

mesosoma is reddish, and queens also have an enlarged petiole and postpetiole (subgenus *Epixenus*). The yellow species can be confused with *Solenopsis* workers but these last species have two segmented antennal clubs. Only *Plagiolepis* workers are of similar size and colour but they have just a petiole (Formicinae), whereas species in the genus *Monomorium* have a petiole and a postpetiole (Myrmicinae).

Habitat

Open habitats on the edges of saline lakes near the coast on muddy or sandy soils. Salt marshes. Can occasionally be found far from the coast.

Where to look

Nests are built directly in the ground, sometimes against a piece of introduced material (such as a piece of wood). Workers forage on the ground.

Monomorium carbonarium queen (left) and worker (right).

Biology

A very rare species that can occasionally be abundant in favoured habitats. Colonies are highly polygynous, with several thousand workers. They are omnivores.

Monomorium of the *salomonis* group

subfamily Myrmicinae

Monomorium salomonis colony.

Identification

Size: 2 mm. The head and mesosoma are never completely smooth but finely sculpted, which gives the body a matt appearance. The front of the body is orange-yellow to reddish. Gaster is brown. This group is more diverse in Africa and there are four species in Southern Europe: *Monomorium salomonis* (Linnaeus, 1758), recorded in the south of Spain and the Balearic Islands; *M. subopacum* (F. Smith, 1858) more widespread, occuring from Spain to Greece; *M. sommieri* (Emery, 1908) recorded from Lampedusa island in Italy; and *M. phoenicum* (Santschi, 1927) in the Greek islands.

Possible confusion

Monomorium pharaonis (Linneaus, 1758) is a species of tropical origin that can be found in blocks of flats over much of Europe. *Temnothorax* species have spines on the propodeum.

Swarming

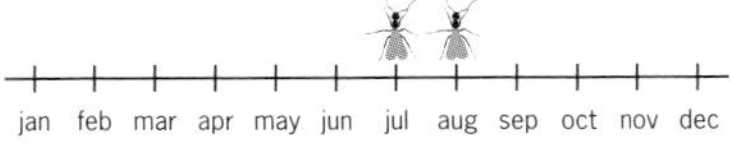

Distribution

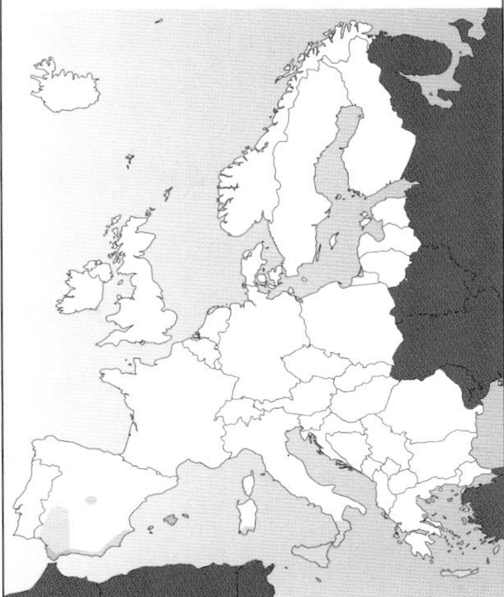

Range of *Monomorium subopacum* (pink) and *M. salomonis* (grey).

Monomorium phoenicum worker.

Habitat

Hot, dry, open habitats.

Where to look

The top edges of beaches, but also in towns: pavements, lawn edges, brownfield sites, under rooves and in cardboard boxes.

Biology

Can be locally very common. Within a colony, workers are numerous and very active. These species are polygynous and omnivorous, hunting various arthropods and also appreciating aphid honeydew.

In Europe *Monomorium pharaonis* occurs only in heated buildings. This photograph was taken in the tropics, where this species introduced in Europe occupies natural habitats.

Myrmecina genus Curtis, 1829

subfamily Myrmicinae

Myrmecina graminicola workers and queen.

Identification

Size: 3.5–5 mm. Body entirely black or reddish, with paler legs and antennae. The abdomen tip tends to be yellowish. The cuticle is more or less highly wrinkled, depending on species. They have a characteristic cube-shaped petiole. The genus *Myrmecina* contains some 50 species, of which only three are found in Europe. One of the three is widespread throughout: *Myrmecina graminicola* (Latreille, 1802). The other two have a much more limited distribution: *Myrmecina sicula* (André, 1882) occurs in Sicily, and *M. melonii* (Rigato, 1990) in Sardinia. These last two species are paler and less sculpted.

Swarming

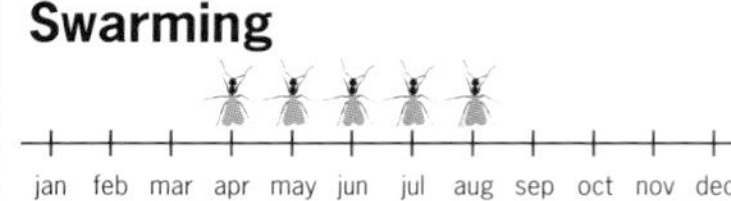

Possible confusion

Tetramorium workers are slightly smaller, more lively and their petiole is of a different shape.

Habitat

Wooded environments, generally quite closed areas. Sometimes on woodland edges receiving little sun. To an altitude of 1,000 m.

Where to look

Nests are under large stones, under moss or directly in the ground. Colonies come to the surface during damp weather but go deeper in the soil when it is hot and dry. Workers hunt in the ground litter.

Biology

Common species, but secretive. Colonies are generally monogynous, with a few dozen workers, as many as a hundred. Some colonies with inter-caste queens (intermediate between queen and worker) are polygynous. Founding is independent, by a single queen. Workers hunt individually for small arthropods in the ground litter. They move about slowly, and stop and form a ball when disturbed.

Distribution

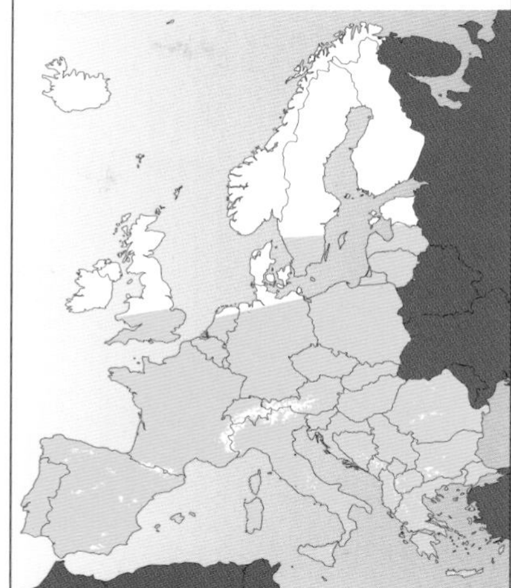

Range of *Myrmecina graminicola*.

Myrmecina graminicola worker.

Myrmica of the *bergi* group

subfamily Myrmicinae

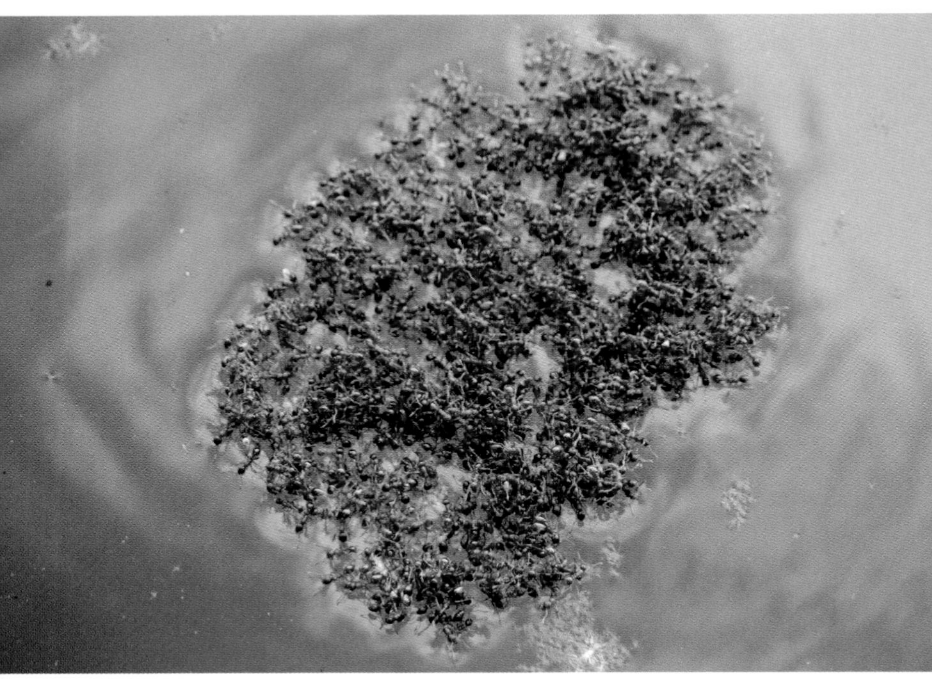

Myrmica gallienii colony forming a raft after flooding.

Identification

Size: 4–5.5 mm. The body is mainly red. The scape base is markedly curved, without a visible angle. Two species of this group occur in Europe: *Myrmica gallienii* (Bondroit, 1920), which is widely distributed; and *M. bergi* (Ruzsky, 1902), which only occurs in eastern Romania, on the shores of the Black Sea.

Possible confusion

Myrmica of the *rugulosa* group have a scape more strongly arched at the base and their petiole tegument is less sculpted. However, *Myrmica sulcinodis* has a very sculpted tegument, with deep grooves on the mesosoma and petiole. In *Myrmica ruginodis* and *M. rubra*, the bend of the scape is only slightly curved.

Swarming

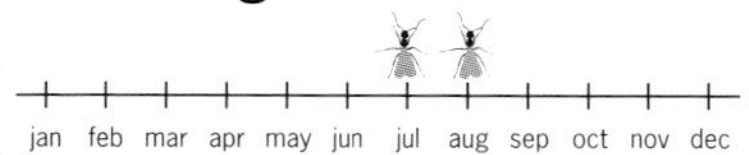

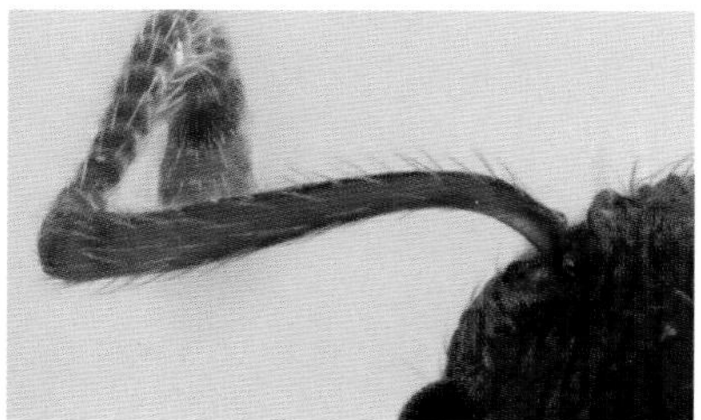

Incurved scape of *Myrmica gallienii*, without any hint of a longitudinal ridge.

Habitat

Generally in wetlands (floating peat bogs) or areas susceptible to flooding (river and stream banks).

Where to look

Nests are on the top of tufts of vegetation, under stones or directly in the ground. Workers forage on the ground or in low vegetation.

Biology

Myrmica gallienii is quite a rare species but in appropriate sites nest density can be high. Colonies are monogynous or polygynous, with several hundred workers. Founding can de independent or by adoption in a colony. They are omnivores: eat invertebrates, Hemiptera honeydew, nectar and more. Very aggressive species. It can be host to blue butterflies of the genus *Phengaris* (= *Maculinea*, Lycaenidae) whose caterpillars develop at the expense of the colony. When flooding occurs, *Myrmica gallienii* workers come together to form a raft which allows them to survive in such conditions.

Distribution

Range of *Myrmica gallienii*.

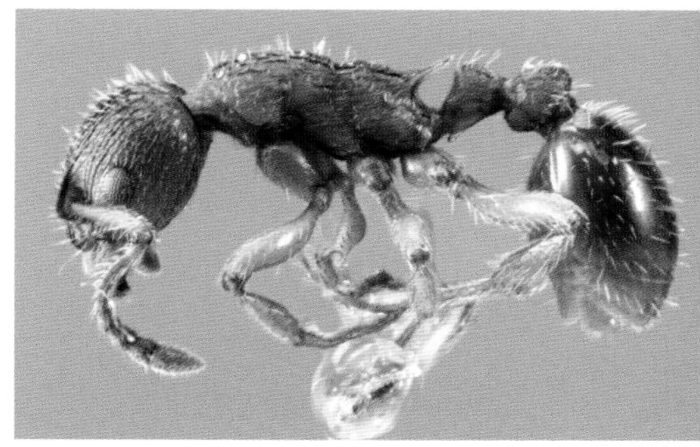

Myrmica gallienii worker.

Myrmica of the ***lobicornis*** group

subfamily Myrmicinae

Myrmica sulcinodis worker.

Identification

Size: 3.5–4.5 mm. Body generally dark red to almost black. The base of the scape has a vertical lobe. There are five species of this group in Europe. They are cold-climate ants, only occurring at altitude in the south. *Myrmica lobicornis* (Nylander, 1846) is the most widespread species. *Myrmica lobulicornis* (Nylander, 1857) is only present in western mountain ranges (Pyrenees, Massif Central and western Alps); *M. wesmaeli* (Bondroit, 1918) in the Iberian Peninsula and the Pyrenees; *M. xavieri* (Radchenko, Elmes & Savolainen, 2008) only in Spain. *Myrmica sulcinodis* (Nylander, 1846) has no vertical extension at the scape base but from the male's morphology it does belong to the *lobicornis* group.

Swarming

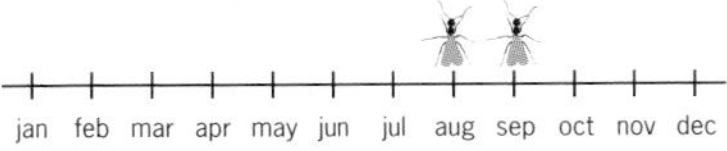

Possible confusion

Other species of *Myrmica* are normally of a less dark red and do not have a vertical lobe at the scape base, except for species in the *schencki* group.

Habitat

A preference for open habitats at altitude: forest edges, well-exposed grassland with short vegetation, peat bogs and heather moors. Sometimes in forests. A typical species of low and middle mountain habitat, to 2,000 m altitude.

Where to look

Nests are under stones or moss or directly in the ground. Workers forage individually on the ground.

Biology

Quite a common species in appropriate habitats. Colonies are monogynous and not very populous, with at most a few hundred workers. Founding is independent. These species probably feed on small invertebrates (flies, small worms, caterpillars, etc.).

Distribution

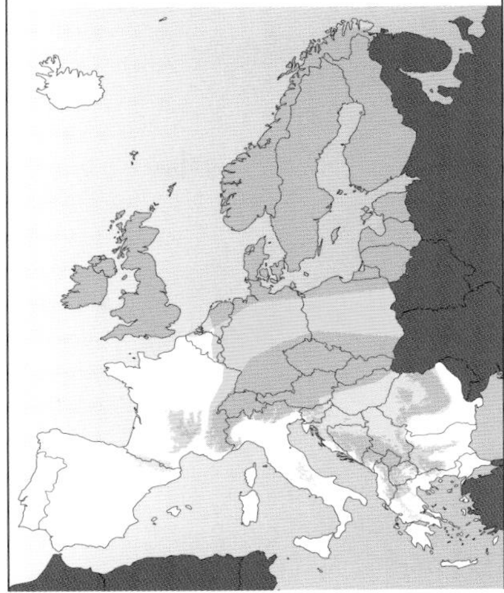

Range of *Myrmica lobicornis* (pink) and *M. sulcinodis* (grey).

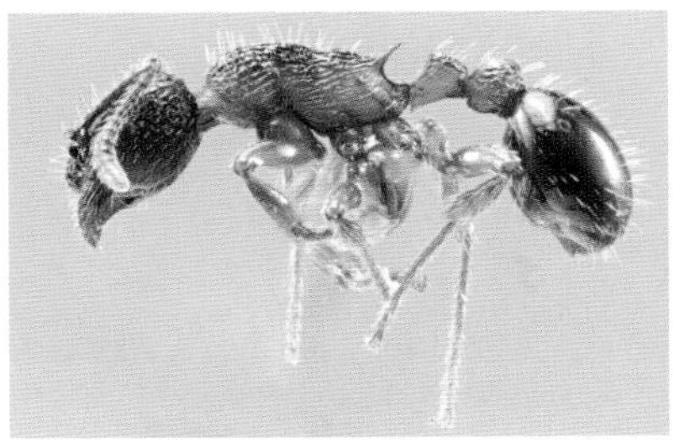

Profile view of *Myrmica lobicornis* worker.

Myrmica lobulicornis queen (left) and male (right).

Myrmica rubra Linnaeus, 1758

subfamily Myrmicinae

Myrmica rubra worker carrying a larva.

Identification

Size: 3.5–5 mm. Body entirely red. The first segment of the gaster is slightly darker than the rest. The base of the scape is uniformly curved. The propodeum spines are relatively short.

Possible confusion

Myrmica ruginodis has longer propodeum spines. In other *Myrmica* species there is a more abrupt curve at the scape base or it forms an obvious angle. *Aphaenogaster subterranea* has a much more elongated petiole and is generally of a browner colour.

Habitat

A quite omnipresent species that prefers cool, damp sites. It appears, however, to avoid peat bogs. It occurs in natural as well as human-made habitats (parks,

Swarming

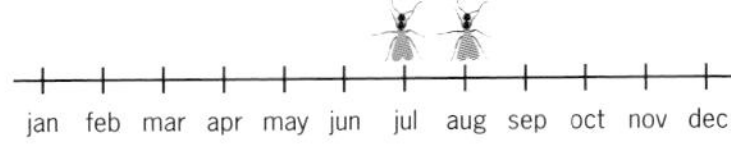

gardens, copses, tracks and footpaths). More common at lower altitudes, but it can occur up to 1,500 m.

Where to look

Nests are often under stones, flower pots or in dead branches on the ground, or simply in ground litter. Workers forage for food on the ground and in vegetation.

Distribution

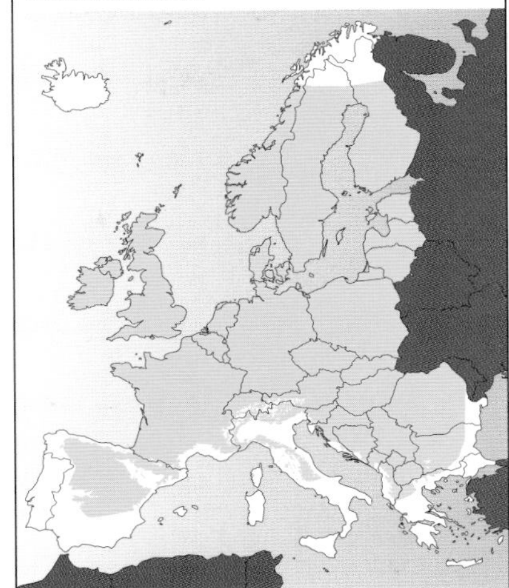

Range of *Myrmica rubra*.

Biology

A very common species. Colonies are polygynous, with many hundreds of workers. The same colony may contain several interconnected nests. There are two forms of queen: small queens (microgynes) and large queens (macrogynes). After the nuptial flight queens are often integrated into an already established nest. New colonies can be formed by budding. An omnivorous species, it feeds on small invertebrates (aphids, flies, small worms, etc.) and Hemiptera honeydew. Workers are very aggressive, freely using their sting. They ferociously defend their nests when disturbed. This species is a regular host of blue butterflies of the genus *Phengaris* (= *Maculinea*), whose caterpillars live at the expense of the colony.

Myrmica rubra queen among her workers.

Myrmica ruginodis Nylander, 1846

subfamily Myrmicinae

Myrmica ruginodis queen.

Identification

Size: 4–5.5 mm. Body entirely red. The first segment of the gaster is slightly darker than the rest. The scape base is in the form of a progressive curve. The propodeum spines are relatively long.

Possible confusion

Myrmica rubra has shorter propodeum spines. In other *Myrmica* species the curve at the scape base is more abrupt or obviously angled. *Aphaenogaster subterranea* has a rounded, smooth pronotum, an obviously longer petiole and is generally a browner colour.

Habitat

A widespread species that can occur as frequently in forest as in open habitats, as long as they are damp. Occurs in peat bogs. It is also found in human-made habitats (parks, gardens, copses, tracks and footpaths). It occurs at all altitudes to 2,000 m.

Swarming

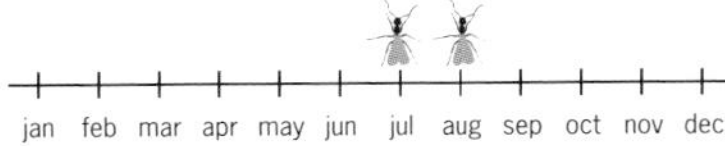

Where to look

Nests are under stones, directly in the ground or in a grass or moss (peat bog) tussocks, in dead branches on the ground, against or under a tree stump or simply in ground litter. Sometimes nests have a small dome of vegetation debris on them, difficult to see if surrounding foliage is long. Workers forage on the ground or in vegetation, even in trees.

Distribution

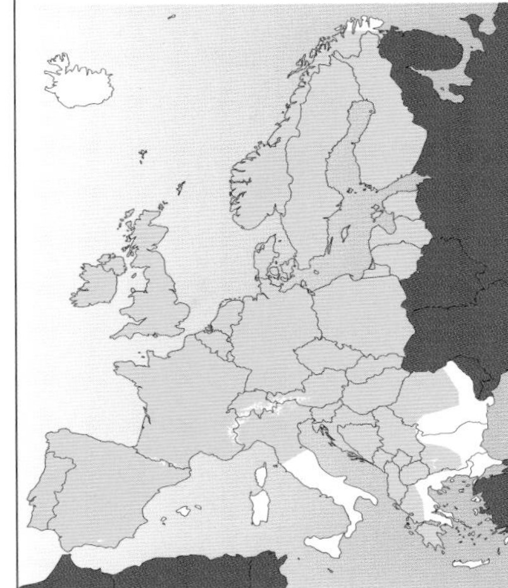

Range of *Myrmica ruginodis*.

Biology

A very common species. Nest density can be very high in cool, humid habitats – conditions to which *Myrmica ruginodis* is very well adapted. Colonies are either monogynous or polygynous, with several hundred workers. A single colony may consist of several interconnected nests. There are two forms of queens: small queens (microgynes), with which colonies are polygynous; and large queens (macrogynes), which are found in monogynous colonies – these are founded independently. They are omnivores, feeding on small invertebrates (aphids, flies, small worms, etc.) and Hemiptera honeydew. Workers are very aggressive and ferociously defend their nests when disturbed; they freely use their sting. This species is a regular host of blue butterflies of the genus *Phengaris* (= *Maculinea*), whose caterpillars develop at the expense of the colony.

Myrmica ruginodis workers and brood.

Myrmica of the *rugulosa* group

subfamily Myrmicinae

Myrmica constricta worker.

Identification

Size: 3.1–4.5 mm. Reddish-brown body. The rear part of the rectangular petiole slopes downwards in a regular manner. The antennae scapes are highly but regularly bent near their base, sometimes with the trace of a lobe or a ridge. This group includes three species. *Myrmica rugulosa* (Nylander, 1849) has a vast distribution throughout Europe; the scapes are highly incurved, without a longitudinal ridge. On the other hand, *Myrmica constricta* (Karawajew, 1934) and *Myrmica hellenica* (Finzi, 1926) have visible longitudinal ridges on their scapes, and occur only in Eastern Europe.

Swarming

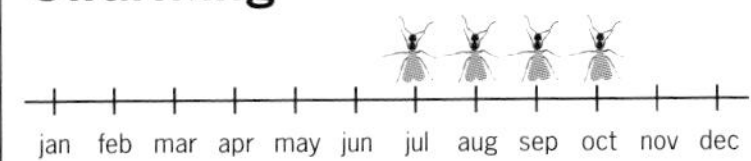

Possible confusion

Myrmica gallienii has a less incurved scape without any trace of a ridge. In *Myrmica specioides* the ridges are more obvious and outline a small lobe.

Habitat

Occurs in warm habitats, in sunny sites, especially on sandy ground with short vegetation: short grassland, intensively grazed sheep-walks and meadows with a majority of short sward. It occurs in clearings in woodland areas near water. It can appear in gardens and urban areas.

Where to look

In dry, rocky or sandy ground, and open borders of large water bodies. The simple nests, nearly always made of earth, are often built under stones. Their entrances are typically marked by small quantities of excavated matter.

Biology

These species are generally polygynous, sometimes with multi-domed nests containing thousands of workers. Workers can sometimes be seen collecting dead or injured invertebrates on the sides of water bodies or roads. Winged individuals swarm during late afternoons in hot weather, especially in September. Males mate with queens on the ground often just after leaving the nest.

Distribution

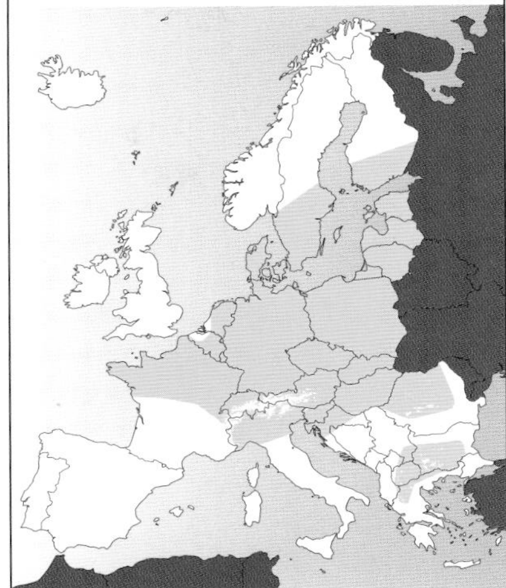

Range of *Myrmica rugulosa*.

Myrmica rugulosa worker.

Myrmica of the ***sabuleti*** group

subfamily Myrmicinae

Myrmica sabuleti worker.

Identification

Size: 4–5 mm. A red body. The scape base is angular with a wide, backward-pointing lobe. *Myrmica sabuleti* (Meinert, 1860) is widely distributed in Europe. Two other species are closely related: *Myrmica spinosior* (Santschi, 1931) occurs in Mediterranean habitats in Western Europe, and *M. lonae* (Finzi, 1926) in Central Europe in cool, wet habitats. *Myrmica lonae* has well-developed scape lobes. *Myrmica bibikoffi* (Kutter, 1963) also belongs to the *M. sabuleti* group; it is a temporary social parasite of *M. sabuleti* and *M. spinosior*.

Swarming

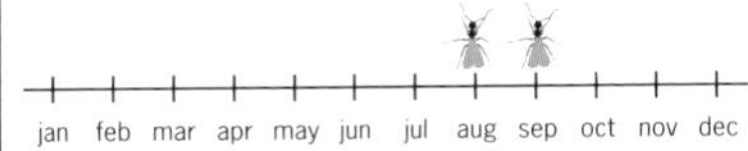

Possible confusion

Myrmica tulinae (Elmes, Radchenko & Aktaç, 2002) superficially resembles *M. sabuleti* but the males with short scapes look more similar to species of the *scabrinodis* group. In species of the *specioides* group of *Myrmica*, the rear part of the petiole becomes gradually lower, whereas it is in the form of a step in *M. sabuleti*.

Habitat

Open, warm and dry areas: sandy sites, heaths, calcareous grassland. These species occur to 2,000 m.

Where to look

Nests are under stones or directly in the ground. Workers forage on the ground or in low vegetation.

Biology

Common species. Colonies are generally polygynous. Founding is either independent or by adoption into a colony. An omnivorous species, workers hunt for invertebrates and collect Hemiptera honeydew. They are a relatively non-aggressive species. They are regularly hosts of blue butterflies of the genus *Phengaris* (= *Maculinea*), whose caterpillars develop at the expense of the colony. Species of the *sabuleti* group of *Myrmica* may also be the host of social parasites of the genus *Myrmica* (see page 326).

Distribution

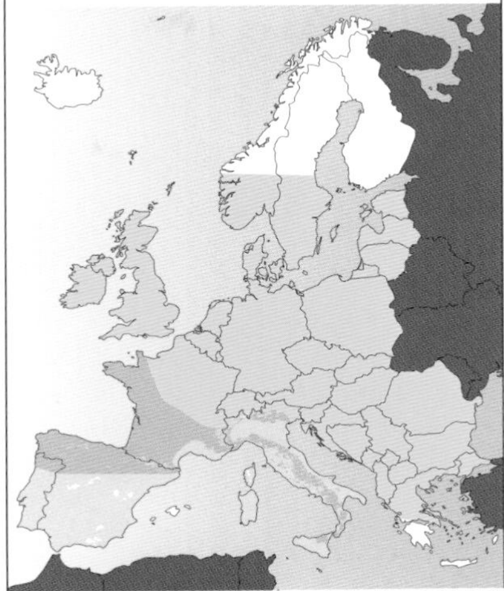

Range of *Myrmica sabuleti* (pink) and *M. spinosior* (grey).

Myrmica lonae worker.

Myrmica of the *scabrinodis* group

subfamily Myrmicinae

Myrmica scabrinodis worker carrying a pupa.

Identification

Size: 3.5–5 mm. Body entirely red. The scape base is angular and has a very small lobe pointing backwards. *Myrmica scabrinodis* (Nylander, 1846) is quite a common species in Europe, widely distributed in all but some Mediterranean habitats. The most western populations have recently been given species status (*Myrmica martini* [Seifert, Yazdi & Schultz, 2014]). *Myrmica aloba* (Forel, 1909) is a closely related species found in Spain and along the Mediterranean coast of France; it is distinguished by the lobe at the scape base being very small, reduced to a simple keel. *Myrmica vandeli* (Bondroit, 1920) is sometimes a temporary social parasite in *M. scabrinodis* nests; it is present in much of Europe and is distinguished from *M. scabrinodis* by being more hairy, its tegument sculpting consists of fine longitudinal wrinkles on the mesosoma.

Possible confusion

In *Myrmica specioides* the rear part of the petiole progressively slopes downwards, whereas it forms a step in *Myrmica* species of the *scabrinodis* group. The lobe at the scape base is horizontal and bigger in *Myrmica sabuleti* and *M. spinosior*.

Habitat

Widespread species: all types of open habitat (meadows, heather moors, peat bogs, etc.), and also forest (clearings). In lowlands and in mountainous areas to 2,000 m altitude.

Swarming

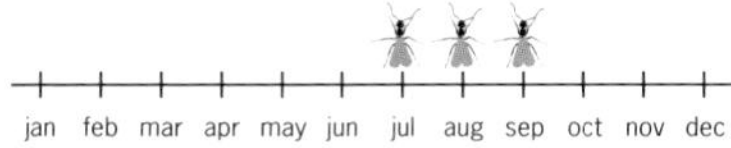

Where to look

Nests are generally under stones, in stumps or under the bark of dead wood. In hot sites (e.g. in Mediterranean areas) nests are directly in the ground and can be very difficult to find. In peat bogs and wet meadows nests are in hummocks or tufts of grass or moss, where the ants construct small domes of plant debris or earth visible at the base of grass stems. Workers forage on the ground or in low vegetation.

Distribution

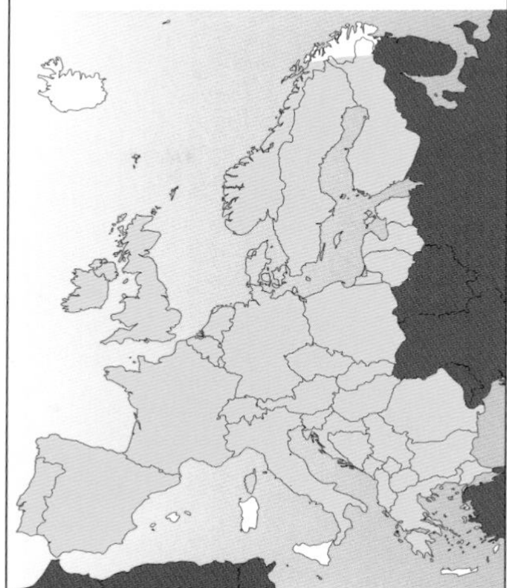

Range of *Myrmica scabrinodis sensu lato*.

Biology

Common species. Nest density can be very high. Colonies are either monogynous or polygynous, with several hundred workers. Founding can be independent or by adoption in another colony. These species feed on small vertebrates (flies, small worms, caterpillars, etc.). They can be hosts of blue butterflies of the genus *Phengaris* (= *Maculinea*), whose caterpillars grow at the expense of the colony. Parasitic fly larvae of the genus *Microdon* may also be found in nests. *Myrmica scabrinodis* can also be the host of social parasites of the genus *Myrmica* (see page 326).

Comparison of the mesosoma sculpting of *Myrmica vandeli (left)* and *M. scabrinodis (right)*.

Myrmica of the *schencki* group

subfamily Myrmicinae

Myrmica schencki workers.

Identification

Size: 4–5.5 mm. Body generally a very dark red but the mesosoma is sometimes pale. The scape base has a vertical lobe with a lateral extension that forms a plate. Six species in this group occur in Europe. *Myrmica schencki* (Emery, 1895) is the most widespread. The other species are more localised: *Myrmica obscura* (Finzi, 1926) in the southern Alps and Italy; *M. siciliana* (Radchenko, Elmes & Alicata, 2006) in Sicily; *M. ravasinii* (Finzi, 1923) in the Balkans; *M. pelops* (Seifert 2003) in the Peloponnese (Greece); and *M. deplanata* (Emery, 1921) in Central and Eastern Europe.

Swarming

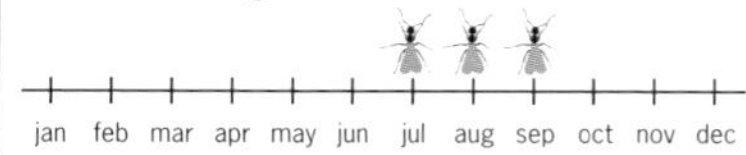

Possible confusion

Myrmica species of the *lobicornis* group also have a vertical lobe at the scape base but the petiole is shorter and more angular on top. Other *Myrmica* species do not have a vertical lobe at the scape base.

Habitat

Open, dry habitats: calcareous grassland, rocky escarpments and sometimes riverbanks. To 2,600 m altitude.

Where to look

Nests are under stones or directly in the ground. In the latter case each nest entrance may be covered with a typical and recognisable small chimney of plant debris. Workers forage on the ground and in low vegetation.

Biology

Uncommon species. Colonies are monogynous or polygynous, with a few hundred workers. These species feed on small invertebrates (flies, small worms, caterpillars, etc.) and aphid honeydew. *Myrmica schencki* is a regular host of blue butterflies of the genus *Phengaris* (= *Maculinea*), whose caterpillars grow at the expense of the colony.

Distribution

Range of *Myrmica schencki*.

Head of *Myrmica schencki* worker.

Myrmica schencki worker.

Myrmica of the *specioides* group

subfamily Myrmicinae

Myrmica specioides worker.

Identification

Size: 3.5–5 mm. Body entirely red. The profile of the rear of the petiole slopes gently downwards. The scape base is obviously angular and has a more or less developed, backward-pointing, horizontal lobe. Two species of this group are present in Europe: *Myrmica specioides* (Bondroit, 1918), widely distributed and common throughout Europe; and *M. curvithorax* (Bondroit, 1920), also with a vast distribution but more rarely encountered. This last species has well-developed lobes at the base of the antennal scapes.

Possible confusion

In *Myrmica constricta* and *M. hellenica* (which belong to the *rugulosa* group) the ridges at the base of the antenna do not demarcate the lobe-shaped swelling. Species in the *sabuleti* and *scabrinodis* groups have different petioles.

Habitat

Generally in warm situations: calcareous grasslands, coastal

Swarming

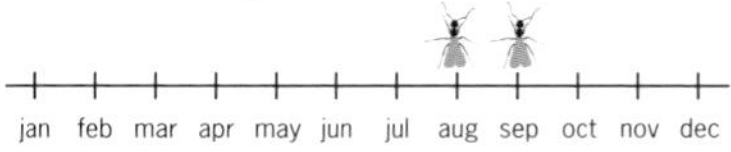

dunes, edgeland habitats, clearings and quarries. These species are quite drought-tolerant.

Where to look

Nests are under stones or directly in the ground. Workers forage on the ground or in low vegetation.

Distribution

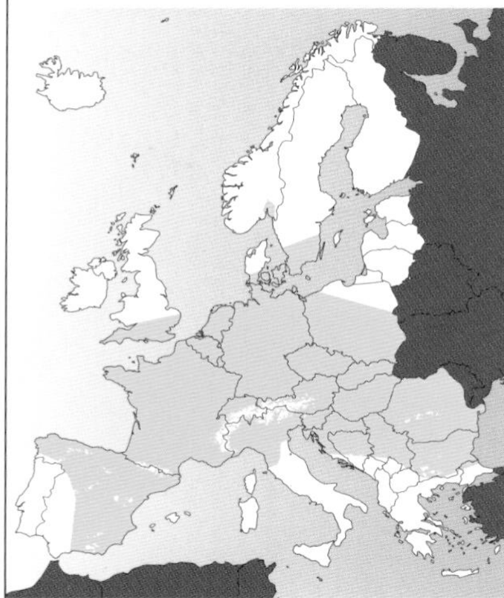

Range of *Myrmica specioides.*

Biology

Myrmica specioides is quite a common species. Colonies are monogynous or polygynous, with several hundred workers. Founding may be independent or by adoption in another colony. They are omnivorous: eat invertebrates, Hemiptera honeydew, nectar, etc. They are very aggressive. Can be the host of blue butterflies of the genus *Phengaris* (= *Maculinea*), whose caterpillars grow at the expense of the colony.

Myrmica curvithorax worker.

Myrmica specioides mating.

Parasitic species of the ***Myrmica* genus** Latreille, 1804 subfamily Myrmicinae

Myrmica karavajevi worker.

Identification

Size of queens: 3–4 mm. Body entirely red. Workers are either rare or absent. Often have a well-developed cover of hairs. In Europe there are five species, all permanent social parasites. These species differ, as in other *Myrmica* species, partly in the shape of their scapes: these are either incurved, without any lobe or extension – as in *M. karavajevi* (Arnold, 1930), present throughout Europe; *M. lemasnei* (Bernard, 1967), which occurs in the Pyrenees; and *M. laurae* (Emery, 1907), in central Italy; or, angular with a lobe delimited by a ridge – as in *M. hirsuta* (Elmes, 1978) present in temperate Europe; and *M. myrmicoxena* (Forel, 1895), in the western Alps. Parasite queens can be distinguished from host queens by their small size, similar to that of the host workers.

Possible confusion

Other species of *Myrmica* can be temporary social parasites, such as *M. bibikoffi* or *M. vandeli* (see pages 315 and 320).

Swarming

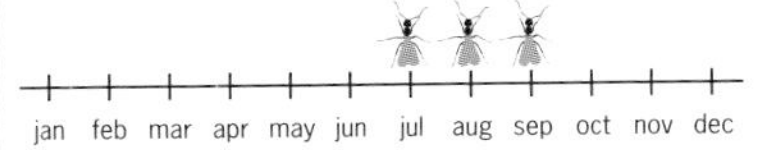

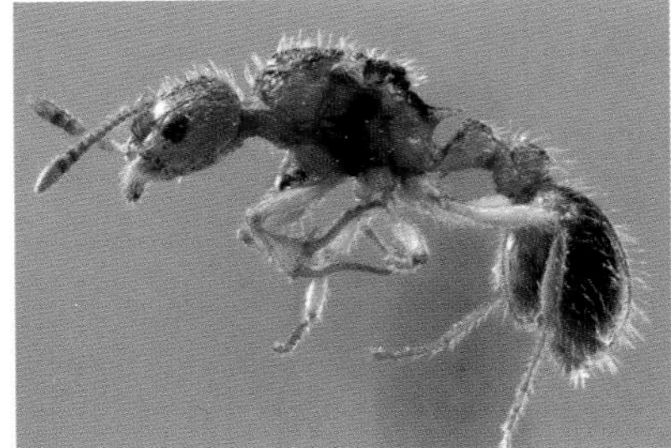

Myrmica hirsuta queen.

Distribution

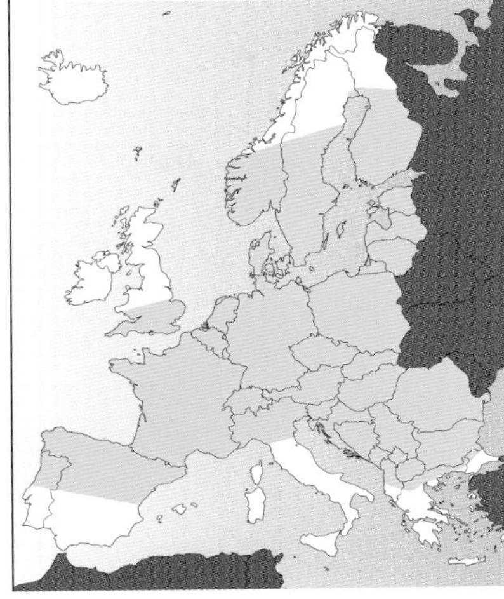

Range of *Myrmica karavajevi*.

Myrmica hirsuta male.

Habitat

Same habitats as their hosts.

Where to look

In the host's nests.

Biology

These are five rare species of permanent social parasites. It would appear that *Myrmica karavajevi* is commoner than the others. Density of parasitised nests is always low. Their biology is little known. *Myrmica lemasnei*, *M. laurae* and *M. karavajevi* produce only sexual individuals. *Myrmica karavajevi* uses several species as hosts: *M. scabrinodis*, *M. sabuleti*, *M. gallienii*, *M. rugulosa* and *M. lonae*. *Myrmica myrmicoxena* parasitises *M. lobicornis*. *Myrmica laurae* parasitises *M. scabrinodis*. *Myrmica hirsuta* and *M. lemasnei* use mainly *M. sabuleti* and *M. spinosior* as hosts.

Myrmoxenus genus Ruzsky, 1902

subfamily Myrmicinae

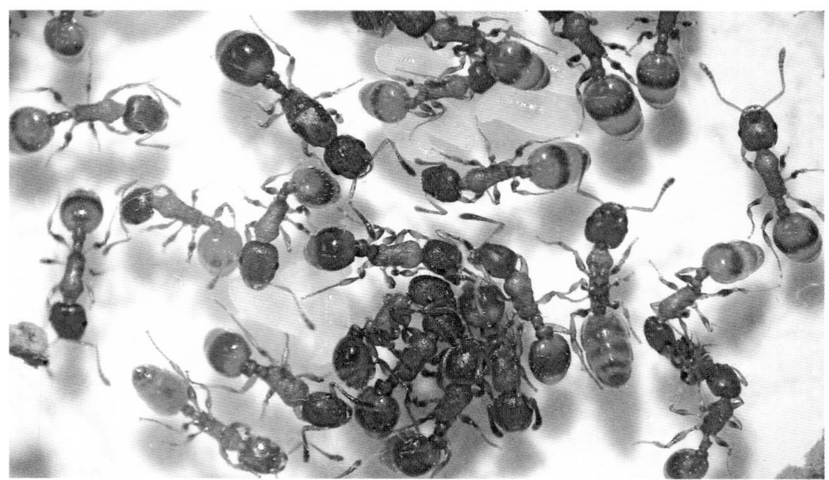

Myrmoxenus ravouxi is a slavemaker species in which colonies are made up of a few slavemaker workers and numerous host workers. Seven *Myrmoxenus ravouxi* workers are grouped together in the centre of the photograph. The queen (right) is hardly bigger than the workers. The other ants are host species *Temnothorax aveli* workers.

Identification

Size: workers about 2.5 mm; queens about 3 mm. A yellow-beige thorax. The antennae tips are darker than the rest. The dark band on the first segment of the gaster is faint and its edges imprecise. All 12 species in the genus *Myrmoxenus* are social parasites with *Temnothorax* species as hosts. Seven species occur in Europe. Two of these are fairly widely distributed: *Myrmoxenus kraussei* (Emery, 1915), which parasitises *Temnothorax recedens*; and *M. ravouxi* (André, 1896), which parasitises several *Temnothorax* species (*T. unifasciatus*, *T. aveli*, etc.). The other species have more restricted distributions: *Myrmoxenus adlerzi* (Douwes, Jessen & Buschinger, 1988) parasitises *Temnothorax exilis* in Greece; *M. bernardi* (Espadaler, 1982) parasitises *T. gredosi* in Spain; *M. corsica* (Emery, 1895) parasitises *T. exilis* in Corsica; *M. gordiagini* (Ruzsky, 1902) parasitises *T. lichensteini* in the Balkans and *T. graecus* in Greece; *M. stumperi* (Kutter, 1950) parasitises *T. tuberum* in the western Alps.

Swarming

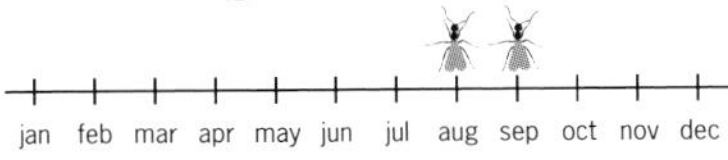

Note: According to recent genetic research, the genus *Mymoxenus* should be included in the genus *Temnothorax*. These species should thus be named: *Temnothorax adlerzi*, *T. bernardi*, *T. corsica*, *T. gordiagini*, *T. kraussei*, *T. ravouxi* and *T. stumperi*.

Possible confusion

Myrmoxenus species can be distinguished from their *Temnothorax* hosts by the presence of an obvious rounded growth under the postpetiole. The parasites and the hosts are very difficult to differentiate in the field. The parasite queens are obviously smaller than the host queens and the workers appear to be less clumsy.

Habitat

Same habitat as their respective hosts.

> **Where to look**
> In the nests of their respective hosts.

Biology

All the species of this genus are social parasites of *Temnothorax* species. Where *Myrmoxenus* species occur, the proportion of parasitised nests can be high (as high as one nest in five). Certain species do not produce workers. In all *Myrmoxenus* species the queen founds a new colony by penetrating the host species' nest and killing the resident queen by grasping her neck for several days.

Distribution

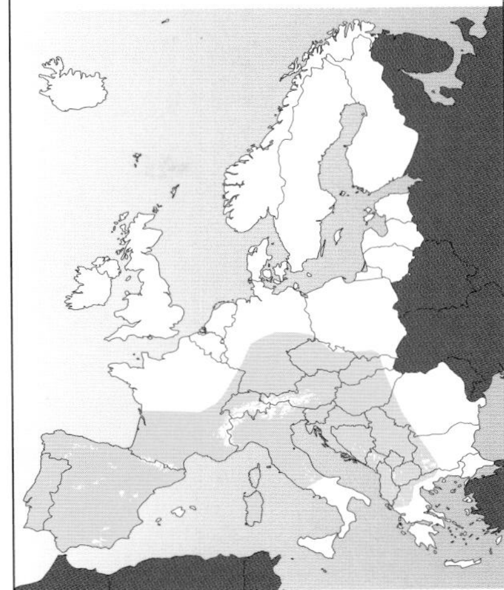

Range of *Myrmoxenus ravouxi*.

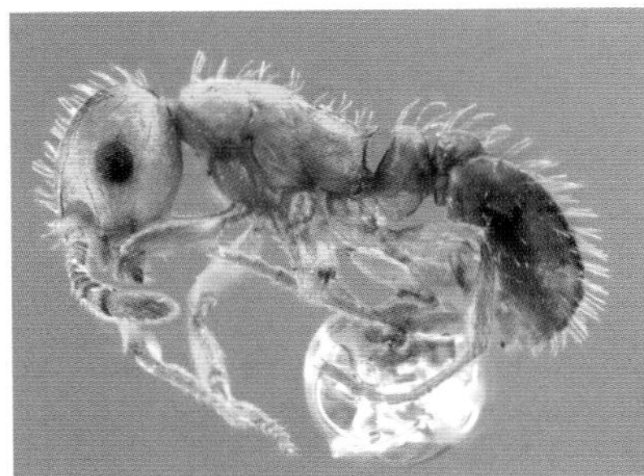

Myrmoxenus kraussei worker.

Oxyopomyrmex genus André, 1881

subfamily Myrmicinae

Two *Oxyopomyrmex saulcyi* workers at the nest entrance.

Identification

Size: 1.8–2.2 mm. Body totally matt and black. Appendages and mesosoma slightly paler. Eleven segments to the antennae. They have a psammophore that helps in carrying seeds. A genus endemic to the Mediterranean Basin. They have the particularity, along with species of the genus *Goniomma*, of possessing comma-shaped eyes. The genus contains 15 species, five of which are found in Southern Europe: *Oxyopomyrmex saulcyi* (Emery, 1889), from the Iberian Peninsula to Sicily; *O. krueperi* (Forel, 1911) in the Balkans; *O. magnus* (Salata & Borowiec, 2015) in Spain; *O. laevidus* (Salata & Borowiec, 2015) in Crete; and *O. polybotesii* in the eastern Greek islands.

Possible confusion

Workers of the genus *Goniomma* are bigger and have 12 segments to their antennae.

Habitat

Tracks, sunny paths or Mediterranean vegetation such as low garrigue.

Swarming

jan	feb	mar	apr	may	jun	jul	aug	sep	oct	nov	dec
		✓	✓								

Where to look

The nest entrance is very small. The nest, at a depth of 20–40 cm, consists of four or five chambers with storage areas. There are always low grasses nearby.

Distribution

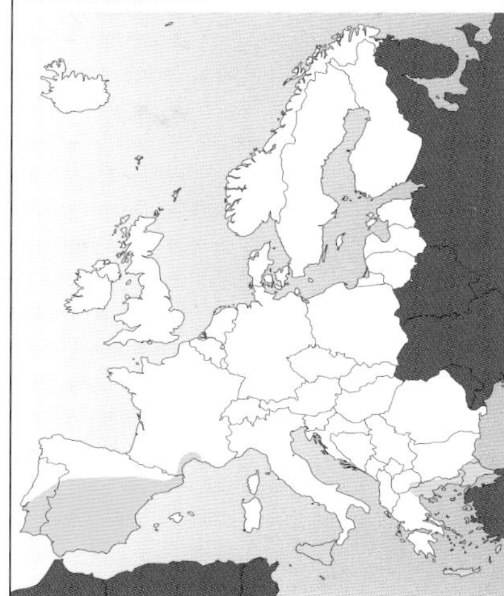

Range of the genus *Oxyopomyrmex*.

Biology

Nest density can be high. Colonies are monogynous or polygynous, with about a hundred workers. Workers forage near the nest by moving in circles. This type of foraging allows them to have regular contact with fellow workers. When faced with danger, workers feign death. Essentially granivores, these species fill small stores and also bringing back arthropod corpses or various insect larvae.

Oxyopomyrmex saulcyi worker.

Pheidole genus Westwood, 1841

subfamily Myrmicinae

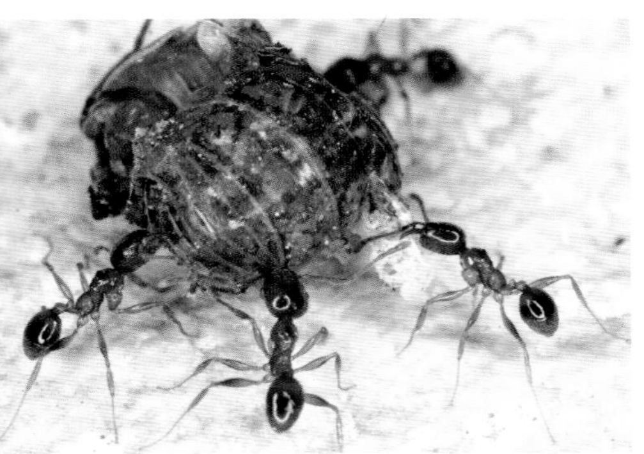

Pheidole pallidula minor workers carrying prey.

Identification

Two morphologically distinct castes: minor workers, 1.5–2.5 mm, and major workers 3.5–5 mm with a much larger head. Colour varies from pale yellow to dark brown. Minor workers have very long antennae. The genus *Pheidole* is widespread around the world. Only three species have been recorded in Europe: *Pheidole pallidula* (Nylander, 1848) is widely distributed; *P. megacephala* (Fabricius, 1793) and *P. teneriffana* (Forel, 1893), of various tropical origins, have colonised sites on the Mediterranean coast or heated buildings elsewhere. *Pheidole teneriffana* can be distinguished from the two other species by having an entirely wrinkled head.

Possible confusion

Confusion with other genera is impossible if both castes are seen in the same nest. Minor workers closely resemble *Temnothorax recedens* but *Pheidole* species move about much more quickly. Certain *Tetramorium* species are of a similar size and colour but have obvious longitudinally striped heads and the front of the thorax has angular 'shoulders'.

Habitat

Quite ubiquitous but especially in warm sites, *Pheidole pallidula* occurs in stony sites, vineyards, heath and sunny areas of garrigue and maquis and also in forests. It is well adapted to living in human-made habitats: green spaces in towns, pavements and so on. Does not occur at altitude.

Where to look

Nests are directly in the ground or under a stone of any size. In urban areas, nest entrances are in cracks in ground covering. Workers forage on the ground and in low vegetation.

Swarming

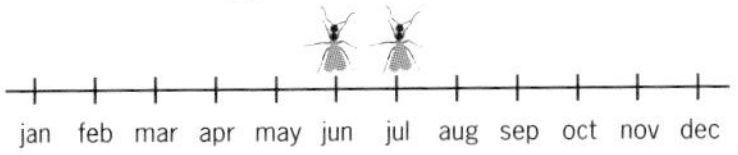

jan feb mar apr may jun jul aug sep oct nov dec

Pheidole teneriffana major worker.

Distribution

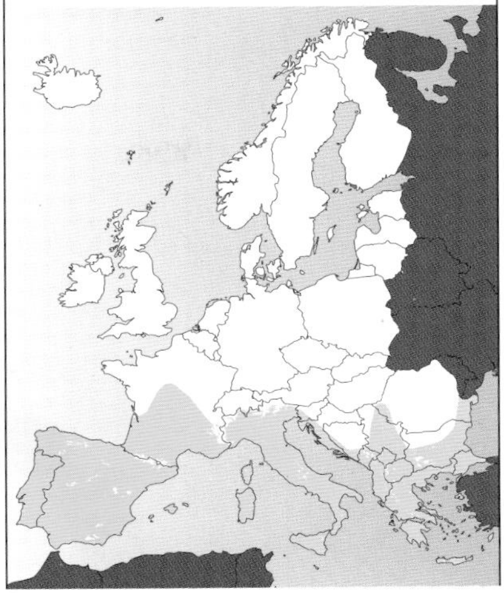

Range of *Pheidole pallidula*.

Biology

Pheidole pallidula is a very common species along the Mediterranean coast. Nest density is often very high. It is an opportunistic species, a fighter and often dominant. Nests contain several thousand workers and one to four queens (two thirds are monogynous). Founding is essentially independent, by one queen, but colony multiplication by budding after adoption of the queen is probable. They are omnivores; they search principally for invertebrates, and any corpses are attacked by many individuals. They also eat seeds. This is the first species of ant to find picnic remains. The major workers rarely leave the nest. They defend the nest entrance and use their strong mandibles to cut any food item carried there into pieces. They may sometimes help in carrying large or heavy food items.

Pheidole pallidula major worker (soldier) and minor worker.

Solenopsis genus Mayr, 1851

subfamily Myrmicinae

Solenopsis fugax colony.

Identification

Size: 1.5–2.2 mm, with some variation within a colony. Body entirely pale yellow. The largest individuals have a darker head and first gaster segment. The body is smooth and shiny, the eyes very small. Separating *Solenopsis* species is difficult. As workers are very similar morphologically, it is important to have either males or queens for determining species. Several groups of species are defined according to the size of winged individuals. *Solenopsis fugax* (Latreille, 1798) has large wings and is widely distributed across Europe. On the contrary, *Solenopsis orbula* (Emery, 1875) of Corsica and Italy and *S. oraniensis* (Forel, 1984), which occurs in southern Spain, have much smaller wings. The other species have intermediately-sized wings: *Solenopsis lusitanica* (Emery, 1915) and *S. fairchildi* (Wheeler, 1926) of the Iberian Peninsula; *S. gallica* (Santschi, 1934) of southern France; *S. latro* (Forel, 1894) of southern Italy; and *S. crivellarii* (Menozzi, 1936) and *S. wolfi* (Emery, 1915) of Greece.

Possible confusion

Leptanilla revelierii appears similar to *Solenopsis* species even though it belongs to another subfamily (Leptanillinae). However, it is slimmer, its head is twice as long as wide and it is very rare. Species of the genus *Strumigenys* are of similar size but are reddish rather than yellow and have an obviously triangular head. The genus *Carebara* is closely related to the genus *Solenopsis*; a single species occurs in Greece, *C. oertzeni* (Forel, 1886), which lives underground, is very secretive and scarcely ever found.

Swarming

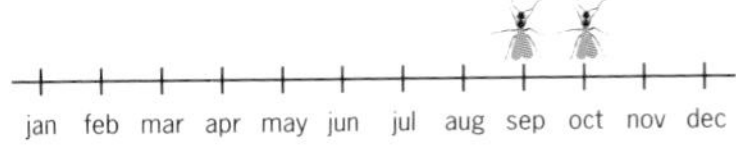

Solenopsis fugax in September–October.

Solenopsis latro sexual individuals exiting the nest before swarming.

Distribution

Range of *Solenopsis fugax*.

Habitat

A wide range of warm habitats as high as 1,500 m.

Where to look

Nests are under stones or directly in the ground. Due to the underground habits of these species, workers do not come to the surface. These species can therefore only be found by lifting stones or digging in the soil, or seeing them above ground when swarming.

Winged *Solenopsis fugax* individuals exiting the nest before swarming.

Biology

Solenopsis fugax is very common. Nest density can be very high. Colonies are polygynous and very populous, with the presence of as many as tens of thousands of workers. They are omnivorous. *Solenopsis fugax* forages for small invertebrates and takes the honeydew of underground root-sucking Hemiptera. It is known to feed on broods stolen from the colonies of other species.

Stenamma genus Westwood, 1840

subfamily Myrmicinae

Stenamma debile workers.

Identification

Size: 3–4 mm. Body entirely reddish. The eyes are very small. There are 85 species in the genus *Stenamma*, seven of which occur in Europe. Specific identification is difficult and depends on the tegument sculpting, which is in the form of longitudinal or interconnected furrows. Two species are widely distributed: *Stenamma debile* (Foerster, 1850) throughout Europe, and *S. striatulum* (Emery, 1895) in Southern Europe. The other species have more reduced ranges: *Solenopsis petiolatum* (Emery, 1897) occurs in central Italy; *S. sardoum* (Emery, 1915) in Sardinia; *S. sicilum* (Rigato, 2011) in Sicily; *S. westwoodii* (Westwood, 1839) in France and Northern Europe; and *S. zanoni* (Rigato, 2011) in northern Italy and Corsica.

Possible confusion

Workers of the genus *Stenamma* can be confused with

Swarming

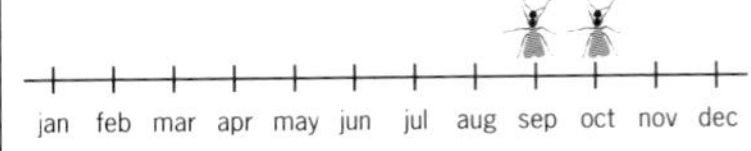

Stenamma sp. worker.

Distribution

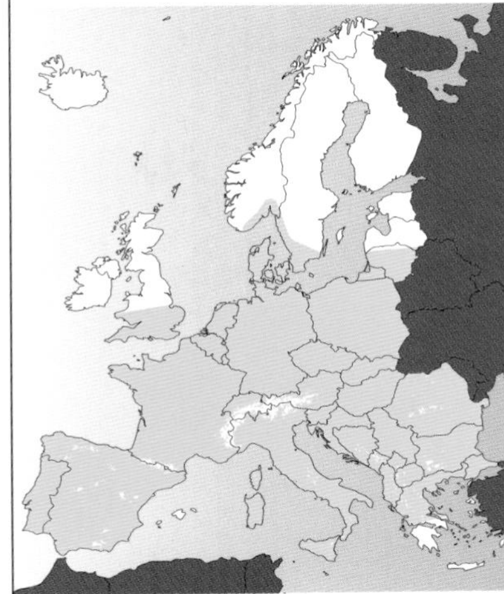

Range of *Stenamma debile*.

Aphaenogaster subterranea workers; however, the latter have bigger eyes and their tegument is smoother.

Habitat

Dense, cool, humid forests. Mainly a lowland species that can, however, occur above 1,000 m.

Where to look

Nests are under large stones, under moss or directly in the ground. Workers forage in the ground litter and probably underground in the same manner as underground species.

Stenamma debile worker.

Biology

Common species but their real status is probably underestimated due to their secretive habits. They can be locally abundant. In *Stenamma debile,* colonies are monogynous or polygynous, with a few dozen workers. Diet consists mainly of small invertebrates (especially springtails) found dead or captured alive. *Stenamma debile* also consumes seed elaiosomes. *Stenamma* workers move around slowly and stop and curl up if disturbed.

Strongylognathus genus Mayr, 1853

subfamily Myrmicinae

Strongylognathus testaceus workers (pale red) among *Tetramorium* sp. workers (dark brown).

Identification

Size: 2–3.5 mm. Quite pale body, between pale brown and yellow. The characteristic mandibles are sabre-shaped, without teeth. There are 25 species in the genus *Strongylognathus* within the Palearctic region. Eleven of these are found in Europe. *Strongylognathus testaceus* (Schenck, 1852) is the only European species with a head with a very indented rear edge; it occurs throughout Europe. The other ten species have a rounded edge; these are closely related species and separation is difficult, but they have restricted ranges: *Strongylognathus huberi* (Forel, 1874) occurs in Spain, Italy and France; *S. alboini* (Finzi, 1924) and *S. alpines* (Wheeler, 1909) occur in the Swiss and French Alps; *S. caeciliae* (Forel, 1897) in the south of Spain; *S. destefanii* (Emery, 1915) in the south of Italy and Sicily; *S. italicus* (Finzi, 1924) in the Apennines; *S. pisarskii* (Poldi, 1994) in the south of Italy; *S. dalmaticus* (Baroni Urbani, 1969) and *S. silvestrii* (Menozzi, 1936) in the Balkans and in Greece; and *S. kratochvili* in Central Europe.

Possible confusion

Species of the genus *Strongylognathus* are distinguished from those of the genus *Tetramorium* by their sabre-shaped mandibles. Recent genetic studies have confirmed the close relationship of the genus *Strongylognathus* with certain species in the genus *Tetramorium*. The grouping of these two genera is being studied.

Swarming

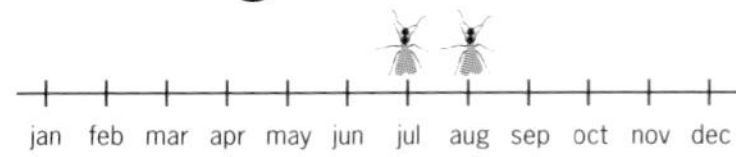

Habitat

Same habitat as their hosts.

Where to look

In *Tetramorium* nests of the *caespitum-impurum* or *semilaeve* groups. They are more easily found in early spring and again when sexual individuals appear.

Biology

All the species of the genus are obligate social parasites of ants of the genus *Tetramorium*. They form colonies of a few dozen workers mixed with hundreds or thousands of host workers. *Strongylognathus* species of the *huberi* group are slavemakers: workers leave the nest in large numbers organised into columns; they then move towards neighbouring *Tetramorium* colonies that they enter to rob of pupae and larvae which are taken back to the nest to become slaves. *Strongylognathus testaceus* has an inquiline lifestyle within the host colony; this results in there being far fewer workers than in *S. huberi*. Founding of a new society in *Strongylognathus* species is of the independent type; it cannot be achieved by an isolated queen. The newly mated queens have to be adopted by a *Tetramorium* colony.

Distribution

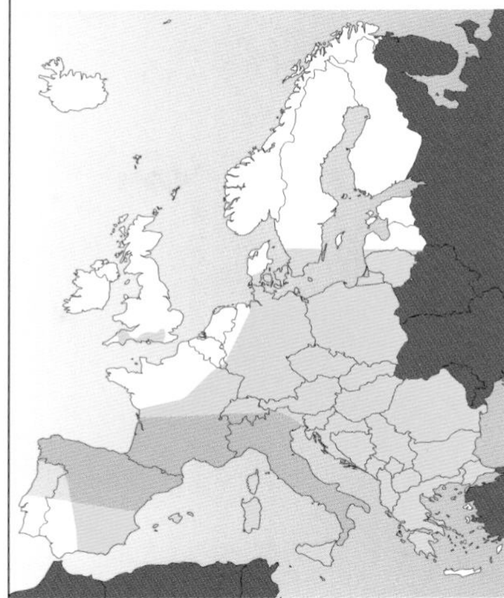

Range of *Strongylognathus testaceus* (pink) and *S. huberi* (grey).

Strongylognathus alpinus queen.

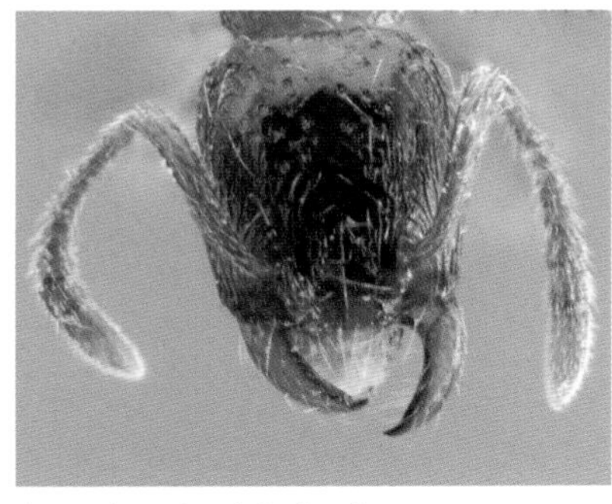

Strongylognathus huberi worker.

Strumigenys genus F. Smith, 1860

subfamily Myrmicinae

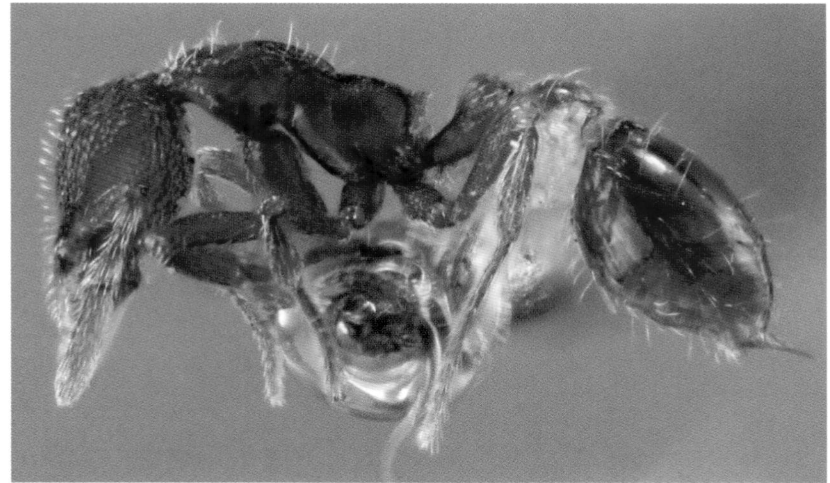

Strumigenys tenuipilis worker.

Identification

Size: 1.8–2 mm. Body entirely reddish. Triangular head, much narrower in front than at the rear. *Pyramica* (Rogers, 1862) is a later synonym of *Strumigenys*. A vast tropical and subtropical genus. Only five species have been recorded from Europe: *Strumigenys argiola* (Emery, 1869), *S. baudueri* (Emery, 1875), *S. membranifera (*Emery, 1869), *S. tenuipilis* (Emery, 1915) and *S. tenuissima* (Brown, 1953), known only from the Greek islands. Their distribution is not well known due to their secretive habits, but they probably all occur widely.

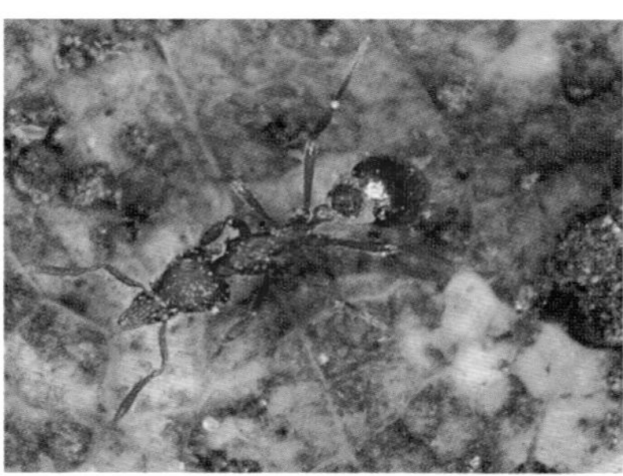

Strumigenys sp. worker in ground litter.

Possible confusion

From their size and colour, species of the genus *Strumigenys* could possibly be confused with those of the genera *Solenopsis* and

Swarming

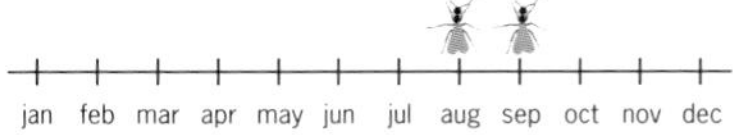

Strumigenys baudueri worker.

Leptanilla. However, *Strumigenys* workers have a triangular head.

Habitat

Probably quite a ubiquitous species. Their ecology is little known.

Where to look

The probably underground habits of these species means they are difficult to find. The workers forage at least part of the time in the ground litter. Trapping techniques (litter sieving, Berlese and Winkler traps) allow them to be found more easily. Winged individuals are easier to find than workers.

Biology

All species of the genus *Strumigenys* are rarely collected. They are probably commoner than supposed and our knowledge would almost certainly increase with the use of collecting methods aimed specifically at underground species. Their biology is little known. They forage for small invertebrates on the ground, with an apparent preference for springtails.

Distribution

Range of the genus *Strumigenys*.

Head of *Strumigenys tenuipilis* worker.

Temnothorax affinis Mayr, 1855

subfamily Myrmicinae

Temnothorox affinis worker.

Identification

Size: 2.5–3.5 mm. Yellow-orange thorax, darker head and gaster. The antennal clubs are dusky, sometimes only slightly in certain individuals. Each gaster segment has a black band with blurred edges on its rear part. In some individuals the black band is only apparent on the first gaster segment. The spines on the propodeum are thin and of variable size but generally longer than those of other *Temnothorax* species. *Temnothorax affinis* is widespread in Europe. It can be quite variable but is distinguished from other *Temnothorax* species by having a roughly triangular and very sculpted petiole.

Possible confusion

Other species have similar characters but these are not a sign of their being closely related. *Temnothorax graecus* (Forel, 1911) in the southern Balkans has a less sculpted head with smooth

Swarming

jan feb mar apr may jun jul aug sep oct nov dec

patches. *Temnothorax minozzii* (Santschi, 1922) and *T. leviceps* are distinguished from *T. affinis* by having entirely glossy, smooth heads and an obviously angular top to their petiole. *Temnothorax leviceps* is related to the *exilis* group.

Habitat

In the southern half of Europe *Temnothorax affinis* is found equally in open sunny habitats and in closed forest. In the very south the species becomes rare and is more often found in damp, cool forest. It is encountered in lowlands and foothills but not at altitude.

Where to look

Essentially tree-dwelling, *Temnothorax affinis* nests are found in cavities in dead branches still on the tree. Lower nests can also be found in hollow stems (straw, brambles, etc.). Workers forage in vegetation.

Biology

An uncommon species. Nest density is very variable but usually low. Colonies are monogynous, rarely having more than 200 workers. Founding is independent and claustral. This species feeds on small invertebrates (small caterpillars, aphids, gnats, mites, etc.) which they capture on the leaves and branches of the nest tree.

Distribution

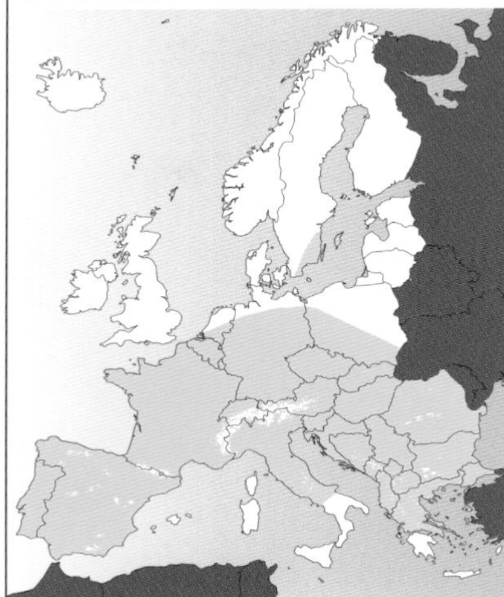

Range of *Temnothorax affinis*.

Temnothorax affinis often make their nest under bark or in hollow stems.

Temnothorax of the *angustulus* group

subfamily Myrmicinae

Temnothorax angustulus worker.

Identification

Size: 2.5–3 mm. Body entirely black or with reddish mesosoma. Presence of a mesopropodeal ridge. There is quite strong sculpting on the mesosoma, with large longitudinal furrows. This group of *Temnothorax* species tends to be tree-dwelling, with at least five species present in Southern Europe. The most visible differences are seen in the sculpting on the head, mesosoma colour and length of the propodeal spines. Species identification can be difficult due to quite a large variability in workers from one nest to another. *Temnothorax angustulus* (Nylander, 1856) has a dark body and only slightly sculpted head. *Temnothorax algiricus* (Forel, 1894) from southern Spain, has a more sculpted head and very long spines. *Temnothorax dessyi* (Menozzi, 1936), described from Greece, has a dark body and short spines. *Temnothorax atlantis* (Santschi, 1911) and *T. mediterraneus* (Ward, Brady, Fisher & Schultz, 2014) have a partly reddish mesosoma.

Note: Following a change in their nomenclature, species of the genus *Myrmoxenus* have been transferred to the genus *Temnothorax*. *Myrmoxenus kraussei* (Emery, 1915) thus becomes *Temnothorax kraussei* (Emery, 1915). It was therefore necessary to rename the previous *Temnothorax kraussei* (Emery, 1916), part of the *angustulus* group, as *T. mediterraneus*.

Swarming

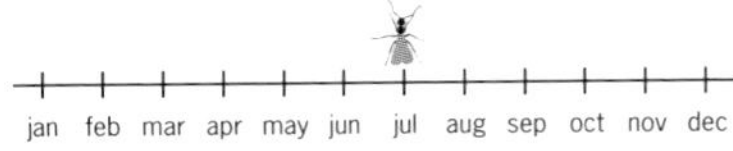

Distribution

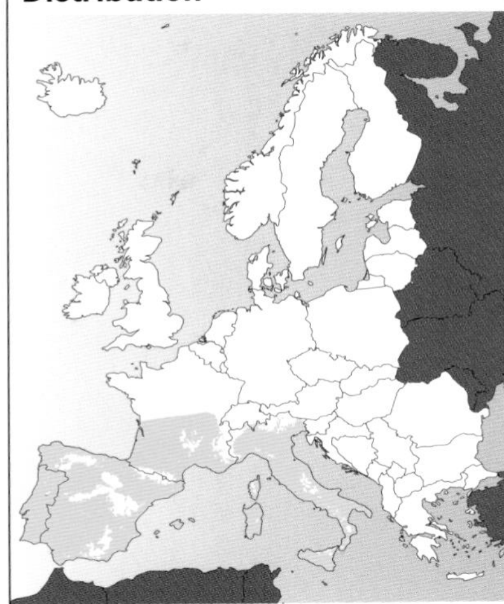

Range of *Temnothorax* species of the *angustulus* group.

Possible confusion

There are other very dark-coloured *Temnothorax* species that can be confused with species of the *angustulus* group but they are not tree-dwelling – such as those of the *exilis* (see page 350), *niger* (see page 364) or even *sordidulus* (see page 374) groups. *Temnothorax angulinodis* (Csösz, Heinze & Miko, 2015) also has a mesopropodeal ridge and a very angular top to the petiole but less sculpting on the mesosoma; this species is only known from the Peloponnese (Greece).

Habitat

Oak forest is their preferred habitat but these species can be found in other biotopes as long as there are trees. A warmth-loving, low-altitude species.

Where to look

Nests are built in dead branches still on the tree (not on the ground), especially on oaks, on branches with a diameter of 1–2 cm. Sometimes found under bark of standing dead trees, always far from the ground.

Biology

Quite a common species in their preferred habitat. Nest density is generally quite low; many branches have to be opened to find a nest. Colonies have a few dozen workers. They are quite docile; at the slightest sign of danger they squeeze into a crack. If a branch containing a colony is broken, most workers will normally freeze.

Workers of a *Temnothorax* species of the *angustulus* group.

Temnothorax clypeatus Mayr, 1853

subfamily Myrmicinae

Temnothorax clypeatus worker.

Identification

Size: 2.5–3.5 mm. Reddish-yellow body. Brown band on each of the gaster's tergites. Head highly grooved, thin longitudinal lines on the forehead. Characteristically, there is a hollow in the centre of the clypeus which has a ridge forming a fold on its edge. It has big spines that are long and wide. The petiole is dome-shaped.

Possible confusion

Temnothorax clypeatus can be distinguished from other *Temnothorax* species by the characters given in the key. The uniform colour and large size of the mesosoma may lead to confusion with *Leptothorax acervorum*.

Habitat

A tree-dwelling species which can be found on oaks, beeches, poplars and fruit trees. Trees must be exposed to the sun. In cold climates, they occur in deciduous trees, whose leaves capture the warmth of the sun's rays.

Swarming

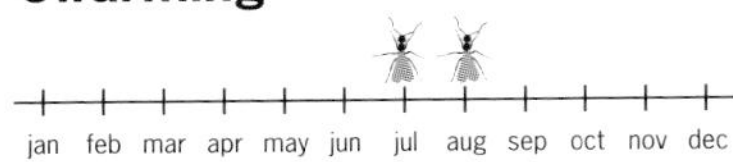

Where to look

Nests are built under the bark of oak or fruit trees, in ancient beams and in beehives.

Biology

Workers forage individually on tree trunks by searching in cracks in the bark. At the slightest sign of danger they crouch into a crack or enter a small hole, which means they are very difficult to observe. Colonies are not populous and have a single queen.

Distribution

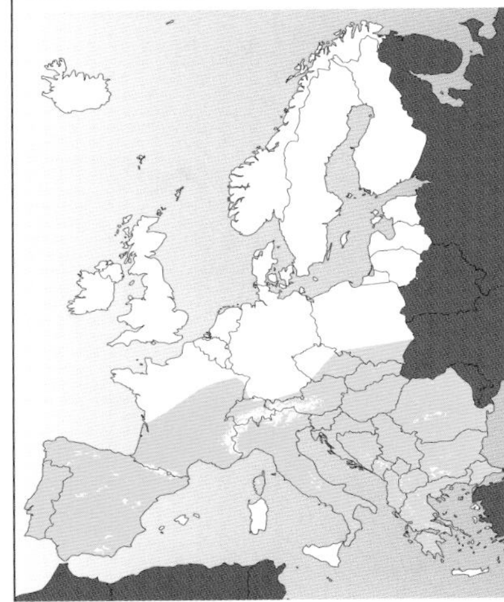

Range of *Temnothorax clypeatus*.

Temnothorax clypeatus worker.

Temnothorax of the *corticalis* group

subfamily Myrmicinae

Temnothorax aveli colony.

Identification

Size: 2.5–3 mm. An orange-yellow thorax, with slightly darker head and gaster. The petiole is in the form of a right angle at its top. The femora can be slightly paler than the other appendage parts. Individuals may be very variable from one nest to another, which makes identification difficult. *Temnothorax corticalis* (Schenck, 1852) has very short spines, reduced to simple spurs. *Temnothorax aveli* (Bondroit, 1918) is variable in colour and length of spines. *Temnothorax italicus* (Consani & Zangheri, 1952), from Italy, has a slightly less triangular petiole. *Temnothorax jailensis* (Arnol'di, 1977), described from Ukraine, occurs in Eastern Europe.

Possible confusion

Other ant species are arboreal, such as *Temnothorax clypeatus* which is significantly bigger and has a larger and raised petiole with a rounded top. *Temnothorax affinis* also has a vaguely triangular petiole but its antennal clubs are dusky.

Swarming

jan feb mar apr may jun jul aug sep oct nov dec

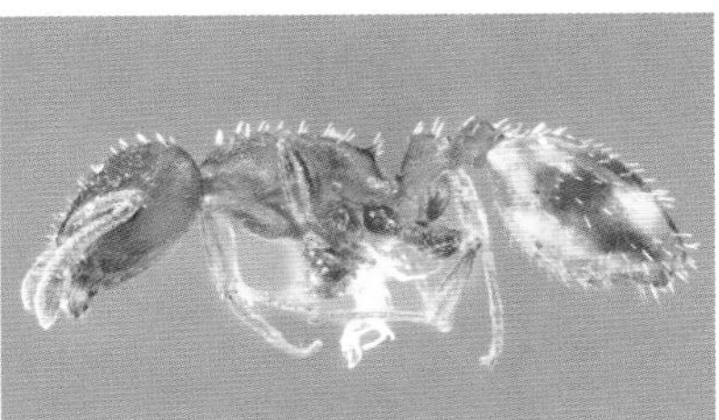

Temnothorax aveli worker.

Habitat

A ubiquitous species but generally requires the presence of trees (open forest, copses, etc.). In the northern part of its range it is more frequent in warmer, well-exposed sites. These species occur in lowlands and foothills but not at altitude.

Where to look

Nests usually occur in small dead, hollow branches, on the ground as well as in situ. They also occur under the bark of stumps or dead trunks, or sometimes even in cracks in rocks or gaps between stones. Workers forage on rocks, low plants, in the ground litter and in trees.

Biology

Common species. In certain sites there may be several nests per square metre. Colonies are monogynous, with a few hundred workers. Founding is independent, by a single queen. Theses species hunt small arthropods. They may be used as hosts by the social parasitic ants *Chalepoxenus muellerianus* and *Myrmoxenus ravouxi*.

Distribution

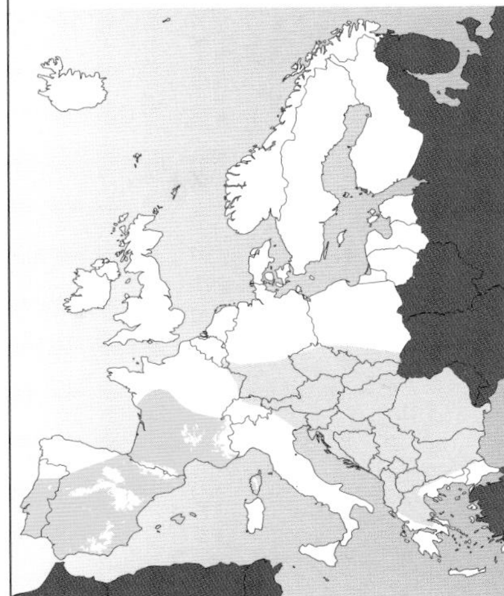

Range of *Temnothorax aveli* (pink) and *T. corticalis* (grey).

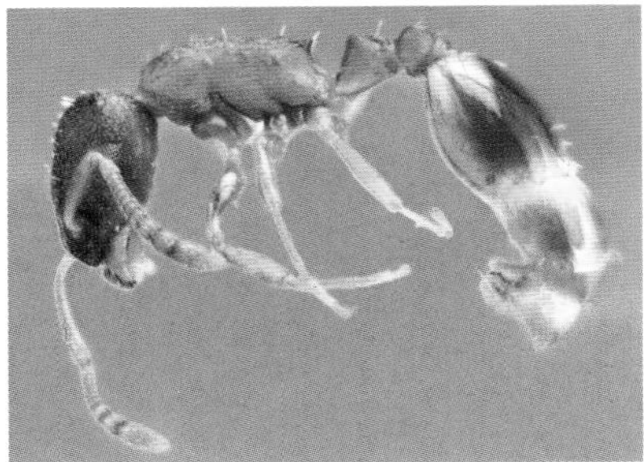

Temnothorax corticalis worker.

Temnothorax of the *exilis* group

subfamily Myrmicinae

Temnothorax exilis colony in a hollow stem.

Identification

Size: 2–3 mm. Entirely black body. Petiole is angular on the top. Smooth head, with shiny aspect. No mesopropodeum ridge. *Temnothorax exilis* (Emery, 1869) and *T. specularis* (Emery, 1916) are two closely related species of Mediterranean habitats. *Temnothorax specularis* has a very smooth, shinier, less sculpted tegument. *Temnothorax tyndalei* (Forel, 1909), from Spain and Portugal, has a reddish head and petiole, its mesosoma is brown, sometimes quite pale, and it has a dark gaster. *Temnothorax leviceps* (Emery, 1898) is a pale *Temnothorax* but it does belong to the *exilis* group.

Possible confusion

In their habitat these *Temnothorax* species can be confused with other dark species. *Temnothorax melas* is a rare Corsican endemic; it has a

Swarming

jan feb mar apr may jun jul aug sep oct nov dec

Temnothorax specularis worker.

mesopropodeum ridge and is restricted to the wooded banks of fast-flowing streams. *Temnothorax niger* and *T. grouvellei* have a very rounded top to the petiole. *Temnothorax angustulus* has a mesopropodeum ridge and is arboreal.

Habitat

Hot, dry habitats exposed to the sun.

Where to look

Nests are built in rock crevices, between stones in walls, in dead branches on the ground and sometimes under the bark of dead wood.

Biology

Common species. Colonies are monogynous. *Temnothorax exilis* is a host to the social parasite *Myrmoxenus corsica*.

Distribution

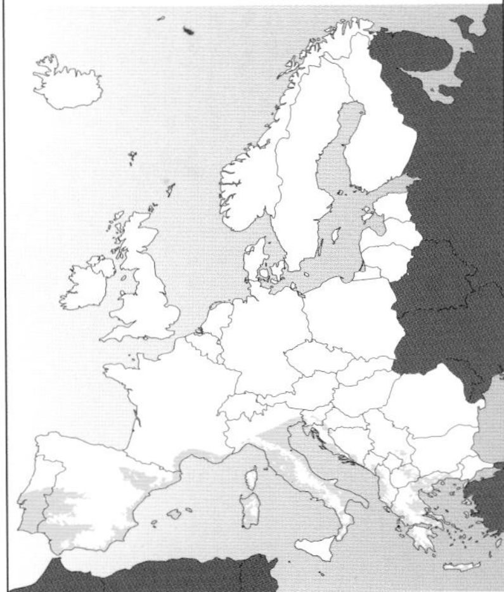

Range of *Temnothorax* species of the *exilis* group.

Temnothorax exilis worker.

Temnothorax flavicornis Emery, 1870

subfamily Myrmicinae

Temnothorax flavicornis worker.

Identification

Size: 1.7–2 mm. Pale yellow except for the last tergite, which can be darker. The propodeum spines are long and thin. The very thick petiole and head sculpting, with lines on the forehead and reticulations near the frontal lobes, are also characteristic features. The gaster is shiny. The mesosoma has deep crevices along its whole length. The mesopropodeum ridge is well developed. It is the only European member of the *Temnothorax* genus to have only 11 segments to the antennae; all the others have 12.

Possible confusion

Without verifying the number of antenna segments, this species could easily be confused with other yellow species of *Temnothorax*.

Swarming

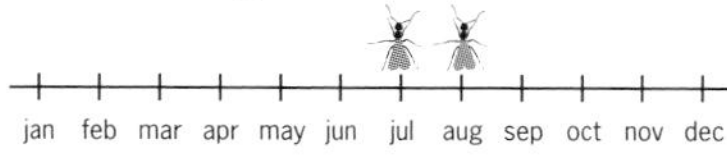

Habitat

Low-lying Mediterranean habitats. Free-lying rocks on the ground and drystone walls.

Where to look

They usually occur under stones but can reside in acorns.

Biology

A rare species. Colonies are monogynous and nests have few occupants. They feed on sugary substances on euphorbias or other ground-dwelling plants.

Distribution

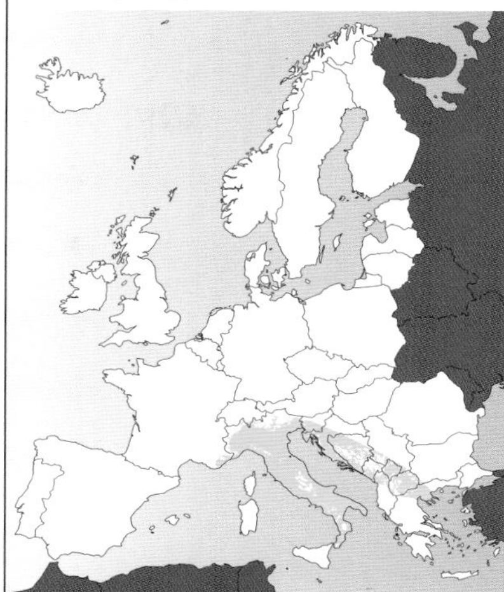

Range of *Temnothorax flavicornis*.

Temnothorax flavicornis worker.

Temnothorax gredosi

Espadaler & Collingwood, 1982 subfamily Myrmicinae

Temnothorax gredosi worker.

Identification

Size: 2.5–3 mm. Slightly bicoloured, dusky head and gaster with paler mesosoma. There is a slight ridge on the mesopropodeum. The dorsal part of the mesosoma is only slightly sculpted, almost smooth. Reduced propodeum spines. The petiole is quite high, with an angular top.

Possible confusion

Due to its having an mesopropodeum ridge and dusky gaster, this species resembles species of the *nylanderi* group but can be distinguished by its being much darker and the sculpting of the mesosoma. Body colour is similar to that of *Temnothorax recedens* but its antennae are shorter and the body hairs thicker.

Swarming

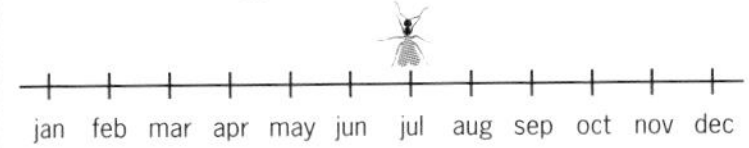

Temnothorax gredosi worker.

Habitat

Woodland edges at altitude, mainly between 800 and 1,800 m. It occurs in various situations, from exposed open ridges to open woodland undergrowth.

Where to look

Nests are in dead wood or under stones. Workers can be found in the plant layer with the use of a sweep net.

Biology

Quite a rare species, and its biology is little known. Colonies are monogynous and contain around a hundred individuals. It appears that mating occurs in the nest and that newly fertilised queens stay in their natal nest until spring. They leave the nest after the winter to found new colonies individually. It is the specific host species of the social parasite *Myrmoxenus bernardi*. The speed with which workers cross sunny stones is reminiscent of that of *Temnothorax recedens* or small *Temnothorax pallidula*. It forages for small arthropods in the ground litter.

Distribution

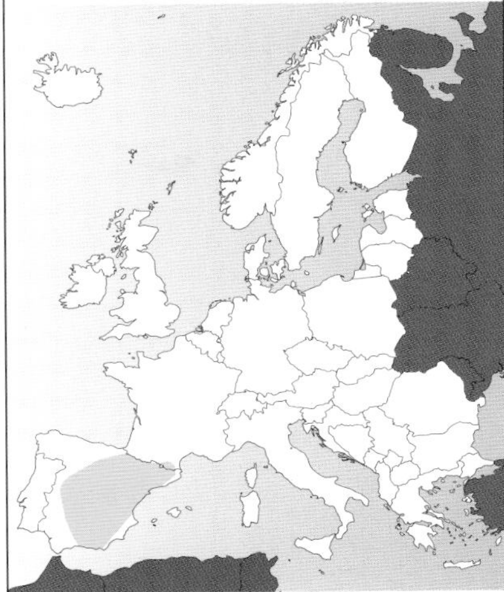

Range of *Temnothorax gredosi*.

Temnothorax gredosi colony under a stone.

Temnothorax interruptus Schenck, 1852

subfamily Myrmicinae

Temnothorax interruptus worker.

Identification

Size: 2.5–3 mm. Generally a pale colour. The antennae and often the underside of the head are darker. There are widened frontal blades in the area of antennal insertions. The mesosoma has no mesopropodeum ridge. Long propodeum spines. Petiole quite high.

Possible confusion

Temnothorax interruptus is widely distributed in Europe and can be mistaken for other yellow *Temnothorax* species. The distinctive character is the wide, angular frontal blades; in other species they form a slightly sinuous curve.

Habitat

Temnothorax interruptus colonises hot, dry open areas with only light, low vegetation cover.

Swarming

jan feb mar apr may jun jul aug sep oct nov dec

Head of *Temnothorax interruptus* worker.

Distribution

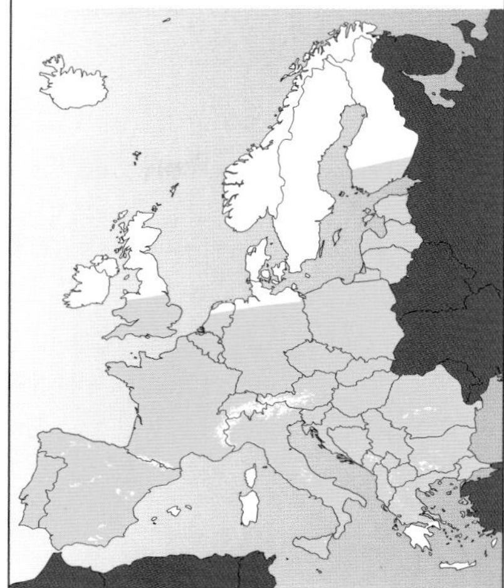

Range of *Temnothorax interruptus*.

Where to look

Nests are often under stones, in cracks in rocks or directly in the ground. In the last case, the nest entrance is a simple hole in the ground. They can also be found under moss, lichens or small, flat stones. Workers can be caught in the plant layer with the use of a sweep net.

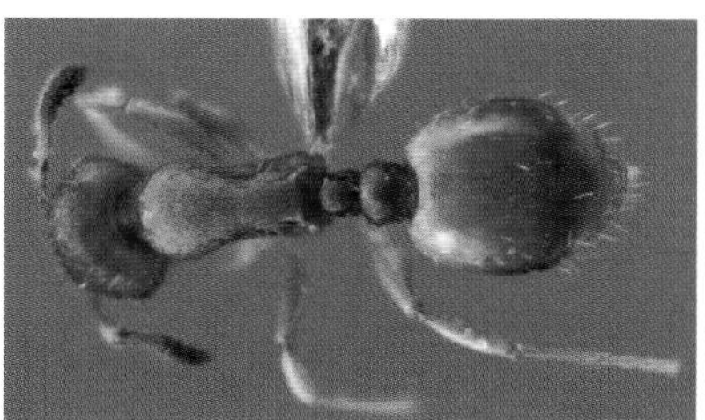

Gaster of *Temnothorax interruptus* worker, showing the dark hind part of the first tergite.

Biology

A quite common species. Colonies are regularly polygynous (up to 13 queens) with about a hundred workers. Workers forage for small arthropods on rocks or on the ground. When a food source is abundant a worker may recruit other workers. This species uses a chemical repellent to protect itself from other ants.

Temnothorax of the *lichtensteini* group

subfamily Myrmicinae

Temnothorax lichtensteini workers.

Identification

Size: 2–3 mm. Body, antennae and legs are pale yellow, with only a single black band on the first segment of the gaster. The first sternite is not dusky. It has a slight groove in the mesopropodeum. Large spines on the propodeum. The *lichtensteini* group contains two very closely related species which are difficult to separate morphologically: *Temnothorax lichtensteini* (Bondroit, 1918) is widespread, and *T. laconicus* (Csösz, Seifert, Müller, Trindl, Schultz & Heinze, 2013) occurs almost exclusively in the southern Balkans.

Possible confusion

Two other groups are closely related: the *nylanderi* and the *parvulus* groups. In *Temnothorax parvulus* the dark band on the gaster is paler and the mesopropodeum groove is more obvious. *Temnothorax nylanderi* is generally darker and its first gaster sternite is dusky.

Habitat

A quite ubiquitous species but particularly common in moderately shaded areas in the Mediterranean zone, such as forest edges, open forests, copses and scrub. Warmth-loving species of low altitudes.

Swarming

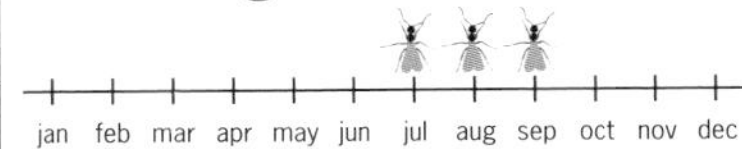

Where to look

Nests occur mainly in crevices in rocks and spaces between stones above the ground. They can be found on crumbling rocky outcrops and ancient stone walls. They are also often found in dead branches on the ground, particularly those with a diameter of 1–3 cm. Workers forage on rocks, in low plants and in the ground litter.

Biology

Very common species in the Mediterranean region. In favourable habitats nest density can be very high (several nests per square metre). Colonies are monogynous and can contain a few hundred workers. Founding is independent, by a single queen. These species hunt small arthropods on rocks and in the ground litter.

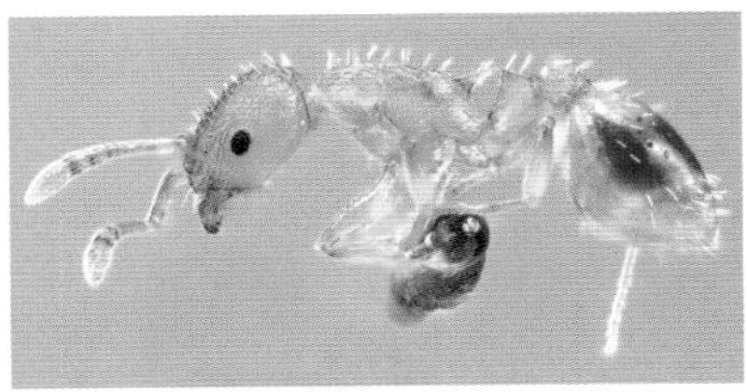

Temnothorax lichtensteini worker.

Distribution

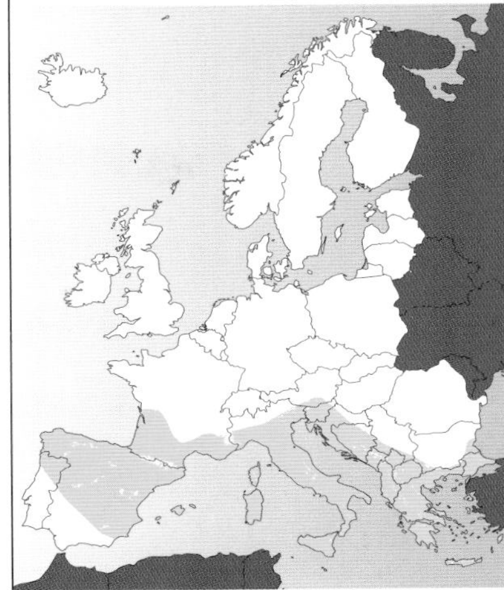

Range of *Temnothorax* species of the *lichtensteini* group.

Temnothorax lichtensteini worker carrying a larva from its nest.

Temnothorax of the *luteus* group

subfamily Myrmicinae

Temnothorax luteus worker.

Identification

Size: 2–3 mm. Yellow body. The gaster has a slightly darker band on the first tergite (which is not visible on the sternite). The occiput of the head is smooth and sometimes a little darker than the thorax. The propodeum spines are relatively large and often curved slightly downwards. This group contains many closely related species that have the common features of a very pale body and antennal clubs that are not darker. *Temnothorax luteus* (Forel, 1874) is the reference species of this group, largely distributed around the Mediterranean area of Western Europe. Several more strictly Mediterranean species have a less sculpted body. These include: *Temnothorax racovitzai* (Bondroit, 1918), *T. subcingulatus* (Emery, 1924) in southern Spain, *T. pelagosanus* (Müller, 1923) in Italy, and *T. lagrecai* (Baroni Urbani, 1964) in Sicily.

Swarming

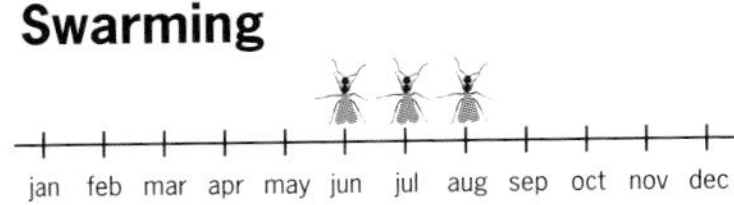

Possible confusion

Temnothorax pardoi (Tinaut, 1987), from Spain and the west coast of France, has a small lump under the postpetiole. *Temnothorax cristinae* (Espadaler, 1997) and *T. bejaraniensis* (Reyes-Lopez & Carpintero-Ortega, 2013) have slightly sculpted bodies and more angular petiole, they occur in Spain. *Temnothorax alienus* (Schulz, Heinze & Pusch, 2007), from Italy, has a darker, pale brown body.

Habitat

A ubiquitous group: open forest, woodland edges, open areas, garrigues. In lowlands and foothills, never at altitude.

Where to look

Most nests occur in cracks in rocks, between stones or in dead wood. Workers search for food on the ground, on stones and in the ground litter.

Biology

Quite common species and nests can be numerous. Colonies are monogynous, containing about 150–200 individuals. *Temnothorax racovitzai* is the main host species of the social parasite *Chalepoxenus kutteri*, which is very rare.

Distribution

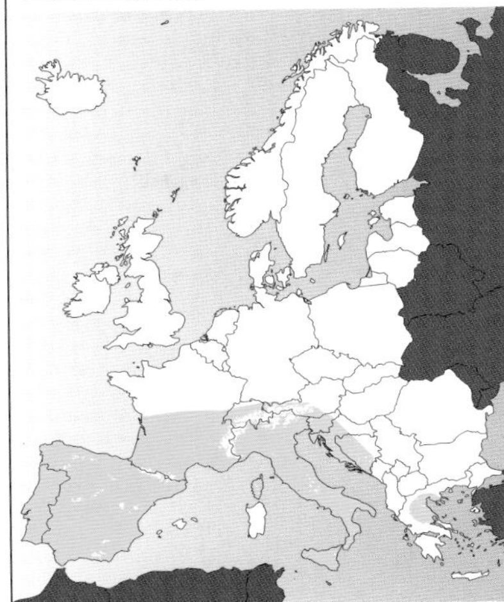

Range of *Temnothorax luteus*.

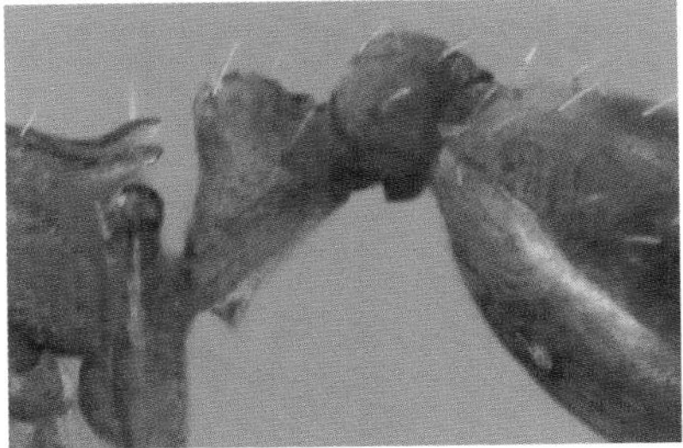

Petiole of *Temnothorax racovitzai* showing the small lump under the postpetiole.

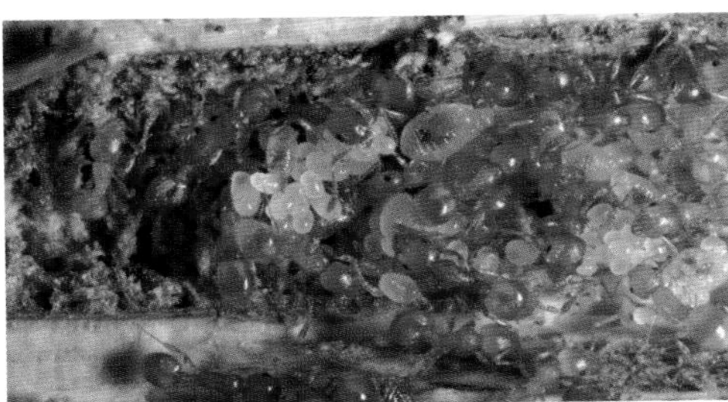

Temnothorax subcingulatus colony in a hollow stem.

Temnothorax nadigi Kutter, 1925

subfamily Myrmicinae

Temnothorax nadigi worker.

Identification

Size: 2.5–3 mm. Generally a brown colour. The tips of the antennae are darker. The propodeum spines are reduced to two thick, tooth-shaped projections. The truncated petiole is clearly longer than it is high.

Possible confusion

Temnothorax bulgaricus (Forel, 1892) occurs in Bulgaria and Greece; it has dusky clubs and only rudimentary spines but its head is entirely smooth and shiny. *Temnothorax corticalis* also has very reduced propodeum spines but seen in profile it has a clearly triangular petiole and pale antennal clubs. *Temnothorax tuberum* has a relatively higher petiole and more pronounced propodeum spines.

Habitat

Woodland edges at altitude.

Swarming

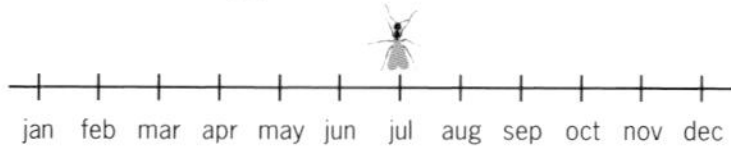

Where to look

Nests occur in dead wood or under stones. Workers can be found in low vegetation with the use of a sweep net.

Biology

Quite a rare species, and its biology is little known. Colonies are monogynous and contain around a hundred workers.

Distribution

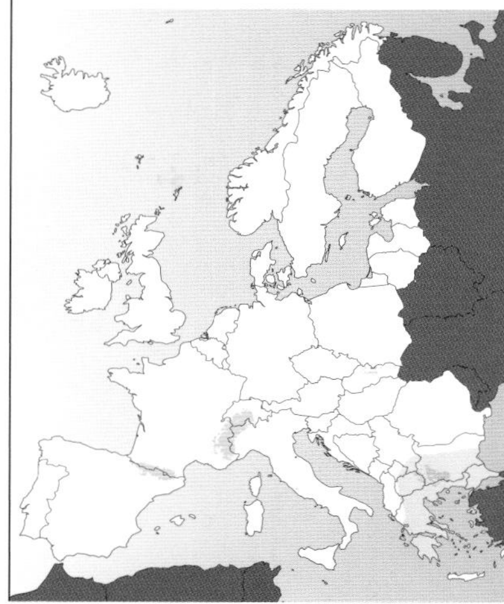

Range of *Temnothorax nadigi* (pink) and *T. bulgaricus* (grey).

Three *Temnothorax nadigi* castes. From left to right: a queen, a worker and a male.

Temnothorax nadigi worker.

Temnothorax of the *niger* group

subfamily Myrmicinae

Temnothorax niger colony.

Identification

Size: 2–3 mm. Body entirely black. Petiole has a rounded top. A large part of the head is striped longitudinally. *Temnothorax niger* (Forel, 1894) is quite common in the eastern part of the Mediterranean Basin. Other species with similar characteristics also occur in Europe. *Temnothorax grouvellei* (Bondroit, 1918) differs from *T. niger* by having longer propodeum spines. *Temnothorax ibericus* (Menozzi, 1922) occurs only in Spain, is paler-bodied and more sculpted. *Temnothorax platycephalus* (Espadaler, 1997), also present in Spain, has a distinctively elongated head. *Temnothorax laestrygon* (Santschi, 1931) is the only representative of the group occurring in Sicily.

Swarming

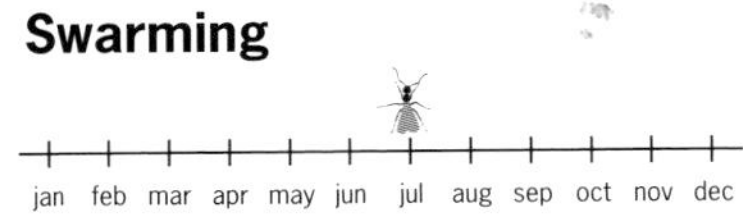

Possible confusion

These species can be confused with other dark-coloured *Temnothorax* species (see characters given in the key for this genus).

Habitat

Ubiquitous species found in open woodland, meadows and garrigues. They occur in warm, dry habitats and can be found as high as 1,000 m in the south of their range.

Where to look

Usually nests are built directly in the ground or under stones and in hollow stems. Workers forage on the ground, under stones and in vegetation. They can be difficult to find as nests built directly in the ground have a small entrance and workers are secretive. Contrary to most *Temnothorax* species, they are more likely to be found by searching for foraging workers rather than nests.

Biology

Common species in the Mediterranean zone. It would appear that nest density is generally low. Colonies are monogynous and contain around 200 workers.

Distribution

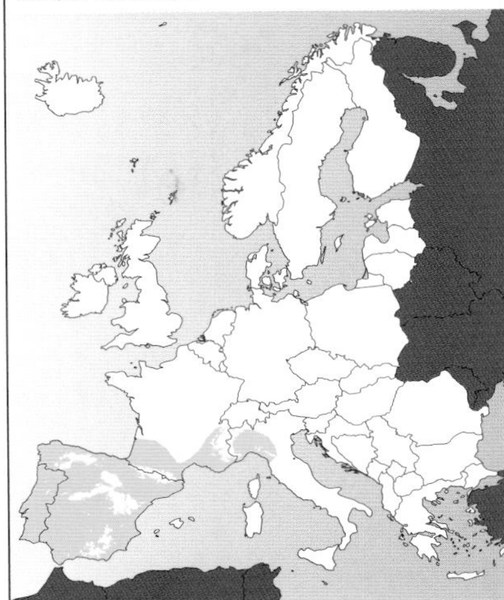

Range of *Temnothorax niger*.

Temnothorax grouvellei worker.

Temnothorax niger worker.

Temnothorax of the ***nylanderi*** group

subfamily Myrmicinae

Temnothorax nylanderi worker.

Identification

Size: 2–3.5 mm. Orangish thorax with darker head and gaster. The hind part of each gaster tergite is also dusky. They have a mesopropodeum ridge. The antennae are a uniform orange colour. This group encompasses three relatively common species of temperate Europe: *Temnothorax nylanderi* (Foerster, 1850); *T. crassispinus* (Karavaiev, 1926), which have longer propodeum spines; and *T. crasecundus* (Seifert & Csösz, 2015), which occur only in the Balkans.

Possible confusion

Temnothorax tergestinus (of the *sordidulus* group) has a more elongated head and shorter and more upright spines than

Swarming

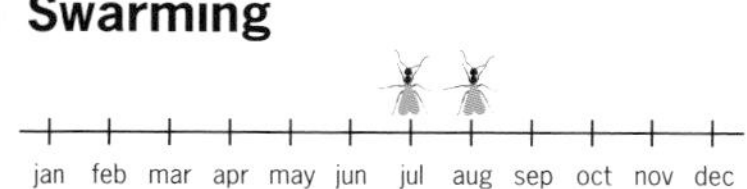

T. nylanderi. *Temnothorax parvulus* and *T. lichtensteini* are paler and only the first tergite of the gaster has a dusky zone. Other *Temnothorax* species of a similar colour have no mesopropodeal ridge. *Temnothorax gredosi* of the Iberian Peninsula has a darker body and the back of the mesosoma is almost smooth.

Habitat

Woodland habitats: forest, woods and wooded parks. These species inhabit damp, cool areas in lowlands and foothills.

Where to look

Nests are usually built in dead wood on the ground, but also in other cavities such as those of old acorns, old sweet chestnuts and empty snail shells. They are more rarely found under stones or among leaves in the ground litter. Workers forage in the ground litter and on dead wood.

Biology

Temnothorax nylanderi is a very common species except in the Mediterranean region. Nest density can often be as high as several nests per square metre. Colonies are monogynous, with

Distribution

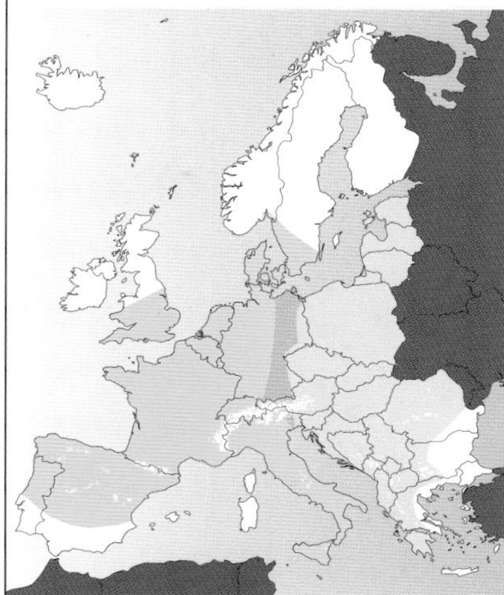

Ranges of *Temnothorax nylanderi* (pink) and *T. crassispinus* (grey).

Temnothorax crassispinus worker.

about a hundred workers. Founding is either independent or by intraspecific parasitism (the young queen penetrates an already established colony and replaces the resident queen). Certain colonies carry out fusion before the winter but generally only a single queen persists; the colonies split in spring. Species of this group feed on small invertebrates (mites, worms, etc.) and have also been observed stealing spider eggs.

Temnothorax of the *parvulus* group

subfamily Myrmicinae

Temnothorax parvulus workers.

Identification

Size: 2–3 mm. Orange-yellow body only punctuated by a dark band on the first segment of the gaster. The antennae are a uniform orange-yellow. The mesopropodeum ridge is well developed. This group contains three related species: *Temnothorax parvulus* (Schenck, 1852), with a wide distribution in Europe; *T. ariadnae* (Csösz, Heinze & Mikó, 2015), endemic to Crete; and *T. helenae* (Csösz, Heinze & Mikó, 2015), present in Greece.

Possible confusion

These species are related to those of the *nylanderi* and *lichtensteini* groups. They are distinguished by having a pale body and well-pronounced mesopropodeum ridge. *Temnothorax lucidus* (Csösz, Heinze & Mikó, 2015) and *T. subtilis* (Csösz, Heinze & Mikó, 2015), present on Crete, can be distinguished from species of the *parvulus* group by being less sculpted on the head – leaving a large, smooth patch. *Temnothorax*

Swarming

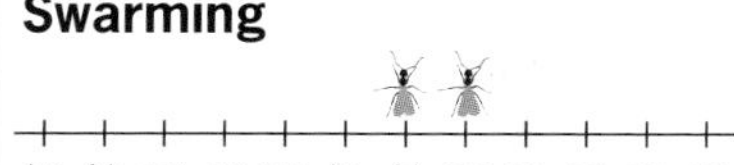

flavicornis can be distinguished from other *Temnothorax* species, including *T. parvulus* which it resembles, by having 11 segments, not 12, to the antennae.

Habitat

In Northern Europe *Temnothorax parvulus* generally inhabits warm sites such as well-exposed hillsides and woodland edges. In Southern Europe it prefers cooler, wooded areas. Found mainly in lowlands.

Where to look

Nests are found in dead wood on the ground, under moss or in cracks in rocks. Workers forage in the ground litter, on dead wood and on rocks.

Distribution

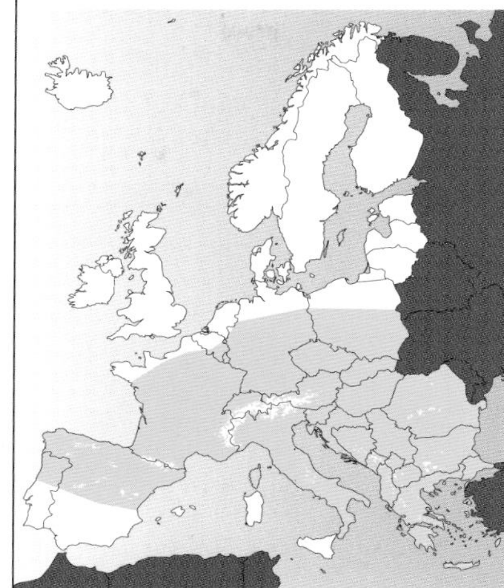

Range of *Temnothorax* species of the *parvulus* group.

Biology

Uncommon species. Colonies are monogynous and contain around one hundred workers. They probably feed on small invertebrates (mites, worms, etc.).

Temnothorax parvulus worker.

Temnothorax of the *recedens* and *laurae* groups

subfamily Myrmicinae

Temnothorax recedens worker.

Identification

Size: 2.5–3 mm. Body colour between yellow and brown. The gaster is darker than the rest of the body. A very pronounced mesopropodeal ridge. Contrary to other *Temnothorax* species, this group has long, thin hairs that finish in a point. Four closely related members of the *recedens* group occur in Europe. *Temnothorax recedens* (Nylander, 1856) is widely distributed throughout Southern Europe. The three other species occur in Greece: *Temnothorax rogeri* (Emery, 1869), which has very long propodeum spines; *T. solerii* (Menozzi, 1936), with a dark brown body; and *T. antigoni* (Forel, 1911), which is paler than *T. recedens* and is only found on the western Greek islands. Species of the *laurae* group also have long, thin hairs all over their bodies. They are different in having large eyes which measure about a quarter of the head length. One species occurs in Italy, *Temnothorax finzii* (Menozzi, 1925), and four species in Spain: *T. blascoi* (Espadaler, 1997); *T. caesari* (Espadaler, 1997); *T. crepuscularis* (Tinaut, 1994); and *T. universitatis* (Espadaler, 1997).

Possible confusion

Pheidole pallidula minor workers are very similar but have shorter propodeum spines, reduced to tooth-like protrusions, and have longer mandibles with about ten 'teeth' (far fewer in *Temnothorax recedens*).

Habitat

Areas well exposed to the sun or in partial shade: garrigues (shaded parts), edge habitats and open woodland. Warmth-loving species of lowlands.

Swarming

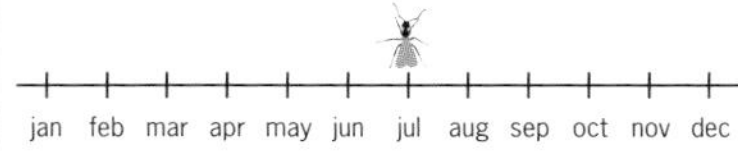

Where to look

Nests are built in rock crevices and spaces between stones, even at ground level. They can be found on crumbling rocky outcrops, in old stone walls and in rock piles. Workers forage on rocks.

Biology

Very common species in the Mediterranean zone. In favourable habitats nest density can be very high (several nests per square metre). Colonies are monogynous and contain rarely more than a hundred workers. Founding is independent, by a single queen. *Temnothorax recedens* can be a host to some social parasite ant species: *Chalepoxenus muellerianus* and *Myrmoxenus kraussei* (and occasionally *M. ravouxi*).

Distribution

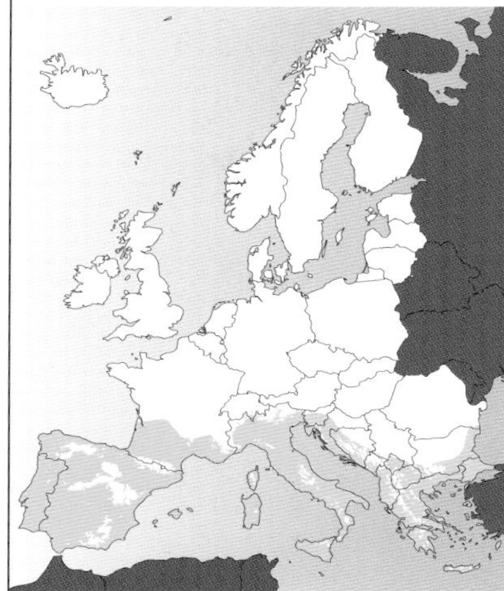

Range of *Temnothorax recedens.*

Temnothorax blascoi worker.

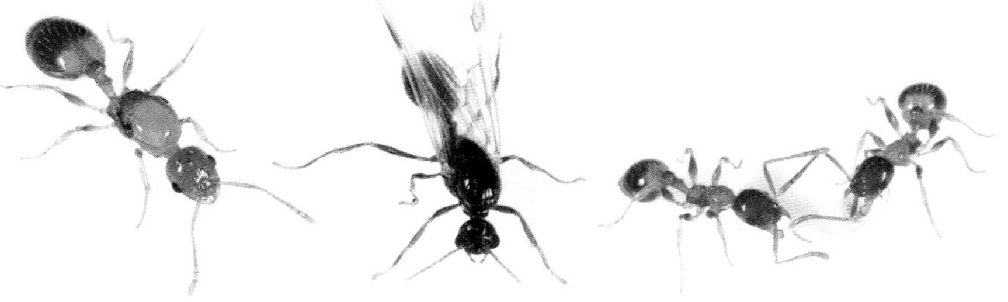

Three *Temnothorax recedens* castes. From left to right: a queen, a male and two workers.

Temnothorax of the ***rottenbergii*** group

subfamily Myrmicinae

Temnothorax formosus worker.

Identification

Size: 3–3.5 mm. Brown-black head and gaster. The brown mesosoma is more or less reticulated. The characteristic rounded petiole is attached by a long stalk. There are five species of this very characteristic group of *Temnothorax* in Europe. *Temnothorax rottenbergii* (Emery, 1870) occurs in southern Italy and Sardinia. *Temnothorax sardous* (Santschi, 1909) occurs only in Sardinia. Two species occur in the Iberian Peninsula: *Temnothorax baeticus* (Emery, 1924) and *T. Formosus* (Santschi, 1909), which reaches the south of France. *Temnothorax semiruber* (André, 1881) is the only bicoloured species; it occurs in the south of the Balkans.

Possible confusion

There is another group of large, dark *Temnothorax species* that occurs only in the south of Spain: *T. schaufussi* (Forel, 1879) and *T. cagnianti* (Tinaut, 1983). Their petiole is also attached by a long stalk but their tegument is only slightly sculpted, almost smooth,

Swarming

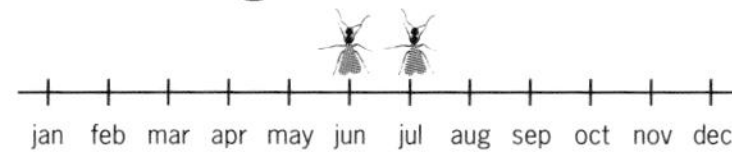

and they have a pronounced mesopropodeum connection.

Habitat

Can occur at altitudes above 1,000 m, sometimes to 1,500 m. Ground-dwelling species which occur in oak forests, along tracks, paths and in clearings. May also be found in garrigues.

Where to look

Nests are built under small stones, in cracks in rocks or directly in the ground.

Biology

Species that live in the ground and do not try to flatten themselves in a crevice. Colonies are monogynous and contain fewer than 1,000 individuals. Workers hunt for small prey that they find on rocks, at the foot of small plants or on the ground. In spring they climb into nectar-rich plants.

Distribution

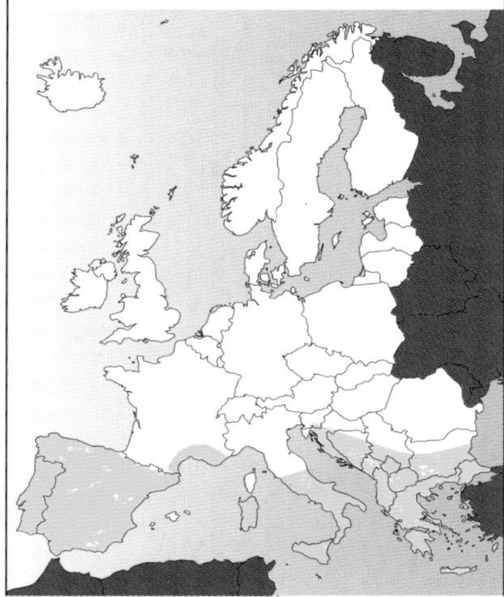

Range of *Temnothorax* species of the *rottenbergii* group.

Temnothorax formosus worker.

Temnothorax of the *sordidulus* group

subfamily Myrmicinae

Temnothorax sordidulus worker.

Identification

Size: 2–3 mm. The head and gaster are quite dark, varying from brown to orange or blackish-brown. Appendages are reddish-brown. There is a mesopropodeal ridge. Three species of this group are found in Europe: *Temnothorax sordidulus* (Müller, 1923) and *T. tergestinus* (Finzi, 1928) occur in Central Europe, and *T. melas* (Espadaler, Plateaux & Casevitz-Weulersse, 1984) is endemic to Corsica.

Possible confusion

As with *Temnothorax nylanderi*, *T. parvulus* and species of the *lichtensteini* group, these species have a mesonotum depression and a high petiole. In contrast, the spines are shorter, straighter and darker.

Habitat

At the edges of warm, dry forests, in open areas with numerous isolated stones or piles of stones and on rocks or drystone walls.

Swarming

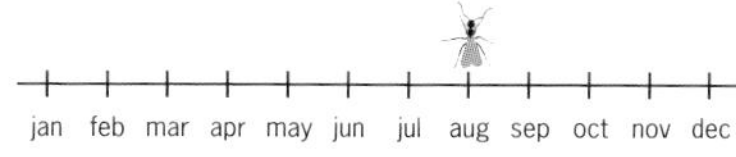

August, towards evening.

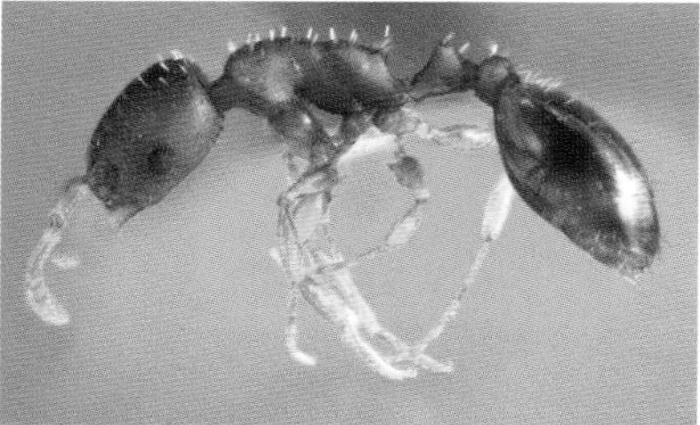

Temnothorax tergestinus worker.

Where to look

Nests are built between stones or in cracks, in sunny positions.

Biology

Workers move about relatively slowly, avoiding contact with other species. Recruiting of aid for exploiting an abundant food resource occurs by tandem running (one worker follows another that knows where the resource is by keeping in physical contact using its antennae). They hunt small arthropods which they find under moss, in rock cracks and crevices. Swarming occurs towards the end of the day during August.

Distribution

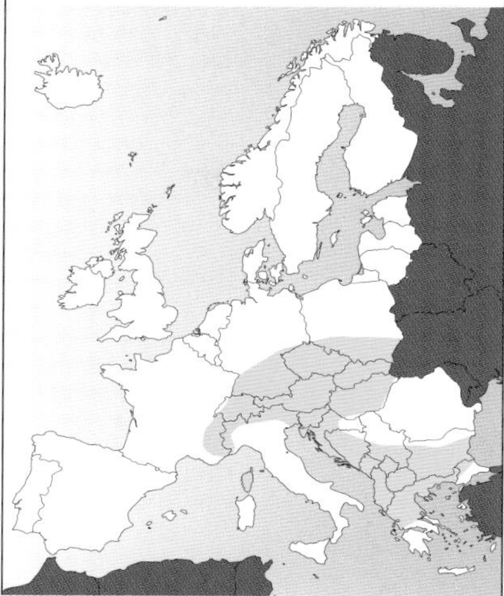

Range of *Temnothorax* species of the *sordidulus* group.

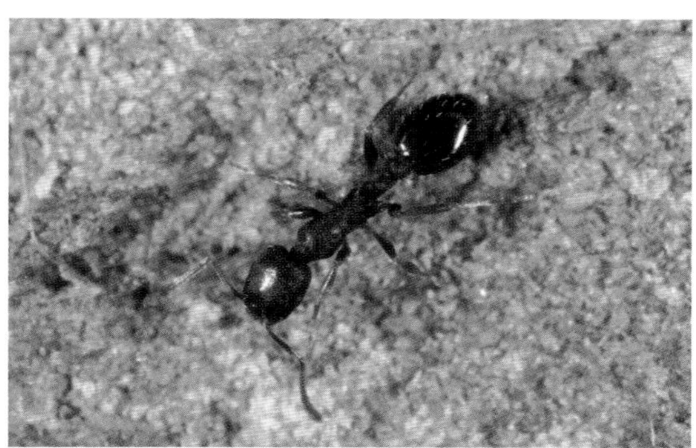

Temnothorax melas worker.

Temnothorax of the *tuberum* group

subfamily Myrmicinae

Temnothorax tuberum colony.

Identification

Size: 2.4–3 mm. Head dark brown to black, contrasting strongly with the orange mesosoma and gaster. Dusky tips to the antennae. *Temnothorax sordidulus* (Fabricius, 1775) and *T. nigriceps* (Mayr, 1855) are two closely related species. *Temnothorax nigriceps* has larger propodeum spines and obviously dark femora. Both are widely distributed in Europe.

Possible confusion

Temnothorax saxatilis (Schulz, Heinze & Pusch, 2007) of southern and central Italy has a more rounded petiole. The closely related *Temnothorax albipennis* and *T. unifasciatus* never have such a dark head. *Temnothorax nadigi* has a much less high petiole and smaller propodeum spines.

Habitat

Sunny, open habitats: meadows, dry grassland, stony areas, woodland edges, hillsides, etc. These species show a preference for mountainous areas. To an altitude of 2,300 m.

Where to look

Nests are built in rock crevices, between stones, in the ground, under stones or moss or other vegetation, and against stones. They can be found under small pieces of detached rock. Workers forage under stones, on the ground or in low vegetation.

Biology

Common species in mountainous areas. Nest density can be high at favourable sites. Colonies are monogynous or polygynous,

Swarming

jan feb mar apr may jun jul aug sep oct nov dec

Temnothorax nigriceps colony.

Distribution

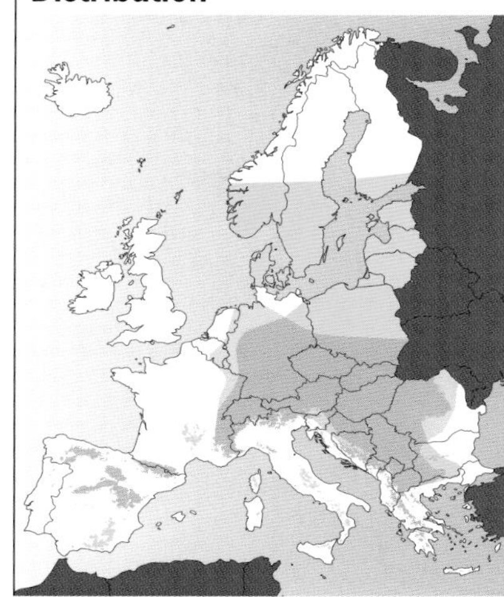

Range of *Temnothorax aveli* (pink) and *T. corticalis* (grey).

never with more than 300 individuals. Founding can be independent and claustral but new queens can also be adopted into an existing colony. These species feed on small invertebrates (mites, small insects, etc.), foraged for on rocks or on the ground, and they also consume flower nectar. They may be used as a host by slavemaker ant species *Myrmoxenus stumperi*, *M. ravouxi* and *Chalepoxenus muellerianus*.

Temnothorax tuberum worker.

Temnothorax nigriceps worker.

Temnothorax of the *unifasciatus* group

subfamily Myrmicinae

Temnothorax unifasciatus workers and males.

Identification

Size: 2–3 mm. Yellow body and appendages. Dusky tips to the antennae. First segment of the gaster has a very well-defined black band. *Temnothorax unifasciatus* (Latreille, 1798) and *T. albipennis* (Curtis, 1854) are two closely related and widespread European species. In *Temnothorax albipennis* the edges of the dark band on the gaster are less well defined and it is generally paler and narrower in the middle; this species often has dusky cheeks, and the rest of the head is yellow.

Possible confusion

In the less common *Temnothorax interruptus* the edges of the band on the gaster are less well defined and it is narrower in its middle. The frontal keels form a net angle behind the antennae (a difficult character to see but diagnostic of *Temnothorax interruptus*).

Swarming

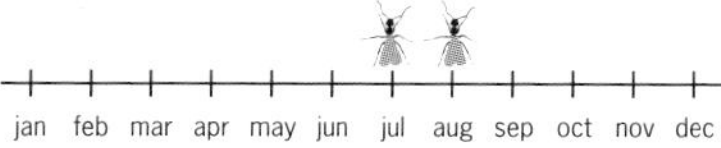

Distribution

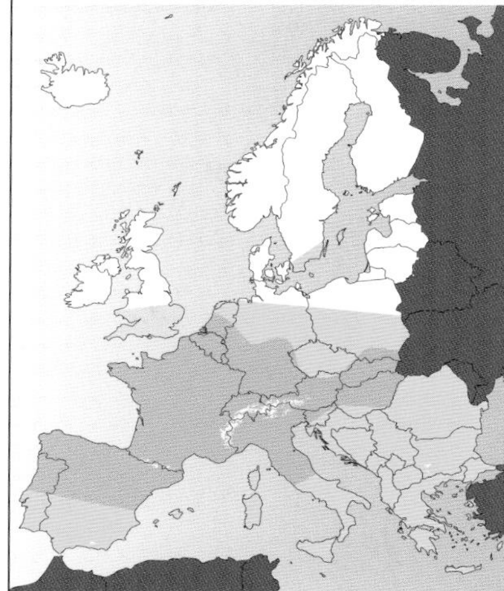

Range of *Temnothorax unifasciatus* (pink) and *T. albipennis* (grey).

Habitat

Very ubiquitous species, occurring in all types of habitats. They are more likely to be found in warm, well-exposed habitats in the north of the range. They can occur at quite high altitude (to 1,700 m) but are then only encountered in sunny sites.

Where to look

Nests are built in a wide variety of natural habitats: rock crevices, cracks between stones, dead branches on the ground, under bark of dead, lying tree trunks, between bark pieces at the base of pines, stems of various plants (including grasses and ferns), stems of dead brambles, hollow acorns, snail shells and more rarely directly in the ground, under dead wood or stones or in trees. Workers forage on rocks, in low vegetation and in ground litter.

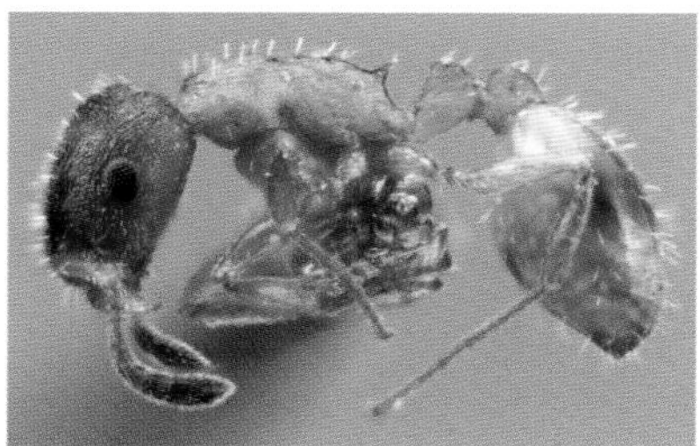

Temnothorax albipennis worker.

Biology

Common species. In certain sites nest density can be as high as several nests per square metre. Colonies are monogynous and can contain several hundred workers. Founding is independent and claustral, by a single queen. Food consists mainly of small arthropods (particularly mites and springtails) but also flower nectar. *Temnothorax unifasciatus* is used as a host by two social parasite ant species: *Chalepoxenus muellerianus* and *Myrmoxenus ravouxi*.

Tetramorium of the ***simillimum*** group and other ***Tetramorium*** groups

subfamily Myrmicinae

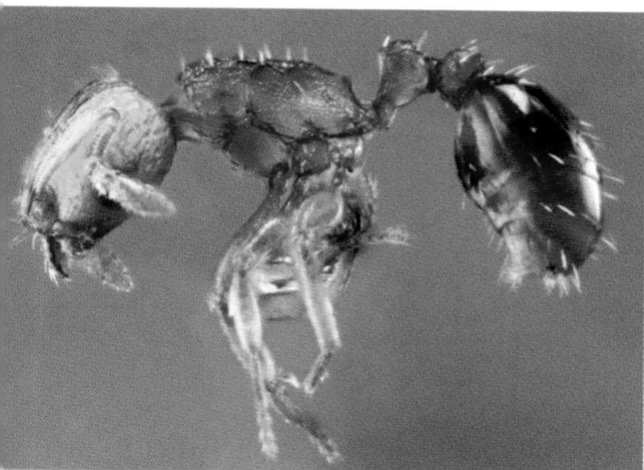

Tetramorium caldarium worker.

Identification

Size: 2–2.5 mm. Quite pale in colour. Quite a well-marked frontal ridge. Mandibles and body are obviously sculpted in the form of hexagonal cells. The petiole is rectangular. Many exotic species can be found in Europe, in heated blocks of flats, for example. *Tetramorium simillimum* (Smith, 1851) and *T. caldarium* (Roger, 1857) are two closely related small, yellow species, and their queens are also very small; these species may occur in the field but only in the warmest parts of Europe. *Tetramorium exasperatum* (Emery, 1891) is established in the Gibraltar area at the extreme south of Spain.

Possible confusion

There are other species that are becoming cosmopolitan: *Tetramorium bicarinatum* (Nylander, 1846) and *T. insolens* (Smith, 1861) belong to another group of species; they are bigger, with well-developed spines. *Tetramorium lanuginosum* (Mayr, 1870) is very small with a very sculpted body and a dense covering of hairs.

Habitat

These species occupy heated buildings, botanic gardens, greenhouses, zoos and so on. Locally, they occur in large ports via which they arrive in a new land. They preferentially remain in humid areas such as gardens and parks.

Where to look

Nests are built directly in the ground, against a pavement slab, for example.

Biology

Tetramorium bicarinatum is one of the most invasive ant species. It occurs in most tropical and subtropical habitats throughout the world. It occurs locally in temperate countries. The species is found in much of the Orient and Indo-Australian regions,

Swarming

jan feb mar apr may jun jul aug sep oct nov dec

Tetramorium bicarinatum worker.

Distribution

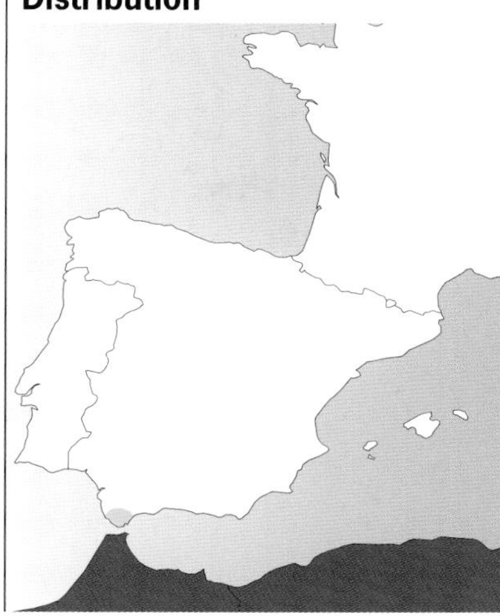

Range of *Tetramorium exasperatum*.

including most of the Pacific island groups, North America, Europe, in the Madagascar region and several Atlantic and Indian Ocean islands. It is an omnivore and opportunist: it eats anything it finds, sometimes being a scavenger of large prey. Colonies contain relatively few individuals.

Tetramorium lanuginosum worker.

Tetramorium of the *biskrense* group

subfamily Myrmicinae

Tetramorium brevicorne worker.

Identification

Size: 2.2–2.6 mm. Black body. Queens are small compared to those of *Tetramorium* species of the *caespitum-impurum* group. *Tetramorium biskrense* (Forel, 1904) is a common ant in North Africa that reaches the south of Spain and the Italian island of Lampedusa. *Tetramorium pelagium* (Mei, 1995) has been described from the island of Linosa, near the Sicilian coast, and closely resembles *T. biskrense*. *Tetramorium brevicorne* (Bondroit, 1918) occurs only on Corsica and Sardinia; in *T. brevicorne* the top of the postpetiole is finely sculpted and the queens of this species have a similar morphology to those of *T. biskrense*.

Swarming

Tetramorium biskrense worker.

Possible confusion

Tetramorium biskrense can be differentiated from workers of *Tetramorium* species of the *caespitum-impurum* group by denser head sculpting with more numerous longitudinal folds.

Habitat

Quite dry, open habitats.

Where to look

Nests are under stones well exposed to the sun.

Distribution

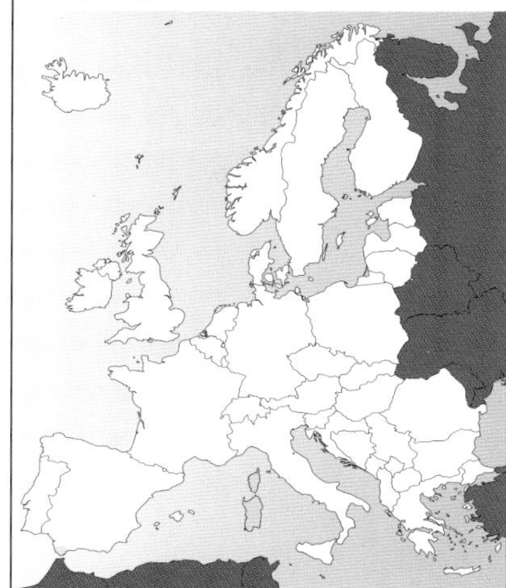

Range of *Tetramorium brevicorne* (pink) and *T. biskrense* (grey).

Tetramorium brevicorne worker.

Biology

Despite the small size of queens, colonies are monogynous. The nest is always superficial, with many workers caring for the brood that is under a stone on the ground surface, exposed to the sun. As in many *Tetramorium* species, these species are omnivores. Their main source of food is small dead arthropods found at the foot of low plants. They also bring seeds back to the nest, which are stored in one or several larders.

Tetramorium of the *caesptum-impurum* group

subfamily Myrmicinae

Tetramorium species colony.

Identification

Size: 2–3.5 mm. Entirely black body. Sometimes the mesosoma is paler is some individuals, especially in hot sites. The head has complete longitudinal stripes. The upper surfaces of the petiole and postpetiole always have a smooth patch without any sculpting. *Tetramorium caespitum* (Linnaeus, 1758) and *T. impurum* (Foerster, 1850) are the earliest described taxa belonging to this species complex. In 2006, a team of researchers using molecular data showed that there were at least five additional species; the description of some of these is still underway. *Tetramorium alpestre* (Steiner, Schlick-Steiner & Seifert, 2010) is known from alpine habitats between altitudes of 900 and 2,300 m in Austria, France, Italy and Switzerland. *Tetramorium alpestre* is the only polygynous species of the West Palearctic and forms super-colonies. *Tetramorium hungaricum* (Röszler, 1935) of Central Europe and the Balkans is more or less

Swarming

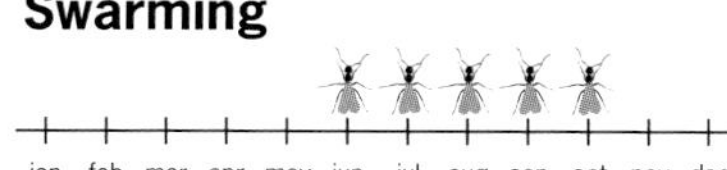

smooth or has very fine longitudinal stripes on the head.

Possible confusion

Tetramorium semilaeve is altogether paler and its head is less clearly striped. Other dark *Tetramorium* species have a sculpted upper surface to the petiole.

Habitat

These ants are found in a wide variety of habitats but normally open and well exposed to the sun. They occur equally in urban environments – such as in gardens, green spaces and in cracks in pavements – as in natural ones, mainly in meadows. From sea level to 2,400 m.

Where to look

Nests are built under stones or directly in the ground, sometimes in dead wood.

Biology

Very common species. Nest density can be very high. Colonies are monogynous. Nests are always very populous, with as many as several thousand workers in a nest. They are omnivores, feeding on dead invertebrates, seeds and the honeydew of root-sucking

Distribution

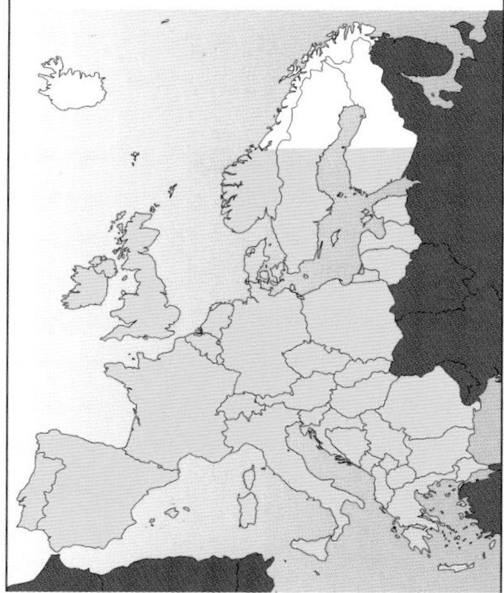

Range of *Tetramorium* species of the *caespitum-impurum* group.

Tetramorium workers of the *caespitum-impurum* group.

Hemiptera. Workers are always very aggressive. These species are hosts to the following parasitic species: *Teleutomyrmex schneideri* (see page 396), *Anergates atratulus* (see page 394) and *Strongylognathus* species (see page 338).

Tetramorium of the *chefteki* group

subfamily Myrmicinae

Tetramorium forte workers.

Identification

Size: 2.5–3.5 mm. Body entirely dark brown. The head has complete longitudinal stripes. The upper surfaces of the petiole and postpetiole are entirely sculpted. Five species of this group occur in Europe, and differentiation between these species is difficult. *Tetramorium moravicum* (Kratochvil, 1941) has the widest distribution; *T. chefteki* (Forel, 1911) occurs only in the Balkans; *T. forte* (Forel, 1904) in Spain and the south of France; *T. sanetrai* (Schulz & Csösz, 2007) is found in the south of Italy, and *T. rhodium* (Emery, 1924) on the eastern Greek islands.

Possible confusion

Tetramorium ferox also has a slightly sculpted top to the petiole and postpetiole, but the spines are very short and placed lower on the propodeum.

Habitat

Dry meadows and sandy areas on the Mediterranean coast.

Swarming

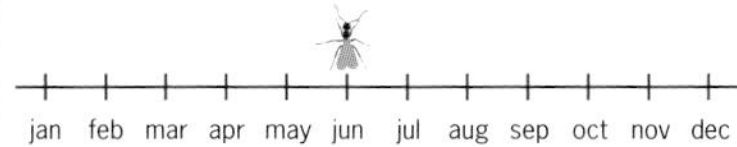

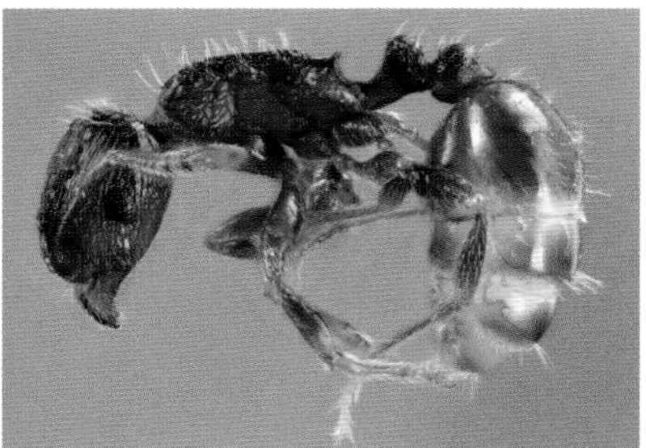

Tetramorium moravicum worker.

Tetramorium forte queen with a very large postpetiole.

Where to look

Nests are built under stones, directly in the ground or at the foot of bushes.

Biology

Species can be common. Colonies can be polygynous and are always very populous. Winged individuals are small compared to those of *Tetramorium* species of the *caespitum-impurum* group.

Distribution

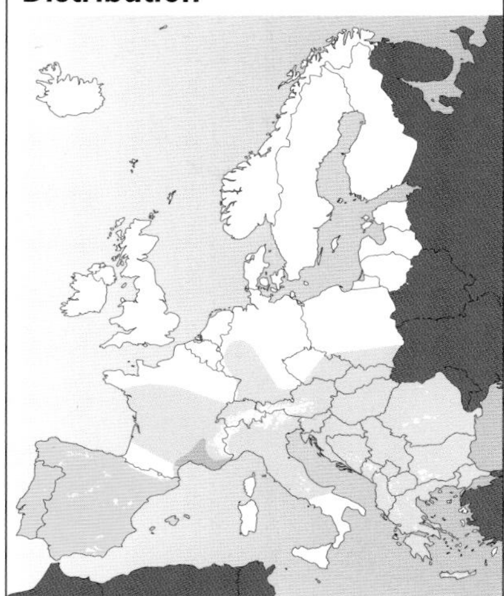

Range of *Tetramorium forte* (pink) and *T. moravicum* (grey).

Three castes of *Tetramorium forte*. From top to bottom: a queen, a male and a worker.

Tetramorium of the ***ferox*** group

subfamily Myrmicinae

Tetramorium ferox worker.

Identification

Size: 2.8–3.5 mm. Body colour brown to yellow. The head is sculpted but the wrinkles can be very fine in *Tetramorium diomedeum*. The propodeal spines are short and placed at a low position. The petiole and postpetiole are proportionally bigger than in other species, particularly in winged individuals.

This is an oriental *Tetramorium* group represented by just two species in Europe: *T. ferox* (Ruzsky, 1903) in Central Europe and the Balkans; and *T. diomedeum* (Emery, 1908), which is more southerly, occuring in the south of Italy and the south of the Balkans. The tegument of *Tetramorium diomedeum* is paler and less sculpted that that of *T. ferox*.

Swarming

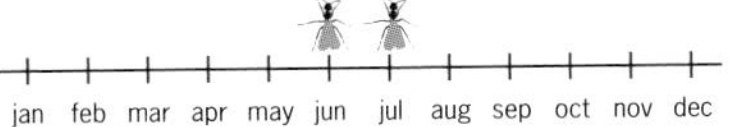

Distribution

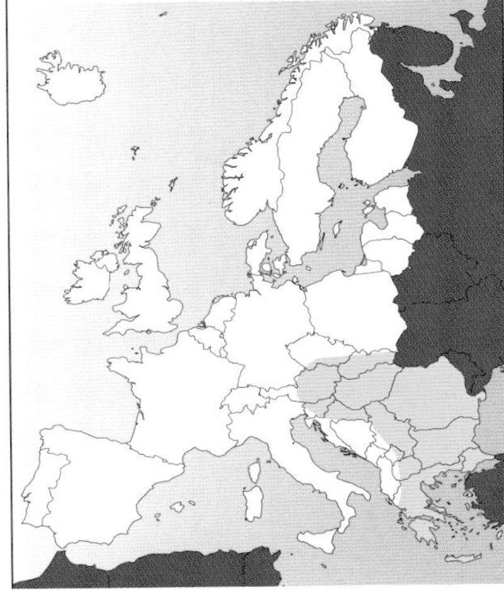

Range of *Tetramorium ferox*.

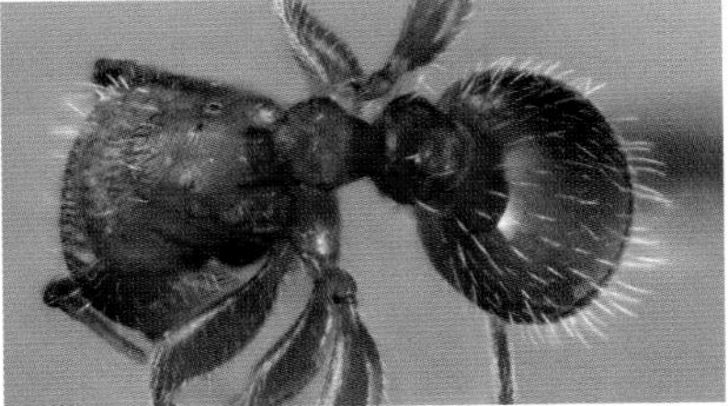

Large petiole and postpetiole of *Tetramorium ferox*.

Possible confusion

The low position of the propodeal spines and large petiole and postpetiole separates these species from other groups of *Tetramorium*.

Habitat

Open, dry habitats.

Where to look

Under stones where the brood may be placed to be warmed in order to optimise development. The nests are in the ground, with the ants visible in the spring, after heavy rain or during swarming.

Tetramorium diomedeum worker.

Biology

The nests have few occupants. Monogynous species. They are omnivores, feeding without preference on seeds, dead insects or the honeydew of white aphids which they rear on roots.

Tetramorium meridionale Emery, 1870

subfamily Myrmicinae

Tetramorium meridionale queen; note the transverse wrinkles at the back of the head.

Identification

Size: 2–2.8 mm. The body is yellow, often reddish-yellow, and the gaster and sometimes the head are darker. It is the only European *Tetramorium* that has transverse wrinkles on the occiput. *Tetramorium meridionale*, described from Corsica, also occurs in Spain and southern Italy. Reported from Greece.

Possible confusion

Tetramorium semilaeve may also be found in Mediterranean regions; it can be distinguished by being paler, with a less brown gaster and a smooth or only slightly wrinkled forehead. *Tetramorium* of the *caespitum-impurum* group always have longitudinal wrinkles on the whole head.

Swarming

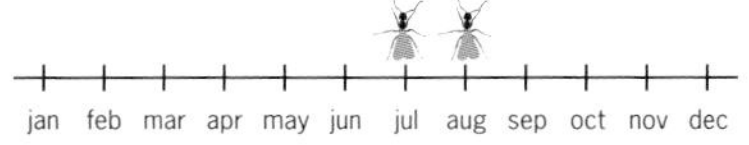

Tetramorium meridionale queen and workers.

Distribution

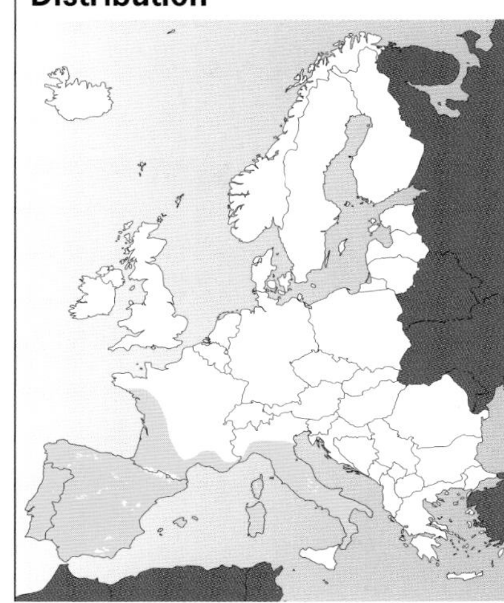

Range of *Tetramorium meridionale*.

Habitat

Damp areas: springs, fountains, meadows, beaches and dunes in coastal Mediterranean regions.

Where to look

Nests are under stones or directly in the ground.

Biology

A quite common species but difficult to find during hot weather. Colonies are polygynous and very populous. Workers rarely leave the nest. They feed on small arthropods living in the ground and rear aphids on plant roots.

Tetramorium meridionale worker.

Tetramorium of the *semilaeve* group

subfamily Myrmicinae

Tetramorium semilaeve workers, winged males and queens.

Identification

Size: 2–3 mm. The body is generally quite a pale reddish colour but can vary from one colony to another: all individuals might be pale yellow or dark reddish or brown (rarer). The rear of the head is quite smooth.

Tetramorium semilaeve (André, 1883) is the reference species for this group. It is present in Western Mediterranean regions, between Spain and Italy. There exist several more or less closely related species in Greece which are difficult to differentiate, for example:

Swarming

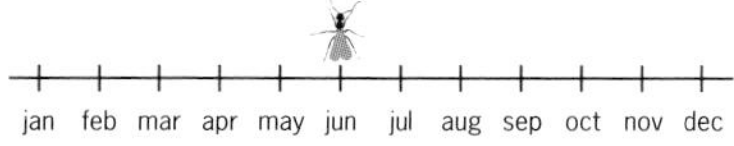

Tetramorium semilaeve worker.

Tetramorium schmidti (Forel, 1904), *T. hippocratis* (Agosti & Collingwood, 1987) or *T. sahlbergi* (Finzi, 1936). *Tetramorium punctatum* (Santschi, 1927), which occurs in the south of Italy, Sicily and Greece, can be distinguished by its smaller size and smoother tegument. It is the same for *Tetramorium lucidulum* (Menozzi, 1933) from Greece.

Possible confusion

Tetramorium meridionale is also found in Mediterranean regions; it is distinguished from *T. semilaeve* by having transverse wrinkles on the occipital border of the head. *Tetramorium* species of the *caespitum-impurum* group have the whole head wrinkled. In *Tetramorium semilaeve* the wrinkles diminish on the occiput, which is almost smooth.

Habitat

Warm habitats: dry meadows, garrigue, forest edges on the Mediterranean coast. Only at low altitudes.

Distribution

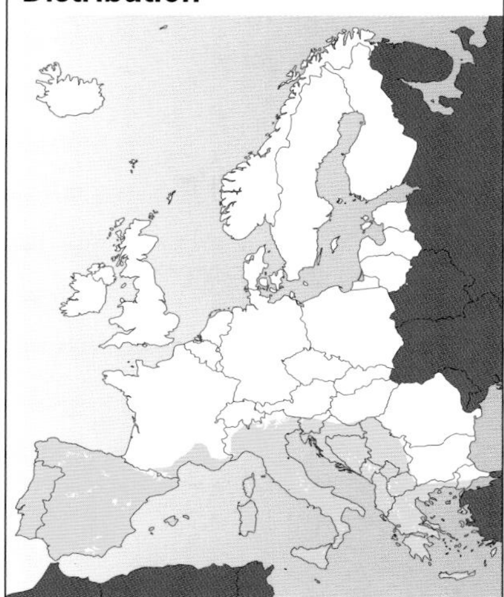
Range of *Tetramorium* species of the *semilaeve* group.

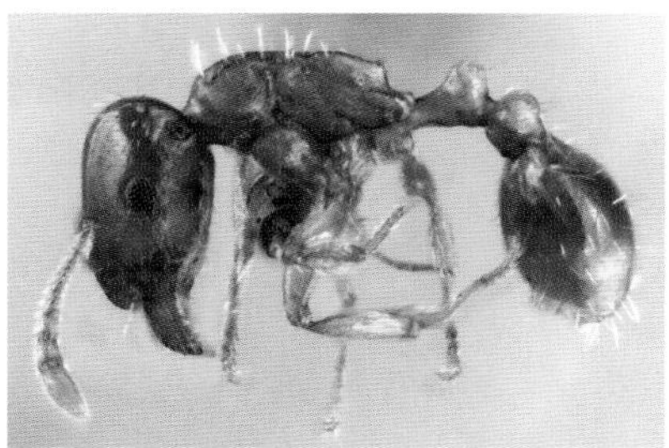
Tetramorium lucidulum worker.

Where to look

Nests are built under stones or directly in the ground.

Biology

Quite common species. Nest density can be very high. Colonies are polygynous and very populous.

Anergates genus Forel, 1874

subfamily Myrmicinae

Anergates atratulus queen (arrow) with *Tetramorium* sp. workers.

Identification

There are no workers (an inquiline parasite). Size: queen 2.5–3 mm, dark brown. Non egg-laying females (winged) have a dorsal depression on the gaster. Egg-laying queens are physogastric. Males are 2.5–3 mm, yellowish and wingless. This genus contains just one species: *Anergates atratulus* (Schenck, 1852).

Note: According to recent genetic studies, the genus *Anergates* should be included in the genus *Tetramorium*. This species' correct name should therefore be *Tetramorium atratulum*.

Possible confusion

The wingless males are very recognisable and cannot be confused with those of any other

Swarming

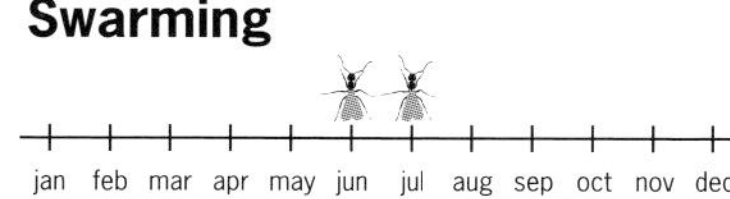

species. Ants of the genus *Teleutomyrmex* are also social parasites (inquilines) of *Tetramorium* species but are rarer and smaller than *Anergates atratulus* and have winged males.

Habitat

Same habitats as its host.

> **Where to look**
> In the nests of *Tetramorium* species of the *caespitum-impurum* group.

Distribution

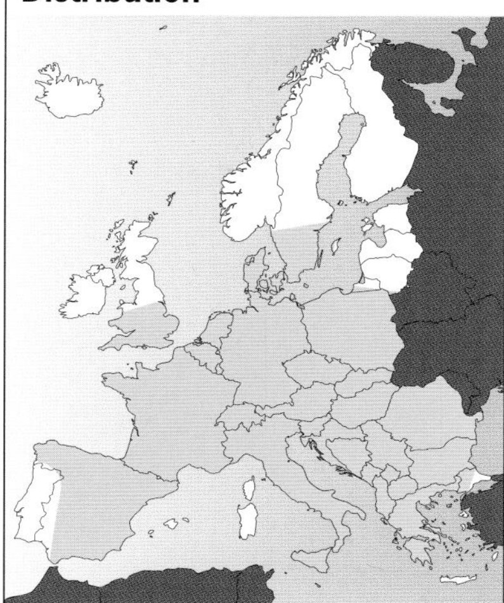

Range of *Anergates atratulus.*

Biology

Anergates atratulus is an obligate parasite of *Tetramorium* of the *caespitum-impurum* group. It is apparently a rare species. At sites where it occurs, the proportion of parasitised nests is low. It is an inquiline species, without workers. The colony can produce several hundreds, even thousands, of males and winged females. This species' biology is little known. It appears possible that new queens can only start a new colony by penetrating an orphan *Tetramorium* colony (without a queen). Sexual individuals can be found in the nest between early May and early September.

Anergates atratulus male (left) with a *Tetramorium* sp. worker (right).

Teleutomyrmex genus Kutter, 1950

subfamily Myrmicinae

Teleutomyrmex schneideri male.

Identification

Species of this genus do not possess workers. Individuals of both sexes (males and queens) have wings. The queen's gaster is circular and concave underneath. Queens are generally a dark brown colour, whereas the males are a paler brown.
This genus contains just two species: *Teleutomyrmex schneideri* (Kutter, 1950) and *T. kutteri* (Tinaut, 1990); the latter has only been found in Spain (Sierra Nevada and Andalusia), at least for the present. The two species are morphologically very similar and cannot be separated in the field. Recent genetic data show that species of this genus should be considered to be in the genus *Tetramorium*. Thus, the correct nomenclature should be *Tetramorium kutteri* (Tinaut, 1990) for one of these two species. For the other, as *Tetramorium schneideri* has already been used for another species, another name has necessarily been given: *Teleutomyrmex schneideri* becomes *Tetramorium inquilinum* (Ward, Brady, Fisher & Schultz, 2014).

Possible confusion

These two species can be confused with *Anergates atratulus*, another species that parasitises species of the genus *Tetramorium* but which is slightly bigger and its males do not have wings.

Habitat

These species are generally found at around 2,000 m altitude. Habitats vary from alpine meadows (French Alps) to forest edges and sides of sunny tracks (Swiss Alps) and coppice (Spain). Sites must contain a good number of host nests.

Swarming

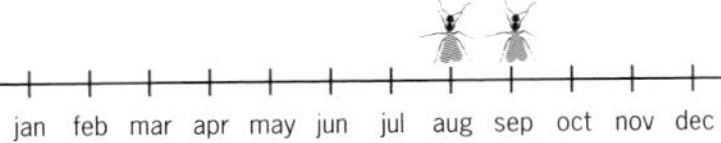

Where to look

They occur in *Tetramorium* nests, which may be under stones, under moss or among the roots of species of *Vaccinium*.

Biology

Even though the two sexes have wings, it would appear that mating often occurs in the nest. Their morphological adaptations (circular, concave gaster and strong claws) and also the fact that the host queen retains the ability to produce sexual individuals suggest that dispersion of *Teleutomyrmex* queens can take place at the same time as the dispersion of *Tetramorium* queens.

Distribution

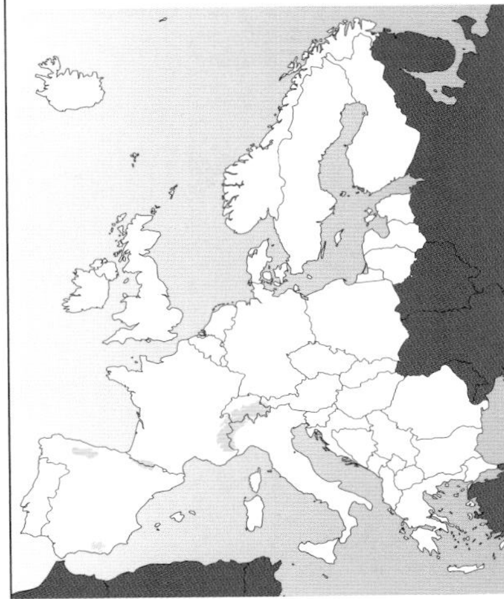

Range of *Teleutomyrmex schneideri* (pink) and *T. kutteri* (grey).

The parasite queen stays gripped onto her host during its exit from the nest. The new founding is done together with that of the host species.

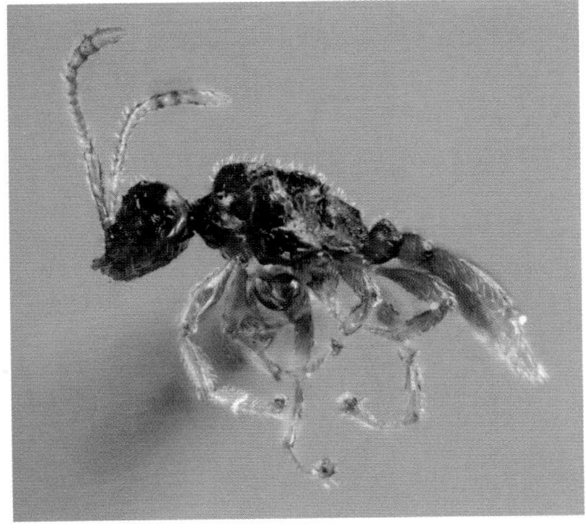

Teleutomyrmex schneideri queen.

Trichomyrmex genus Mayr, 1865

subfamily Myrmicinae

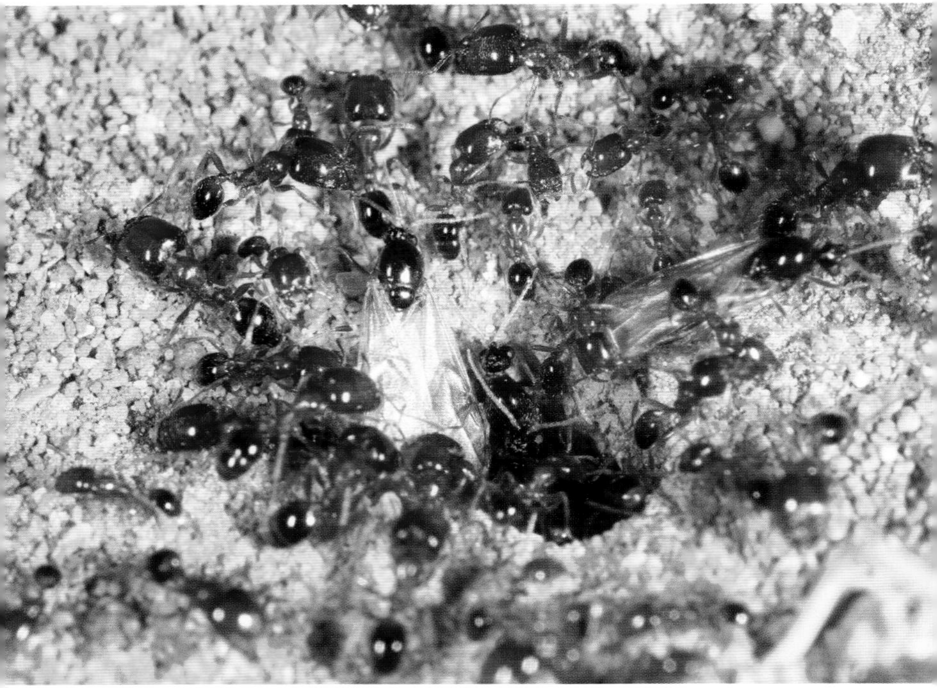

Trichomyrmex perplexus swarming.

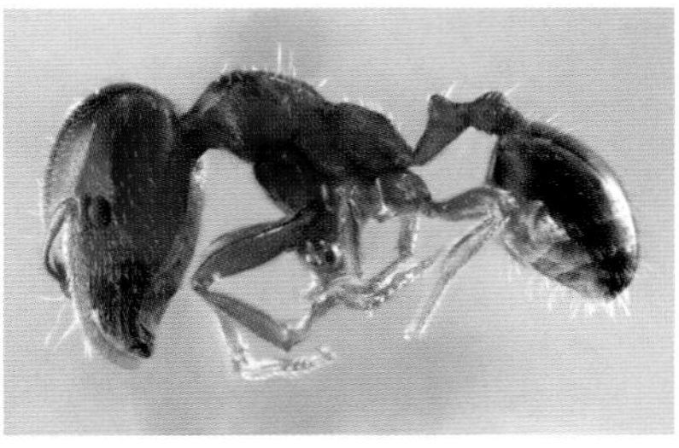

Trichomyrmex perplexus worker.

Taxonomy

Size: 4 mm, dark brown body. There are no spines. An enlarged head, recalling that of *Messor* species. A mainly African and Asiatic genus containing about 20 species. Only one occurs in Europe, in Greece: *Trichomyrmex perplexus* (Radchenko, 1997).

Swarming

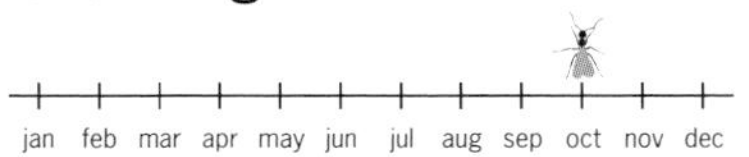

Trichomyrmex perplexus head.

Distribution

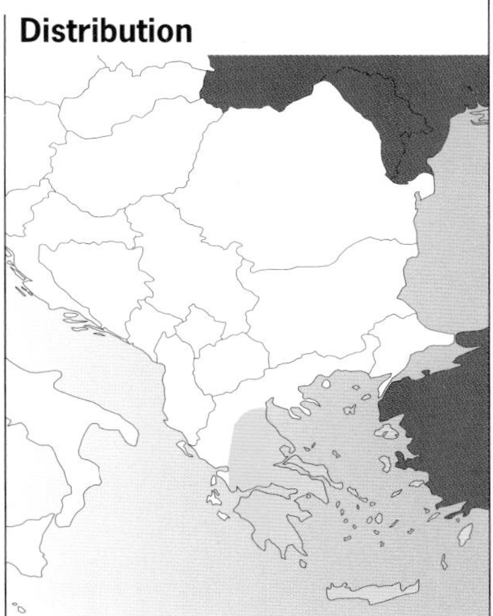

Range of *Trichomyrmex perplexus*.

Possible confusion

Messor species are bigger. *Pheidole* major workers are accompanied by morphologically different smaller workers and they are yellower.

Habitat

Open habitats, short grassland, bare ground, edges of roads and tracks, areas of steppe and the top of beaches.

Habitat occupied by *Trichomyrmex perplexus*.

Where to look

Nests occur directly in the ground. The nest entrance is in the form of a small hole.

Biology

Workers can take on the same role as those of seed-eating species in steppe-like ecosystems. They may also recover dead insects to be eaten. They forage for food in columns, as with the *Messor* species.

Anochetus genus Mayr, 1861

subfamily Ponerinae

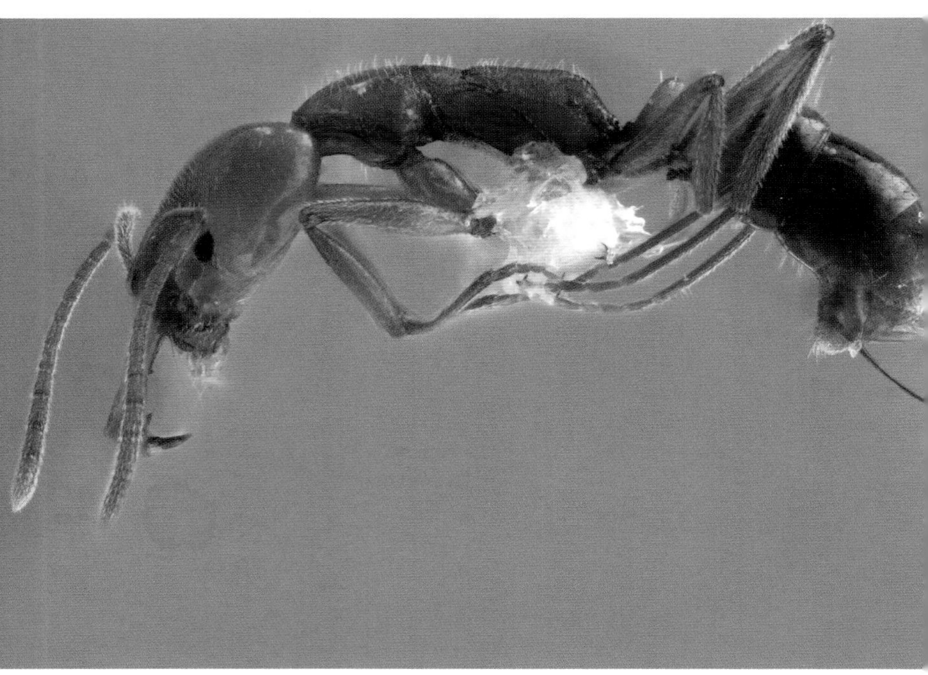

Anochetus ghilianii worker.

Identification

Size: 4–5 mm. Dark body. The well-developed mandibles only have teeth at their extremities. A large tropical genus with around a hundred species. Just one species reaches the European Mediterranean basin: *Anochetus ghilianii* (Spinola, 1851), in the extreme south of Spain.

Possible confusion

This genus cannot be confused with any other in the European fauna.

Habitat

Anochetus ghilianii is found between Cadiz and the Straits of Gibraltar in areas near the coast. It also occurs in Morocco.

Swarming

Where to look

Under stones and in the ground litter.

Biology

Anochetus ghilianii is a predatory species that moves about with wide-open mandibles. As soon as it detects a prey item, it closes its mandibles on it – this movement is one of the most rapid in the animal kingdom. Workers feed on insects. There is no nuptial flight; mating takes place in the nest.

Distribution

Range of *Anochetus ghilianii*.

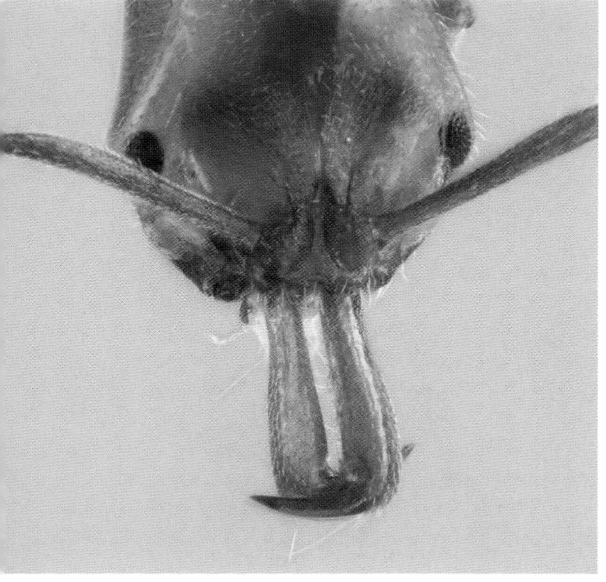

Head of a *Anochetus ghilianii* worker.

Cryptopone genus Emery, 1893

subfamily Ponerinae

Cryptopone ochracea winged queen.

Identification

Size: about 3 mm. The body is entirely pale reddish. Workers have no eyes. The mandibles have well-developed teeth. This genus occurs worldwide but only a single species occurs in the Mediterranean basin: *Cryptopone ochracea* (Mayr, 1855).

Possible confusion

They can be distinguished from species of the *Ponera* and *Hypoponera* genera by having a depression at the base of the mandibles.

Habitat

Cryptopone ochracea is a widespread underground species.

Where to look

Under stones and in the ground litter.

Swarming

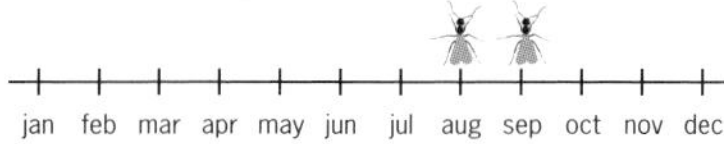

Distribution

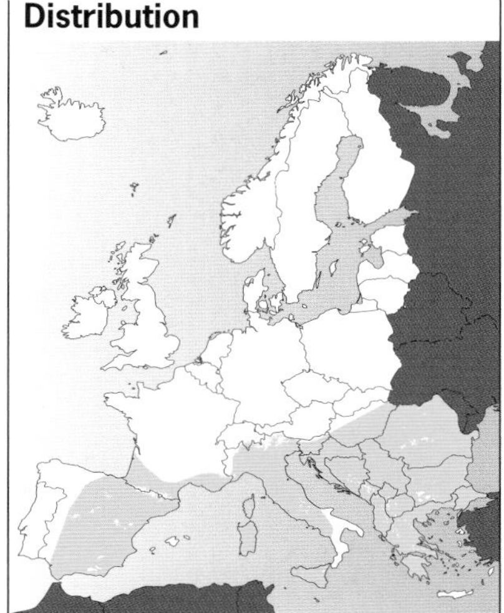

Range of *Cryptopone ochracea*.

Biology

Cryptopone species form small, more or less nomadic colonies. They are a genus of predatory species that hunt small arthropods on the ground. *Cryptopone ochracea*'s biology is little known. Colonies occur deep in the ground and workers rarely come to the surface. It is more common to find winged queens during swarming than to find workers.

Cryptopone ochracea queen.

Hypoponera genus Santschi, 1938

subfamily Ponerinae

Three castes of *Hypoponera eduardi*. From left to right a queen, a male and a worker

Identification

Size: 2.5–3 mm. Generally, the body is entirely black but pale brown or yellow individuals sometimes occur. They have an elongated, thin body. The genus *Hypoponera* contains more than 150 mainly tropical species. Five species occur in Europe. *Hypoponera eduardi* (Forel, 1894), which is the most frequent, especially in Southern Europe, has an entirely dark body. *Hypoponera abeillei* (André, 1881), reported from the Iberian Peninsula, Corsica and Italy, has no eyes and lacks a metanotal groove. Three other introduced and cosmopolitan species can be found in inhabited buildings and botanical greenhouses, rarely outside buildings: *Hypoponera punctatissima* (Roger, 1859), *H. ergatandria* (Forel, 1893) and *H. ragusai* (Emery, 1895), which are difficult to separate without precise biometric data.

Possible confusion

Species of the genus *Ponera* are very similar to those of the genus *Hypoponera* but can be separated by the presence of a small, circular, transparent window in the ventral extension of the petiole (criteria only visible using a binocular microscope). The closely related genus *Cryptopone* has just one uncommon representative in Europe: *C. ochracea*; *Cryptopone* species are generally paler (reddish-yellow and not brown-black).

Swarming

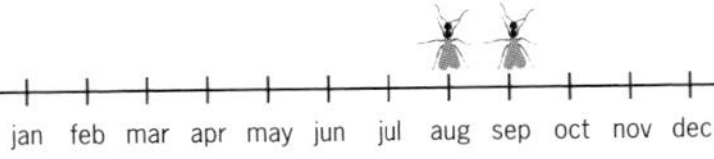

Habitat

A quite ubiquitous species: wooded or open habitats, often on riverbanks. They appear to seek out damp soil. They live underground.

Where to look

Nests are built directly in the ground or under large stones in the soil. The ants move to the surface when it is wet. Thus, in the south these species are most easily found when it rains. Certain species, such as *Hypoponera punctatissima*, can occur in the basements of heated buildings, sewage systems, slag heaps or horticultural greenhouses.

Biology

Hypoponera eduardi is generally fairly uncommon but can be locally abundant in the southern part of its range. It forms small colonies of a few dozen individuals, sometimes more. The other species are much rarer. All *Hypoponera* species forage for small arthropods on the ground.

Hypoponera ergatandria worker.

Distribution

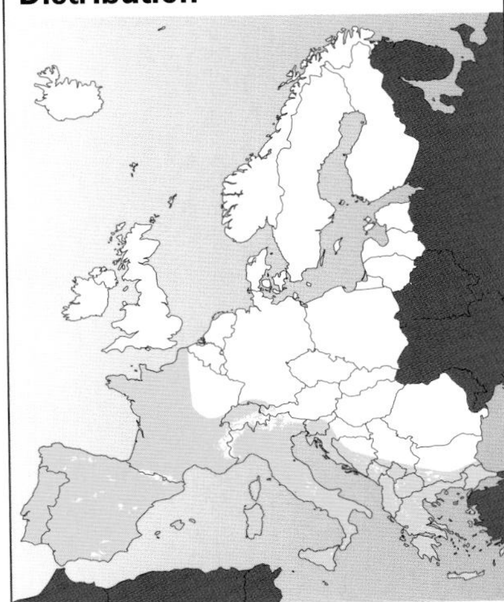

Range of *Hypoponera eduardi*.

Hypoponera punctatissima worker.

Ponera genus Latreille, 1804

subfamily Ponerinae

Ponera coarctata worker.

Identification

Size: 2.5–3.5 mm. Body reddish-brown to black. Immature individuals are a dirty white. Overall, the body has a slim appearance. There are two species of the genus *Ponera* in Europe: *P. coarctata* (Latreille, 1802) and *P. testacea* (Emery, 1895). The second is generally a little paler then the first but certain differentiation of the two species necessitates a biometrical study.

Possible confusion

Species of the genus *Hypoponera* are very similar to those of the genus *Ponera* but can be distinguished by the absence of a small, transparent, circular

Swarming

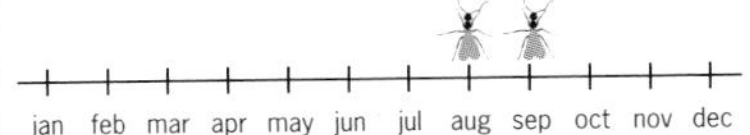

Ponera coarctata queen and workers.

window in the ventral extension of the petiole (only visible under a binocular microscope). *Cryptopone* species are generally paler (reddish-yellow) and their mandibles are different.

Habitat

Essentially in forested areas. *Ponera testacea* replaces *P. coarctata* in Mediterranean forests. Shaded areas with a modicum of dampness in the ground.

Where to look

Nests are built quite deep in the ground, under large stones, in dead wood or under bark of tree trunks on the ground. Workers forage in the ground litter.

Biology

These are the most often encountered Ponerinae species.

Distribution

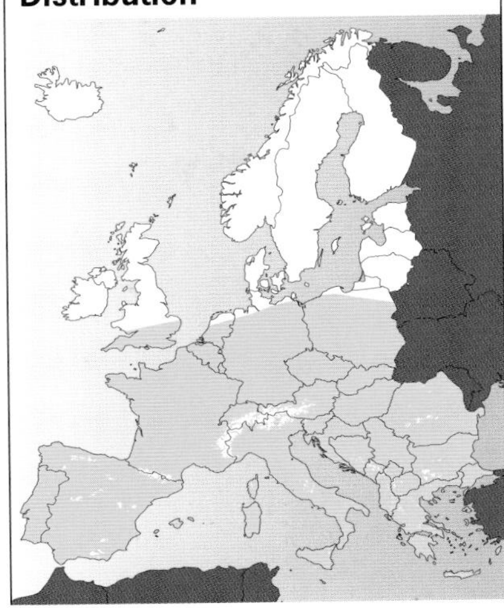

Range of the genus *Ponera*.

Ponera testacea worker.

Globally they are quite uncommon but can be common locally. Colonies are small with a maximum of a few dozen individuals, and they are optionally polygynous. Queens closely resemble workers. They prey on small arthropods.

***Proceratium* genus** Roger, 1863

subfamily Proceratiinae

Proceratium algiricum queen.

Identification

Size: 3–4.5 mm. Workers are orange-yellow, the queen darker, sometimes brown. As in the Ponerinae, there is a constriction between the first and second tergites. The rest of the gaster is very rounded. The eyes are very reduced. *Proceratium* is a very big genus, containing more than 80 species distributed throughout all the regions of the globe. Only four are found in Europe, in the south. *Proceratium melinum* (Roger, 1860) has the largest distribution, from the Iberian peninsula to Greece – the front edge of its clypeus is in the form of a triangular point. The following two species are very similar: *Proceratium algiricum* (Forel, 1899) has been reported from Italy, Croatia and Greece; *Proceratium melitense* (De Andrade, 2003) is present on Sicily and Malta. *Proceratium numidicum* (Santschi, 1912) has a scale-shaped petiole, differentiating it from the preceding species; it has been reported from Turkey and Cyprus, but its presence in the Balkans needs to be confirmed.

Swarming

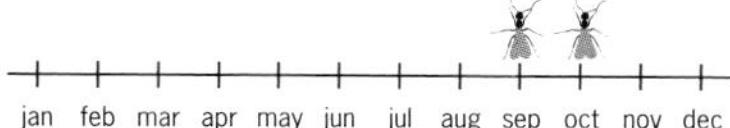

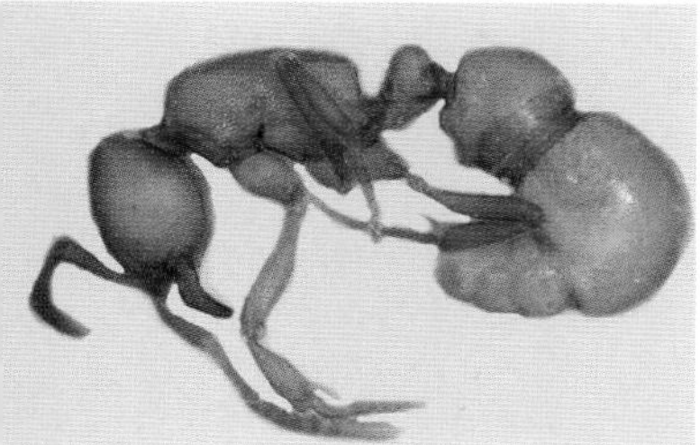

'roceratium melinum worker.

'ossible confusion

ipecies of the genus *Proceratium* :an be confused with individuals of the *Cryptopone*, *Hypoponera* or *Ponera* genera but these others lo not have a rounded last tergite o the gaster.

Habitat

These species appear to be .ssociated with oak woods but hey may be more ubiquitous than hought. Any ground with a cover of vegetation is favourable as this .llows the maintaining of a elatively high soil humidity and a ertain freshness.

Where to look

Nests are built under very large stones, among the leaf litter of trees under which they are implanted.

Distribution

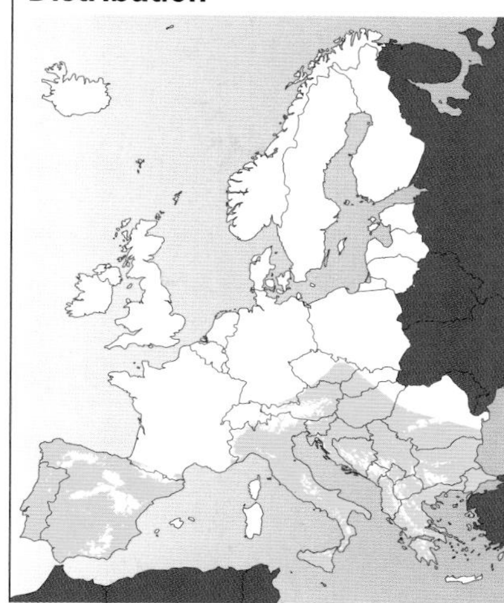

Range of the genus *Proceratium*.

Biology

Underground-dwelling species that are very difficult to find. Nests are built deep in the ground. They lead a concealed lifestyle. Colonies contain 30 to 50 workers. The nest is formed of small, rounded chambers dug in rotten wood or directly in the ground. Workers forage for the eggs of other insects and also especially spiders. As with *Myrmecina* species, if they feel threatened they can roll up into a ball. Swarming occurs at the end of the day.

Glossary

Certain terms shown in the general diagram of worker morphology are not included again here.

Acidopore: A conical structure with a small terminal opening, at the posterior end of an ant's gaster, through which it sprays formic acid and associated hydrocarbons, collectively comprising the venom.

Brood: All young stages in the nest (eggs, larvae and pupae).

Claustral: A species in which the queen builds a small nest chamber, seals herself in it and feeds on the food store inside until the first workers appear.

Elaiosome: Fleshy structures rich in lipids and proteins attached to the seeds of many plant species and attractive to ants.

Ergatoid: With the form of a worker. Said of functional queens or males that have the outward appearance of a worker ant.

Eusocial: A social species in which generations overlap. There is cooperation in rearing the brood, only certain individuals reproduce, and tasks (caring for the brood, nest defence, etc.) are divided.

Extrafloral nectaries: Nectar-secreting plant glands that develop outside of flowers, many providing food for ants.

Haemolymph: A fluid, analogous to the blood in vertebrates, that circulates in the interior of an arthropod's body.

Inquiline: A social parasite species that lives in the nest of another species, the host, and only produces sexual individuals.

Macrogyne: With a large queen that produces many workers.

Major: A caste of ant morphologicall different from others in the colony; a large worker.

Microgyne: With a small queen that produces more microgynes and males.

Minor: A caste of ant morphologicall different from others in the colony; a small worker.

Monogynous: In which the colony contains just a single queen.

Mutualism: A symbiosis in which two different species (e.g. an ant and an aphid) both gain from associating with each other.

Myrmecochory: Seed dispersal by nts.

Myrmecophile: Concerning another rganism that lives within an ants' est.

Nuptial flight: In many social insects, iture queens and males are winged nd fly in swarms to mate; a nuptial ight is one during which mating ccurs.

ligogynous: With a few queens, but ot living together.

mmatidia: Units of an arthropod's ompound eye.

arasitoid: Species whose evelopment occurs within the host's ody. The host subsequently dies and e adult parasitoid has no ependence on the host.

hytogastric: Describing an ant with highly enlarged gaster, due to evelopment of the ovaries (queens) dilation for stocking food orkers).

Pleometrosis: Colony founding by several queens.

Polygynous: Nests containing more than one reproductive queen.

Psammophore: Long hairs under the head used to hold seeds.

Rubicole: Living in hollow stems.

Sternite: Ventral part of an insect's body segment; each segment consists of a sternite and a tergite.

Stipule: Growth at the base of the petiole (leaf stalk) of certain plants.

Swarming: In ants, the period during which future queens and males leave their colony of origin to mate and disperse.

Tergite: Dorsal part of an insect's body segment; each segment consists of a tergite and a sternite.

Trophallaxis: Transfer of food from one individual to another by regurgitation.

Xenobiotic (social parasitism): Ant species obligated to live in another species' nest but in a separate chamber.

Index